GUATEMALA

Never Again!

DIRECTORY

Próspero Penados del Barrio
Archbishop of Guatemala City

Advisory Council

Julio Cabrera, Bishop of El Quiché
Álvaro Ramazzini, Bishop of San Marcos
Ronalth Ochaeta, Director of ODHAG
Carlos Gehlert Mata

Juan Gerardi, Auxiliary Bishop of Guatemala City
and General Coordinator of ODHAG
Dr. Julio Penados del Barrio
Gonzalo de Villa, SJ

Diocesan Coordinators

Father Rigoberto Pérez Garrido, Catarina
Sánchez Yaz and Roberto Tepaz López,
El Quiché
Sister Rosario Celis, Pilar Hoyos, and Oscar
Pacay, Las Verapaces
Francisco Leiva and Toñi Tecles, Petén
Edgar Hernández, Huehuetenango
José Antonio Puac, Guatemala

Francisco Recancoj Mendoza, Los Altos
Rodolfo Godínez, San Marcos
Sister María Estela López, Chimaltenango
Eugenia Juárez and Jeffrey Falk, Izabal
Rosa M. Aleman and Father Alberto Gighlia,
Ixcán
Otto Castellanos, Escuintla
Carlos Morfín, SJR-Campeche

General Coordinator

Edgar Gutiérrez

Team Coordinators

Fernando Suazo and Michael Moerth

Information System

Oliver Estuardo Mazariegos Zetina

Report Coordinator

Carlos Martín Beristain

Technical Team (field liaisons, analysts, data processors)

Claudia Ágreda
Graciela Azmitia
Marco Tulio Ajquejay Chiquiyá
Candelaria Batz
Rosa Cana de Mollineda
Ofelia Chirix
Pilar Clúa
José Benedicto Cúa Xicay
Ruth del Valle Cóbar
Claudia Estrada

Marta Gutiérrez
Marco Antonio Gutiérrez
Ana Patricia Hernández
Elisa Hyvönen
Teresa Laines
Mayra Méndez
Marcie Mersky
Juan Manuel Merino
Rocío Mézquita
Fernando Morales

Victor Moreira
Manuel Esaú Pérez
John Ramírez
Gaspar Reanda Pablo
Rodrigo Salvadó
Marja Savolainen
Mervi Solkakoski
Domingo Vásquez Gómez
Diego Zaparolli
Rebeca Zúñiga

Special Support/Independent Advisors and Consultants

Enrique Ortego
Pilar Yoldi
Yolanda Aguilar
Darío Pérez Rovira
Lucía Onaindia Olalde
Joseba Iraugi Castillo
Santiago Otero
Cirilo Santamaría

Alfonso Huet
Francisca Álvarez
Ricardo Falla
Pau Pérez Sales
Nekane Basabe Barañain
Benjamín Cuéllar
Luis Mario Martínez
Daniel Saxon

Javier Esquembre
Edelberto Torres Escobar
Germain Alberto Véliz Zepeda
Coindi
Acesa
Ignacio Cano
National Security Archive

Administrative Support

Mauricio Peñalba

René Zamora

Guillermo Escobar

GUATEMALA
Never Again!

REMHI
RECOVERY OF HISTORICAL MEMORY PROJECT
THE OFFICIAL REPORT OF THE HUMAN RIGHTS OFFICE,
ARCHDIOCESE OF GUATEMALA

ORBIS BOOKS

Maryknoll, New York 10545

The Catholic Foreign Mission Society of America (Maryknoll) recruits and trains people for overseas missionary service. Through Orbis Books, Maryknoll aims to foster the international dialogue that is essential to mission. The books published, however, reflect the opinions of their authors and are not meant to represent the official position of the society. To obtain more information about Maryknoll and Orbis Books, please visit our website at www.maryknoll.org.

The Catholic Institute for International Relations (CIIR) tackles the causes of poverty and injustice internationally through advocacy and skill sharing. An independent charity, CIIR works with people of all faiths and none.

The Latin America Bureau (LAB) is an independent research and publishing organisation. It works to broaden public understanding of issues of human rights and social and economic justice in Latin America and the Caribbean.

Copyright ©1999 by ODHAG (Human Rights Office of the Archdiocese of Guatemala)

This is an abridged English translation of Guatemala: Nunca Más (4 vols.), Informe proyecto interdiocesano de recuperación de la memoria histórica, ©1998 by the Oficina de Derechos Humanos del Arzobispado de Guatemala (ODHAG), 6 Calle 7-70 Zona 1, 01001, Guatemala City, Guatemala.

Gretta Tovar Siebentritt translated this abridged edition into English.

Cover photo by Daniel Hernández.

First published in the United States of America by Orbis Books, Maryknoll, NY 10545-0308.

First published in the UK in 1999 by: Catholic Institute for International Relations (CIIR), Unit 3 Canonbury Yard, 190a New North Road, London N1 7BJ in association with The Latin America Bureau (Research and Action) Ltd, 1 Amwell Street, London EC1R 1UL.

Manufactured in the United States of America.
Copy editing and typesetting by Joan Weber Laflamme.

A CIP catalogue record for this book is available from the British Library.
ISBN 1 899 365 44 3 (pbk)

CONTENTS

PART ONE
THE IMPACT OF THE VIOLENCE

PART TWO
THE METHODOLOGY OF HORROR

PART THREE
THE HISTORICAL CONTEXT

PART FOUR
THE VICTIMS OF THE CONFLICT

FOREWORD TO THE ENGLISH EDITION

This is a book of martyrs, a martyrology. It is an account, not exhaustive but fully representative, of the suffering and death of a martyred people, the preponderantly Mayan victims of nearly four decades of civil conflict in Guatemala.

It is also an outstanding example of a literary genre that, given the horrors of this century, has become increasingly widespread, the gathered data and analysis of a nation's crimes that are commonly referred to as truth commission reports.

It can also be considered a theological work. It is an expression of the pastoral mission of the Catholic church of Guatemala, whose bishops seized the momentum of the 1994 Oslo Agreement, leading to the 1996 definitive Peace Accord, to begin the process of healing and national reconciliation. Fully recognizing that healing and reconciliation cannot even be talked about until the truth of what went before is brought to light and acknowledged by all, the bishops undertook an imaginative and daring initiative—the Recovery of Historical Memory project (REMHI)—to seek out and present the truth.

In a number of countries in Latin America the church has written some of the most lucid chapters in the modern story of the defense of basic human rights, of faithful Christians standing up, sometimes at the cost of their own lives, to the forces of repression and control that typified many countries of the hemisphere since the 1950s. The modern human rights movement, well established nearly everywhere today, owes an immeasurable debt to the pioneering work of human rights groups in Latin America, and especially to the many groups inspired by the church's social teachings. If the flagship of this movement was the Chilean church's Vicariate of Solidarity, equal praise must be given today to the Guatemalan Archdiocesan Human Rights Office (ODHAG), the guiding light and coordinator of the REMHI project under the inspired leadership of murdered Bishop Juan Gerardi Conedera.

Some countries emerging from military dictatorship, such as Chile, Argentina, and El Salvador, formed truth commissions, which resulted in important and often shocking reports. In Brazil, Catholic and Protestant church leaders conspired to produce a most unusual "truth commission" report without benefit of an actual truth commission. Cardinal Paulo Evaristo Arns and Presbyterian pastor Jaime Wright secreted from police headquarters the meticulously detailed reports on the numerous atrocities committed by the government, carefully returning the files after copying them, and finally published a sensational and bestselling report, *Brasil: Nunca Mais.*

In Guatemala, a still more extraordinary thing occurred. As agreed upon by the government and the URNG guerrilla commanders in Oslo in 1994, a Historical Clarification Commission (*Comisión para el Esclarecimiento Histórico—CEH*) was to be created under UN auspices, following the definitive end of hostilities. It was to accomplish its work of studying nearly four decades within a single year after beginning, a seemingly impossible limitation. And it was prohibited from "individualizing responsibility"; no names, thank you.

The wonder is that the CEH report, "Guatemala: Memory of Silence," is as powerful and devastating a report as it is. Issued February 1999, the CEH report assigns blame for fully 93 percent of the atrocities to the government forces and their allied paramilitary bands, and only 3 percent to the guerrillas, contrasted with the REMHI findings of 89.7 percent and 4.8 percent respectively. Even more strikingly, it found that acts of genocide were committed against specific Mayan communities. Because Guatemala's postwar National Reconciliation Law excludes genocide from its amnesty provisions, the CEH's finding leaves open the possibility of future prosecutions.

The CEH report had at least three advantages over the REMHI report, *Guatemala: Nunca Más*. First, it followed by almost a year the release of *Nunca Más*, and thus reflected the benefit of REMHI's work. Second, it benefited greatly from the decision of the U.S. administration to declassify and release roughly a thousand sensitive documents, ironically enabling the report to cite the unhelpful role of certain U.S. agencies during the war. Third, the CEH had a budget of almost $10 million, giving it far greater resources than REMHI or any comparable NGO project.

The extraordinary thing, then, is that Guatemala, having suffered one of the longest and cruelest civil conflicts of our times, has been able to mount two independent yet complementary inquiries that leave future historians no doubt as to what happened in the Guatemalan killing fields. Even more than establishing the truth, the REMHI project offered the voiceless victims a chance to find their voices, perhaps for the first time, and, with that, the courage to continue speaking out and the long denied hope that tomorrow can be better.

This English-language condensation of the four-volume, thousand-page *Guatemala: Nunca Más*, offers a unique window onto the landscape of this martyred land and people. The victims' accounts of what they experienced are often shocking and painful to read, made no easier by the repetition of the same horrors recounted by different people in different places. The banality of evil. Some of the most dramatic testimonies are those of soldiers who confessed their participation in the horrors. Unlike the South African truth commission process, only a few of the guilty have come forward to seek forgiveness and healing, but those who did have left unforgettable testimony.

In addition to the voices of the people, and all the statistics, maps, graphs, analyses, and lists of unfamiliar names, *Nunca Más* presents a rich historical overview of Guatemala over the past four decades, which even knowledgeable students of the area will find both interesting and challenging. The severe constraints involved in reducing some fourteen hundred pages of text to slightly under four hundred pages make it impossible fully to reflect the richness of the original, but it provides the English-speaking reader with a unique opportunity to understand, especially through the voices of the victims and perpetrators themselves, the horror of Guatemala's recent history and the ways people responded to it.

I have said this is a martyrology, an alternative truth commission report, and a work of pastoral theology. This last point is underlined by Bishop Juan Gerardi's final public talk, the presentation in the Cathedral of *Guatemala: Nunca Más* on April 24, 1998, two days before he was killed (and which we can compare to Archbishop Romero's final sermon on March 23, 1980, the day before his martyrdom). This document, like much of the Latin American church's preaching, especially during the golden years of liberation theology, seeks to combine both *denuncia,* the denouncing of the sin, the evil that is being described, and *anuncio,* the announcing of the gospel's good news of liberation, redemption, salvation.

This is a book replete with horrors that merit the world's unequivocal denunciation. It is a book that serves as a reminder, if any is needed in this time of Kosovo, Sudan, and Burundi, that the genocide we have come to euphemize as ethnic cleansing has occurred in our hemisphere as well, and as recently as just yesterday in Guatemala. But above all, it is an account of the indomitable spirit of a people who have risen from the depths of unimaginable suffering and are seeking to refashion their society along the paths of peace, justice, and reconciliation. It is a book of hope.

THOMAS QUIGLEY
U.S. Catholic Conference
WASHINGTON, D.C.

PREFACE TO THE INTERNATIONAL EDITION

Dear Reader:

The international abridged version of the REMHI report you have before you addresses three main issues: (1) the suffering of the population; (2) how repression functioned; and, (3) the consequences of repression and demands for the future. We have selected key chapters from the report and condensed them with an emphasis on victims' testimonies and an analysis of the repressive apparatus.

Because this is a summary, it leaves out most of the psychosocial aspects of the events, their impact on both victims and perpetrators, and a detailed analysis of incidents, massacres, and repressive strategies. Rich statistical information and graphics included in the original four-volume report are also omitted.

In order to reduce the REMHI report to approximately one-sixth of its original length, we were obliged to exclude most of the victims' testimonies as well as the psychological and political analysis that make this document unique in the human rights field worldwide. This has been a painful task for the editorial staff. We constantly had to ask ourselves, "Can we really take responsibility for excluding this testimony or that critical aspect of the history of Guatemala's internal armed conflict?"

We hope that this summary is useful and contributes to the international community's increased solidarity with, and understanding of, what happened in Guatemala. And we hope that it affords non-Spanish speakers a degree of access to the valuable human rights work carried out by different institutions of the Guatemalan Catholic church. And finally, we hope that it inspires Spanish-speaking readers to read the full report. It is worth the effort!

THE EDITORIAL STAFF
GUATEMALA,
APRIL 24, 1998

ACKNOWLEDGMENTS

We would like to express our gratitude to the following people and institutions:

- The individuals and communities who gave their testimonies; the promoters (*animadores*) of reconciliation; the pastoral workers and bishops of the Guatemalan Catholic church; the translators, transcribers, and support staff of the Human Rights Office of the Archdiocese of Guatemala; the participating Diocese, the Archdiocese of Los Altos and Guatemala City, the data processors, consultants, field liaisons, and Guatemalan and international volunteers;

- the Swedish International Development Cooperation Agency (SIDA) and the Norwegian Agency for Development Assistance (NORAD) for their support throughout the implementation of the project;

- the European Union (EU), the Protestant Association for Development Cooperation (EZE), Misereor of Germany, the Danish International Development Agency (DANIDA), OXFAM UK, Project Counseling Service, the Heinrich Böll Foundation, the German Development Service (DED), and the German Society for Technical Cooperation (GTZ) for their support at different stages of the project;

- the Swedish government, INKOTA-Medical International of Germany for funding the publication of the REMHI report;

- all those who, through their invaluable and unconditional commitment and support, have made it possible to recover the people's memories of suffering during the armed conflict and to accompany the Guatemalan people, in their grief and their hope, as they face the challenge of reconstruction and peace.

The German Society for Technical Cooperation (GTZ) provided funding for the English translation of the abridged REMHI report. The Robert F. Kennedy Memorial Center for Human Rights facilitated the publication in English. Gretta Tovar Siebentritt translated the abridged report into English. Shannon Kathleen Lockhart reviewed the entire manuscript for the ODHAG in Guatemala. Margaret Popkin supervised and edited the translation. Ann Butwell, Elizabeth McMeekin, and Victoria Rich also assisted in editing the translation.

SPEECH BY MONSENOR JUAN GERARDI

ON THE OCCASION OF THE PRESENTATION OF THE REMHI REPORT
METROPOLITAN CATHEDRAL OF GUATEMALA CITY, APRIL 24, 1998

The REMHI project has been an effort within the human rights ministry, which is itself part of the social ministry of the church. It is a mission of service to people and to society. When faced with political or economic issues, many people react by saying, "Why does the church get involved in this?" They would like us to dedicate ourselves strictly to spiritual ministries. But the church has a mission to accomplish in terms of constructing the social order, and that includes ethical, moral, and evangelical values. What do the commandments tell us? They say, "You shall love your neighbor as yourself." And it is precisely to that neighbor that the church has to direct its mission.

Speaking to lay people, Pope John Paul II said, "An essential task of the church is to rediscover the dignity of the human person." This was also the evangelizing work of Jesus. The Lord put the dignity of human beings at the center of the gospel.

Within the pastoral work of the church, the REMHI project is a legitimate and painful denunciation that we must listen to with profound respect and a spirit of solidarity. But it is also an announcement. It is an alternative aimed at finding new ways for human beings to live with one another. When we began this project, we were interested in discovering the truth in order to share it. We were interested in reconstructing the history of pain and death, understanding the reasons for it, the why and the how. We sought to show the human drama and to share with others the sorrow and the anguish of the thousands of dead, disappeared, and tortured. We sought to look at the roots of injustice and the absence of values.

This is a pastoral approach. It is working with the light of faith to discover the face of God, the presence of the Lord. In all of these events it is God who is speaking to us. We are called to reconciliation. Christ's mission is one of reconciliation. His presence calls us to be agents of reconciliation in this broken society and to try to place the victims and perpetrators within the framework of justice. People have died for their beliefs. Killers were often used as instruments. Conversion is necessary, and it is up to us to open spaces to bring about that conversion. It is not enough simply to accept the facts. It is necessary to reflect on them and to recover lost values.

We are collecting the people's memories because we want to contribute to the construction of a different country. This path was and continues to be full of risks, but the construction of the Kingdom of God entails risks, and only those who have the strength to confront those risks can be its builders.

On June 23, 1994, the parties who negotiated the Peace Accords expressed their conviction that "all of the people of Guatemala [have] the right to know the full truth" about the events that occurred during the armed conflict, and that "this clarification will help to ensure that these sad and painful pages of history will not be repeated and that the process of democratization in this country will be strengthened." They emphasized that [knowing the truth] is an indispensable condition for achieving peace. This is part of the preamble of the accord that created the Commission for Historical Clarification, which is also in the process of concluding its important work.

The church resonated with this desire and committed itself to the search to "know the truth," convinced, as Pope John Paul II said, that "truth is the strength behind peace" (World Day of Peace, 1980). As a church, we collectively and responsibly took on the task of breaking the silence that thousands of war victims have kept for years. We opened up the possibility for them to speak and have their say, to tell their stories of suffering and pain, so they might feel liberated from the burden that has weighed them down for so many years.

The essential objective behind the REMHI project during its three years of work has been to know the truth that will make us all free (Jn 8:32). Reflecting on the Historical Clarification Accord, we, as people of faith, discovered a call from God for our mission as church—that truth should be the vocation of all humanity. If we orient ourselves according to the Word of God, we cannot hide or cover up reality. We cannot distort history, nor should we silence the truth.

Twenty centuries ago St. Paul made an affirmation that our recent history has unequivocally confirmed: "The wrath of God is revealed from heaven against all ungodliness and wickedness of men who suppress the truth with injustices" (Rom 1:18). In our country, the truth has been twisted and silenced. God is inflexibly opposed to evil in any form. The root of the downfall and the misfortune of humanity comes from the deliberate opposition to truth, which is the fundamental reality of God and of human beings. This reality has been intentionally distorted in our country throughout thirty-six years of war against the people.

That is why in our bishops' pastoral letter entitled "True Peace Is Urgent!" we stated that historical clarification was "not just necessary, but crucial to ensuring that the past, with all of its serious consequences, not be repeated. As long as the truth is not known, the wounds of the past remain open and do not begin to heal."

As a church, we do not doubt that the work we have carried out in these past few years has been part of a story of grace and salvation, a real step toward peace stemming from justice. It has lightly scattered the seeds of life and dignity throughout the country—and the advocates and participants in the work have been the suffering people themselves. It has been a beautiful service of veneration for the martyrs and has brought dignity to the victims who were the targets of the plans for destruction and death.

To open ourselves to truth and to face our personal and collective reality are not options that can be accepted or rejected. They are indispensable requirements for all people and societies that seek to humanize themselves and to be free. They make us face our most essential human condition: that we are sons and daughters of God, called to participate in our Father's freedom.

Years of terror and death have displaced and reduced the majority of Guatemalans to fear and silence. *Truth* is the primary word, the serious and mature action that makes it possible for us to break this cycle of death and violence and to open ourselves to a future of hope and light for all.

REMHI's work has been an astonishing endeavor of discovery, exploration, and appropriation of our personal and collective history. It has been an open door for people to breathe and speak in freedom and for the creation of communities with hope. Peace is possible—a peace that is born from the truth that comes from each one of us and from all of us. It is a painful truth, full of memories of the country's deep and bloody wounds. It is a liberating and humanizing truth that makes it possible for all men and women to come to terms with themselves and their life stories. It is a truth that challenges each one of us to recognize our individual and collective responsibility and to commit ourselves to action so that those abominable acts never happen again.

This project has made a commitment to the people who gave their testimonies to assemble their experiences in this report and to support all the victims' demands. But our commitment is also to return these collected memories to the people. The search for truth does not end here. It must return to its birthplace and support the use of memory as an instrument of social reconstruction through the creation of materials, ceremonies, monuments, etc.

Pope John Paul II tell us, "It is necessary to keep alive the memory of what has happened. It is a specific duty. We have been better able to comprehend what World War II has meant for Europeans and for the world during these fifty years thanks to the acquisition of new information that has allowed us a better understanding of the suffering caused" (50th anniversary of the end of World War II). This is what the REMHI project has done in Guatemala.

Discovering the truth is painful, but it is without doubt a healthy and liberating action. The thousands of testimonies of the victims and the recounting of the horrific crimes are today's manifestations of the figure of the "suffering servant of Yahweh," brought to life in the people of Guatemala. "Behold my servant," says Isaiah, " . . . many were afraid of him. He was so disfigured he was beyond human semblance, and his form beyond that of sons of man. He has borne our griefs and carried our sorrows, yet we esteemed him stricken, smitten by God and afflicted" (Is 52:13–53:4).

Bringing the memory of these painful events into the present leads us to confront some of the first words of our faith, "Cain, where is your brother Abel?"

"I don't know," he answered. "Am I my brother's keeper?"

Yahweh replied, "What have you done? The voice of your brother's blood is crying to me from the ground" (Gn 4: 9-10).

—Translated by EPICA

INTRODUCTORY REMARKS

Dear Brothers and Sisters:

In October 1994, I asked the Archdiocesan Human Rights Office to present the Recovery of Historical Memory (REMHI) project to the bishops of the Guatemalan Episcopal Conference. The support of my brothers and their dioceses have made this an interdiocesan effort. We regarded it as a contribution to peace and reconciliation that involved acknowledging the suffering of the people, giving voice to those who had not been heard, and bearing witness to their martyrdom so as to honor the memory of the dead and restore the self-esteem of their relatives.

The pastoral teams of eleven dioceses and countless others conducted this study, *Guatemala: Never Again!,* whose findings are presented to you here. In a fragile and uncertain climate, they devoted themselves to the task of repairing the social fabric that begins by discerning the truth.

This effort commenced prior to the establishment of the Historical Clarification Commission, and we envisioned it as an initial form of support for the commission's activities. Our search for information centered on rural communities whose physical inaccessibility and linguistic diversity would complicate the commission's task.

We do not wish to imply that we have come even close to exhausting this subject. The violations committed against urban residents should be analyzed separately, given the unique characteristics of the individuals or social groups that were targeted. Moreover, following extremely rigorous criteria, we let the people freely and spontaneously describe their memories and firsthand experiences in order to avoid bias in the collection of testimonies.

The purpose of this report is to conserve the historical memory of political violence, of the egregious human rights violations suffered by indigenous people and communities over the past thirty-six years of fratricidal struggle, which left incalculable social polarization.

The armed conflict that afflicted us for so long, bringing about the loss of moral and ethical values that ultimately led to our breakdown as a society, has ended. It is time now to face the truth in order to morally rebuild our society, mangled and torn apart by an unjust war whose legacy is an excessively high toll in human lives. Many were victims of a "dirty war" that terrorized the population, the effects of which persist to this day. This is apparent in each and every chapter of the report.

One asks oneself, How was it possible to arrive at this depth of degradation? How was it possible to achieve this degree of disregard for the human person, the handiwork of a loving creator? How was it possible for nature, the product of the evolution and improvement of the species, to be so mercilessly destroyed?

What were the roots of this conflict? We must consider the living conditions of the vast majority, deprived of their basic needs (access to food, health, education, housing, a fair wage, the right to organize, respect for political opinions, etc.) so that they were unable to develop in conditions befitting human beings. We must reflect on the prevailing anarchy in our country at that time and the enduring wound inflicted by an armed intervention that allowed a glimpse of humankind's hidden capacity for destruction. And we must consider that some groups felt that the political space had closed. We can then understand that the war launched by young civilians and army officers could no longer be averted. People joined the insurgency out of their desire to bring about a more just society and the impossibility of accomplishing it through the established system. This went beyond those seeking to install a socialist state to include many who—without being Marxists or espousing a particular political position—became convinced by, and felt compelled to support, a movement that seemed to represent the only possible path: armed struggle.

The army, for its part, had been shaped by the Cold War policy of confrontation that had permeated armies throughout Latin America. Its rallying cry as it undertook the counterinsurgency struggle was the imperative to uphold and defend the status quo against the threatened installation of a socialist government on *terra firma*. (Remember that the Batista regime had recently been overthrown in Cuba and a confrontation was gradually heating up between the Cuban and United States governments.) In this way the army was removed from its assigned role under Guatemalan law, which is to safeguard territorial integrity and national sovereignty, in part by international pressure, and in part by the political parties then in power. The latter transformed the army into a political police force and an instrument for the persecution, harassment, and murder of their enemies. These observations are not directed against the institution of the army established by our Constitution. They refer instead to those military leaders who lent themselves to the political machinations of the controlling parties and compromised the entire armed institution by participating in actions contrary to the most elemental standards of human existence.

This war was characterized by torture and murder. Entire communities were obliterated, terrorized, and defenseless in the crossfire, and nature, which the indigenous cosmovision holds sacred, was destroyed. Like a maniacal windstorm, the war swept away the cream of Guatemala's intellectual community. The country was orphaned abruptly by the loss of valuable citizens whose absence is still being felt.

Who was the victor in this war? We all lost. I do not believe that anyone is cynical enough to raise the flag of victory over the remains of thousands of Guatemalans—fathers, mothers, brothers and sisters, and young children—innocent of the inferno that consumed them. Our country's social fabric was devastated, as demonstrated by the thousands of testimonies in this report. Those directly and indirectly responsible for the suffering must read and interpret these findings as the people's utter and unequivocal rejection of the culture of violence. It is ethically and morally imperative that the acts of Guatemala's recent past never again come to pass. Those directly involved in the armed conflict and the dirty war must acknowledge openly their errors and excesses and ask forgiveness for their crimes against innocent victims. The church teaches us that "no one is so perverse and so guilty that they cannot trust that they will be forgiven as long as their behavior is sincere." But they are not the only ones; society as a whole must engage in a process of reflection that reaches into the far corners of the collective conscience in order to enter into a period of transformation in the aftermath of horrors that are only beginning to come to light. For this transformation to be genuine, however, we all—each sector of society—must acknowledge our faults, by commission or omission, and radically change our attitude toward our fellow human beings. The hierarchical church has done this; we have taken the opportunity to ask forgiveness for not having known how to defend properly those battered by injustice (*Urge la Verdadera Paz,* no. 18; *Joint Pastoral Letter, July 15, 1995*).

Despite the profound sorrow with which we have heard these testimonies of human suffering, the memory and image of Christ crucified anew, we can do no less than hope that by renouncing this dark past of horror, and with our determination to rebuild our country, a new climate of hope will emerge with fraternity, solidarity, and understanding; with respect for our fellow human beings, social harmony, and resource-sharing; and with a clear conscience and firm resolve that as children of God we are required to build a society based on justice and solidarity. With our feet on the ground and our eyes raised toward heaven. Amen.

MONS. PRÓSPERO PENADOS DEL BARRIO
ARCHBISHOP PRIMATE OF GUATEMALA

INTRODUCTION

This report is based on an analysis of testimonies compiled by the REMHI project. The first part examines the effects of violent ordeals, diverse forms of resistance, and the survivors' demands on government and society. This is followed by a discussion of the types of violence employed against the civilian population, the impact of militarization, and the mechanisms that made such atrocities possible. Finally, an overview of distinct historical periods is presented, as well as general information about the victims and statistics on human rights violations culled from the testimonies.

This effort to reconstruct the historical memory is the product of a complex preparatory phase involving the project's outreach workers (*animadores*) and coordinators. It is the result of a collective movement to reclaim memory, which often journeyed silently along roads and footpaths, from the hands of the people who came to give their testimony. The report endeavors to reassemble this collective memory and to fulfill the people's expectations of the REMHI project.

THE VALUE OF TESTIMONY

Besides the individual and collective impact of violence and terror, political repression deprived the people of their right to a voice. For many years they were unable to share their experience, to reveal what had happened, or to accuse those responsible. These testimonies represent the first time that many victims and survivors have spoken of their experiences.

Remembrance frequently aroused emotions. The act of giving testimony about what happened led many people to relive, in some form, their pain. Many tears accompany these testimonies, tears that we were unable to transcribe in the report. The interview format, the outreach worker training, and the information-gathering tools were all designed to create a space, albeit limited, that acknowledged and supported the witnesses.

Even remembering this makes you want to cry. You really feel what the people felt. Case 6102 (murder and refugee flight), Barillas, Huehuetenango, 1982.

Despite this atmosphere of trust, many feared that giving their testimony could have adverse consequences. At the time, the military still maintained pressure on communities, and there was no certainty that a signed agreement to end the war would be reached. Most people who gave their testimony found the experience to be beneficial as an emotional catharsis and as a way of acting on their suffering, restoring the dignity of their murdered or disappeared family members, and articulating their demands and needs.

> *Now I am content because the testimony I have given will become part of history. I have no more misgivings; now I have released my pain by giving my testimony.* Case 3967, Caserío Pal, Quiché, 1981.

The compiled testimonies are imbued with the virtue of the victims' own words. On some occasions it was impossible to record more than a partial account of the facts. In many others, people's experiences were replete with different intersecting episodes and violent ordeals. Thus, the report is an attempt to piece together, in their own words, the many complex and divergent experiences of the populations touched by the war. It can be read as a book, it can be heard as a story, but above all it can be learned from as a collective memory that reclaims the victims' dignity and the survivors' hopes for change. Besides examining past events, this memory sustains the demands for truth, respect, justice, and reparation that must be part of Guatemala's social reconstruction process.

SOCIAL AND POLITICAL VIOLENCE IN GUATEMALA

PERIODS OF VIOLENCE

Guatemala's geography, like the memory of her people, is crisscrossed by massive displacements and ruptures. The roots of social conflict in Guatemala are found in a tradition of political exclusion, ethnic discrimination, and social injustice that permeates the state structure. During the sixties, in addition to combat between the guerrillas and the army, government violence targeted peasants in the eastern part of the country. In the seventies, state violence was particularly virulent in the cities. It was trained on leaders of social movements and sectors opposing the successive military regimes, in addition to the guerrilla infrastructure. In the early eighties, counterinsurgency policy took the form of state-sponsored terrorism featuring systematic, mass destruction, particularly of indigenous communities and organized peasant groups. The magnitude of the destruction went beyond all conceivable horror and extinguished any hopes for change.

Faced with increasingly indiscriminate repression, many people saw the revolutionary movement as a means of bringing about change and realizing their demands for justice and freedom. At the same time, some guerrilla organizations adopted strategies to expand their bases and incorporate large numbers of people into their military support structures. These strategies had a strong influence on community dynamics. The guerrillas used violence to eliminate army collaborators and, on other occasions, to eliminate the opposition in zones under their control.

THE IMPACT OF MILITARIZATION

The army's strategy was to militarize the social fabric. This was accomplished through widespread forced recruitment and the establishment of Civilian Self-defense Patrols *(Patrullas de Autodefensa Civil—PAC)* and military commissioners responsible for maintaining control over the population and fighting the guerrillas. This strategy dragged the civilian population into the war. Militarized structures dominated the daily life of every village or neighborhood, trampling local values and culture. Civil patrols and military commissioners implicated neighbors and community leaders by making them directly responsible for numerous murders and massacres. People's lives were transformed into a battleground.

IMPUNITY

The term *impunity* appears throughout this book to describe a pervasive reality in which government agents operated, and continue to operate, without fear of punishment. Impunity is presented as a cause and a consequence of violence, as well as a central obstacle to justice and reconciliation.

The ability of government forces to operate without fear of punishment has been a central feature of the Guatemalan conflict. The absolute power of military and police forces, their frequent clandestine activities, and the substitution of military power for civilian authority have contributed to what is widely referred to as a state of impunity. Throughout the years, virtually no one has been investigated or prosecuted for committing crimes against humanity. To the contrary, many of those primarily responsible for the violence have retained their powerful posts and privileges. The ability of perpetrators to commit crimes with impunity has been a constant factor influencing the conduct of the army, police, military commissioners, and civil patrol, and has contributed to further violence against the people. The inability to obtain justice frequently evokes a sense of powerlessness among victims and survivors. Long-lasting effects observed today include the lack of trust in the justice system, the reality that victims live next door to perpetrators in many communities, and the emergence of new forms of social violence, still protected by a mantle of impunity.

THE STRUGGLE FOR MEMORY

Historical memory has an important role to play in dismantling the mechanisms that made state terrorism possible and in exposing the role terrorism plays in an exclusive political and economic system. The story of people's suffering cannot be treated as if it were a page in a book. The distortion of events and of accountability for them elevates the risk that new ways will be found to legitimize the instigators of the war, placing Guatemala's future in grave jeopardy. In addition to enforcing the law, future atrocities must be prevented by abolishing systems and ideologies that make obedience a virtue and countenance horror as a means of attaining social objectives.

GLOSSARY

Acronyms, Abbreviations, Organizations, and Spanish Words

AED	Law Students' Association (*Asociación de Estudiantes de Derecho*)
AEU	University Students Association (*Asociación de Estudiantes Universitarios*)
AGA	General Association of Growers (*Asociación General de Agricultores*)
AID	U.S. Agency for International Development
ANACAFE	Coffee Exporters Association (*Asociación Nacional del Café*)
APRI	Patriotic Action for Institutional Recovery (*Acción Patriótica de Recuperación Institucional*)
Archivo	Intelligence division of the Presidential General Staff (EMP); also known as the DSP
ASECSA	Association of Community Health Services (*Asociación de Servicios Comunitarios de Salud*)
ASIES	Research and Social Studies Association (*Asociación de Investigación y Estudios Sociales*)
BIEN	Special Narcotics Investigation Brigade (*Brigada de Investigaciones Especiales en Narcóticos*)
BROE	Reaction and Special Operations Battalion (*Batallón de Reacción y Operaciones Especiales*); a police rapid response unit also known as *Comando Seis* and SWAT
CACIF	Coordinating Committee of Agricultural, Commercial, Industrial, and Financial Associations (*Comité Coordinador de Asociaciones Agrícolas, Comerciales, Industriales y Financieras*)
CADEG	Anticommunist Council of Guatemala (*Consejo Anticomunista de Guatemala*)
CAN	Nationalist Authentic Central (*Central Auténtico Nacionalista*)
CAPS	Social Promoter's Training.Program (*Centro de Adiestramiento de Promotores Sociales*)
CAVISA	Central American Glass Industry, Inc. (*Centro Americana Industria de Vidrio, S.A.*
CCL	Local Clandestine Committees (*Comités Clandestinos Locales*)

CDC	Civil Defense Committees (*Comités de Defensa Civil*); also known as PACs
CDHG	Guatemalan Human Rights Commission (*Comisión de Derechos Humanos de Guatemala*); a nongovernmental human rights group
CEAR	Special Committee for Attention to Refugees (*Comité Especial de Atención a Refugiados*); a government agency
CEG	Guatemalan Bishops' Conference (*Conferencia Episcopal de Guatemala*)
CEH	Historical Clarification Commission (*Comisión para el Esclarecimiento Histórico*); United Nations-sponsored truth commission mandated by the Peace Accords
CEM	Military Studies Center (*Centro de Estudios Militares*)
CERJ	Council of Ethnic Communities Runujel Junam (social movement founded in 1986 to protest civil patrols)
CETE	Emergency Committee of Public Employees *(Comité de Emergencia de Trabajadores del Estado*)
CGTG	General Confederation of Guatemalan Workers (*Confederación General de Trabajadores Guatemaltecos*)
CIAS	Center for Investigation and Social Action *(Centro de Investigación y Acción Social*); a Jesuit institution
CLAT	Latin American Workers Central (*Central Latinoamericana de Trabajadores*)
CMU/URNG	Unified Coordinator of the Masses (*Coordinadora Unitaria de Masas*); an organization of the URNG
CNCG	National Peasant Confederation of Guatemala *(Confederación Nacional Campesina de Guatemala*)
CNT	National Workers Central (*Central Nacional de Trabajadores*)
CNUS	National Committee of Labor Unity (*Comité Nacional de Unidad Sindical*)
Comando Seis	National Police Rapid Response Team that operated in the capital; also known as BROE and SWAT
CONAVIGUA	National Coordination of Guatemalan Widows (*Coordinadora Nacional de Viudas de Guatemala*)
CONFREGUA	Guatemalan Conference of Religious; founded in June 1961
COPAZ	Peace Commission (*Comisión de la Paz*)
COPREDEH	Presidential Human Rights Commission *(Comisión Presidencial de Derechos Humanos*)
CPR	Communities of Population in Resistance *(Comunidades de Población en Resistencia*)
CRAG	Committee for Anticommunist Resistance (*Comité de Resistencia Anticomunista de Guatemala*)

CRN	National Reconstruction Committee (*Comité de Reconstrucción Nacional*)
CUC	Committee of Peasant Unity (*Comité de Unidad Campesina*)
CUSG	Guatemalan Labor Unity Central *(Central de Unidad Sindical Guatemalteca)*
D-1	Army Personnel Directorate
D-2	Army Intelligence Directorate; also known as *La 2*
D-3	Army Operations Directorate
D-4	Army Logistics Directorate
D-5	Army Civil Affairs Directorate
DC	Christian Democratic Party
DECAP	Department of Administrative Oversight of the Presidency (*Departamento de Control Administrativo de la Presidencia*)
DIC	Criminal Investigations Department *(Departamento de Investigaciones Criminológicas)*; National Police detective branch in the nineties (see DIT)
DIDE	Army Public Relations Department (*Departamento de Información y Divulgación del Ejército)*
DIT	Technical Investigations Department (*Departamento de Investigaciones Técnicas);* National detective branch created under Ríos Montt; predecessor to DIC
DSP	Public Security Department (*Departamento de Seguridad Pública)*; a division of the EMP, also known as *Archivo*
EAFG	Guatemalan Forensic Anthropology Team (*Equipo de Antropología Forense de Guatemala)*
ECLAC	Economic Commission on Latin America and the Caribbean
EGP	Guerrilla Army of the Poor (*Ejército Guerrillero de los Pobres)*; one of four guerrilla groups comprising the URNG
EMDN	National Defense Staff (*Estado Mayor de la Defensa Nacional*); known as EMGE prior to the mid-eighties
EMGE	Army General Staff (*Estado Mayor General del Ejército*); known as EMDN as of the mid-eighties
EMP	Presidential General Staff (*Estado Mayor Presidencial*); military staff attached to the presidency
ESA	Secret Anticommunist Army (*Ejército Secreto Anticomunista*); a death squad
ESTNA	Center for Studies on National Stability *(Centro de Estudios de la Estabilidad Nacional*); founded in September 1988
FACS	Augusto César Sandino Front (*Frente Augusto César Sandino*); an EGP unit

FAMDEGUA	Association of Families of the Disappeared and Detained of Guatemala (*Asociación de Familias de los Desaparecidos y Detenidos de Guatemala*)
FAR	Rebel Armed Forces (*Fuerzas Armadas Rebeldes*); one of four guerrilla groups comprising the URNG
FDNG	New Guatemala Democratic Front (*Frente Democrático Nueva Guatemala*); a political party formed in the mid-nineties
FERG	Robin García Revolutionary Student Front *(Frente Estudiantil Revolucionario Robin García)*
FGEI	Edgar Ibarra Guerrilla Front (*Frente Guerrillero Edgar Ibarra*); formed out of the GEI
FIL	Local Irregular Forces (*Fuerzas Irregulares Locales*); part of the guerrilla infrastructure in many communities; known by the army as "local political-military organizations"
FMLN-FDR	Salvadoran political and military opposition alliance
FONAPAZ	National Fund for Peace (*Fondo Nacional por la Paz*); government assistance program
FOSA	Organized Front of Unions in Amatitlán *(Frente Organizado de Sindicatos de Amatitlán)*
FP31	Popular Front "January 31" (*Frente Popular 31 de enero)*
FPL	Popular Liberating Front (*Frente Popular Libertador*)
FRG	Guatemalan Republican Front (*Frente Republicano Guatemalteco*); a political party
FRN	National Resistance Front (*Frente de Resistencia Nacional)*
FUEGO	United Front of Organized Guatemalan Students (*Frente Unido del Estudiantado Guatemalteco Organizado)*
FUN	National Unity Front (*Frente de Unidad Nacional*)
FUNA	United Anticommunist Front (*Frente Unido Anticomunista*)
FUNDAPI	Foundation to Assist the Indigenous People (*Fundación de Ayuda al Pueblo Indígena*); created by the Church of the Word, an evangelical church to which Efraín Ríos Montt belonged
FUR	United Revolutionary Front (*Frente Unido de la Revolución)*
FYDEP	Progress and Development in the Petén *(Fomento y Desarrollo en El Petén*); a development organization
G-2	Army intelligence (see D-2)
GAM	Mutual Support Group (*Grupo de Apoyo Mutuo*)
GEI	Edgar Ibarra Guerrilla [unit] (*Guerrilla Edgar Ibarra*); later became the FGEI

GUATEL	Guatemalan national telephone company
IEME	Spanish Institute of Foreign Missions (*Instituto Español de Misiones Extranjeras)*
IGE	Guatemalan Church in Exile (*Iglesia Guatemalteca en Exilio*)
IGSS	Guatemalan Social Security Institute *(Instituto Guatemalteco de Seguridad Social*)
INAP	National Public Administration Institute *(Instituto Nacional de Administración Pública*)
INCAE	Central American Business Administration Institute (*Instituto Centroamericano de Administración Económica)*
INTA	National Agrarian Reform Institute (*Instituto Nacional de Transformación Agraria*)
JPT	Patriotic Youth Workers (*Juventud Patriótica del Trabajo*); an affiliate of the PGT
La 2	Army Intelligence (see D-2)
La Cofradía	The Brotherhood; a fraternal network of military intelligence officers
La Judicial	Guatemalan secret police; a plainclothes detective unit
La Regional	Regional Telecommunications Office (military communications part of the Guatemalan intelligence and security apparatus); predecessor to *Archivo*
M-20 de Octubre	Movement "October 20" (*Movimiento 20 de Octubre*)
MAG	Anticommunist Movement of Guatemala *(Movimiento Anticomunista de Guatemala*)
MAP	Military Assistance Program (United States)
MANO	National Organized Anticommunist Movement *(Movimiento Anticomunista Nacional Organizado*); a death squad
Mano Blanca, la	The White Hand; a death squad; also known as MANO
MAYS	Marco Antonio Yon Sosa Front (*Frente Marco Antonio Yon Sosa);* a guerrilla unit
MDN	National Democratic Movement (*Movimiento Democrático Nacional*)
MEU	University Student Movement (*Movimiento Estudiantil Universitario*)
MINUGUA	United Nations Verification Mission in Guatemala *(Misión de Verificación de las Naciones Unidas en Guatemala*)
MLN	National Liberation Movement (*Movimiento de Liberación Nacional*)
MPMMMM	Movement in Memory of Mario Méndez Montenegro *(Movimiento por la Memoria de Mario Méndez Montenegro*)

MR-12 de Abril	Revolutionary Movement "April 12" (*Movimiento Revolucionario 12 de Abril*)
MR-13 de Noviembre	Revolutionary Movement "November 13" (*Movimiento Revolucionario 13 de Noviembre*)
MRP-Ixim	Popular Revolutionary Movement-*Ixim* (*Movimiento Revolucionario Popular- Ixim*); *Ixim* means corn
NOA	New Anticommunist Organization (*Nueva Organización Anticomunista*); a death squad
ODHA	also ODHAG: Human Rights Office of the Archdiocese of Guatemala (*Oficina de Derechos Humanos del Arzobispado de Guatemala*)
OPA	Armed Political Organization (*Organización Política Armada*)
ORPA	Revolutionary Organization of the People in Arms (*Organización Revolucionaria del Pueblo en Armas*); one of four groups comprising the URNG
PAAC	Program of Aid to Conflictive Areas (*Programa de Ayuda a Áreas en Conflicto*)
PAC	Civilian Self-defense Patrols (*Patrullas de Autodefensa Civil*); also known as Voluntary Civil Defense Committees; see also CDC
PAN	National Advancement Party (*Partido Avanzada Nacional*)
PGT	Guatemalan Workers Party (*Partido Guatemalteco de Trabajo*); one of four groups comprising the URNG
PID	Democratic Institutional Party (*Partido Institucional Democrático*)
PMA	Mobil Military Police (*Policía Militar Ambulante*)
PR	Revolutionary Party (*Partido Revolucionario*)
PRES	Economic and Social Adjustment Program (*Programa de Reajuste Económico y Social*)
PRN	National Reorganization Plan (*Plan de Reorganización Nacional*)
PROMIKA	Kaqchiquel Missionary Program (*Programa Misionero Kaqchiquel*)
PSD	Social Democratic Party (*Partido Social Democrática*)
PURD	Revolutionary Democratic Unity Party (*Partido de Unidad Revolucionaria Democrática*)
RUOG	United Representation of Guatemalan Opposition (*Representación Unitaria Opositora de Guatemala*)
S-2	Intelligence section (at the army base and unit level)
S-5	Civil affairs section (at the army base and unit level)
SIPROCI	Civilian Protection System (*Sistema de Protección Civil*); a military-police coordination on public security matters

SWAT	Police rapid response unit; see *Comando Seis* and BROE
UASP	Union for Popular and Labor Action (*Unidad de Acción Sindical y Popular*)
UCN	National Centrist Union (*Unión del Centro Nacional*)
UNAGRO	National Agricultural Exporters Union (*Unión Nacional de Agroexportadores*)
UPM	Permanent Military Units (*Unidades Permanentes Militares*)
URNG	National Revolutionary Union of Guatemala (*Unidad Revolucionaria Nacional Guatemalteca*); the umbrella group comprising four guerrilla factions (EGP, FAR, ORPA, PGT), founded in 1982
USAC	San Carlos University *(Universidad de San Carlos)*

Part One

THE IMPACT OF THE VIOLENCE

Chapter One

INDIVIDUAL EFFECTS OF THE VIOLENCE

I wanted to tell you this, about what hurt me so terribly. Most of all, before starting, when I said I was going to tell it to you, I was very tense. And even now I feel it more here, by thinking about all of these things. Because now I see it from another perspective; now it doesn't hurt me more than when I was going through it. Of course I experienced it another way. And sometimes I even get—I don't know how this resentment wells up in me and who to retaliate against sometimes. Case 5017, San Pedro Necta, Huehuetenango, 1982.

THE IMMEDIATE IMPACT

First, in the vast majority of cases, repression caused mortal danger and sorrow over what had happened and frequently left behind feelings of injustice, extreme hunger, and ill health.[1] A second group of effects includes altered grieving processes for deceased family members, a sense of humiliation, and powerlessness and uncertainty about the future, all indications that the meaning of life has been totally altered. While undoubtedly quite severe on an individual basis, acute traumatic reactions immediately following the ordeal (such as serious mental health problems) were probably less significant than the above-mentioned effects.

Most of the individual effects reported are similar in men's and women's testimonies. Descriptions of effects associated with powerlessness and their social role as males tend to predominate in men's testimonies, while women emphasize the personal impact (health problems, altered grieving) and other effects on them as women. In terms of the incidents, men were more likely to speak of massacres, while women spoke more of murders and individual acts of violence, describing the direct loss of family members.

---

[1] We point out that these are open-ended interviews based on a questionnaire rather than closed interviews. Therefore these findings discuss the most salient aspects of people's testimonies rather than the precise frequency of problems (for example, it is unlikely that fewer than 1 percent have had nightmares or recurrent memories after experiencing the repressive act; according to various studies, when direct questions are asked about these recurring memories, the frequency rises to 20-40 percent).

ONGOING TRAUMA

In general, the global effects of repression have diminished, although most people still exhibit symptoms of the violence they suffered. These lingering symptoms probably have as much to do with recurring experiences of violence as with the persistence of the most serious effects.

The most common individual effects that survivors still experience are feelings of sorrow and injustice, altered grieving processes and, less frequently (one out of three who reported experiencing such symptoms at the time of the incidents continue to report them as problematic), psychosomatic complaints, hunger, loneliness, traumatic memories, nightmares, and alcoholism.

Problems such as loneliness, however, may last longer or increase as time passes. Altered grieving processes are also reported more frequently now (for each person who described this at the time of the incident, two report it currently). Survivors are more likely to describe symptoms associated with traumatic memories now, and may find themselves becoming very emotional when giving their testimony. Although this could indicate a significant long-term impact on a particular group, it is also probably the people's response to having their memory triggered and the atmosphere of political violence and intimidation that prevailed when the testimonies were taken.

FROM FEAR TO TERROR

At the nine-day mass they were told about some corpses in Verbena. The corpses were in a terrible state. They saw a burned corpse. They took the dentist...to look at that corpse, and he said it wasn't him. A birth certificate was needed to process the social security [IGSS] pension and she decided to go by the National Police to ask about the car. That same night they called to threaten her to stop looking for the car and viewing corpses, or they would kill her and the child. The house was still being watched. She went on with her life but stopped seeing her friends so as not to cause them problems. Twice they threatened her. She sought psychological help. She was very young and what she had seen in the morgues had affected her terribly. Case 5080, Guatemala, 1980.

A STRATEGY OF TERROR

Human rights violations have been used as a strategy of social control in Guatemala. Society as a whole has been touched by fear, whether during periods of rampant and indiscriminate violence or times of more selective forms of repression. More than simply a byproduct of armed confrontation, terror has been the goal of a counterinsurgency policy that utilized different means at different times (fear is the effect most frequently reported in the testimonies).

Selective Repression against Leaders

The strategy of forced disappearances and murders of leaders of social organizations, while employed throughout the conflict, was particularly prevalent from 1965 to 1968 and 1978 to 1983. The goal of selective repression has been to crush organizational efforts viewed as threatening to the government. In such cases, the police and security forces chose methods and actions designed to prevent the perpetrators from being identified and to make a pointed display of violence and the omnipresent repressive apparatus. These actions were accompanied by the conspicuous absence of public protection such as judicial institutions, the media, and so forth.

> *They held him for two nights at the public jail. That was where they interrogated him; the authorities did whatever they wanted to him, and later they sent him home to rest. Intelligence agents from the G-2 arrived about midnight. At the command headquarters, they had a tape player on with the volume turned way up. Later they put a hood over his head to interrogate him. The next day, they removed him, dying, from the jail, and they took him in a G-2 vehicle, tied up with all-purpose ropes, toward Salamá. They left my dead father bound and riddled with bullets; and his face totally destroyed so that we family members wouldn't be able to identify him. They left him in that place called El Palmar. This was because the deceased was extremely religious, very active, and he liked to be part of improvement committees, and he was highly regarded by the community.* Case 2024, San Miguel Chicaj, Baja Verapaz, 1982.

Harassment of Family Members

The selective murder of leaders was often accompanied by the harassment of their families either before or after the violent incidents. On some occasions, the strategy of terror was trained directly on the families after the fact in order to discourage them from reporting the incidents.

> *So afterward the people from the army found out and called us to a meeting in the village of El Culeque. They threatened us, and they told us "if anyone is leaving from here to complain to Mutual Support, we're going to leave them strung up on a pole on the mountain where we find them." And so we stopped going with the group. And when we do go, we sit in the back; and we are only now beginning to give our testimony again.* Case 1509 (forced disappearance), Santa Ana, Petén, 1984.

Family members also became the direct targets of repression; in some cases they were abducted or murdered when the person actually being sought could not be found.

FAMILY IMPACT

The data

The primary impact at the time of the events was the loss of one or more family members, which was compounded by economic hardship and the fact that survivors, particularly women, are overwhelmed by their new roles and responsibilities. This was followed by a series of trauma-related effects that appear with moderate frequency: persecution, family breakdown, and forced separation.

Currently, the most severe impact on families is economic hardship and being overloaded by responsibilities. Although efforts to keep families going were crucial during the years following the events, many families, and particularly widows, feel emotionally and socially overwhelmed to this day. For every two testimonies that described a responsibility overload and economic hardship at the time of the events, one reports that these problems persist.

These effects are interrelated, and fall into three patterns in the testimonies: the *loss* of different family members, often multiple losses—loss of spouse (21 percent), of parents (22 percent), of children (12 percent), and others (21 percent); *persecution of families*, which causes further breakdown of family life; *family crisis*, brought on by an overload of responsibilities, financial hardships, and family disintegration, since the affected families have had to cope with multiple crises—economic (poverty), social (roles and responsibilities), and emotional (separation)—that often persist to this day. This has had a particularly forceful impact on women. Women appear more affected by loss of family members and more frequently reported the loss of their spouse, greater economic hardship, family conflicts, overload and additional responsibilities, and the inability to rebuild their lives.[2] Added to a pattern of family losses that have affected female survivors the most, this suggests that the overall impact of the war on families has been felt most strongly by women. Specifically, our data confirm the need to provide psychological and social support to widows.[3]

_____

[2] The differences are loss of family members (24.6 percent *vs.* 31.2 percent); loss of spouse (16.8 percent of men and 25.1 of women); financial hardship (4.3 percent *vs.* 6.4 percent); family conflicts (0.4 percent *vs.* 1.1 percent); overload and extra roles (6.6 percent *vs.* 18.5 percent); and inability to rebuild their lives (2.1 percent and 3. 4 percent).

[3] Widows experience feelings of intense sorrow and injustice, together with fear, altered grieving, and the effects on themselves as women. Compared to the rest of the testimonies, widows also describe more traumatic memories, feelings of solitude and uncertainty, and hunger. This demonstrates the impact of the losses as well as the negative aftermath, especially in terms of deprivation and lack of control over their own lives.

Harassment of Entire Communities

Military harassment of the civilian population acquired a community dimension in many areas of the country. Accusations of participation in, or support of, the guerrillas often encompassed entire communities denounced as "guerrilla communities." In this way, a person's place of origin or point of departure led to accusations, if not direct aggression.

> *We were fleeing to Santa Clara (1982-90), but always on an emergency basis, and we could not return to the village because there was no life there. Upon arriving at that community, we began to plant corn, malanga, and sugarcane. We were always persecuted; when the army came in, it chopped everything down and burned the houses. This was in September 1985. In 1987, the army arrived at Amachel and constantly entered the community; we were always fleeing into the mountains.* Case 4524, Santa Clara, Chajul, Quiché, 1985-87.

From 1978 to 1983, persecution in the form of military incursions, bombing raids, and massacres was particularly widespread in communities located in what the army viewed as "red" areas (Ixcán, Alta and Baja Verapaz, the Ixil region, the central highlands). Beginning in 1984, community-wide persecution primarily targeted displaced groups in the Alta Verapaz and Cuchumatanes mountains, and the Ixcán and Petén jungle regions, especially the Communities of Popular Resistance (CPRs).

Exemplary Terror (Terror as a Warning to Others)

The strategy of terror in Guatemala degenerated into the most extreme displays of disregard for human life with public torture sessions, public display of corpses, and the appearance of mutilated bodies bearing signs of torture.

> *They had cut out his tongue. His eyes were blindfolded with a wide bandage or wide tape and there were punctures everywhere on his rib cage, and it seemed that one of his arms was broken. They left him unrecognizable. And I could tell that it was him only because I had lived with him for many years and I knew about certain scars. I also took a recent photo that showed his whole body and I told the forensic doctor that he was my husband. Then "yes," he told me, "he was your husband. Yes, you may take him."* Case 3031 (abduction in Salamá and murder in Cuilapa), Cuilapa, Santa Rosa, 1981.

Fear-induced Collaboration

Certain aspects of the strategy of terror could affect the perpetrators themselves. There are numerous examples in the compiled testimonies that show how fear acted as an internal control mechanism among perpetrators.

And that officer told us that if we didn't kill them, they were going to kill all of us. And that's how it came about that we had to do it. I don't deny that, yes, we had to do it, because they threatened us. Case 1944 (civil patroller), Chiché, Quiché, 1983.

Most of the testimonies describe tremendous military pressure on the communities between 1980 and 1983. The activities of military commissioners and the obligatory organization of civil patrols contributed to this pressure. From that time on, the strategy of fear stressed internal control mechanisms based on civil patrol actions.

There was great fear in those days. We had to take turns patrolling but with tremendous fear. At the same time, the guerrillas also came to say that we should please not patrol. And so you were really afraid; because one came to organize the patrol, and the other came to block it; so you had a serious problem. From that time on, we began to understand that it was not going to be possible to live in that place anymore. Case 2267, Aldea Nojoyá, Huehuetenango, 1980.

No Way Out

In 1980 and 1981, when the people congregated in Cobán—when the guerrillas were getting rid of the bosses and all that—the guerrillas were already making contact with the people, and the people with the guerrillas. The people felt threatened; that is, we joined forces with the guerrillas. We believed they were our arms to resist, because the truth was that we had no one to stand up for us. The situation, as we saw it, was the same one in which the guerrillas walked, talked, and fought. And based on this we joined them, because our struggle was the same as their struggle. Then the army repression began. Sahakok Case, El Calvario, Cobán, Alta Verapaz, not dated.

The social polarization created by the armed conflict, combined with the lack of space for civilian opposition, led many people in certain areas to join the war effort, either voluntarily or by force of circumstance.

People here did not join the guerrillas. They passed through but did not achieve their goal....We began to feel insecure when the warning was given that it was dangerous to walk at night. Because of these problems, it was decided during a meeting that fourteen compañeros *would go talk to the army so that it wouldn't do anything to our community. And the fourteen* compañeros *never returned....They killed them in the school in Paley.* Workshop, San José Poaquil, Chimaltenango, November 23, 1996 (p. 1).

In many rural areas, widespread fear of the army led some people to flee. The same fear caused others to support the guerrillas directly or indirectly, either for protection or as a way to participate actively in the conflict. Testimonies concerning the 1980 to 1982 period recount how, as the situation became increasingly critical, the guerrillas also pressured some families or communities either to participate actively in the war or to refrain from giving any support to the army. In some areas, the fear of being taken for a "spy" [*oreja*, literally "ear"—TRANS.] is a typical example of the stranglehold on communities that compelled people to take sides.

Some of us, out of fear that they would kill us, you know, forced ourselves to attend the meetings that they would hold. Because whoever did not attend was a spy to them; we were considered traitors. Case 5334, Aldea Pozo de Agua, Baja Verapaz, 1983.

CLIMATE OF TERROR

During the early eighties, a climate of terror spread across the country, characterized by extreme violence against communities and organized movements against which the people were completely defenseless. An atmosphere of constant danger totally disrupted the daily life of many families. Whether in the form of mass killings or the appearance of corpses bearing signs of torture, the horror was so massive and so flagrant that it defied the imagination.

This outrageous display of violence by the army and police forces at the time was accompanied by the absence of any possibility of recourse to judicial or other civilian authorities capable of stopping the assaults on the population. These authorities had either been eliminated or were under military control.

CLIMATE OF TERROR

Constant tension
No one went to bed and we stayed there together throughout that night. In the morning, we were sad and exhausted from lack of sleep; all the people were terrified. Case 2299, Santa Ana Huista, Huehuetenango, 1981.

Generalized violence
The soldiers had begun to kill, without a word. They weren't asking whether anyone had done something wrong or not; they were killing that day. Case 6629, Cobán, Alta Verapaz, 1981.

Public nature of the horror
What we have seen has been terrible: burned corpses, women impaled and buried as if they were animals ready for the spit, all doubled up, and children

massacred and carved up with machetes. The women too, murdered like Christ. Case 0839, Cuarto Pueblo, Ixcán, Quiché, 1985.

Blatant impunity
Well the truth is, a feeling of powerlessness, at that moment, in front of those corpses, because it was overwhelming. And the people stood there, no one said a word, because there were vendors there on the sidewalk. Everyone was paralyzed, terrified. Case 5374 (abduction by army intelligence, G-2), Guatemala City, 1982.

THE SOCIAL EFFECTS OF FEAR

But when you realize just how many people have been murdered, then you share this sorrow. And you know that it is a moral obligation, a duty too, not only for the voiceless, but for the whole society that has been terrorized. Because that psychology of terror is part of the abductions, right? Since they took so and so, they are also going to take others who were his friends. Case 5449, Guatemala City, 1979.

THE SOCIAL EFFECTS OF FEAR

Restricted communication
It was very dangerous and risky to get through the day; it was very dangerous. You couldn't speak or say anything. There were constant calls for silence, to keep from discussing anything. That's what I heard, every single person's daily life was filled with danger. Case 553, Chiquisis, Alta Verapaz, 1982.

Withdrawal from organizational processes
Since at that time, the dead were beginning to appear, people were extremely afraid and began to withdraw. Case 2267, Nojoyá, Huehuetenango, 1980.

Social isolation
Sometimes I thought I was dying. Who could comfort me? I no longer had my mother; my father was afraid to be with me. Because the only consolation they offered me was that they were going to come and kill me and my children. Case 5334, Pozo de Agua, Baja Verapaz, 1983.

Humiliation
They terrified you, and so you felt humiliated. You couldn't say anything. Case 6259, Nentón, Huehuetenango, 1983.

> **Community distrust**
> *The army began to change people's ideas. It became difficult to trust in them.*
> Case 771, Ixcán, Quiché, 1975.

Despite the far-reaching impact of social disintegration and demobilization, the cruelty and arbitrariness of the violence also had the effect of raising people's awareness of violence and the army's conduct. Paradoxically, this awareness of terror fostered the development of various forms of resistance.

It was terrifying for us, because the army came and took away a mute person from the village, bound hand and foot. They asked him something, but he was a mute; he couldn't answer. They grabbed him, they kicked him a lot, and then they tied him up. They dragged him back; they called all the people together and threw him into the middle of the crowd, and asked if we knew that person. We said, "Yes, he is a mute." Everyone loved him and respected him because he was a defenseless person. This caused tremendous fear and anger because he was such a humble person for them to do that to him. He deserved more respect. Case 2267, Nojoyá, Huehuetenango, 1980.

THE INDIVIDUAL EFFECTS OF FEAR

The descriptions of how terror affected people's everyday lives include the individual effects of fear, which often went beyond an acute reaction to the atmosphere of violence. The lasting effects of fear are still present today, owing to years of unrelenting intimidation and military control.

So then we experienced the time of dread. We lived with dread for ten years, and believe me, it was hard for me in that sort of deteriorated state. Because everything was taken over, any vendor, anyone who came, you considered him suspect. So you couldn't work in peace. No one even wanted to go out to work. Case 5362 (attempted abduction/threats), Santa Lucía Cotzumalguapa, Escuintla, 1979.

INDIVIDUAL EFFECTS OF FEAR

Living in a threatening climate
In a reality that has turned threatening, the boundaries between the real and the imagined are grossly distorted.

Feeling of powerlessness

The counterinsurgency strategy, and the impunity with which actions were carried out, paralyzed people and they began to adapt their behavior to a hostile environment. Fear diminishes the capacity to take control of one's life and is a significant factor in psychological and social vulnerability.

State of alert

Living under a state of alert has helped people survive in dire circumstances, but it also entails substantial risk of physical and psychological damage. While there may be physical reactions at the time of the events, the health effects of chronic tension are even more damaging in the medium term.

Behavioral disorders

The effects of fear include involuntary reactions that can range from paralysis to acute behavioral disorders (panic attacks), creating even greater vulnerability in tense situations.

Health problems

Fear is portrayed in many testimonies as a shock (*susto*) or an illness whose effects outlast the initial threat (ailments affecting various organs, psychosomatic and affective health disorders, immunological dysfunctions, pain, and generalized somatic complaints). In Mayan culture particularly, this shock is perceived as an illness that occurs following a violent incident or when the person is in a vulnerable state. It must be removed from the body with specific cures.

FEAR AS A SELF-DEFENSE MECHANISM

Fear can also be a self-defense mechanism. As crisis situations intensified, the sensation of mortal danger drove many individuals and communities to flee or to band together for protection and support. Fear in this context is an adaptive strategy that, despite causing certain difficulties, enables people to survive.

The Decision to Flee

There was fear everywhere, throughout the village; no one slept at home. We went there to look; we only spent the mornings at home. In the afternoons we went to the woods, because we thought that the same thing was going to happen to all of us. Case 0553, Chiquisis, Alta Verapaz, 1982.

Precautions Taken

We'll go to work together; if we stick together, nothing will happen to us. With several of us together, in a little group, they can't screw us so easily. Because we all have to watch out for each other. We'll go to work together, and maybe that way nothing will happen to us, they told me. Case 7392, Petén, 1982-90.

Acts of Solidarity

It was both a very beautiful thing and a very sad thing for us. Some relatives and friends avoided us in the street as if we were lepers. And some family members risked the state of siege, the state of martial law, all those "states," and visited us, even at night. They risked their lives. Case 5444, Guatemala City, 1979.

ONGOING EXPERIENCES OF FEAR

Ongoing fear is described spontaneously in testimonies in considerably smaller proportions. In a significant number of cases, however, people reported that they continued to be afraid due to past experiences, traumatic memories, and the intimidating atmosphere in which REMHI carried out its work. Even so, it must be noted that people who stepped forward to offer their testimonies had already made enormous strides in overcoming their fear of relating what had happened to them.

And so some [women] are still afraid, and have not wanted to give their testimony. Case 1509, Santa Ana, Petén, 1984.

An analysis of witnesses' current fears found four different but partially overlapping situations.

Fear of the Perpetrators

Witnesses reported being terrified by the fact that perpetrators known to the affected families lived in the same communities and often retained positions of power.

I am a little anxious because if the ones who have caused harm in our communities find out, well, they could harm me too, because we have reported what they have done. Case 1376, Río Pajarito, Quiché, 1983.

I would rather that the identity of the witness not be revealed because the perpetrator is still alive. Case 5042, Santa Lucía Cotzumalguapa, Escuintla, 1984.

Fear of the Repercussions of Giving Testimony

Although many witnesses overcame their fear of speaking out, they continued to view giving testimony as a risk. In some cases, the witnesses themselves reported that many people did not want to give their testimony for fear of the consequences.

What if death comes for me after this interview, tomorrow or the next day?
I want to live with my family. That is why I'm afraid; and I'm concerned
about discussing what happened during those years. Case 6102, Barillas,
Huehuetenango, 1982.

Fear of Rekindling Social Conflicts in the Post-conflict Period

People's traumatic memories of their ordeals often foster a widespread demand
and desire that "the violence never return." This fear is quite pronounced in some
areas where ongoing social conflicts call to mind the severe social polarization or
militarization of daily life that prevailed at different times during the war.

Fear, like many others feel, that the division in the Ixcán, that what hap-
pened in the eighties, will happen again. Case 0839, Cuarto Pueblo, Ixcán,
Quiché, 1986.

The Lingering Threat

Finally, there is the selective repression of particular social movements in recent years, or the impact of incidents that had been relegated to past memory
and, instead, have continued into the final stages of the armed conflict.

In this sense, fear is the most damaging thing. Sometimes, when I see that he
is late based on the time he leaves work—he usually comes home at a cer-
tain time—the anxiety is tremendous, the tension you live with. And my
father is very ill because of this. The life you live is terribly changed, and this
has a lot of consequences: family disintegration, orphans, nervous psycho-
sis. Because, forget it, you live with that kind of stress all day. You see a
strange person and you think that they're already following you. You are
always afraid that something is going to happen to you. Case 0141,
Quetzaltenango, 1994.

ALTERED GRIEVING PROCESSES

All cultures have rituals, customs, and expressions of grief that emanate from
their particular beliefs about life and death. In Mayan culture, death is not understood as the absence of life, and relationships with the ancestors are part of daily
life.

It was necessary to leave the ancestors behind, the dead were far away, the
sacred sites too. Case 569, Cobán, Alta Verapaz, 1981.

In situations of extreme sociopolitical violence and displacement, mourning
also becomes a means of confronting many other losses, and it involves a sense of

community. People have not only lost friends and family members but also may feel a loss of respect for the victims and survivors.

We saw how they killed people, young people, young women. So many people were left grieving—wives for their husbands; people who were poor and couldn't provide for their children. We grieved for all of those things. Case 2230 (massacre), Jolomhuitz, Huehuetenango, 1981.

The meaning of grief is broader than the loss of loved ones. There is mourning for the destruction of the quintessential family purpose. Grief often had significant political and economic ramifications, loss of status, and loss of the land and the feeling of connection to it. The destruction of corn and nature represented more than deprivation or the loss of food; it was an assault on community identity.

We were sad for a year. We no longer cleared our cornfield; the corn died among the weeds. It was hard to get through that year—our hearts were no longer happy after they killed my father. That is what happened. It was hard to raise our spirits; everyone was very sad. All of our relatives were grief-stricken. One girl survived, and she is now a grown woman. She cries whenever she remembers. Case 553 (massacre), Chiquisis, Alta Verapaz, 1982.

The destruction of material goods caused individual and family suffering but also affected the communal meaning of life. Mourning the loss of material things takes on a *human form* in people's descriptions.

His clothing was left in sorrow. Case 1343, Chicamán, Quiché, 1982.

By nightfall on Saturday, we couldn't see anyone. All of the houses were sad because there were no longer any people inside them. Case 10583 (murder of parents), Chisec, Alta Verapaz, 1982.

Cultural differences may influence the impact of violence on the grieving process. In the *ladino* culture, the mourning process includes the initial wake, burial in the cemetery, and accompaniment of the family; this is followed by anniversary ceremonies and commemorations. Although some of these rituals are similar in other cultures, the manner of death (the position of the body, for example) is especially important in the Mayan culture, as are the preparation of the corpse and the objects that accompany the deceased. The relationship between the living and the ancestors is more tangible in subsequent ceremonies and commemorations.

Some information provided by key sources suggests that, in recent years, the suicide rate has increased significantly in certain areas where massacres occurred. Although there are no definitive studies, and other important factors may be involved, an analysis of the death records in Rabinal municipality revealed a significant increase in deaths by suicide. As in most indigenous cultures, suicides were rare prior to the eighties (only one case during the ten preceding years, compared to more than eight cases in a two-year period).

SOCIOPOLITICAL VIOLENCE AND ALTERED GRIEF

The Magnitude and Brutality of the Violence

In cases of massacres and sociopolitical violence, bereavement processes are often interrupted by the massive, abrupt, and brutal nature of the killings. Most of the testimonies gathered by the REMHI project demonstrate the brutality of the killings, which at times took on massive proportions, whether in the form of individual murders, collective murders, or massacres.

We went for five or six months without tasting a single tortilla. My mother and father died; their remains were left on the mountain. They hacked the children to pieces with machetes. If they found sick people, bloated with the cold, they finished them off. Sometimes they set them on fire. I feel it deep in my heart. I have no one left. My parents are dead, and I feel as if I have a knife in my heart. We have been dragging the dead; we had to bury them in our fright. My mother died in Sexalaché, and my father somewhere else. The bodies were not together; they were scattered all over, lost on the mountain. When the patrol came, they hacked them apart with machetes, and some were drawn and quartered. Well, we waited until they had finished killing them, and then we went back to look for them. We found them and gave them a burial of sorts. And there were people who died that it was impossible to bury. Case 2052, Chamá, Alta Verapaz, 1982.

The brutality of the killings has deepened the suffering of the survivors, leaving them with health problems and recurrent traumatic memories of what their loved one suffered before death.

We were crowded onto the patio of the house. On the fifth or sixth day, the army ordered us to bury the dead. We went and buried them, but they didn't go to the cemetery. We buried them all in one place. We found a hole in a ravine, piled them up, and set them on fire. It made us ill to do this. We have lost our appetites. Among them, I saw one whose thorax was opened up; his heart, his lung, everything was hanging out. Another's head was twisted around backward, his face toward the sun. Two or three months later they were dug up by their relatives. They were moved to the cemetery, but it wasn't any use by then, it was just water and bone. They were just stacked in boxes; five boxes were put together. We took them to the cemetery, but it made us ill. This is what I saw personally in those times. Case 1368, Tierra Caliente, Quiché, 1981.

They removed his teeth when they killed him and his nose swelled up a lot. I've never seen a dead person look anything like what they did to my son. I'll never forget it, because they pulled out all of my poor son's teeth. Case 2988, Nebaj, Quiché, 1983.

Since massacres were usually public spectacles, the impact of death was magnified by having witnessed the atrocities. Many of those who gave their testimony were eyewitnesses to the aftermath of the massacres. Others lived with critically wounded victims who didn't die immediately, and they experienced their agony firsthand.

When the army returned, [the soldiers] came out of that house. And they went by to tell my uncle, who is the military commissioner: "Look, you, go and bury those people, we finished off a whole family. They are bad folks, we finished them off and now go and bury them. Some are not quite dead yet, they're still twitching; wait until they die, so they're not jumping, and then bury them." When we got there, oh, but it was horrible. I can't forget it. Even though some say you have to put the past behind you, I can't. I remember...we went to the kitchen and there was the whole family, my aunt, my daughter-in-law, her sons and daughters; there were two little children hacked to pieces with machetes. They were still alive. The boy, Romualdo, lived for a few more days. The one who couldn't last any longer was Santa, the one with her guts hanging out. She only lasted half a day and then she died. Case 9014 (massacre), San José Xix, Chajul, Quiché, 1982.

The Senselessness of Death

The senselessness of violent deaths is usually compounded by a profound feeling of injustice that endures to this day.

This is why we are still sad. Because if it had been because of an illness, it would have been all right, but he was fine and healthy. Case 6006, San Mateo Ixtatán, Huehuetenango, 1982.

In some cases of guerrilla executions of community members, this sense of injustice is accompanied by disappointment with guerrilla treatment of community members.

Andrés Miguel Mateo—because he spoke after Tomás Felipe's death. He asked why those "brothers" had killed that man. And just because he said that, they went to get him and they killed him. So the people—like I said, there are many people I know in other villages who, because of problems over land "this brother of mine wants to take my land, let's take his life." And then the killing started, and once it started, the people started to get disillusioned. Case 6257, Tzalá, Huehuetenango, 1983.

Although people have sought to explain these senseless deaths through their cultural beliefs, past experience, or ideology, it is important to note the impact that feelings of powerlessness and guilt over the inability to prevent what happened may have had on the grieving process.

My heart is heavy because of this suffering and pain. I grieve for my son, but I can do nothing now. I don't know where his body and his blood might have been left. I ask God to keep him, to shine his light on him, to gather up his soul. Why did he have to go buy corn that day? The corn would have been there another day! Case 2195, Tactic, Alta Verapaz, 1981.

The overpowering violence, and the direct involvement of relatives or neighbors in the killings, make it more difficult to deal with grief and make sense of what happened.

We thought that God had to do justice. But what hurts the most—I was never able to see his face in the casket, because his face was disfigured. They treated him very badly. What hurts me the most is that his own uncle had him killed, like H.C. who was the biggest murderer here in Salamá. Case 3077 (murder) Salamá, Baja Verapaz, 1981.

Obstacles to Burials and Rituals

The effect of terror on those closest to it sometimes inhibited and paralyzed the grieving process. Many people were unable to find and bury their family members, or were prevented by threats from even acknowledging their violent deaths. Only half of the survivors who gave their testimonies knew where their relatives were left (49.5 percent knew where the bodies were) and only one-third (34 percent) were able to hold a funeral service or burial.

The emergency situation itself, or the repressive social climate, interfered with rituals and ceremonies to honor the dead, say goodbye, and support and accompany the family. These types of commemorations often were obstructed deliberately in order to terrorize the survivors or prevent public acknowledgment of the facts. The Guatemalan army's *Counterinsurgency Manual*[4] contains explicit instructions on how to conceal the whereabouts of deceased individuals:

Dead civilians, friends and enemies, will be buried by military personnel as quickly as possible to keep subversive elements from using them for purposes of provocation or propaganda.

This strategy was sometimes superseded, however, by the tactic of exemplary terror. At times, the risks associated with ongoing military operations were com-

---

[4] *Manual de contrainsurgencia,* Guatemalan Army (1983), 208.

pounded by explicit military orders not to touch or inter the victims. Many people were unable to bury their murdered loved ones or tend to their corpses in any way at all.

The frequency of such orders, and the fact that the army meticulously studied the social and cultural traits of the Mayan population in its effort to assert its control in rural areas, indicate that these tactics emanated from a clear political intent to sow terror.

> *The ones who died there rotted. There they remained. No one collected them; no one buried them. Because they had said that anyone who picked them up or went to see them would be killed right there. Whoever buried them was one of them. Even now I don't know what happened to them—if some animal or dog ate them. I don't know. That is the violence that my mother and father suffered. There is a constant ache in my heart, and I always think about the violence they endured.* Case 2198, San Pedro Carchá, Alta Verapaz, 1982.

The mutilation of corpses, with distinct cultural overtones, was another way of denigrating people and undermining the victims' dignity. The symbolism associated with mutilation (burning, hacking with machetes, impalement, etc.), abandoned corpses eaten by animals, and the use of sacred sites as killing fields appear in the testimonies as illustrations of how the survivors' grieving processes were distorted.

FORCED DISAPPEARANCES

During the late seventies, the security forces carried out numerous individual forced disappearances in the course of their operations. Shrouded in secrecy, these actions were never acknowledged, and the families were never able to discover the fate of their loved ones.

Forced disappearance was a systematic practice even in rural areas, where people frequently were disappeared during military operations or after being detained by clearly identified perpetrators. In many of the cases collected, there are eyewitnesses to the detention itself and even to the time the victims were held in military detachments.

Living with this type of loss is much more difficult, even in cases where it is clear that the victim was ultimately killed. Disappearance creates a sense of ambiguity and heightened distress and anxiety over what actually happened and the whereabouts of the body.

> *Like everyone else, he was a patroller. He was in the park when he was captured by the soldiers in front of his six-year-old son, Victor Clemente, together with the teacher, Jacinto de Paz. His wife asked the soldiers, who were holding him at the Catholic convent, to release him, but they always*

refused. Three days later they released Jacinto, and he talked about how Alberto's hands were swollen from the torture. No one ever knew when they killed him or where they took him....Who knows where they threw him? So many times we went looking for them; so many dead in the cemetery. Case 2978, Nebaj, Quiché, 1982.

The inability to hold a wake makes it more difficult to face the loss and bring closure to the grieving process, although some people find ways to symbolize the presence of the disappeared person or find a memento to remember them by.

For three days I cried, crying that I wanted to see him. I sat there below that piece of ground. Just a little bit of earth to be able to say there he is. There is the little cross, he is there, everything is there. There is our little bit of dust and we will go to show our respect, leave a candle...but when are we going to light the candle? and where are we going to...? There isn't any place. I feel so much pain. Each night I get up to pray, every night. Where can we go? Case 8673, Sibinal, San Marcos, 1982.

THE DISAPPEARANCE OF A CHILD
Marco Antonio Molina Theissen

On October 6, 1981, Marco Antonio Molina Theissen, aged fourteen, was abducted. This incident is related to the illegal detention of his sister, Emma Guadalupe Molina Theissen.[5]

One day after her escape from the location where she had been held, three heavily armed men in civilian dress arrived at the family home (in a car with license plates P-16765). Two of the men entered the house and threatened the family with their weapons while they searched the house for one hour. They shackled Marco Antonio on one of the sofas in the living room and gagged him with masking tape. They put a sack over his head, threw him into the back of the pickup truck, and took him away, ignoring his mother's pleas. We never found out anything about what happened to him.

_____

[5] Emma was a secondary-school student leader from 1974 to 1978. She moved to the western part of the country after the death of her boyfriend. She was captured, at an army checkpoint in Santa Lucía Utatlán. She was interrogated and tortured; her head was punctured with needles, and she was raped repeatedly. From the moment she was captured she was denied food and water. She was shown photographs of university students. They took her out to drive around (*ruletear*): they put a wig on her and drove along the streets of Quetzaltenango in a car so that she would turn in the people who supposedly had contact with her. She escaped from the Manuel Lisandro Barillas Military Brigade in that city. The commander of the base was Colonel Luis Gordillo Martínez, who was later replaced by Colonel Quintero.

Marco Antonio's parents looked for him. They went to Quetzaltenango to speak with Colonel Quintero; they sought the support of the Catholic church hierarchy but did not obtain it. Archbishop Casariego offered to intercede before then-president of the Republic, General Lucas, whom he said he ate breakfast with every Wednesday. They later requested assistance from other bishops, journalists, the police chief, and the next president, General Ríos Montt, but to no avail. The response of the military authorities was always the same: your son was abducted by the guerrillas. The entire family had to flee the country due to threats. Case 11826, Guatemala City, 1981.

In most cases, the official response varied between denying the detention or any knowledge of the person's whereabouts, and offering contradictory versions that only increased the family's confusion. In addition, the very fact of making such inquiries often led to direct or indirect threats against the survivors. Many families were painfully torn between their need to know what happened and the need to do nothing so as to avoid further danger.

Testimonies given by several eyewitnesses corroborate the belief that many disappeared people were actually held by the security forces. In some cases, family ties between civilians and individual soldiers became a source of information about the fate of detainees. Despite all of their efforts, however, in most cases relatives were unable to learn the fate of the disappeared person. Many of these people may be in clandestine cemeteries and common graves that are located, according to the testimonies gathered, on the grounds of various military bases.

THE IMPACT OF ALTERED GRIEVING PATTERNS

The facts

A quantitative analysis offers some insights about the people who had the most difficulty mourning their dead family members.

1. People currently experiencing the greatest hardship are those who lost a family member in the collective massacres and could not bury the body, which was left in an unknown location or perhaps in a common grave. The individual cannot assimilate the loss without knowing where the family member was killed or where the body might be, since these circumstances leave a glimmer of hope (real or imagined) that the person may still be alive. Any attempt to bring closure to the grieving process, therefore, would be tantamount to betrayal. Therein lies the social significance of the exhumation process. Still, some families may be ambivalent toward this issue. While exhumations may offer certainty regarding the death and a reference point for rituals, they can also be seen as a threat to the equilibrium that the person has gradually achieved with the passage of time.

> 2. In contrast, people who were able to learn where their relatives were killed generally do not continue to grieve in this way. They experienced more illnesses and health problems during the years when the events occurred. Confirming the death and losing hope—particularly when the body could not be buried, according to the data—caused many people to "become ill," which is how people commonly refer to the physical breakdown induced by grief.
>
> 3. Finally, there are families who knew about the death and were able to bury the body. Besides sorrow over the death, the predominant emotions reported by these families are a sense of injustice and anger over what happened. The burial completes the cycle of death and allows the survivors to articulate their anger and indignation toward the perpetrators.

Our data also clearly indicate that, given the nature of the incidents and the social dynamics of violence, the following elements are essential to the grieving process: clear information about the fate of family members; public acknowledgment of the facts and of the institutional responsibility; and acts of social restitution and measures to honor the victims.

BLAMING THE VICTIMS

A central feature of the counterinsurgency strategy has been to place the blame and the responsibility on victims and survivors. To this end, the army's key tactics were propaganda and psychological warfare; structures such as civil patrols to militarize society and encourage conformity; and religious sects. The manipulation of Mayan cultural beliefs—such as attributing events to their own conduct, changing the equilibrium in the community, and redefining the concept of sin from a religious standpoint—was aimed at blaming the people for incidents and concealing the deliberate nature of repressive strategies. Survivors of traumatic events frequently report feelings of guilt over whether they could have done something to prevent the incident.

Sometimes I think that if she had listened to me, perhaps she would be here now. Case 10757, San Cristóbal Verapaz, Alta Verapaz, 1982.

FORCED COLLABORATION

This is evident mostly in the cases of some civil patrollers who exhibit great personal distress over their participation in killings or massacres. In general, however, patrollers' testimonies about their involvement in the civil patrols describe the events themselves, without relating them to their personal experience.

We acted on the army's orders, if it weren't for them, we wouldn't have done it. We allied ourselves with the army to survive; and also because the guerrillas killed the father-in-law, who was a military commissioner. At that time you didn't know what to do, and we had to obey the army. Case 2463 (patrol chief), Chutuj, Quiché, 1982.

These sentiments have tormented the people involved for years. The diverse forms of forced collaboration have often traumatized people who participated directly in repression. Giving testimony has been helpful in these cases because it has offered the possibility of sharing the experience, placing it in a social context, and seeking some kind of solace.

Maybe God will forgive me...that is why I have come to tell it. If I die one day, I can't take it all with me. It feels good to tell it, it's like a confession. It is a great relief to get out what you have held in your heart for so long. Patroller case, Sacapulas, Quiché [not dated].

As part of the strategy of guilt, the army took advantage of any minor infraction of military order to justify a punishment that would serve as an example to others; this was a way of maintaining control over the population and commanding absolute obedience. Guilt also contributed to internal control within the community.

Forcing people to participate in the murder of fellow community members was a collective approach to encouraging complicity. Forced participation in atrocities meant that violence became the norm and its source was internalized; this redefined social values and the very meaning of community. In some cases, the testimonies provide details that reveal the extent to which forced collaboration in atrocities was intended to destroy the social fabric.

"We don't do the killing now. Instead the patrollers from here in this community, they are the ones who will kill them. These people here, twelve men are going to die. It is clearly written in the Bible: 'The father against the son and the son against the father.'" *That is what the man said. So they made them begin and some of the patrollers carried knives and others sticks. And with just sticks and knives they killed those twelve men they referred to there. After they had killed the twelve men—they killed them and they tortured them, and they went to get gasoline and they gathered them together. They sent the patrollers to pile them up together, and they said to them:* *"You are going to burn them yourselves."* *"They told us to put them in two stacks of six. We went to get sticks and pine needles, and they put gasoline on them and burned them to ashes right in front of us."* *That is what the man who saw it said, and he told it to me. When they were all burned up, everyone applauded, and they began to eat.* Case 2811, Chinique, Quiché, 1982.

A new identity as a patroller was forged in order to quash potential resistance or guilt feelings on the part of the perpetrators, increase their acceptance of the incidents, and reinforce aggressive behavior toward people. This was accomplished by rewarding their conduct and replacing feelings of grief with a new type of group revelry.

> *When we left Zacualpa, they gave a big pig to the patrol chief, and to us too. And the lieutenant said: "You're going to make a stew when it is the ninth day of mourning for those twelve men; prepare a big stew there in Chinique. This is for the patrollers because the Chinique patrollers 'have balls.'" They also gave us money for a seventeen* octavo *box [an* octavo *is a measure of volume—*TRANS.]. Case 2811, Chinique, Quiché, 1982.

POLITICAL ACTIVISM: A SENSE OF RESPONSIBILITY AND GUILT

The few testimonies that discuss ways of blaming the victims allude to their involvement with one of the parties to the conflict. In many cases, survivors still wonder about their own culpability as they try to make sense out of how the incidents came about.

> *And the one who made the accusation is L.O.; Doña Teresa said to me, "Don't you realize that he is the one with a handkerchief tied around his face?" And my mother answered: "What is our crime and what is it that we are supposed to have done? What they are doing to us is terribly painful."* Case 10583 (murder of the father and torture of the mother), Chisec, Alta Verapaz, 1982.

The testimonies contain diverse opinions about blame or responsibility for incidents in light of the civilian population's active, and usually forced, participation in the armed conflict. The perception of guilt in the testimonies tends to be colored by whether or not the victims were known to be active, armed agents in the conflict.

> *The people in Nojoyá were the most upset about those three deaths because they felt that there was no reason to kill those people. They didn't have any problems; there were no grounds to kill them. Well, about the other deaths, people take into account that they died in combat since they went out on a search mission to look for the guerrillas, with weapons and everything for fighting. They say that the army wasn't even there at the time. The patrol went alone, which means they went of their own volition. So the people themselves evaluate, and they say that it is sort of their own fault. But they blame the guerrillas for those three deaths.* Case 2267, Nojoyá, Huehuetenango, 1980.

In other cases, minor acts of collaboration with the guerrillas are viewed with disapproval after the fact, depending on their repercussions on people's lives.

The following case describes how the guerrillas are blamed after the army abducted and disappeared a family member.

That's how I knew that it was for giving food to the guerrillas. Yes, he gave them food, according to my mother. Later, my mother was looking for him. She asked about him and found out that he was in the Cotzal detachment. They later transferred him to Nebaj. My father sent a letter saying that he was already with the soldiers and that he had already joined that group in Huehuetenango. My mother told the guerrillas that they had taken him, and they responded that the family of the victim had to go to the mountains. And my mother said to them: "How can that be, since it was your fault this happened because you just come here...from now on, I'm not giving you anything to eat." Case 3627 (torture and forced disappearance by the army and guerrilla recruitment), Cotzal, Quiché, 1980.

BETWEEN WORDS AND SILENCE

The use of fear to induce conformity may also lead to guilt feelings over the failure to act in the face of violence; this is especially true of people who were helpless witnesses to incidents.

I felt weighed down after watching the deceased die. I also saw that the community didn't support him. I was just about to come forward when the judge arrived—when they registered the death. But for work-related reasons I decided against it. Because what if I'm the only one who speaks up? And his family didn't say anything, and that's how it was left. So I was left with this feeling forever. Case 6009 (murder witness), Jolomar, Huehuetenango, 1993.

THE WRATH OF INJUSTICE

We don't want vengeance, because otherwise there is no end to the violence. At first I wished I were a poisonous snake, but now I have thought it over. What I ask for is their repentance. Case 9909, Dolores, Petén, not dated.

FROM SENSELESSNESS TO INJUSTICE

The senselessness of death frequently arises in the interviews. The most common attitude among family members is a sense of injustice stemming from their high opinion of the victim. These favorable opinions include recognition of the victim's social stature, which is consistent with the fact that many of those who suffered repression played important roles in their communities. There are also strong feelings of injustice when the person was significant to the community or was in a vulnerable position or under obvious duress.

> *Why did they take my brother-in-law, when he had done nothing to deserve it? He was a hard worker, he was Catholic, and he was a catechist in charge of baptism. And, because he had that responsibility, the soldiers went to get him and they killed him. This man was no criminal; he worked in the community.* Case 1316, Parraxtut, Quiché, 1983.

> *It isn't fair that people in positions of power bring about these kinds of deplorable situations.* Case 046 (farm administrator who had dealt with both the guerrillas and the army, murdered by the latter), Santa Bárbara, Suchitepéquez, 1983.

The testimonies also contain numerous opinions and reflections about the fact that the person "was good [and] did not deserve it." This indicates a positive image of the family member as well as an inability to reconcile the repression suffered with their prior experiences.

POWERLESSNESS AGAINST IMPUNITY

In this harsh context, in virtually every case, family members have faced the government's failure to acknowledge the incidents, provide social restitution, and punish those responsible. This is one of the reasons that survivors continue to harbor a strong sense of injustice.

> *They burned our homes down, they ate our livestock, they murdered our children; the women, the men, oh! oh! Who is going to rebuild all the houses? The army isn't going to do it.* Cuarto Pueblo, Ixcán, Quiché, 1985.

Two key factors commonly associated with ongoing feelings of rage are that the victims and survivors were condemned to powerlessness from the outset and that those responsible for the violence remain unpunished. And while this rage may not have led to acts of violence, it generally remains deeply embedded in the personal experience of some victims.

> *My family and I think, since I am a person, that they are attacking my honor. In that moment I had thoughts against them; that I am somebody; I am capable of doing something to one of them. But then I thought about my family, my brothers and sisters, and the neighbors. Of course if I do something, we'll all be killed, including my family, so I decided to restrain myself.* Case 2273 (torture and threats), Jacaltenango, Huehuetenango, 1981.

A VENEER OF NORMALCY

The impunity with which crimes were committed coupled with the lack of public acknowledgment have left many victims living behind a veneer of normalcy, constrained by ongoing social control, militarization, and their dependent position within the community power hierarchy.

Everything goes on as usual in our community, as if nothing had happened. What happened is that the authorities at the time threatened us, and all the disappearances, abductions, and massacres have gone unreported. This is why I want to denounce it nationally and internationally, so it all comes out clearly. Like a story written down on paper that relates everything that happened to the Mayan Achí people. Case 2024, San Miguel Chicaj, Baja Verapaz, 1982.

Power hierarchies based on militarization and the social stature enjoyed by many perpetrators have enabled the latter to retain coercive power over their victims, who expect renewed threats if they denounce the situation.

They still come to intimidate my granddaughters, my daughter-in-law. And this cannot be and I would be willing to say so, but the problem is that I can't speak Spanish very well. I am already tired of listening to them. Case 3164, Aldea Najtilaguaj, Alta Verapaz, 1982.

This means that many victims may continue to experience rage, even though they may keep it contained.

QUESTIONING THE STRUGGLE

In the case of extrajudicial executions by the guerrillas, the sense of injustice is frequently expressed in terms of the incongruence between such actions and the values these armed groups supposedly espoused, as well as misgivings about guerrilla tactics.

So at the time I was very sorry since I, too, had known him well; because we used to do things together. I began to cry and I said to myself: Why, if they talk so much about human rights? Why do they say that we are struggling for peace, that we are striving for equality, to end injustice? Why did they not respect the rights of that young man now? Why did they kill him? That young man had spent three or four years risking his life, enduring hunger, rain, all of the feelings associated with living in the hills. He went through all of those things, saying that it was necessary to struggle for your children, the family, the people. Why didn't they respect his rights? Why should we keep on struggling? Case 8352, (murder of a youth in a CPR), Mayalán, Ixcán, Quiché, 1981.

In such cases, the predominance of the military aspects of the guerrilla struggle, coupled with organizational rigidity, bred insensitivity toward suffering and a disregard for people's lives, which were subordinated to military interests.

I was left an orphan and I went to tell my grandmother: "They just killed my uncle." Later they called my grandmother and told her that they had killed him for being an "army informer." It seems that my uncle's wife denounced him to her father because he didn't want to stay in the resistance; he wanted to move to a cooler climate, and she didn't want to. The people in our camp complained to those responsible, but without success. I kept working, but sadly. A month later, the army killed my mom, my little sister, and then my grandmother. I was left alone, and I went to Mexico. Case 723 (murder, according to the witness, the victim was hounded to join the guerrillas and, when he refused, was denounced as an army informer), Ixcán, Quiché, 1984.

Chapter Two

DESTROYING THE SEED

The army's plan was to get rid of the seeds. Even if it was a little one- or two-year-old child, they are all bad seeds, so they say. This was the army's plan. This is what I have seen. Case 4017, Las Majadas, Aguacatán, Huehuetenango, 1982.

Children are present in most of the testimonies. Children, as a social group, have been deeply affected by violence and political repression whether as indirect victims of violence against family members, as witnesses to numerous traumatic events, or through their firsthand experiences of violence and death.

Children are less equipped to protect themselves when faced with a threatening reality. They resent more strongly the lack of family support, and their ability to make sense of what is happening depends on their individual developmental level. The security, trust, and care they require are drastically altered, even after the most intense violence is over. In this context, children can cope more effectively with traumatic experiences if they have adequate family support, can remain active (attend school, and so on), reestablish their daily routines, and if their families provide love, understanding, and age-appropriate information about what happened.

He was fourteen years old when he was wounded in this village. He hurt himself on tree trunks and thorns—he was out of his mind when he fled. And little by little he recovered. Later he got married and now he lives in Quiché, in the capital. Case 1351, Parraxtut, Quiché, 1982.

VIOLENCE AGAINST CHILDREN

Children were killed and wounded in the course of indiscriminate attacks on the civilian population. Under the circumstances, they had more difficulty fleeing, were less aware of the risk, and had little grasp of the mechanics of violence. They were also more dependent on the family, which could not support them under the circumstances. Soldiers and civil patrollers killed many children directly, particularly between 1980 and 1983. They were an easy target in the course of strategic military operations against the civilian population. And because they tended to remain close to their mothers, violence against women is often associated with violence against children.

When we reached the Yaltoya path, the women and children were all thrown down on the ground. They were all killed by the bomb that they set off. But they were all women and children. There were males, but they were just children. Case 6065, Nentón, Huehuetenango, 1982.

Without asking a single question, the soldiers tied them up inside the house. They poured gasoline on the house and lit it. They all perished in the fire, including a child about two years old. My mother, sister, brother-in-law, and their three children were all massacred. Case 3164, San Cristóbal Verapaz, Alta Verapaz, 1982.

Half of the massacres recorded include the collective murder of children. In keeping with the indiscriminate violence of massacres, descriptions of children's deaths often contain atrocities (incineration, machete wounds, and drawing and quartering, and most frequently, severe head trauma). Many young girls were raped during massacres or while detained. Cases of children killed by indiscriminate fire or machine-gun strafing of communities are reported less frequently. This suggests direct, deliberate aggression consistent with the overall treatment suffered by communities in these situations.

A thirteen-year-old girl was handed over to me, the poor girl crying bitterly. "What's wrong with you, girl?" "Only God knows where they will take me!" the child said. I took out my handkerchief and gave it to her. "Clean yourself up instead." So a certain military instructor, Basilio Velásquez, comes over: "What's up, and what's with her? She should be 'vaccinated,' no? She's good." That vile individual raped her, and after raping her, sent her to the well. How was it that they executed those poor people? Look, they blindfolded her—and clubbed her on the head all the way to the well. Collective Testimony 27, Massacre at Dos Erres, Petén, 1982.

The woman lived in the house with her little ones. And they grabbed the woman; they stuck a knife in her neck. I was nearby, watching what the soldiers did there. They had the poor woman and she was bleeding because they had already stuck the knife in her throat. She was still able to escape, and they grabbed her and a soldier hit her in the face. They set the house on fire with all the little ones inside. Case 600, Chajul, Quiché, 1982.

During the massacres, the violence against pregnant women sometimes included extreme cruelty toward the children they carried in their wombs. Many infant victims of the horror never appeared in the statistics on violence because they never had a name: they were murdered before they were born.

They threw bombs, grenades...they approached through a ravine. That was when more children died. And they captured the pregnant women alive, they sliced them open and removed the baby. Key source 11, Chimaltenango, 1967-68.

In many massacres, however, violence against children was not only part of the violence against the community in general but also had a deliberate purpose. In the testimonies gathered by REMHI, soldiers or patrollers frequently refer to the killing of children as a way of eliminating the possibility of rebuilding the community and of circumventing the victims' efforts to attain justice.

> *Well, they told my sister—since among the soldiers there was one who spoke our language—and he told my sister that they had to finish off all the men and all the male children in order to eliminate the guerrillas. "And why?" she asked, "and why are you killing the children?" "Because those wretches are going to come some day and screw us over." That was their intention when they killed the little ones too.* Case 1944 (ex-patroller), Chiché, Quiché, 1983.

Information on the deaths of children and survivors' accounts of atrocities also are consistent with testimonies about military training methods and the instruction that was given at that time to soldiers in order to implement the scorched-earth policy. During those years (1980-82), regarding the entire civilian population of many villages as members of guerrilla groups and physically eliminating them, including the children, was part of a carefully designed strategy.

> *When it was time to patrol, they told us, "Okay, guys, we're going to an area where there are only guerrillas. Everyone is a guerrilla there. Children there have killed soldiers, and supposedly pregnant women have just come and thrown a bomb and killed; they have killed soldiers. And so you all must distrust everyone. No one is a friend where we are going. So, they are all guerrillas and all of them must be killed."* Key source 80 (former soldier and intelligence officer [G-2]), 1980.

Massive displacement of the population, which frequently resulted in family separation, posed even greater risks for children. The simple fact of not finding family members was tantamount to a death threat for the children, just as it was for many women. For the perpetrators, at that time, the mere suspicion that they could be the offspring of guerrillas was considered sufficient reason to kill these children.

> *When they got to the place, they (civil patrollers) asked the children if they knew anyone there [who could take care of them] and the children said yes, but Doña Candelaria already had her son-in-law, two brothers-in-law, and her uncle [with her, to take care of]. And when the patrol asked the people "which of you know these children? If someone knows them, take them, and if you don't know them, we're going to leave them here dead," they said.* Case 0717, Senococh, Ixcán, Quiché, 1988.

Many children in rural communities witnessed the atrocities committed against their family members in the context of indiscriminate violence against the civilian population. Children were present during most of the collective massacres and witnessed acts of violence against their relatives. This may have been a deliberate part of the strategy of terror against the population, or it may have occurred as the children were trying to save themselves. Today, children who were eyewitnesses to this violence may be the group most afflicted with problems such as traumatic memories of the death of their family members.

> *I was playing there when I saw the soldiers coming up. As they came, my mom told me to run. Since my dad's house had two doors, one in front and the other leading out among the coffee bushes, I fled; I knew that they had already started killing. I ran alone among the coffee bushes, and my mother did not follow me. At about four o'clock in the afternoon, I went back to the village. They had already burned the house and my family. No one was left.* Case 10066 (massacre), Aldea Kajchijlaj, Chajul, Quiché, 1982.

Threatening and torturing children was also a means of torturing their families. The torture of children was a means of forcing people to collaborate, inducing people to denounce others, and destroying community. It was a form of exemplary terror for their families and was an extreme demonstration of contempt for people's lives and dignity. Some people even stated that they preferred to die when confronted with the possibility of this kind of suffering.

> *I did beg God that, if they were going to kill me, that they kill me first. I didn't want to see what they were going to do to my children, because they always did it like that. First they killed the children. It was a way of torturing the people, the parents. And I thought about all of that, but thank God it didn't happen. And so someone was still able to escape. They took the baby out of the woman. She was alive and they took out the child she was expecting, in front of her husband and her children. And the woman died and her children died too. They killed the others; the only one who remained was the one who escaped.* Case 2173, Buena Vista, Huehuetenango, 1981.

In addition to its power to terrorize, the army used violence against children as a way of eliciting accusations and information about guerrilla movements or sympathizers. Some witnesses described these atrocities against children as persistent traumatic memories of such things as mutilation of corpses and, in some cases, disembowelment. The ways in which children were killed epitomize the impact of terror, and they are remembered today with tremendous suffering.

> *I still dream; I still see it. Because my heart is still afflicted by the persecution. Because they have pointed their guns at us. Because the patrol has gone after us. And this means that I am still deeply distressed by everything we have suffered. What do they do to the children? They cut them into pieces. I mean, they cut them up with machetes; they cut them into pieces.* Case 2052, Chamá, Cobán, Alta Verapaz, 1982.

They buried the ones that the army killed. They were decapitated with a tourniquet around the throat. They crumpled them up, they handled them like little balls. There were three-year-old children. We went to see. We saw them, three kids, they were hanging there without any heads. Their little dolls were behind them. Case 1367, Sacapulas, Quiché, 1981.

On September 5, 1985, they went after six people and, just then, a plane arrived circling. Later a group of soldiers arrived. They started shooting. My cousin R.J. died there, and I. and E., about thirteen years old (they are cousins). H.J.S. wasn't killed by the bullets; they pulled out his heart. Case 3083, Chitucán, Rabinal, Baja Verapaz, 1981.

The murder of children has had an enormous impact on the survivors. It is accompanied by an even deeper feeling of injustice and symbolizes utter destruction. Such violence against children is an assault on community identity, which encompasses the ancestors and descendants. It is even apparent in the language. For example, in the case of the Achí Mayan Indians, the word *Mam* refers equally to grandparents-ancestors and to their newborn grandchildren.[1]

Because the truth is, so many innocent children died! They didn't even know why this happened. The truth is, when you went to places like that, you saw dead people all over. They left them all cut up, an arm here, a leg there; that's how it was. Case 3024, Aldea Panacal, Rabinal, Baja Verapaz, 1981.

WITNESSES TO THE VOID AND THE INFERNO

I was twelve years old when they abducted my father. I was the eldest of the children. We didn't have the courage to say anything, we were crying when they took him. And after a while my father returned and said: "Look Mario, don't cry, I'll be right back." That was around ten or eleven at night. I was in the fourth grade then. I went to school the next day, and I told the teacher that they had abducted my father and that I wouldn't be going to school anymore because I didn't have anyone to buy my notebooks. That was how the family was destroyed.

My stepmother went to look for work in Pajapita and I was left alone with my little brother. Thanks to my aunt, who was called Lorenza—she fed us, and the neighbors did too. Shortly after my father was abducted, they burned our house down. That night we had gone over to my aunt's house to eat and we

---

[1] A. Breton, *Rabinal Achí: une dynastique maya du quinzième siècle* (Paris: Société d'Ethnologie, 1994).

were passing the time playing ball. My brother ran ahead, and when he got to the house a group of men were waiting for us. They grabbed him by the neck and they said to him: "Are you Mario? No? We're going to wait for him."

I was coming up behind. Then they sat him down and they began to pour gasoline on the house. Ismael thought that they were going to kill us both and so he thought: "It would be better if they only kill me, I'm going to run." He got up and said to them: "I'm going to urinate." And they told him: "Don't move, urinate in front of us." And they grabbed him, but he resisted, and they fired two shots so he wouldn't go. But he didn't care if they killed him to save my life. And he did save it because I was coming up from below and when I heard the shots I said, "What's going on?"

That was when I heard the crackle of the shot in the gorge and I sat down. And he was crying as he went. Well, they didn't hit him! He was smaller. Then I followed him because he was running, and that was when I said to him: "Hey, hey, what is it?" "Mario," he told me, "look, there are some men there who want to talk to you, but what they really want is to kill us." I started to shake because we were innocent, and we went back to our aunt's house. We were just arriving when we saw the flames shoot up, and I said to him, "Look, they burned down the house!" Our childhood was nothing but suffering. They left us with nothing. Case 8586, Aldea Ixcahin, Nuevo Progreso, San Marcos, 1973.

CHILDREN ON THE RUN

We left under cover of the coffee bushes, myself and my six children. That night we headed for the river, feeling our way along it so they wouldn't hear the sound of my baby's crying. Afterward, when we were in the Suchiate River, my children cried from the cold. Oh, my little boys! When morning came, they had turned really blue with the cold. They had no clothes on, and I took off my blouse and wrapped it around my baby. We walked through the forest to get to Toquian Grande. Case 8632, Bullaj, Tajamulco, San Marcos, 1982.

The extreme hardship associated with persecution and flight into the hills or into exile caused rampant disease and death among children. They suffered deprivation and hunger, exposure, and traumatic stress.

Many testimonies about the first months of flight into the hills include descriptions of children who became bloated from hunger, a symptom of severe malnutrition.[2] Many of these children died. Their families felt completely helpless and

---

[2] These descriptions of malnutrition are consistent with kwashiorkor, which is caused by severe protein and vitamin deficiencies.

anguished by their inability to feed and care for their children. In some cases, these feelings persist to this day.

And that time, like I said, there was no nylon cover; and there was a huge storm so that even the newborn baby boy was close to death because of the rain. We had nothing to cover ourselves with because we were so poor. We had nothing. Case 1280, Palob, Quiché, 1980.

The women and children were already getting bloated. Our children were getting bloated because of the weather and the cold. When we left, the woman was also pregnant and her baby was born in the hills. And after its birth, the baby only cried, maybe because he had no milk and his mother wasn't eating well. Case 4521, Salinas Magdalena, Caserío La Montaña, Sacapulas, Quiché, 1980.

It was so sad because we couldn't find any more to eat. The children were screaming from hunger. Case 10681, San Cristóbal Verapaz, Alta Verapaz, 1983.

The children presented enormous difficulties for communities in emergency situations requiring rapid flight or other lifesaving measures. Many small children were lost, murdered, or perished because it was hard for them to flee and their families had difficulty taking them along. The tragedy of parents who had to abandon children in order to flee may exacerbate their feelings of guilt over the death or disappearance of their offspring.

When they were persecuted, there were a few among them who had three or five children. If they couldn't run or walk, they left them behind, because the parents didn't want to die. They couldn't take their children, because they left in the middle of gunfire. Case 10004, Chajul, Quiché, 1982.

There are babies lying under the trees. They died all over the place. There are babies hanging in the tree branches. It's like what they do with them when they're at home and they wrap them in a piece of cloth [the Mayans commonly hang pieces of cloth as makeshift hammocks for babies to sleep in—TRANS.]. They're hanging like that from the tree branches. And the babies are alive, but you can't take them. Where are you going to leave them if you don't know where their mother is? Collective Case 17, Santa Cruz, Verapaz, 1980.

These dramatic stories are repeated over and over again in different areas where people had to take refuge in mountainous areas or jungles. The presence of small children increased the risk that the communities would be discovered. For months, and sometimes for years—often subsisting in extremely precarious circumstances—the children could not even cry, play, or develop on their own. Families had to control their children strictly and even stifle their cries when the soldiers were nearby. This sometimes caused death or serious neurological damage due to asphyxiation.

And the children could not cry; we had to cover their mouths. We stuffed handkerchiefs in their mouths so they wouldn't cry. Case 3804, Cotzal, Quiché, 1976.

The child was crying and our companions scolded us. They said, "Man, please look after your child, he is going to give us away." And since he would get irritable, we would cover his mouth with a rag. And now something is wrong with him. Case 4521, Salinas Magdalena, Caserío La Montaña, Sacapulas, Quiché, 1980.

THE MILITARIZATION OF CHILDHOOD

The militarization of communities throughout the armed conflict also had an impact on childhood. With diminishing frequency, this included the influence of the civil patrols, forced recruitment, and life in army bases or *model villages*. The mere presence of civil patrols as permanent armed entities in many communities had its effect on the children. From fear of aggression or death to the *normalization* of violence as a way of life, children were influenced by the warlike socialization patterns of life in a militarized environment. Especially in the early years, there are cases describing the participation of minors in the civil war as the norm in many communities. When it occurred, this participation forcibly militarized children and carried with it a high risk of death, as the patrols were used for search missions and to fight the guerrillas. Virtually throughout the armed conflict, the army was responsible for numerous instances of forcible recruitment of minors.[3]

During that time, even the children were required to patrol. My son said: "Mom, I want to leave the patrol. I don't want to go out to patrol with those people because the guerrillas could kill me. Because the first time I went to patrol, I saw twelve dead bodies." (They later killed him.) Case 2988, Cantón Vitzal, Nebaj, Quiché, 1983.

THE CHILDREN OF VIOLENCE

Although there are many testimonies about the rape of women, the consequences of those rapes are rarely discussed. The stigma attached to rape is probably compounded by the community sense of shame about such incidents. Many women have faced the dilemma of what to do with children conceived during

---

[3] Although there are no references to this in the testimonies collected by REMHI, there have been cases of child guerrillas. There is no evidence that this occurred by force, however, and it most likely was a result of the murder of the child's family.

rape. Given that mass rapes took place during certain periods, whether as part of the overall treatment of civilian populations considered subversive, during detentions and massacres, or because women were widowed and bereft of support, the problem of these children cannot be considered insignificant. When women kept the children, the explanations about their fathers forced them to confront the dilemma of their own lives and seek explanations that affirmed their own dignity and helped their children to better understand their situation.

> *Often I remained sleeping in the street, and because I was sleeping in the street I had my son. I don't know who the father is because two men came and raped me. And when I realized it I was fourteen. I turned fifteen just a month before my son was born. And that child, well there he is. He sometimes asks me: "And my father?" And I tell him, "There he is, my son." I try to tell him that a person who wanted to help me so much gave him a name; and I tell him that is his father. But he is not his father.* Case 0425, Uspantán, Quiché, 1983.

Some testimonies contain descriptions of what ultimately happened to these children. These descriptions are consistent with some research findings in the sense that the children conceived of rape tend to be rejected socially, as a form of community resistance.[4] The women also tend to be shunned as the embodiment of the community's shame. One way or another, the children of rape who have been turned over to charitable groups or orphanages are a significant consequence of the violence against women and communities in many parts of the country.

> *Some of those responsible from Baja Verapaz raped the women, even though the women were carrying their children on their backs. They grabbed the children and threw them to the ground, and the men lined up to take their turn with the women. Some of those women became pregnant. The ones who became pregnant had their babies and went to give the children to the nuns. I went to register a child [to give him a name] in Guatemala City since the Sister asked me to do it. This child was abandoned by the mother because he was from the patrollers. He was fifteen days old when the mother left him.* Case 5281, Buena Vista, Baja Verapaz, 1982.

Most of these children appear to have ended up in special homes that also took in children directly orphaned by the violence.

FROM ADOPTION TO ABDUCTION

In most instances, family arrangements or different forms of intra-community adoption are examples of the cohesion and solidarity that provided orphaned

---

[4] "La expresión del trauma en los jóvenes: Guatemala," in *Trauma psicosocial y adolescentes latinoamericanos: formas de acción grupal* (Chile: ILAS, 1994).

children with the family and community support essential to their development, health, and socialization.

> *My son climbed a tree. There in the yard he said: "Mom has died, she has died. I am going to go to Doña Luz, since she wants me to go and live with her."* Case 5281, Buena Vista, Baja Verapaz, 1982.

Families "gave" their children to others with more wherewithal to care for them, and with whom they believed the children would enjoy a brighter future, particularly when the mother was killed. When the mothers survived, however, this practice was much less common.

But being taken in by other families was not always an act of solidarity with the orphans. In the testimonies examined, there are abductions of children who were later used as servants by families who, far from being harmed by the violence, had used it to improve their social status. There have also been accusations of forced separation of families, in which children were subjected to reeducation in special homes.

> *In 1984, the mayor of Rabinal ordered the auxiliary mayors to take children between the ages of five and ten from the Pacux settlement to the Children's Home of the Church of the Nazarene in San Miguel Chicaj. They took twenty boys and girls against their parents' wishes. I was thirteen years old. Later, in 1988, the families complained to the parish priest that their children had been turned into evangelical Christians; they wanted their children returned to them. They were returned that same year.* Rabinal Collective Testimony and Case 3213, Sa'chal Cooperative, Las Conchas, Cobán, Alta Verapaz, 1984.

There are also cases of children who were separated from their families or communities, abducted, and fraudulently adopted by the perpetrators of violence against their families. This practice has condemned these children to living, unknowingly, with their families' murderers. According to statements made by the then–defense minister, General Héctor Gramajo, this practice was common during certain periods, and may have affected many children.

> *The families of many army officers have grown with the adoption of victims of the violence since, at certain times, it was popular among army soldiers to take responsibility for little three or four year olds found wandering in the mountains.* General Héctor Alejandro Gramajo, Prensa Libre, April 6, 1989.

THE WILL TO LIVE

Despite the violence they endured, extraordinarily harsh living conditions, and militarization, children who received sufficient family and social support may be relatively well-adjusted today. Many witnesses, even those who witnessed incidents during their childhood, have reestablished family and social ties, and are now functioning individuals. And, notwithstanding the image of childhood as a vulnerable period, some boys and girls have been active in stressful situations and have faced life's difficulties by helping each other and supporting their families.

And so all of the brothers and sisters pulled together and kept on living, even though they didn't have a father or mother anymore. Full of sorrow and with only a grandmother who also lived with them. The grandfather had already died. Case 5180, Jutiapa, 1987.

While adults sometimes responded to potential attacks by refusing to believe they were in danger, the children sometimes had the instinct to flee when they intuited that danger was near.[5] Many children were able to escape situations of extreme emergency, inform other communities about what was happening, and warn their families in time to save their lives.

For some children, this type of behavior surfaced later when they protested incidents that their families dared not mention. This may have placed them in danger on some occasions, especially in cases where they were living with perpetrators who remained in positions of authority.

The children told the police, "You people killed my father." "I am going to report you," my kid said, since he doesn't forget things. Only my children were there when they arrived to ask questions. And one of my children said to them: "Yes, you were the ones who killed my father; it was you." And after that the police officers didn't say anything. Case 2987, Nebaj, Quiché, 1985.

Children need to understand what happened to them and to their families. When their search for meaning is met with lack of communication, silence, or contradictory explanations from adults, the impact of violence may be exacerbated. In contrast, clear explanations adapted to their needs, together with efforts to preserve the memory of their family members, can help them reconstruct their sense of identity.

---

[5] According to Ricardo Falla, this mechanism was in play during some massacres in the Ixcán, such as Nueva Concepción, Kaibil, and Piedras Blancas (Falla 1987).

Chapter Three

THE ASSAULT ON COMMUNITY

COLLECTIVE AND COMMUNITY DESTRUCTION AND LOSS

Political violence damaged the social fabric of communities. This was particularly true of rural areas where collective murders and massacres had a strong impact on the social structure of indigenous communities, and on power relationships and culture.

The most common effects of the violence are *community destruction,* which is reported in one out of five testimonies, the *destruction of nature,* and *collective persecution.* These are followed by effects associated with profound *community and social crises,* including distrust and internal breakdown. Massacres had the most forceful impact on community life.[1] Specific *religious and cultural changes* are reported to a lesser degree, perhaps because community crises and losses are more vivid in the memory of violence than the perceived cultural effects.[2]

COMMUNITY DESTRUCTION

The army and civil patrols employed diverse strategies of mass destruction to eliminate communities considered to be guerrilla support bases: they burned homes; slashed and burned crops and livestock; destroyed household goods, tools, and symbols; and conducted bombing raids. Generalized losses such as these frequently appear in testimonies of massacres and descriptions of persecution of communities living in the hills and forests. Often homes were destroyed and burned down with people still inside them.

In addition to its capacity for devastation, destruction by fire is highly symbolic for the indigenous population. The burning of everyday objects linked to human life also destroys their *mwel* or *dioxil,* the principle underlying the continuity of

---

[1] There is evidence of community destruction in nearly two-thirds of the massacres, and collective persecution in one of every three. Symptoms of social breakdown are described in one in five testimonies overall.

[2] Social losses and sociopolitical changes in the communities predominate in men's testimonies (they describe group destruction, community breakdown and persecution, and the destruction of people's means of subsistence). Nevertheless, there are no statistically significant differences regarding the collective effects described by men and by women.

life, among other things. This is true of corn and grinding stones, and the human body or any of its parts, such as hair.

They destroyed our houses, they stole our possessions, they burned our clothing and took the livestock, they cut down the cornfield; they perse-cuted us day and night. Case 5339 (Achí man), Plan de Sánchez, Baja Verapaz, 1982.

Material possessions or livestock were not always destroyed, however. Soldiers and officers routinely stole cattle and household items during massacres. The army treated people's belongings as war plunder. Many survivors retain vivid memories of these losses and can even itemize them.

There was nothing but death. They took my only seven head of cattle. They stole eighty cuerdas [13.3 acres—TRANS.] *of corn, twenty-four sheets of tin roofing, a handsaw, a manual saw to cut trees, pigs, clothing, a grinding stone, and a hatchet.* Case 3909 (Kiché man), Aldea Xemal, Quiché, 1980.

The Impact of Material Losses

The destruction of goods essential for survival (villages in ruins, properties destroyed, livestock dead or lost, and so on) not only further impoverished the affected families, but also left them with a sense of defeat and despair. Many people feel that their economic sacrifices, the struggles and work of generations, have been lost, and that these losses are not only detrimental to them personally but also affect future generations. For example, it will not be easy to continue the traditional system of inheritance in indigenous communities.

The Destruction of Nature

In Mayan culture, the earth has a profound significance linked to the collective identity; it is Qachu Alom (our Mother Earth). Thus, an assault on nature is also an assault on the community. Moreover, the purpose of this type of destruction was to eliminate the people's means of survival.

Societies based on traditional corn farming attend to the important cultural aspects of their work: land, seeds, technology, organization of labor, expertise, and symbolic rites (Dary 1997). When crops were destroyed, part of the seed supply that communities had inherited and preserved for generations was also lost. This interfered with the production cycle and reduced the quality of corn and other crops. Also lost was the wisdom and genetic inputs contained in seeds that had been selected and tended for generations. The diverse and depraved strategies used to destroy communities also damaged their basic means of survival and their symbols of life.

Whenever the army camped, it left several pounds of poisoned salt behind when it moved on; [community] leaders tried to figure out how to tell if it was poisoned; a hen would eat it. In Sumal they tried to poison the creek to kill the people. They tried to kill people, not only with bombs, but also by poisoning them. Case 7907 (Kiché man), Aldea Xix, Quiché, 1981.

The Significance of the Losses

The destruction of communities involved countless material losses for the survivors. In this chapter we focus on the collective meaning of community destruction. Besides their economic and social impact, material and social losses often represent symbolic wounds. This woundedness affects the feelings, dignity, and aspirations of communities, as well as subjective, important aspects of their cultural, social, political, and traditional life. The imposition of armed force destroyed community systems of governance: traditional leaders and authorities were killed, basic social organization destroyed, and ethical and moral principles and convictions trampled upon. This confused the population. The most respected, valued members of the community, those revered as examples, were the first ones the army killed because it considered such individuals guilty (sinners) and accused them of being communists and guerrillas.

That which was sacred was profaned. They took away the land, slashed and burned the crops, the hills, nature in general; they destroyed and burned down houses with the family altars inside, they poisoned the water, burned the church, killed loved ones in places where ancestral rites were observed. They desecrated burial sites and trampled dignity; they attacked the struggle, hope, and life itself.

The Elimination of Leaders and Authorities

Community structures responsible for conflict resolution or development were eliminated by the criminalization of any type of leadership not under military control. This loss also had an impact in the medium term because anyone who tried to step into a significant organizing or community role was harassed and denounced.

The people they took were the leaders, like teachers and secretaries—the people who had a voice and knew how to speak up for themselves. Francisco was abducted because he was a leader and had a strong commitment to getting ahead, and he wasn't ashamed of his culture. Case 5017, San Pedro Necta, Huehuetenango, 1982.

The army also attacked civilian authorities in its effort to establish control over the social fabric of communities. The army exercised control over the population by eliminating the civilian authorities, ensuring their obedience and submission to military authority, or replacing them. As a result, many auxiliary mayors and local authorities were killed.

Whether through the use of force, its overriding military capacity against the army, or its credibility among some population groups, the guerrilla presence weakened civilian authority. Guerrillas committed selective murders of community authorities who refused to collaborate with the insurgency or who were alleged to be army collaborators. In other instances, the guerrillas' military power to fight the army also permeated the social fabric of communities through the de facto replacement of civilian authorities.

Community leaders were lost or changed, replaced, or subordinated to the military authorities. Besides imposing values and customs foreign to the community, this led to abuses of authority. Community checks and balances on authority were also suppressed, as no one could disobey the new authorities or dispute their actions. Military commissioners and civil patrols drastically altered community power relationships, which came to be determined by the possession of weapons and the use of force.

COMMUNITY BREAKDOWN AND CRISIS

SOCIAL POLARIZATION

Escalating tensions and open conflict forced people to take sides in a threatening and polarized atmosphere, particularly during the years of generalized violence. Divisions often began with family discord over support for a particular military force. This process was repeated at the community level, leading to social tensions and fissures.

Close relationships that were betrayed in the schism caused by belonging to, or sympathizing with, either the guerrilla forces or the army are often difficult to repair. Militarization distorted and challenged community values such as loyalty and respect.

There was a lot of evil in the commissioners' behavior toward the people in the community. The people didn't do anything; they didn't cause problems. But at the whim of the commissioner, of the army, someone would be accused of being a guerrilla, even if it wasn't so. But they killed people for this reason. The guerrillas used the same method. That's how people were divided. Some were with the guerrillas and others with the army; and both sides deceived us. Case 8008 (Mam Indian man), Ixcán, Quiché, 1981.

PERSECUTION AND DISRUPTION OF DAILY LIFE

Persecution began with strictures on the daily routines of community life such as trade and transport. Curbed marketing opportunities, the isolation of communities, and control over people's movements often preceded collective murders and community destruction.

In 1981 and 1982, the market was closed; you couldn't buy any kind of medicine or anything to eat in the stores. Our work—we couldn't sell our crop, no one was buying anymore. It was only for us and our children. Case

2297 (Mam man, community leader), Santa Ana Huista, Huehuetenango, 1981.

A REGIMENTED EXISTENCE

In the eighties, the army routinely concentrated civilian populations into designated areas, thereby increasing their social isolation and enhancing military control over them. According to the testimonies gathered, at least one out of five communities where massacres took place subsequently remained under military control. This control, which was achieved through the presence of the army, military commissioners, or civil patrols, had an enormous influence on community dynamics, which, for years, were subordinated to military logic. Model villages and development poles were extreme examples of the changes imposed on daily life, although other rural populations experienced such changes to a lesser degree.

We used to live in Sebás, but now we're from Xacomoch. I took my wife and my children there because their objective was to round up all the villages and put us there in Sebás. They had measured it out so that each house could be no more than two meters from the next. Case 3344 (Qeqchi man), Caserío Chimoxán, Cahabón, Alta Verapaz, 1982.

SOCIAL BREAKDOWN

The social support usually found in relationships between families and neighbors was another casualty of community breakdown. Whether because of the losses suffered or out of fear, existing support systems vanished, as did solidarity on issues of vital importance to community members. The likelihood of being accused as a guerrilla collaborator for the slightest reason made any attempt at solidarity extremely risky.

Violence also destroyed many social customs, such as marriages and extended family systems, which determine socioeconomic and political relationships and confer social identity, particularly in Mayan communities.

I was left in the street, no one left to look out for me. I have two other daughters—all of the violence we suffered frightened them. They never came back to visit me, since they were also raped by the ones responsible. They left me alone. I am barely surviving. If I die I don't know who will bury me. Case 535 (Achí woman), Buena Vista, Rabinal, Baja Verapaz, 1981.

Any form of social order requires at least a minimum of cooperation among its members. Without this minimum cooperation—observance of certain group rules, solidarity, basic trust, elemental respect, for example—it becomes impossible to live together (Martín-Baró 1989). These experiences of solidarity traditionally formed the basis for life in rural communities.

> *The army's fear was that the people were united; they knew how to share, to live together in their own village. If someone was sick, people did his work for him. Twenty or thirty people—everyone would go over to do his work. If a widow wanted to build her house, we would all do it together. When you build a house for other relatives, all the people go. They take wood. Other communities don't do this. They became suspicious and they considered us communists.* Case 2297, Aldea Buena Vista, Santa Ana Huista, Huehuetenango, 1981.

Nonetheless, many people continued to act in solidarity and accepted the negative repercussions that their decision to help others might bring them. Alongside the terrifying massacres and horrific acts of terrorism, there are repeated examples of solidarity and profound altruism.

THE MILITARIZATION OF DAILY LIFE: THE IMPACT OF THE CIVIL PATROLS

Obligatory participation in the Civilian Self-defense Patrols (PACs) shattered community life. The patrols' militarized hierarchical structure imposed new forms of authority and a new set of rules and values distinguished by the possession of weapons and the use of force. The patrol chief, and hence the army, directly or indirectly controlled or supervised all social activity. This militarized authority elevated the social status of some community members and was frequently used for personal gain. The civil patrol system was imposed throughout rural Guatemala, although its characteristics and impact on communities varied from place to place.

Obligatory participation in the civil patrols changed daily life in the communities to the detriment of the family economy. Men lost work on the days they had to patrol and, over time, this strained the family finances. Moreover, the dictates of the civil patrol system impeded strategies—such as trade or seasonal migratory labor—by which families customarily supplemented their income. Men had to request permission to travel and often had to pay for missed patrol duty. The patrols thus became an economic drain.

> *They did as the army ordered for fear of losing their lives and those of their families, as had occurred in other communities. They did not have time to work the land. They realized that they had been taken there to serve the army.* Case 847, Ixcán, Quiché, 1982.

The patrol system also relied on group control and militaristic socialization methods by pressuring its members to take part in, and even distinguish themselves by, violent actions such as arbitrary attacks on defenseless individuals.

Other patrol members acted under pressure because failure to comply with orders was severely punished, and could result in death.

The militarization of communities has had consequences beyond the scope of the demobilization process that accompanied the end of the armed conflict. The continued reliance on force—either because people are still armed or due to other forms of social control by those responsible for the civil patrol structures—makes it imperative to rethink power structures at the community level. Real demilitarization, together with mechanisms to ensure social restitution and justice, and to honor the victims, is essential for the social reconstruction of the communities most affected by the war.

SOCIAL IDENTITY: VIOLENCE AGAINST RELIGION AND CULTURE

Violence has also had an impact on religious and cultural practices central to the social identity of people and communities. The counterinsurgency policy sought to change people's attitudes and feelings, not only about the army or military operations, but also about beliefs, social perspectives, and customs that the State considered dangerous. Some of the changes described below have to do with this deliberate attempt to destroy social identity. Others are part of the traditional discrimination and racism against indigenous populations that was intensified by counterinsurgency. Finally, some of these descriptions fit into the broader framework of social changes in recent decades brought about by economic and social factors.

RELIGIOUS CHANGES

We had to leave behind the ancestors and the dead. They separated us from sacred sites and, also, you couldn't practice anymore, you couldn't be religious. There was military control; we had to ask permission to go out to work. Case 567, Cobán, Alta Verapaz, 1981.

Community breakdown and displacement made it very difficult to continue to practice religious rituals and ceremonies. Fear of professing the Catholic faith, which the army considered subversive doctrine, was the most common obstacle to religious expression in rural areas. Mayan and Catholic religious practices were inevitably altered by the loss of places of worship and sacred sites. At the same time, other religious traditions based on collective rituals, such as evangelical Christians and charismatic Catholics, were less visible during that period.

They sent a letter to the house saying that we shouldn't go to the chapel anymore, that we shouldn't pray. So I didn't stop praying; what I did was to pray at home, with my father, every Saturday and Sunday, because we could no longer go to the chapel. They closed the church. Case 5308 (Achí man), Aldea El Nance, Salamá, Baja Verapaz, 1982.

With the exception of some Protestant churches that stood by the affected populations, influential evangelical sects increasingly found that the repression had created a religious vacuum. The army encouraged these sects as a way of controlling the population.[3] The sects broadcast their own version of the violence and blamed the victims. They advocated structural changes in the religious life of the communities based on separation into small groups, messages legitimizing the army's power, and individual salvation. Their ceremonies involved mass emotional catharsis. Violence thus became the motivating force behind these evangelical sects, which installed themselves throughout much of the country.

Inés clearly explained the word of God; he talked about injustice, about fairness, about the poor. The people labeled him for this. The "brothers" from other churches told us, "It would be better to change religions now. You should go with us, because they could come and take you away in front of your children, or they could kill all of you." Case 059 (Mam Indian woman), Aldea La Victoria, San Juan Ostuncalco, Quetzaltenango, 1983.

The military authorities frequently desecrated sacred sites. During military operations against rural populations, many people were murdered in places that were held sacred and have been part of Mayan rituals for generations.

So since they had taken the son of a woman from here, she followed them. And there is a pile of stones where they pray to the ancestors; she went there to pray and that was exactly where [he] was tied among the trees. There they set fire to him and set him aflame. And they were burning him, his tongue, his feet, and they were flogging him. Then they threw away the shoes and, finally, they left him there. Case 6257, Caserío Tzalá, San Sebastián Coatán, Huehuetenango, not dated.

Many churches were destroyed and desecrated during the early eighties. In some regions, such as the Quiché, the army went so far as to occupy churches, turning them into detention and torture centers.

The patrollers and the army arrived at Chisis village, in the Cotzal municipality. They entered each house and took the men from their respective homes, searching for Mateo López. They rounded up a total of about one hundred people. They took some of them into the church, already beaten up. And then they set the house of God on fire, with all the people inside. Case 1440 (Ixil woman), Aldea Chisis, San Juan Cotzal, Quiché, 1980.

---

[3] Membership in Protestant and evangelical churches and the like increased for several reasons: (a) persecution of the Catholic church and branding of its catechists as subversives; (b) the individualistic, salvationist (anti-alcohol, individual rebirth) and apolitical message of the evangelical sects; (c) these churches used Mayan languages and respected some of their traditions; and (d) the army supported and encouraged some sects.

The town was abandoned in 1982, and so the church property was deserted. When we returned on August 15, 1982, I realized that the army was using the temple as a barracks. Inside there were three rows of beds for all the troops, and they also had a huge pile of fertilizer that the captain told me was from El Aguacate farm. Case 2300, Nentón, Huehuetenango, 1982.

LOSS OF TRADITIONAL AUTHORITIES

Many communities lost their elders and traditional authorities. With them, they lost memory of their ancestors and the experience of the Mayan traditional approach to resolving community problems with its emphasis on reparations for damages rather than punitive measures. These systems, in which the offender does something constructive for the victim or for nature, were an integral part of the social life of the community.[4]

LOSS OF LANGUAGE

And so there was a woman named Dominga; she was a Qeqchi. And they always ridiculed her because she didn't speak Spanish, or "Castilian" very well. Case 1280 (Kiché man), Palob, Quiché, 1980.

People who were displaced to different areas had to learn another language, usually Spanish. Even among families who were able to reestablish their own routines, such as those living in refugee settlements or Communities of Popular Resistance (CPRs), Spanish was the common language for communication. This has proved an obstacle to teaching children their native language as part of their socialization process.

Rosa and her children can't speak their own language anymore; they have learned to speak other languages. Because of the violence they lost their tradition. Case 10004, Chacalté village, Chajul, Quiché, 1982.

THE COLORS OF IDENTITY

Traditional weaves are imbued with symbolism, artistry, and emotion; they are intertwined with Mayan identity and beliefs. Mayan dress, as an ethnic marker, has multiple, contradictory meanings as "an object that is experienced with particular intensity; it is created by the women themselves and is part of their social

---

[4] "In Mayan tradition whoever committed an act outside of the public order, now referred to as a crime, was immersed in society instead of paying for his or her mistake in isolation: this person had to make some form of reparation for the misdeed" (Dary 1997).

being. Ultimately, its meaning is so powerful that it has permeated the daily life of the Guatemalan population in general" (Camús 1997).

Traditional costumes were frequently lost in the generalized destruction. Because of the difficulty of obtaining thread, and of weaving or purchasing the needed materials, the recovery of traditional clothing was a costly process given the precarious economic and living conditions of the affected populations.

> *I left my things there, my clothing, my* cortes [traditional skirts]. *I left my house with my daughter, with the one* corte, *with one* guipil [traditional blouse]. *I took none of my daughter's things, everything was left behind in the house.* Case 579, (Qeqchi woman), Cobán, Alta Verapaz, 1981.

Some testimonies reflect the women's shame at having to wear nontraditional clothing or rags. In light of the symbolism and sense of identity associated with traditional dress, particularly for women, its loss is more than a material one and must be understood in terms of personal dignity.

> *We didn't have clothing either; we were ashamed to go around like that. We only found thread for mending from some old sacks that had been thrown away. We ate food from the woods that the animals ate; they showed us what was edible.* Case 7916 (Kiché man), Salinas, Magdalena, Quiché, 1983.

It was also dangerous for women to wear traditional clothing, because its association with their communities of origin was an obvious form of identification. Many women had to change their attire or avoid their traditional dress in order to conceal their identity. Similarly, many men had to conceal their origins to avoid being denounced as guerrillas.

REPAIRING THE SOCIAL FABRIC

Living Together in the Future

The victims and survivors themselves have already begun to repair the social fabric by reinstating the role of improvement committees, catechists, and grassroots and labor organizations, as well as health and education outreach workers. Traditional authorities, to a certain degree, are also reclaiming their former status. The emergence of new leadership and social groups and movements in recent years exemplifies this slowly evolving process and represents hope for the future.

This future is threatened, however, by ongoing community conflicts, primarily land disputes that have been exacerbated by the situation of uprooted displaced persons and refugees. The armed conflict greatly escalated historic conflicts over land.

Other ongoing conflicts associated with the violence have to do with the climate created by the presence in many communities of perpetrators who have never been punished. According to our information, known perpetrators who were involved in accusations, murders, or other acts against the population are identified in one out of three testimonies (17.3 percent of them were from the community and 15.2 percent from outside the community). In some cases, the perpetrator was related in some way to the victim (2 percent).

> *The ones who harmed us are alive. They are living in the village of Salina Magdalena.* Case 1368 (Kiché man), Tierra Caliente, Sacapulas, Quiché, 1981.

Although some testimonies speak of forgiveness for religious reasons, the majority of those describing a situation of coexistence with perpetrators explicitly demand justice and punishment of those responsible. Customary legal remedies must be enforced, perpetrators must acknowledge their actions, and local authorities must be reconstituted as part of the process necessary to rebuild the foundations for living together as a society.

Finally, the social reintegration of the civilian population and ex-combatants constitutes an enormous challenge in the coming years in the context of repairing the social fabric destroyed by the war.

> *Because I feel so much, it hits me anew. More so when my current neighbors are always pointing me out as a bad person. It is painful to remember all this, it makes us sad. Since, in reality, we left the area. We returned—and to hear the same problems again, to be singled out, to be threatened again, to be told we are murderers, that we are a bunch of guerrillas, that we are demons, that we have killed many people.* Case 1642 (Qeqchi man), Cahabón, Alta Verapaz, 1980.

Chapter Four

COPING WITH VIOLENCE

THE POPULATION'S VARIED EXPERIENCES

The strategies people have used to cope with the effects of violence are an important facet of their experience. Many individuals and groups assumed a very active posture despite the risk involved.

CULTURE

Mayan culture distinguishes different ways of coping with violence. The following chart summarizes some of these cultural traits.

CONCEPTS FOUND IN THE MAYAN CULTURE[1]

Analogical thought: An important resource comprising images and metaphors found in thought and language.

The q'eqchi'es, for example, speak of the mwel *of things. The* mwel *could be described as the inner core of each being that gives it its own unique "dignity" as well as the "ability" to serve its innate purpose (corn, for instance, has its* mwel*).*

Time: Time is circular, there is no linear past-present division. It is harmonious with the rhythms of nature, slow paced, and is dependent upon community social life.

All things have, then, their mystery, their lord [ajaw]. Time as well. Therefore, it has been, and continues to be so important for the Mayas to be able to

---

[1] Compiled by the authors based on Breton 1989; J. Solares, comp., *Estado y Nación en Guatemala* (Guatemala: FLACSO, 1993); Ak'kutan 1993.

understand and use their calendar properly. Each day has its "lord," as do the different calendar periods.

The relationship between life and death: A daily relationship between the living and the dead and ancestors. The continuous presence of this relationship in rituals, dreams, celebrations, and ceremonies.

In fact, the Maya conceives his or her identity as a spiritual wholeness of belonging that encompasses both ancestors and living descendants. Thus, for the Achí Indians, the word Mam *refers both to ancestors and to newborn grandchildren.*

Cosmovision: The vision of the interconnectedness of person-nature-community. These relationships have their own set of unique meanings.

Mayan culture regards individuals as destined to form part of a Reality that transcends them; it preceded them and will outlast their temporal state. This perception informs the Maya's approach to nature, the community, history, the spirits, and the ajaw.

The value of the individual and the community: The individual is considered with respect, as part of the community. The sense of community identity is important.

Respect means to take into account the other's dignity and to act accordingly. The first "sin" that Popol Vuh *(the sacred and classic work of the Quiché Maya) describes is that of the "men of wood" who did not know how to respect the cooking pots, clay griddles, grinding stones, and dogs.*

Reciprocity: The people's relationship with nature, with others, and with the spirits is based on reciprocity. This relationship is based on interdependence and has implications for the concept of reparations for victims.

In the Popol Vuh, *even the "Creators and Makers"* [Creadores y Formadores] *of men expect the people to feed them. The Mayans burn candles in their ceremonies to restore this relationship and to feed (*huelan, kesiqonik*) God and the ancestors.*

COPING STRATEGIES

One in three testimonies describes displacement and, at least half of the time, the survivors tried to cope directly with the situation, within their realm of possibilities. These reactions were followed in frequency by acts of solidarity, special precautions, and security measures. A series of highly diverse methods of coping with very different types of experiences subsequently emerges (sharing experiences, return from displacement, exercising restraint, restoring family ties, enduring extreme hardship, refusal to discuss what happened, religious coping mechanisms, political commitment, resignation, and interpretation of dreams).[2]

Living in the Midst of Violence

In general terms, the best explanation of people's experiences was a combination of resistance and adaption to life in a militarized atmosphere. The affected populations relied on several basic resources to cope with the situation, usually as a reaction or a protective instinct on the part of survivors. These included self-defense mechanisms (such as not talking or exercising restraint); mutual support (acts of solidarity); coping through activity (such as searching for relatives); or approaching situations from a religious perspective.

> *It was something very beautiful and also very sad. Some relatives and friends avoided us in the street, as if we were lepers. And some endangered themselves during the state of siege, the martial state, and all of those states, visited us, even at night, risking their lives. People offered to hide us in their homes. We never hid, because we never had reason to hide; we didn't have anything that was outside the law and a normal life, like all human beings, like any innocent and sincere Guatemalan.* Case 5444 (university professor, killed), Guatemala City, 1979.

Fleeing for Life

Group flight is a collective or community-based response that is related primarily to the experience of exile and displacement in the hills and forests (displacement, return, and reestablishing family ties were linked; see section below on displacement).

Two significant patterns emerged in the testimonies gathered:

1. *Collective and community-based displacement:* usually prolonged, to areas not under government control.

2. *Reactive family displacement:* temporary, to another community.

Community Defense

This is a collective response characterized by precautions and security measures in conjunction with the community organization. It is associated with collective

---

[2] Other methods mentioned, such as isolation, eschewing social or political activism, or forgiveness are not considered here, given their low frequency in the testimonies. The low frequency of these reactions, such as isolation or not getting involved, may be due to an inherent bias in that those more likely to utilize such methods did not come forward to give their testimony, or because people tend to emphasize the positive ways they dealt with their situation.

displacement into exile or into the hills (see section below regarding CPR displacement, living in the hills and forests, and exile).

Resistance in Situations of Extreme Hardship

This is a more individualized approach having to do with adapting to stressful and traumatic situations (it combines enduring extreme hardship such as torture or life in the wilderness, with talking and interpreting dreams). Many people report having discussed their experience, such as torture or life in the wilderness, with other people, seeking their support in order to denounce the situation.

> *And this difficult situation is emotional for me. And also for my mother, who suffered greatly also, since they were married for many years. And I'm taking advantage of this opportunity, since it has been offered, to give a testimony so that it is recorded, on tape and in documents. So that this case doesn't remain isolated, but rather joins the many others that everyone knows took place in this country.* Case 0046, Santa Barbara, Suchitepéquez, 1981.

The interpretation of dreams is another of the cultural resources that people have employed to cope with the violence. In Mayan culture, dreams have a cultural interpretation related to the individual's current or past life experience, the direction of his or her future actions, and communication with the ancestors. Dreams are frequently shared among family members, who seek out elders and Mayan priests to interpret them. Survivors of extremely traumatic experiences such as torture describe dreams that had generally positive meanings and helped them remain mentally alert and hopeful.

> *A man came in, a tall man, a white, blond man with his hat on. He asked: "Is Guillermo here? Yes. Oh, good. You or all of you have to follow my path, where I go, where I have been. You all have to follow where I too have gone." There he also told that man that he should not worry, "or are you sad in that jail?" And he said "no." He answered, "I am not sad." "Oh, don't worry, don't worry because your wife came yesterday, your family here in Cobán came yesterday. I was with them, guiding them, the women, too. I am experiencing what you are. You mustn't worry; be happy and I am with you. I am here to help you and your wife too. Don't worry about your family, I am with them and with you. Besides I am witnessing everything they're doing, how they captured you." And he put his hand on his head, on the man's head.* Case 1155, Ixcán, Quiché, 1981.

Attempts to Change the Situation

Other testimonies describe social and political action and reframing what happened in a positive light. In other words, becoming involved in different activities to bring about change was a method of coping with violence. Nonetheless, attempts by people and communities affected by the repression to organize have not been easy. Abductions and threats have been the traditional methods of impeding such efforts.

> *Later, after several months, a human rights organization emerged. I immediately went and signed up, and I entered into an intense struggle. Because my hope was that [he] would appear alive, to be rid of all that uncertainty. Well, if someone is imprisoned, you know where they are and, even if they are given a hundred years in jail, you still have the hope of seeing them again. But unfortunately, it wasn't like that. We entered into this very, very hard struggle. I think that it also heightens your awareness, because it is no longer a struggle for my own relatives, which in my case are six people, but a struggle for all of the disappeared in Guatemala, all of those abducted. Because you realize it's not just you—in the moment of the abduction you think it's just you, right. Sometimes you blaspheme against God: if I am struggling for a better society, why does our Lord allow such things to happen?* Case 5449, Guatemala City, 1984.

The survivors' commitment also involves reclaiming the victims' dignity, their values, and the meaning of life. The sacrifice of many of those murdered or disappeared is not only a sign of pain but also part of the meaning of life and the hope of the survivors. It is just as in the story of *Popol Vuh*, when the youths Hun Hunahpu and Vucub Hunahpu were ridiculed, tortured, murdered, and buried amid the grins of the men of Xibalbá, who told their victims: "Now you will die, you will be destroyed, we will cut you to pieces and here your memory will remain." But the skull of one them was camouflaged among the fruits of a delicious tree when the young girl Ixquic approached. When she extended her hand, the skull let loose a stream of saliva and told her: "In my saliva and in my spit, I have given you my descendants,"...and the young girl became pregnant (*Popol Vuh*, part 2, chaps. 2 and 3) (Corby 1983).

THE EXPERIENCE OF THE DISPLACED

LARGE-SCALE DISPLACEMENT

ESTIMATED FIGURES ON GUATEMALAN DISPLACEMENT

- one million people internally displaced;
- 400,000 exiled in Mexico, Belize, Honduras, Costa Rica, and the United States;
- 45,000 legally recognized refugees in Mexico, the majority living in new communities in camps;

- 150,000 undocumented people in Mexico and some 200,000 undocumenteds in the United States;
- 20,000 people organized in CPRs, another 20,000 may have lived displaced in the wilderness for several years;
- in certain parts of the highlands hardest hit by the scorched-earth policy, up to 80 percent of the population was displaced at certain times.

Displacement has been central to the experience of the populations affected by the violence. Although it occurred throughout the armed conflict, it took on massive proportions during the early eighties. Individual displacement occurred in the sixties and seventies. Displacing the population would later become a counterinsurgency objective rather than simply a collateral effect of the violence, particularly in highly conflictive areas with guerrilla presence or influence. Some groups, however, also used displacement as a self-defense mechanism.

Then at that time I left and I went to spend some time in Mexico. I spent ten years alone in Mexico, with no wife, I was just alone. I saved my money and worked in various places. I went to Tuxtla; I went to the place they call Puebla. Then, when the massacre of '81 and '82 happened, that was when all of the Guatemalan brothers and sisters went to seek refuge in Mexico. And so I found out—I went back to live with my people—I found them in Mexico. Case 0783 (abduction and torture by soldiers), San Juan Ixcán, Quiché, 1975.

Most of the cases compiled by REMHI described collective displacement either of family groups or communities. Massive displacement occurred in parts of northern Quiché, San Marcos, Chimaltenango, Alta Verapaz, Baja Verapaz, and Huehuetenango. It was a veritable exodus of the population.

All the people left in a panic, myself included, and we went to stay in a place called Xolguitz. Later we went to Tajumulco. We spent five months there. Later I returned to Carrizales. There was also violence where I am now. All of the people who lived there went to Mexico and are still there. They sold their land and now they don't have any land. Case 8565 (massacre in Montecristo village), Tajumulco, San Marcos, 1980.

Individual displacement occurred when the threat was directed exclusively at one person, and when that person's family had adequate social support and a minimum degree of security. Nonetheless, in many cases of individual displacement, the family followed afterward in an attempt at family reunification. This type of displacement was commonplace in urban areas.

I don't know what I did, but I told him that he should try to get away, if he could, through a window close to the street. And he, well, he listened to me *and left quickly that way. He opened the window and jumped. When he jumped, one of the ones there yelled to be quiet and made a noise with his weapon as if he were going to fire it. But he did not shoot, and he was able to get away. He zig-zagged across the street and fled. He went into the neighboring houses and ended up at the river's edge. He fled in that direction. I stayed with my children. Oh, it makes me so sad! I was determined that whatever happened to me, so be it, but he had saved his life.* Case 5042 (attempted abduction of husband), Santa Lucía Cotzumalguapa, Escuintla, 1984.

THE DYNAMICS OF DISPLACEMENT: THE PATH OF FLIGHT

Life Became Impossible

Prior to large-scale population movements, living conditions progressively deteriorated because of pervasive fear and the effects of militarization. Although in most cases violence led directly to flight, other factors such as restrictions on movements, community isolation, and the disruption of everyday life figure prominently in the experiences described in the testimonies.

At that time, youths were abducted and taken to the military base; military commissioners helped the army with the captures. We ran that risk; there was no freedom to go out to the markets because suddenly they would close the markets and begin to grab [people]—or at the dances—so it was very difficult to go out. Case 2267, Aldea Nojoya, Nentón, Huehuetenango, 1980.

Firsthand experiences of violence and the pervasive climate of terror led to massive displacement in some parts of the country. Testimonies about the causes of displacement describe knowledge of what was happening in nearby communities, military presence, abductions and murders, and in some cases, guerrilla actions.

Emergency Flight

For communities that suffered massacres, the decision to flee was often abrupt and extremely dangerous. Many families were able to take only a few bare essentials with them, and most people lost everything.

In other cases, the awareness of imminent danger helped many people save their lives. Some groups stayed behind because they didn't feel persecuted or did not believe that the army would harm them. Resistance to leaving their homes or refusal to believe the information coming in from other areas led some families or communities to stay put, and many of these lost their lives. Fleeing for several days and temporary displacement were other examples of people's attempts to cope with danger without totally abandoning their lands. This experience is common to many subsequent situations of displacement to the city, into the hills and forests, or into exile.

It was hard for us to leave because it was our place, where we were born, where we lived, where we grew up. We wouldn't have willingly left that place. The soldiers came often, every day. When we saw how it was, the situation was already getting worse. When we saw that the soldiers were coming, it was best for us to leave our homes, go to the woods, go to the ravines, go to the rivers; so they wouldn't spot us, so they wouldn't kill us. We spent entire nights there, we slept, two or three days enduring the cold, hunger, together with our wives, children, our elderly. We have endured the hardest time of our lives, without homes, without clothing. Case 5106 (murder of brother), Panzós, Alta Verapaz, 1980.

Many people perceived the injustice of being compelled to flee. Families faced the dilemma of fleeing to save their lives, fully aware that if they did so, the army would accuse them of being members of the guerrillas. Families and communities, therefore, were faced with a paradox in which any decision they made could imperil their lives.

In only a few of the cases compiled was the decision to flee preceded by a thorough evaluation of the level of threat, a search for a safe place, and a process of planning for flight. Selective threats and murders during the sixties and seventies, and later from the mid-eighties and into the nineties, led to the displacement of professionals, students, and organized labor sectors, usually into exile. Until a few years ago, certain foreign embassies played an important role in providing protection during the process of leaving the country.

They were in the parish house having a session with public health groups that had problems at the hospital and had formed a commission. That's when they arrived and told them that if they didn't leave they were going to kill them. All of them left. And there were some people in some cars waiting for them. Someone took Dolores, without clothing or anything, to seek asylum in an embassy. I believe that she is still in Canada. Case 6522 (persecution of various leaders), Escuintla, 1982.

In rural areas, information about what was happening caused many people to flee. This type of information was essential for making decisions and saving one's life because rumors spread quickly in a climate of tension, isolation, and uncertainty about the future. In other cases, the guerrillas advised people to move to other areas or accompanied them into the hills. In select cases, moreover, soldiers or civil patrollers alerted people to what was being planned and encouraged them to seek safety.

Sometimes there also were soldiers in the army who didn't want to kill people. So they passed information to the individuals; and they realized that they already had people's names. So what those people did was leave. Case 0977 (threats and murder), Santa María Tzejá, Ixcán, Quiché, 1981-82.

Circumstances of Flight

The main difficulties during flight were the danger of the journey and family separation. For most displaced populations, the horrendous losses they suffered were compounded by an extremely dangerous and arduous escape.

> *Little by little, we went farther away from our community, until one day two men from La Victoria community stayed with us. They wanted us to go with them to Mexico. Finally, we decided to go with them, but on the way we ran into a group of soldiers. That was how I was separated from my husband; they took me to the Cotzal base, where they detained me for two months. Afterward they let me come to Uspantán, where I found my husband, but my children weren't there.* Case 4409, El Caracol, Uspantán, Quiché, 1981.

In many testimonies, the memory of flight in precarious circumstances is quite vivid, including the lack of food, the lack of clothing, nighttime escapes, and avoiding contacts with other communities that could endanger them.

> *So I turned off the light and we left. I very nearly fell into the ravine with my children, because there is a ravine down below there. We left there and we went to the wilds. I got that far, carrying my seven children with me. I stayed there for fifteen days, and from there I went down to Zapote.* Case 5304, Aldea Xibac, Salamá, Baja Verapaz, 1982.

Seeking Social Support

The affected families moved to other areas in search of more security and some degree of social support. Family relationships were an important source of solidarity in receiving people, a process that was often progressive and included various provisional settlements.

> *When the army was stationed here in Nentón, they gave the order for the people to get out of their homes, and we moved. Some went to Guatemala City, others went away—those who had relatives in Mazatenango, in Huehuetenango. And those of us who did not have relatives went to stay in Cajomá Grande. We stayed there for one month.…Then we couldn't make it anymore, so we went to work someplace else instead—to the Guatemalan-Mexican border—to make a living. Out of fear of dying that both sides inspired in us, because we were afraid that the army could kill us.* Case 2300, Nentón, Huehuetenango, 1982.

In the early eighties, army and civil patrol persecution of a significant portion of the civilian population caused this "displacement in stages." This persecution often led to further displacement of the original families as well as of the communities that had taken them in.

There are about five hundred people, and they arrived at a place I have, where I have a coffee plantation. Oh, God, I got there right away, angry, because I don't want to see more people on top of my crops. But I got there, so many poor people. I arrived there angry, but after I saw the first ones I felt sorry for them. "My God, what happened to you people?" I said to them. "Look, mister, this is a child, three or four people are already infested with worms, the head, the knee, the arms." Oh, God! I no longer thought of berating them, I thought about treating them....Then they [the soldiers] started to threaten the people here. Then they burned the whole cooperative and the nixtamal *mill [corn-grinding mill—*TRANS.*]. Well, then the people left, they left their homes, and the soldiers ran us out of here.* Case 3624 (guerrilla-led displacement), El Desengaño, Uspantán, Quiché, 1981.

The First Settlements

The experiences later become increasingly diverse, depending on the conditions that the displaced persons encountered. Their reception and welcome varied greatly depending on the location and whether it was a case of individual or collective displacement.

And so we were already in Las Palmas when the news came that the soldiers were already killing people in San Francisco. They said, "Let's go before they get here." So we left Las Palmas. Then we went into Mexico. We crossed the border; we got to a place called Ciscao there on the border. We settled there and worked with the Mexicans, but sadly because nothing was familiar to us. We didn't have anything, not even our wool blankets [chamarras]. So we began to explain to the Mexicans: "We are poor, they killed our family, they killed everyone, our womenfolk, what are we going to do now?" And since the Mexicans were aware of the situation, they told us: "No, look, compañeros, *we are all children of God, we're going to support each other. Don't worry, we're going to help you here." So they supported us with some clothing, a little money.* Case 6070, Petanac, Huehuetenango, 1982.

There were other cases in which the solidarity of other communities or family support helped the displaced cope with the situation more effectively. However, tens of thousands of people were forced to flee into the hills in dire circumstances. These displaced persons joined together in mutual acknowledgment and support to develop survival mechanisms and collective flight patterns in response to even more difficult situations.

Reestablishing a Daily Routine

In addition to the experiences they had survived, the displaced had to try to reestablish their daily routines in a new place, often in circumstances of political pressure and fear. Besides this, they had to find money, work, and in the case of rural populations, land. Restoring a routine, even under what were often precarious circumstances, helped ameliorate the situation.

A New Identity

Other populations ended up resettling permanently, after several attempts to rebuild their lives in different places. With time—the level of affinity with the receiving community, the living situation, and so forth—displacement brought about its own changes in terms of lifestyle and identity.

Many people felt that they had forfeited their original identity by not remaining in their community ("*I'm not from Nebaj anymore!*") Others, in contrast, acquired a new identity based on their positive experience in the receiving community or their involvement in different movements. Their identity as a refugee or a returnee, or as a CPR member, is an example of how a particular political movement can influence people's lives. Internally displaced persons dispersed in the city may have had more difficulties in this regard, because their self-defense mechanisms included hiding their identity and the receiving communities lacked a group identity.

Despite the fact that, in some cases, these new identities were used to stigmatize politically and to create enmity and conflict among communities, they are usually a common denominator that may be very meaningful to people. Still others developed multilayered identities that might include aspects of both the place of origin and the place of reception.

SEEKING REFUGE IN EXILE

One in five testimonies about displacement actually refers to exile. According to available data, between 125,000 and 500,000 people were obliged to seek refuge in other countries, particularly in Mexico, to avoid persecution by the army or paramilitary groups. What initially appeared to be a transitory measure turned into a protracted experience that required a total change in lifestyle, particularly in refugee camps. This implied the social reorganization of community living and the onset of new family and cultural problems. Refuge, for many, meant always living in the past.

And so my mother said we had to leave for the Mexican border. Many people left; those who didn't go were on the army's side. Since we were on the guerrillas' side, we left. So we left for the border somewhere between four and six o'clock in the afternoon. We left everything behind: chickens, pigs, the corn stalks with ears on them. Everything was left there; we didn't bring a single thing. We lost everything. We were very frightened; my mother was trembling. Case 8391, San Miguel Acatán, Huehuetenango, 1982.

For many people, flight into Mexico was a resort sought only after they had tried everything else. In the Ixcán cooperative region, people's unwillingness to abandon their lands appears to have been the main reason they resisted leaving.

In 1982, the army began to kill people in many places. Many people passed by in February, fleeing into Mexico. They told us that the army was killing people in Xalbal and Santo Tomás. But we stayed. In April the army arrived near the border. The people warned us, but we stayed; we just got ready. In June, the army left the Los Angeles base and retreated to Playa Grande, but later they returned to Los Angeles to kill people, and the people left. We no longer had any corn, and we couldn't take it anymore. So we agreed that we would seek refuge in Mexico. There we suffered from hunger and disease. I was sick for two years. I couldn't work, and my family suffered a lot. We were in Chiapas for ten years. Case 0472, Ixtahuacán Chiquito, Ixcán, Quiché, 1981-82.

Many families separated either over disagreements about what course of action to take or as a survival strategy to have alterative bases of support that might serve them later on.

Some who came here and went on to Mexico. And some women went with their husbands, while others did not. I didn't want to go to Mexico; I stayed here. Those whose women stayed here, they suffered too, because their children are dying little by little. Case 7392 (massacre and life in the hills), CPR Petén, 1982-90.

Most of the refugee population was concentrated into camps, which received most of the humanitarian aid. This afforded them a collective space in which to reestablish their routines and to organize. At the same time, however, it also implied greater control because of the closed lifestyle and government policies. In 1984, the forced relocation of a significant portion of the refugee population from Chiapas to Quintana Roo and Campeche met with resistance and spurred some families to return to Guatemala or to disperse throughout Mexico.

When they came to burn down the refugees huts, the people said: What's the difference between dying in Mexico and dying in Guatemala? To die in Guatemala was to die defending your own land. To die in Mexico was to die eating shit. At that time, the CPR of the Ixcán expanded with a lot of people who preferred to return to a structured resistance situation. Because at that time the CPRs were very structured, very well organized. Key Source 9, Ixcán, Quiché, not dated.

Aside from the government response to their presence, the testimonies reveal numerous references to the solidarity shown to the refugees by the receiving populations. Mexican communities provided support that ranged from material assistance and food to taking people into their homes, concealing them to avoid detection by the authorities, and helping them defend themselves against military incursions. The assistance offered by these communities, and by some institutions such as the Catholic Church of Chiapas, is very present in the collective memory of refuge.

> *And no one helps me, only the Mexican's wife, yes, she is a decent person.* Case 9164 (massacre in Cuarto Pueblo), Ixcán, Quiché, 1991.

> *We were there for three years, very content, very happy there, because the children were given scholarships, they began to study. It was during that short time, and he, well, they gave him a pig farm, close to Mexico City, near Puebla. They gave us a ride there, Father, and were we happy, what we wanted was to stay together.* Case 5042, Santa Lucía Cotzumalguapa, Escuintla, 1984.

Nonetheless, having obtained access to international protection and humanitarian aid, and having survived the worst, did not necessarily mean that the problems were over. The main factors contributing to the refugees' unease were the repression they had experienced, separation from family members, and the negative aspects of life in a refugee camp, such as the daily regimen, relocations, and difficulty finding work. Moreover, holding onto the hope of return, combined with the lack of political changes in the country that would make return possible, cast a pall of perpetual uncertainty over the future. This led a small subset of people to make the decision to return, especially after civilian governments raised their expectations.

As time passed, intergenerational conflicts surfaced within families. These had to do with the young people's experience of working outside the camp setting, as well as their ambivalence toward integration in Mexico or returning to a country like Guatemala that they were unfamiliar with and also perceived as dangerous. While these conflicts were inherent to everyday family and community relationships, they were aggravated by the decision to return. The return experience, therefore, has meant new separations for many families, along with reintegration difficulties associated with economic hardship, the negative attitude of some neighboring communities, and culture shock, particularly for young people.

INTO THE HILLS: FROM FLIGHT TO RESISTANCE

> *The army spread terror and repression throughout the area. Many, or nearly everyone, left the village to take refuge in the wilderness. They resisted for many months, going from one place to another with their little bag packed in case of any emergency with the army since, when the warning comes, everyone leaves. In the end, they couldn't take it anymore and they surrendered. They took them to Las Trojas farm in San Juan Sacatepéquez, on the*

other side of the river, in the mountains facing our village. They eventually returned to their villages. Case 1068 (murder of relatives), San Martín Jilotepeque, Chimaltenango, 1982.

Many of the people who gave their testimony to REMHI had to flee into the wilderness. Although this occurred mostly in areas such as northern Quiché, Alta Verapaz, and Huehuetenango, there were also cases of fleeing into the wilderness in parts of Izabal, Chimaltenango, and Petén. In most cases, fleeing into the wilderness was a last resort to save one's life in inhospitable and inaccessible terrain.

Sometimes people fled into the wilderness in response to an immediate threat and stayed there for only a few days, until they could return home or travel to other, more secure areas. Often, however, this lifestyle lasted for months and even years, settling into a chronic state of extreme instability, hunger, and relentless persecution. Living conditions in such communities were characterized by impermanence, a state of alert, and organization for flight, which were preventive measures to avoid detection or escape the immediate danger of army incursions.

She died after the Cuarto Pueblo massacre, because we had already fled into the wilderness. She was fine, but when the massacre happened she fell ill in the wilderness. It wasn't the same as being at home, and there was no place to get medicine. One person told me "You have to cure your wife" and showed me a medicinal plant. I was just beginning to treat my wife when the soldiers came and I carried my wife out of there. Case 0456, Cuarto Pueblo, Ixcán, Quiché, 1983.

As part of their adaptation to a life of extreme hardship, people had to experiment with different plant species to determine whether or not they were poisonous, or eat wild animals that were not considered edible.

Five or six months without tasting a tortilla. We were dying of hunger, and because of this we began to eat a whole lot of things that we found on the way. Sometimes a little water, sometimes we would eat a banana, and sometimes this led our compañeros to start to kill animals. For example, they ate snakes, they ate rats, they ate other animals; we even ended up eating horsemeat. Why did our people have to come to that and eat things that we might consider disgusting? Because of the conflict—the armed conflict that is going on. Case 2052, Chamá, Alta Verapaz, 1982.

Many communities living in resistance situations in the wilderness had no prior experience to prepare them for it and, what is more, they had often met each other for the first time in the midst of danger and flight. Mutual recognition and support to cope with danger and face their shared needs together led to the formation of new groups and communities that, in some cases, still exist today.

The Experience of the Communities of Popular Resistance (CPRs)

Beginning in late 1982, some of those displaced in the wilderness began to organize new communities, which, by 1984, had become the CPRs of the Ixcán and the Ixil (or Sierra), and later the Petén. The inaccessibility of those areas, and the guerrilla presence, enabled them to sustain a community situation despite severe persecution. Other communities in similar situations, such as those in the highlands of Alta Verapaz, were unable to accomplish this.

We had notebooks where we recorded everything: what day they attacked a community, how many died or were wounded. We kept a record but with the rains, we didn't even have nylon sheets to protect ourselves....Our papers were destroyed little by little and we didn't want them to catch us with any of our lists when we went there with the patrol from Rosario. We didn't want them to find us carrying any list of information because they would kill us. Key Source 33, Sahokak, Alta Verapaz, not dated.

In the case of the CPRs—despite occasional instructions from the guerrillas to the effect that people not take refuge outside of the country or that they stay in the wilderness as a support base—defending the land seems to have been people's primary motivation for choosing a life of resistance. Other contributing factors included the difficulty of fleeing elsewhere without being caught, political convictions, family ties to guerrilla combatants, and the fact that the guerrilla presence often benefited the civilian population by discouraging army attacks.[3]

Those are the groups of people who never became refugees, and they became the seed of resistance. People who defend, who remain to defend their land, because they are determined to die before abandoning their land. And, from plot to plot, because it was all divided into plots, they were constantly on the move. These groups did feel the support, the presence, the company of the guerrillas. And it did have an effect, because the army couldn't act with the same degree of impunity against communities where the guerrillas

---

[3] The coexistence between the guerrillas and the communities was characterized by diverse, and sometimes contradictory, factors: (1) many people looked favorably on the guerrillas because of their courage and their defense of the community; (2) the guerrillas needed a support base, despite the risk that supporters would become targets for the army; (3) people's willingness to remain and defend their lands (especially those who were co-proprietors of the Ixcán Cooperative) and their belief in resistance; (4) efforts by EGP commanders to control community leaders and disagreements with other sectors; (5) guerrilla instructions regarding the need to remain in occupied zones, although its position on this varied at different times; (6) the army encirclement that hampered flight (this was especially true of the CPR of the Sierra); (7) army repression, which caused extreme suffering and flight but also reinforced the decision to resist and preserve relationships with the dead; and (8) the presence of external agents (church, health workers, and others) who helped the population to consolidate and organize their communities.

had weapons in their hands as it could against a community where there wasn't going to be a single shot fired. Key Source 9, Ixcán, Quiché, not dated.

Physical proximity and collaboration did not mean that the population took orders from the guerrillas or was organized with them. Their closest relationships were in the areas of vigilance and defense, which were critical for survival.

The CPR is a civilian community; it is not armed. This distinction must be made: what is civilian, is civilian; what is guerrilla, is guerrilla. It isn't true that the community is a guerrilla community. And many people besides myself have gone to see the communities—[such as] journalists. It is a zone in the wilderness, in conflict. Yes, it's true, we don't deny it, the guerrillas are there, but we are civilians. Key Source 14, Ixcán, Quiché, not dated.

There is no exact data on the number of families who lived in the CPRs, although they appear to have comprised between fifteen thousand and twenty thousand people. Over time, however, various internal and external factors caused their numbers to fluctuate. For example, in the case of the Ixcán, the proximity to the border allowed for movement between the refugee camps and the CPR much of the time. At other times, the hardships associated with the harsh living conditions of resistance over the years led some families to attempt to reestablish themselves in communities that were in a position to receive them.

Every aspect of daily life in the CPRs involved security measures, adaptation to the limitations inherent in the precarious and extremely unstable environment, and the need to support each other in the face of fear and death.

This went on for fourteen years, and the organization was created. And with the support of the refugees in Mexico, little by little we acquired some chickens and seeds. But we could only cook at night, so that they wouldn't detect our smoke. When there was a moon, you couldn't make a fire. Once the people became desperate and made a fire in the daytime. A helicopter came to drop bombs, but we hid in our shelters and no one died. Case 0928, Ixcán, Quiché, not dated.

The basic need for food was a constant struggle throughout those years. On many occasions the army and patrollers destroyed crops or carried off the harvests to cut off supplies to a population that was considered combatant and, hence, to the guerrillas. In this context, collective work and internal distribution of the yield were basic survival mechanisms that, over time, also served as experiments with new community-based values and work-sharing techniques.

During the early years, the guerrillas supported the CPR, with courses on organizing health care, education, and self-defense. Later, the CPRs organized their own structures for these types of services. As time passed, the communities increased their capacity to organize and defend their autonomy, relying on international solidarity and accompaniment and the support of people and institutions affiliated with the church. The organization of labor, security, and provisions, as well as health, education, religion, mail delivery, and moves, became a rich social fabric in and of itself, notwithstanding the precariousness, aerial bombardments, and military incursions.

REINTEGRATION PROCESSES

The reintegration of displaced people and communities has largely hinged on Guatemalan politics. The first returns of displaced populations to their communities were nothing more than a continuation of the political repression. By 1983, some of the groups hiding in the wilderness had started to return spurred by harsh living conditions, relentless persecution, and offers of amnesty. Many people were able to reestablish themselves in their communities. Others who turned themselves in were considered guerrillas and were captured, tortured, and even killed.

An old man said "I'm going to go talk to them and if they kill me, well, we'll see what happens to me, but I am going to go and see," and he left. He arrived alone. "And where are your compañeros?" *the lieutenant asked the man. "Well, they're out there because you are killing them and we are afraid of you because you are killing us." "Killing? We don't kill people anymore. Now we are seeking peace. Now we are going to organize the patrols. Go back and call your* compañeros, *and then come back," the lieutenant told the man. "Okay," the man said, and he went back and informed the others. "It's best that only about twenty-five old people go, and that neither the children nor the young people go; only the elderly will go," they said.* Case 3880, Caserío Choaxán, Quiché, 1982.

As a result, many communities distrusted the government and the army, and they looked for alternatives to improve their miserable situation in the wilderness. Some elected representatives who approached the army; others decided to protect themselves by seeking support from the Catholic church.

One of our brothers representing the group searched for a path. And, persecuted all the while, we crossed the barricades until we arrived. And it was the Catholic church that received and protected us. We turned ourselves in on two occasions. The bishop came to meet us, and we got into a truck, and we stayed in the convent. And there our lives began again, after enduring six years of persecution. Case 3213, Sachal, Alta Verapaz, 1981.

News about a certain normalization of the situation and the expectations raised by the civilian governments in place beginning in 1986 led some refugee groups to repatriate from Mexico. Many of those who returned found themselves living under military control in the receiving communities. In other cases, they had firsthand experiences in concentration centers and "model villages." The army's response to return movements was chiefly influenced by its perception that the population was the social base for the guerrillas, similar to its view of displaced people in the wilderness.

According to a confidential 1987 army document,[4] "Marxist-Leninist ideological indoctrination and the hatred of the country's security forces that was injected into the psyches of children, teenagers, and young adults" were characteristic of most refugees in Mexican camps. Repatriation movements, therefore, would always be closely monitored by the military authorities. This bias underlies the army's overall approach to repatriating refugees as well as numerous instances of army control and harassment of returnee communities between 1992 and 1997.

For peasants, who comprise the majority of the displaced and refugees, reclaiming their land is the prime motivation for returning. Community conflicts over land tenancy, while part of the history of rural communities, are currently strongly influenced by the effects of displacement and militarization and by the repopulation policies implemented by the army as part of its counterinsurgency strategy.

> *I came back to reclaim my grandfather's plot. I have problems because there is no paperwork, CONFREGUA hasn't even been able to get it for me. But I keep trying to get my land despite the political disputes going on in the Ixcán Grande cooperatives.* Case 723, Ixcán, Quiché, not dated.

For many of the internally displaced there is still little chance of returning to their communities because the demilitarization of the civil patrols has not always diminished their power and, in some cases, the problem of land ownership or availability has intensified.

RESTORING FAMILY TIES AND SUPPORT

When families fell apart due to death or displacement to different areas, they tried to find news of their relatives, get in touch with them, or reestablish relationships that had been cut off. Families usually had no information whatsoever about their relatives during periods of detention, refugee flight, or displacement. When basic security was restored, people's first concern was to try to reestablish family ties.

In some cases, people entered into new relationships without knowing for certain whether their husband or wife was dead. Some of them found their origi-

---

[4] Army of Guatemala, "El retorno de los refugiados" (Huehuetenango, March 25, 1987); Marín Golib, then-commander of the Ixcán Military Base, in statements to a foreign journalist, explained with relief that the men who returned would not enter into military service because this would be like "having a scorpion in your shirt."

nal families years later, creating a new set of circumstances that the individuals and families involved had to learn how to deal with.

> *The wife I had before died. So, since we were left alone, we found other people—families where there were some women whose husbands had also died. They had been killed in those massacres of people from other communities where massacres happened, no? So there, well, several of us got together. Once we were there, well, some of us who were alone, widowed, got together with widows or widowers there. A lot of couples got together, but here in this life. Some of us, after so much time, after thirteen or fourteen years of being in the wilderness, well there was nothing for it, we've even had some children. Right now I have two children who were born here in the wilderness. That is all I can tell you about my history.* Case 7392, CPR Petén, 1990.

Often, reestablishing these ties not only has reunited families but has enabled people to deal with the financial straits brought on by the violence.

> *When the incident happened, what we did was separate. At least I was the oldest, I went to work to provide for my brothers' and sisters' needs as they grew. Once they were grown up and could earn a living, we reunited. Even though it was painful, we became a family together again. At the moment we are making it. We are talking about it together because the truth is we are afraid. We were then and we are now. Because the truth is they harm anyone and everything stays the same.* Case 6456, Morales, Izabal, 1968.

IN SEARCH OF AN EXPLANATION

How do people explain the violence they have suffered? In general, their explanations tend to focus on specific causes and individual actions rather than broader interpretations. The explanations compiled in the testimonies, in order of frequency, are, first, accusations related to someone's conduct (*"they killed him because they accused him of collaborating with the guerrillas"*). This is followed by envy, attributing the incident to one's own behavior and being at a loss to explain what happened, and the power and actions of the army and the civil patrols. These are followed in turn by broader explanations, such as government actions, ethnic conflicts, and socioeconomic struggles.[5] These diverse explanations tend to fall into the following four broad areas:

---

[5] From the gender perspective, men tend to offer more sociopolitical interpretations, while women tend to emphasize localized causes. Thus, men more frequently attribute the conflict to previous discord among the group, to the government, the socioeconomic context, and the land situation, or to accusations about individual conduct. In contrast, women tend to place more weight on interpersonal conflicts or to the conduct itself.

NO EXPLANATION OR INDIVIDUALIZED EXPLANATIONS

A significant group either could not explain what had happened or gave an individualized explanation. In other words, many people reported that they did not know why and tried to make sense of it by wondering if the person could have done something to have caused the violence. These are people who adhered to a logic of justice and proportionality that no longer existed: "If I haven't done anything, they can't do anything to me." From this standpoint, the answer "I don't know why this happened" is perfectly logical, because it was impossible for many to understand why so much irrational violence was suddenly unleashed against the people.[6]

> *During that time, 1981-82, we saw a lot of violence against men, women, children, and old people. I also want to ask why there was so much flight from these villages, and how it was that we left. Whether we just left or whether it was because people were nasty, which was why they got into trouble. They brought death and suffering upon us, and now we are alone. Maybe people say that, I don't know, only God knows.* Salaqwil case, 18th witness, Alta Verapaz, not dated.

SOCIOPOLITICAL CONFLICT AND INVOLVEMENT

Another set of explanations had to do with repression caused by the government, land conflicts, and political activity. Such explanations reflect prior experiences with local social conflicts over land or repression against community organization.

> *The reason that they took my brother away, and my father too—since we lived on a farm and they had him there for many days without pay. So he and others began to struggle to see if they would pay them for those days of work they had already done for the boss and also a pay a fair wage for the work they had to do. And that was the problem. The boss didn't like that. But that wasn't it, because the bosses and other people who didn't like it got together and accused them of being bad people, communists. For that reason, the soldiers came to get my brother at home.* Case 5106, Panzós, Alta Verapaz, 1980.

---

[6] The concept of transgression and reparation is based on the logic of individual responsibility in Mayan culture. A person who inflicts harm on the community or on others must make some form of reparation or pay for his or her guilt. According to Dary, the militaristic approach of the conflict trampled traditional community principles governing the commission of crimes: explain the crime, reprimand, dialogue, compensate the victim, and forgive in the presence of a person of authority in the community (Dary 1997, 162 and 171).

INTERPERSONAL EXPLANATIONS

A third group of explanations attributes the repression to envy and accusations against the victim. Envy is common to traditional societies. Military strategies, moreover, sought to divide and to provoke internal clashes, using accusations and finger pointing to pit neighbor against neighbor. These strategies were also used by some people for their own social advancement.

> *He was very energetic, he was very caring, he was well respected and beloved. But since people envied him, they didn't want him around, and so he left. He was accused by the same townspeople, or rather by the man's enemies. Because when someone works for the people, that person is not well regarded. They don't love him; they envy him instead.* Case 1316, Parraxtut, Quiché.

ETHNO-POLITICAL EXPLANATIONS

A fourth and less significant factor is the ethno-political explanation, which connects military power (army, civil patrol) with intergroup conflicts (such as ladino/indigenous). These explanations are more frequent in massacre cases than in individual acts of violence. This perception coincides with the fact that the army implemented the scorched-earth policy and, therefore, was primarily responsible for collective massacres, together with paramilitary forces. The explanations provided by victims and relatives include evaluations of the army's behavior ("*they kill for the sake of killing*") evoked by the experience of indiscriminate killing and atrocities.

> *We all have a right to live, since we are Guatemalans. They practically came from other countries to kill us like that or to remove us. We are Guatemalans, or rather, as our Mayan history tells us, we are indigenous, we are Guatemalans. Just because powerful men came, like the Spaniards, to occupy the land here in Guatemala.* Case 4017, Las Majadas, Huehuetenango, 1982.

The nature of the guerrilla presence in rural communities also influences the explanations of the causes of violence found in many testimonies. Notwithstanding possible biases emanating from the nature of suppressed memories,[7] which served as a self-defense mechanism in those years, most testimonies describe the arrival of the guerrillas as something that came from outside of the community

---

[7] We mean by "suppressed memories" those memories of violent incidents that people have tried to hide as a way of defending themselves from attack and from their own pain. They can be outwardly suppressed but are often retained and shared in one's intimate circle (see Thompson 1988).

and that in some cases corresponded to preexisting demands. In others, it was seen as supporting education and consciousness-raising initiatives, and in still others, was seen as a distortion or constriction of community dynamics.

> *Our first organization was the CUC. Then the EGP came along; it came to advise us. So then we had two choices. But the struggle began with the CUC. Later that organization [the EGP] advised us again, and that is where people got confused; that was where the problem was. Since we are indigenous, we don't know how to read or write. We were organized by the CUC. But this other organization comes along, and that is what confused our thoughts. But our struggle, what I believe in—I am pursuing my struggle as always. I'll never stop.* Case 1311, La Montaña, Parraxtut, Quiché, 1984.

In other words, there is an explanation that tends to be more local than general, in which personal experience dominates attempts to explain a specific incident. Broader, socially oriented explanations appear in a one to four ratio with those based on firsthand experience.

All of this shows that the people call on some of their own cultural beliefs to interpret what happened and give meaning to their firsthand experience of the incidents. There are many local variations—based on the way violence evolved in a particular area, and preexisting social conflicts and their impact on people's lives—including some people's social advancement, or other people's loss of power or economic resources. This confluence of factors is present in most of the testimonies analyzed, over and above any one broad ideological or religious explanation.

Collective memory processes must take all of these perceptions into consideration in order to interpret incidents and to enable individuals and communities to achieve a clearer vision of their experience.

Chapter Five

FROM VIOLENCE TO THE AFFIRMATION OF WOMEN

Women gave half of the testimonies compiled by the REMHI project. In most of these testimonies they describe the experience of violence or the plight of family and community without referring directly to their experience as women. For this analysis, several specific interviews were conducted with key female sources. In addition, collective interviews were conducted in regions strongly affected by the violence, with the goal of fostering understanding of how violence had affected women's lives, social status, and roles.

VIOLENCE AGAINST WOMEN

WOMEN AS VICTIMS

The other girl, maybe about twenty-three years old, was between the kitchen and the bedroom. She also had three gashes here in the neck, and they had taken away her baby girl, who was still nursing. There she was, already dead, and still nursing her. Case 1871 (perpetrator), various locations, 1981.

Horror, death, torture, and abuses affected men and women, boys and girls, and the elderly. Although most of the victims found in the testimonies were men, specific forms of violence were used against women. Because they usually survived, women have had to cope in extremely precarious circumstances with the aftermath of violence.

"THEY TREATED US WORSE THAN ANIMALS"

Terror, in this extremely violent context, included ridiculing the victim. The dehumanization of the perpetrators led them to devalue the humanity of their victims.

They ordered us to eliminate those poor people, you know. You see, the soldiers looked for ways to entertain themselves, and so they made the prisoners they were going to kill, they made them....There were women and men, and some soldiers, and I heard them laughing and I went to see what was going on. They made the male prisoners grab the women right there. I mean, have sex with them. And that's what they were laughing at, you know? At seeing those poor people, who not only hadn't eaten, hadn't slept, were feeling like shit, all beaten up—because it was no picnic to be there—and still, ironically, they made them do that. Key Source 027 (perpetrator), 1982.

USING THEIR MOTHERHOOD AGAINST THEM

One of the most powerful ways of pressuring women was to use their children to control, dominate, or crush the psyches of their mothers; the torture or death of family members and manipulation of emotions were tools used to torture women psychologically.

The children saw everything they did to their mothers, their sisters, and their other family members; and afterward they killed them too. Key Source 027 (perpetrator), 1982.

Reports of atrocities against pregnant women and the babies they carried in their wombs are particularly chilling. This recurrent pattern of behavior clearly demonstrated the army's brutality against the civilian population in its attempt to obliterate even the source of life.

The women who were pregnant. One of them was in her eighth month and they cut her belly, and they took out the little one, and they tossed it around like a ball. Then they cut off one breast, and they left it hanging in a tree. Case 6335, Barillas, Huehuetenango, 1981.

And the fetuses were left hanging by their umbilical cords. There is no doubt that the killing of children in front of their mothers was especially aimed at indigenous women. Interview 0165.

COOKING AND DANCING FOR THEIR ASSAILANTS

Women experienced atrocities and violations in the guise of daily routines; during massacres, with the prospect of certain death awaiting them, practices such as obliging women to serve food, cook, dance, and parade were a form of psychological torture. Taunting and humiliation turned such events into a gala occasion for the killers.

Then the army came and said to them: "Maybe we aren't going to kill you, but each of you bring a hen; there are twelve men and there are twelve of you women, so you will bring twelve of them for lunch." They went quickly and brought the hens from their houses. Then the massacre began: if the son was carrying out his patrol duty, and the father was not, then the son had to kill the father. If the son was the one who wasn't complying, then the father had to stain his hands by killing his son. After that, the clay pots with the twelve hens inside were put on the fire, and the women themselves began to cook. The army ordered them to make sure the food was well prepared after they had killed the twelve men. They killed them and tortured them, and they went to get gasoline. When they were all burned up, they applauded, and they started eating. Case 2811, Chinique, Quiché, 1982.

MASSACRES OF WOMEN

REMHI's testimonies also report some cases of massacres in which only women and children died. The circumstances varied, but the men either were absent from the village at the time (Pexlá Grande, Yalambojoch, Chipal, Chinimaqin, among others), or they had already been killed (Pacoxom).

Pexla Grande, Pulay, Nebaj. Case 5508, February 1982.
Army soldiers reached Pexlá Grande. They seized the people they found, killing some with firearms and burning others. After killing these people, they put their corpses into a deep hole in the ground. Between thirty-eight and eighty victims were reported, all of them women and children.

Yalambojoch, Nentón, Huehuetenango, Cases 766 and 6065, 1982.
This was the base of operations for the San Francisco massacre. Upon returning from San Francisco, [the soldiers] made the women cook two cows for them. Then they made a big hole in the earth, placed explosives in it, and burned the women up. The men were patrolling, and only women and children were there. Upon hearing the loud noise, women, boys, and girls tried to flee. The soldiers chased them, found them, and killed them.

Pacoxom, Rio Negro, Rabinal. Cases 543 and 2026, 1982, Army and civil patrollers from Xoxoc, between 150 and 176 victims.
Those responsible reached Río Negro at six o'clock in the morning. Almost all of the people who remained (after previous massacres) were women, children, and the elderly. They made everyone come out of their houses. They assembled them in the schoolhouse. They made the women cook for them. They took them to Pacoxom, where they made them dance with the patrollers and soldiers. Then they started to rape the women, beginning with the youngest ones, and then they began to kill their victims, beginning with the women. They killed children, but they spared the lives of some of them and adopted them. Some women and children were able to escape.

SEXUAL ASSAULT

ASSAULTS ON BODIES AND ON DIGNITY

> **TESTIMONIES FROM THE REMHI PROJECT**
>
> REMHI's testimonies include 149 victims reported in 92 accounts of sexual assault. These include rape as the cause of death and as a form of torture, and sexual slavery with the repeated rape of the victim. Moreover, in one of every six massacre cases analyzed, the rape of women was part of the soldiers' and civil patrollers' modus operandi.
>
> It must be recalled that, because of the guilt and shame associated with sexual assault, it is under-reported compared to other forms of violence such as torture and murder. Studies on rape in the Western hemisphere have found that an average of just one out of every five sexual assaults is reported; therefore, it can be inferred that under-reporting may be a much more serious problem in the present case.

Individual and collective sexual assaults are reported by witnesses as a specific form of violence against women that was employed in a variety of situations: during abductions and detentions, massacres, military operations, and so on. Rapes were not isolated incidents, but rather—in this war and many others— permeated all forms of violence against women.

On the interminable list of abuses, humiliations, and torture that women endured, sexual assault stands out as one of the cruelest and most frequent. Its complexity lies in its nature as a show of power by the perpetrator and an experience of abuse and humiliation for the victim. In many instances, women suffered additional consequences, including pregnancy and sexually transmitted diseases.

Some soldiers there were sick; they had gonorrhea, syphilis. So he ordered them to go last, when we had all had a turn. The forced prostitution of women was a form of psychosexual control. Case 1871 (perpetrator), various locations, 1981-84.

In REMHI's testimonies, sexual assaults are attributed to army soldiers, patrollers, and paramilitary forces.

Six soldiers raped the wife of a friend of his, in front of her husband. It was very common for the army to rape women. The wife of another acquaintance, and her daughter, were raped by thirty soldiers. Case 7906, Chajul, Quiché, 1981.

MASS RAPES

Soldiers committed mass rapes during massacres or detentions of women. Rape was part of the war machinery and women were frequently sexually assaulted in front of their families.[1]

One day I was able to escape and, while hidden, I saw a woman. They shot her and she fell. All the soldiers left their packs and dragged her like a dog to the riverbank. They raped and killed her. Also, a helicopter that was flying overhead landed, and they all did the same thing to her. Case 11724 (perpetrator), Xecojom, Nebaj, Quiché, 1980.

"Turn in your husband; if you don't, you will die right here." And they grabbed her and forced themselves on her; she was about to have a baby. She said she was thinking: "Who knows what these men are going to do with me." There were about twenty of them, and they did whatever they wanted with her. Case 1791, El Juleque, Santa Elena Petén, 1984.

The public display of sexual violence against women, often by several men at once, reinforced a spirit of *machista* complicity and extolled power and authority as "masculine" traits.

He raped the little one and then left her for the others to keep on raping her. I didn't like participating in that shit because, after you do it, you feel all weak, with no desire to do anything. But they didn't care, and afterward they killed them there among the dug-outs [buzones]. Key Source 027 (perpetrator), 1982.

THE SIGNIFICANCE OF RAPE

A Show of Power

Sexual assault is, above all, a terror tactic used by the perpetrators to demonstrate their power and dominance over female victims. Membership in military structures provided army soldiers and civil patrollers with the violent context and immunity from punishment they required to display their power over women.

---

[1] The rape of women has also been part of the war on civilians in other armed conflicts. Thai pirates intentionally raped Vietnamese women in the presence of their families in order to humiliate everyone involved. During their December 1992 visit to the former Yugoslavia, a team of researchers from the European Union found that many women and teenagers had been raped in Bosnia, Herzegovina, as part of a systematic campaign of terror (UNHCR, "World Refugee Report" [Madrid: Icaria, 1994]).

The PAC and the army raped some children and women. They killed them with bullets, and hung them by the neck, and kicked them in the stomach. Case 8385, Saacté 1, Quiché, 1980.

Using the female body is a central feature of violence against women; it serves to underscore who must be dominant, and who must be subjugated. This type of violence was employed in numerous circumstances and occasions, reflecting social perceptions and behaviors that transcended the armed conflict.

The army would bring down to the zone big native girls with fat braids in their hair and earrings made of wool thread. They brought them because they said they were guerrillas. They would rape them and disappear them. Case 769, San Juan Ixcán, Quiché, 1982.

A Show of Victory over Adversaries

Although women were considered direct military targets because of their potential support for guerrilla activities or structures (mail, information, food, and so forth), they were also used to demonstrate victory over adversaries: they often were valued for what they represented to the other side.

In many places, rape was considered a way to subdue and humiliate communities and families. Soldiers raped "enemy" women for the same reason that they burned down their homes: to signal contempt and victory (Dowdeswell 1987).

There was also a couple. They took her aside to a room adjoining where the husband and the rest of us were. The soldiers said, "Don't worry, we're going to take good care of your wife." The poor man had to watch everything they did to her, torturing the poor woman, [until she] couldn't take anymore. The soldiers raped her one by one. After that they went to ask the husband for money to buy pills because she was in bad shape. Case 710, Santa María Tzejá, Ixcán, Quiché, 1982.

A Bartering Tool

Rape was also a bartering tool: some victims were raped and, in exchange, they or their children were able to survive, or at least avoid being labeled guerrillas by the rapist. In other cases, they lost their lives anyway. Sexual violence was often combined with counterinsurgency violence; that is, accusations that they were guerrillas was used to justify the rape of women.

"If you have a young daughter, we'll let you go," they said. They had me tied up with a cord around my neck. Case 6042, San Miguel Acatán, Huehuetenango, 1981.

War Plunder

The rape of women was also seen as a sort of prize or "perk" for the soldiers; it was a way of "compensating" them for fighting the war. In the context of violence used as a vehicle for acquiring power and property, female bodies were seen as just one more possession.

We found a woman, I called a soldier and I told him: "Take charge of the woman, she is a present from the second lieutenant." "Understood, Corporal," he answered, and he called the boys and said: "There's meat, guys." So they came and grabbed the girl. They took her little boy from her and they all raped her. It was a gang rape. Afterward, I told them to kill the woman first so she wouldn't feel so bad about the death of her son. Key Source 027 (perpetrator), 1982.

OTHER FORMS OF TORTURE ASSOCIATED WITH RAPE

Sexual assault was frequently used to torture women, but it was not the only way in which they were violated or assaulted. Extreme forms of sexual torture, including mutilation, were methods of killing women with the utmost contempt, cruelty, and terror.

There are women hanging. Well, the stick goes into her private parts and then the stick comes out of her mouth. They had her hanging there like a snake. Collective testimony, Huehuetenango.

The purpose of such atrocities was to degrade women through their sexuality, to show the highest contempt for their dignity as people, and to use the intimate aspects of womanhood to add a measure of exemplary terror for the benefit of the population.

Before murdering her, they nailed her to a cross they had made. They stuck huge nails into her hands and chest, then they put her inside the house to burn her up. They found her burned, still on the cross; her son was beside her, also burned—badly burned. Case 1319, Parraxtut, Sacapulas, Quiché.

A COUNTERINSURGENCY METHOD

A premeditated strategy of violence specifically targeting women cannot be inferred from the information compiled by the REMHI project. The testimonies do indicate, however, that the army's counterinsurgency tactics against women were consistent at different places and times and formed part of its strategy of mass destruction.

This counterinsurgency violence acquired certain genocidal characteristics. It attacked the community social fabric at its foundations by attempting to exterminate women and children in their capacity as vessels for the continuity of life and the transmission of culture.

I believe that there was an intentionality in the way women were treated, a policy to harm women and communities: mass rape, the introduction of stakes, the treatment of pregnant women—also when they were detained. All the violence. I feel that women bore the brunt of a lot of it, as mothers, as women, even because of their husbands' attitudes. The issue of disappearances had the strongest social impact. There were things designed just for women—for families—because women are the ones who preserve the family and care for others. Interview 0803.

It is clear that, while there may not have been an explicit counterinsurgency objective that targeted women, there was a deliberate intent to destroy the community social fabric, a fabric woven and sustained primarily by women. Women were also the ones to repair broken social ties, preserving family cohesion even under the most adverse conditions. They were the ones who preserved the essential ingredients for reestablishing life among groups of survivors.

I think that the counterinsurgency policy was very detailed, thought out, and calculated in the case of women. Because women definitely are a symbol, the symbol of life, of the perpetuation of life. In other words, to kill a woman is to kill life. Like in the case of the old people, the idea was to kill the people's wisdom, their historical memory, their roots. Interview 0165.

THE CONSEQUENCES OF CONTEMPT

THE IMPACT OF RAPE

They didn't pay attention to age. They didn't care if they were little girls, teenagers, women, or old ladies. They always took the worst of it, because they could not defend themselves. Collective testimony, Huehuetenango.

The testimonies describe violent acts against women, but there are few firsthand accounts from the women who suffered these abuses. This gap may be due largely to the stigma attached to rape and the difficulty of talking about the experience or its aftermath.

Besides the personal humiliation and family isolation that women may experience, their husbands, brothers, and fathers may also feel powerless and responsible for the rape. When men and women are wounded or killed, they are considered heroes or martyrs; there is no comparable status for a raped woman. This is similar to the case of the disappeared, in which the suffering of the individual or the family cannot be validated. The cultural and religious value attached to "purity" and sexual intimacy, moreover, may make the woman or her family feel even more devastated by this experience.

Other common effects of rape are fear of pregnancy and the ethical dilemmas posed by an unwanted pregnancy by rape. Often, women may experience changes in their self-image following such an experience; they may feel "dirty" or repulsive, or even that they are "possessed by an evil spirit." Concern over personal hygiene, sexual anxiety, and fear of men are common symptoms experienced by rape victims.

WOMEN'S RESISTANCE

PULLING THEIR LIVES TOGETHER: WOMEN'S ROLES AND THE SOCIAL FABRIC

A sense of prevailing over pain and death has been crucial for survivors, and this has certainly been true for most women. Women of all ages and ethnic groups, from divers social backgrounds and geographic locations, with more or less comparable ordeals of losing loved ones to the violence, have had certain common experiences. They have had to search for the disappeared, protect the lives of those left behind, and ensure their own survival and that of their families. Added to this is the tremendous emotional strain accompanying the effects of violence on women, including loneliness, a sense of being overwhelmed, and a negative self-image.

Violence and Changing Roles

The war has had a horrendous impact on women's lives. During the long years of armed conflict, women were the backbone of the family and social structure. However, the armed conflict has tested traditional female roles, obliging women to confront their position in the family and community. Coping with the consequences of violence often meant that women were the sole supporters of their families; social emergencies led them to assume a higher profile in their communities and in society; many women changed their view of themselves and the world as a result of the violence they and their families experienced.

MIDWIVES IN THE WILDERNESS

For twelve years (1982-1994), army persecution and government negligence made births of babies and care of the mothers very difficult in the wilds of the Ixcán. Without medicines or appropriate places, mothers lay down on the leaves to give birth to their children. Sometimes they had to flee, bleeding and

> *in pain. Midwives used plant fibers to tie the umbilical cord, and burned the navel with a knife. Sometimes the mother rested among the roots of a tree. They ate fruits and raw plants during the bombings. Sometimes they ate roots, ground up and cooked.* Case 888 (Midwife) CPR, Ixcán, 1982.

Even in the midst of extreme danger and flight, women's daily routines were governed by concern for their children: carrying them during periods of displacement, finding food for them, obtaining utensils, and so on.

> *When the army came, I was pregnant, but my family and I went into the hills to protect ourselves. My son was born there. But the army came back and we ran. We got to a river and, as I crossed, I lost hold of my son—he was just one day old and I tripped on a rock. I was still able to reach him, but he nearly died because he fell right into the water.* Case 3618, Aldea El Desengaño, Uspantán, Quiché, 1982.

Despite shortages and pressures, for many women maternal duty was stronger than necessity; they fought to safeguard their children and kept them by their side.

> *I am the one who has been with them [referring to six children]. I didn't abandon them for any money; because my duty is to be by their side.* Case 5334, Aldea Pozo de Agua, Baja Verapaz, 1983.

In the case of massacres, many women helped save the lives of boys and girls in the community, even if they weren't their own children.

> *A woman took them to her house. She put them in a bread oven to hide them. Then she decided to change their clothes and dress them as if they were from Cunén. That was the only reason they were saved.* Case 2442, Cunén, Quiché, not dated.

To Be a Woman Alone: "Like a Bird on a Dead Branch"

> *They killed my husband. And from then on, I suffered like a little girl. I couldn't manage money, or work, or support my family. You see, the life of a woman among men is hard; and the life of a woman alone with her children is worse yet. They left me like a bird on a dead branch.* Case 8674, Malacatán, San Marcos, 1982.

Thus, women had to cope alone and see to the material and emotional survival of their families. This feeling of solitude persists for many women who have been unable to put their lives back together.

> *That's what hurts me. Because when my husband was alive, we walked together, we decided what to do together, what to eat. But I was left alone.*

I have to think alone. This is what weighs on my heart, and I can't get over it. It will be with me until I die. My hope is that I will go to wherever my husband is. I'm going to find him, because I don't want to live with another man here on earth. I have decided to suffer, but God willing, if I die I'm going to find him, and then I will be content. Case 5057, San Miguel Chicaj, Baja Verapaz, 1982.

Affirmation of Women

In other cases, however, difficult circumstances have led to increased recognition of women's worth and authority as heads of family. This reassessment of their status reflects the fortitude with which women have coped with the aftermath of violence. This has enhanced the self-esteem of many women, despite the hardships.

I see myself as the head of the household, I am also the head of my parents' household because they are old now. In other words, practically speaking, family life revolves around me. Case 8674, Malacatán, San Marcos, 1982.

In Search of Loved Ones: Finding the Disappeared

The search for relatives who have been disappeared has been one of the most anguishing struggles arising from political repression, and one that has been spearheaded by women. Perpetual uncertainty about what happened, where they are, if they are alive or dead, and if they can be found, are some of the innumerable questions asked by those who day after day have traveled every road, have looked everywhere, in the hope of discovering their loved ones.

Women have spared no cost or sacrifice in their tireless effort to discover the missing persons' whereabouts. When women realized that they no longer had anything to lose, they plunged into these efforts even more vigorously (Fernández 1988). They drew strength to search and denounce from the victim's significance to them. In the face of such dire circumstances, women have displayed an enormous capacity to avoid becoming discouraged, to pull themselves together, and to undertake new strategies.

The pain was so strong that I think we didn't even know what we were doing; the only thing was to rescue our loved one. Our only thought was for the other person, whom we believed was being tortured. We had to do everything possible to rescue him. Interview 015.

The search became the only means of standing up to the army and defying the terror behind the disappearances. It turned into the most unwavering stance in defense of human rights during the worst years of the armed conflict. Mothers, wives, daughters, and sisters of the disappeared were the ones who dared to defy the raging violence. Never before had they been considered protagonists in the political life of the country, yet they displayed courage, resolve, and hope on countless occasions.

I said to my compañeras: "Look, I have news about who they were. Do you all know these people, more or less?"

"Yes," they told me.

"And why don't we say so?" I said to them.

"But you see, you can't talk about anything here because they kill you," they told me.

"Let's stand up to them. Because no matter what, if we don't, they're going to go on killing us, and if they kill us, this is where we'll end up."

"Yes, we'll support you," they said. "But if the other women don't want to go, what will we do?"

"But with one, two, or three, something can be accomplished."

So they told me: "I'll go then," "Me too." And that was how we organized. Case 1791, El Juleque, Santa Ana, Petén, 1984.

Thus, the search for the disappeared became the nucleus of a social movement that protested, investigated, demonstrated, and organized against this inhumane practice. Women led this movement, creating new political space for the struggle against impunity. Particularly during the seventies, family groups began to organize numerous protests and specific actions to learn the whereabouts of their loved ones. Later, as political repression gained momentum in the countryside, women acted collectively to search for their family members. It wasn't until the mid-eighties, however, that these efforts and denunciations became more structured as movements that staged demonstrations and protests in the capital.

Later, when we would go to Guatemala City, to the GAM [Mutual Support Group], we would arrive and we would go to yell at Mejía Víctores to give us back the disappeared; because he knew, he was the one in power there. And what was going on with his army that he didn't investigate what it was doing? And if he didn't know, then he should investigate, because they were killing people unjustly. So we went to the cathedral and we stayed there for about a week. But after a year, they told us that they had taken them from Poptún; a man who was there said that they had been there for a year, and that they had taken them to the Presidential Palace. And we went there, and when they saw us they said: "But, what did you come here to demand, ladies, if there's nothing here?" "We came to demand that you investigate and search in the jails, maybe you have them detained there. What we want is for you to state whether you have already killed them or what you did to them." Case 1791, El Juleque, Santa Ana, Petén, 1984.

CREATING NEW SPACES: WOMEN'S ACTIVISM

The ground-breaking role women played in demanding respect for human rights was the most significant aspect of their activism for social change, both during and after the final stage of political violence in Guatemala. Many women became heads of families as a result of the violence. Still others, out of the strength of their convictions, courageously stood up to the violence and gave birth to new opportunities for social activism.

> *When we women began to call for our disappeared relatives, for life, for freedom from military dictatorships that totally dominated the country, then women's activism began to be more apparent. Even the army was surprised. It was unbelievable that these little women, these little girls, frail as they are, faced up to an army that has always been feared, do you understand me? That's when I think they began to realize that the participation of women is effective, that women are courageous. Because no one could believe that we women could face, harass, and chase away the army. At least that's how it was, it literally was like that: women chased the army away. It wasn't that it could be done, it was that we dared to do it.* Interview 0151.

As the political situation evolved, leadership crises or divergent views about the human rights struggle led to the emergence of new groups like the Association of Families of the Disappeared and Detained of Guatemala (FAMDEGUA). The methods employed also changed, from denunciation to mutual support for the investigation of massacres, accompaniment during exhumations, and demands for justice and restitution.

Some women have become leaders in the struggle for human rights, and their voice has played an important role in raising international awareness about the situation in Guatemala and in the struggle against impunity. They are, among others, Rigoberta Menchú Tum, Helen Mack, Rosalina Tuyuc, and Nineth Montenegro.

Other groups, such as the National Coordination of Guatemalan Widows (CONAVIGUA), have drawn attention to the plight of widows as a large social sector affected by the violence. The demands articulated by these groups have gone beyond the search for relatives to protest the militarization of the countryside and, particularly, forced recruitment. Refugee women also began to organize and reflect on their situation as women. Lastly, many women became active in broader social or political organizations.

The confluence of women's efforts, through divers social movements and groups of women affected by the violence, has revived many groups and contributed to greater social awareness of their demands. And these initiatives have had their share of political problems and disputes, or limitations on participation due to power struggles.

Nonetheless, for some women, this activism served a purpose: women who long have been invisible members of society must now be recognized as protagonists of change, and respected and valued as examples of dignity and defense of life.

Chapter Six

NEVER AGAIN! PREVENTING A RECURRENCE

It must be exposed to get relief. That's the only way to heal the wounds. We have already suffered our history in the flesh; we don't want these events to happen again. Those of us who were wronged must be attended to immediately, to recover our lost possessions. It is also necessary to hold ceremonies or commemorations to remember the dead, those who were massacred in this violence. And the clandestine forces must disappear, like the G-2, paramilitaries—no more weapons. Testimony 0569 (murder, guerrilla). Qeqchí woman, Cobán, September 1981.

Those who gave their testimony to REMHI not only spoke of their experiences of violence but also expressed their demands and opinions about what should be done to avoid a recurrence of the destruction and disregard for human life. These social demands and aspirations must be taken into account in any effort to bring about social reconstruction in Guatemala. The voices of victims and survivors speak of respect for human rights, the value of truth, justice, the struggle against impunity, peace and needed social changes, the importance of different types of social restitution.

TRUTH, JUSTICE, AND HUMAN RIGHTS

THE DEFENSE OF HUMAN RIGHTS

The Value of Awareness

Respect for life is a value evident in testimonies describing the cruelty of actions against the population. The underlying theme of these testimonies reflects not only the destruction of identity but also an effort to affirm human dignity. Outside the formal system, the affected population's recognition of its own rights has given it a sense of individual and group affirmation, and an awareness that the authorities have the obligation to respect these rights.

We hope for greater support to live as human beings. The rights each and every one of us has should not be violated; because we have an identity as people, we have that right. I also hope that this is recorded in a document so that the authorities take notice of the issue and that human rights are respected. Case 6009, Aldea Jolomar, Huehuetenango, 1993.

From the perspective of many of the affected individuals, knowledge of their own individual and collective rights is an important tool to prevent the violence from recurring.

To talk about the truth, to know their individual rights, and to have more ability to know what human rights mean at the level of communities and indigenous peoples. Case 1642, Aldea Chicaj, Cahabón, Alta Verapaz, 1980.

Social reintegration requires respect for human rights. It is part of re-creating community life in the polarized and divided climate left by the war and political repression. The impact of extreme division and polarization, and the ideological indoctrination that much of the population underwent, make it essential to rescue the values of mutual understanding and respect from the authorities and dominant groups. Given the role that accusations of being guerrillas played in attacks on the civilian population, education and effective measures to ensure observance of human rights must center on overcoming prejudice and promoting open-mindedness and solidarity.

Organizing to Defend Life

The government authorities must have effective mechanisms for guaranteeing human rights. Many survivors consider organizing a useful tool for demanding compliance with human rights obligations. Moreover, as a defense against life-threatening living conditions, people see organization as essential to confronting poverty and precarious economic circumstances.

We are willing to keep on struggling for them to listen to us, for us to be free, to be seen as people and not animals. We are human beings, we are people, we are thinking individuals. But who knows what they think about it? [We want] to build a new Guatemala and to live in a truly democratic country. And the army should be punished for the acts it committed...in the poorest society, among the poor peasant people, who struggle for their land, for their food, for their children. Case 7386, Caserío Almolonga, Tiquisate, Escuintla, 1981.

They should respect our rights as the Guatemalans that we are. Because when we speak, when we demonstrate for some reason, we do it because we really need it. We don't have electricity; we don't have roads; we don't have drinking water; we don't have schools. We don't have a lot of things. Case 7727, Caserío Palob, Nebaj, Quiché, 1982.

However, many people still must overcome two serious obstacles in order to consider participating in organized groups again. First, in many places the word *organization* conjures up the memory of their own past experiences with violence. Second, fear continues to stand in the way, given that any social organization not under army control was criminalized.

> *The community should not let itself be fooled again. It should form a good organization to get what we need. Because it isn't fair that the rich person eats and the poor one doesn't. If we need a bus, the community can unite to get it. I want to do this when I get to Guatemala, but the people may think I am a guerrilla because I talk about organization. I have to know how to broach it in my town.* Case 8390 (murder and persecution), Concepción Huista, Huehuetenango, 1979-80.

> *What should be done to keep this from happening again? I think we should organize in grassroots organizations and know what our rights as people are, what our commitment is. And also, put fear aside, because fear is what most affects us. Because we have allowed ourselves to be silenced by fear; but right now a space is being opened for us to speak out. So for me, it's a very important thing that we stop being afraid, because it's the only way to begin to respect each other.* Case 2692 (Threats for refusal to participate in the civil patrols), La Puerta, Chinique, Quiché, 1982.

These demands and efforts to rebuild organizations must be supported by local and regional mechanisms to ensure freedom of association and restore the social-organizational fabric. All of these efforts should conform to traditional forms of grassroots or indigenous organization, and government institutions should recognize the authority of these organizations as representatives of their communities.

Respect vs. Discrimination

The demand for respect for human rights is part of people's broader effort to affirm their dignity. In the context of acute social discrimination against indigenous peoples, reclaiming personal respect is often tied to respect for group identity. References to intercultural dialogue appear frequently in the testimonies. Many indigenous people interpret the attacks on the civilian population, and particularly the scorched-earth policy waged against peasant communities, as a continuation of the historical contempt with which the dominant sectors have always treated them.

The struggle to end discrimination against the poorest sectors, however, is part of a more general demand for respect, and is not limited to ethnic concerns.

> *This situation should never happen again. I think perhaps based on development, on education for us, for all Guatemalan citizens. But they should really respect our rights as indigenous people; because I am indigenous, and I have my rights, and I have a voice to speak with.* Case 2176, Aldea Salquil, Nebaj, Quiché, 1980.

DISCOVERING THE TRUTH

From Truth to Memory

Knowing the truth is a quintessential aspect of the REMHI project and of people's motivations for giving their testimony. In a social context in which denunciation was criminalized and victims had to remain silent to avoid endangering their lives, the need to know the truth and publicize it has remained latent in people's memory. From the perspective of those who gave their testimonies, acknowledging the truth is the first step toward honoring the victims and survivors.

There is still considerable confusion in many people's minds about exactly what happened to their family members; others do not know where their relatives are, or still wonder why they died. Some of these questions will probably never be answered, given the enormous difficulty of assimilating such traumatic episodes. Finding out the truth, however, could clarify the confusion experienced by some relatives.

Therefore, the truth cannot remain private. It must be disseminated throughout society, and the authorities must publicly acknowledge the facts.

Compiling testimonies is a key component of developing a collective memory that enables people to find meaning in what happened and affirm their dignity; remembrance is a way of acknowledging that it happened, that it was unjust, and that it should never happen again (Jodelet 1992).

As I record this, I feel at peace, because I know that this testimony that I am giving is for the good of all of us who suffered those abuses. We feel content. I understand that it is to our benefit. All of our other brothers and sisters will see it like that. They will feel it, and all of those who also gave their testimonies. Case 6029 (murder), San Francisco, Huehuetenango, 1982.

The Social Value of Truth

Clarifying incidents and acknowledging the atrocities committed against the civilian population by the army and other forces are, then, a first step for the victims and for the memory of an entire society. The truth also has social relevance for those not directly affected by losses. After years of censorship, manipulation of information, and social isolation, knowing about the violence and atrocities can help society increase its awareness about what happened (to know one's own history and to avoid distorted versions of reality), promote social condemnation of the perpetrators, and accept the need to compensate the victims.

What I hope is that one day the army will admit all that it has done and that it won't continue, you know, to break the law. It makes you mad; we're still poor. Case 0785 (murders), Cuarto Pueblo, Ixcán, Quiché, 1991.

However, the cathartic effect of the truth could be jeopardized if it is not accompanied by justice. If knowledge of the facts is followed by silence and impunity, truth can become an insult to the victims. In the testimonies analyzed, demands to know the truth are linked to demands for justice.

The Demand for Justice

The desire for justice figures prominently in the testimonies. For victims and survivors, the impact that violence has had on their lives and the lives of their families and communities has left them with a deep sense of injustice, not only because of the painful loss, but because those responsible for the crimes committed against them remain unpunished to this day.

Changing Power Relationships

First, the demand for justice has to do with changing local power relationships and preventing new forms of violence. Without social censure, basic social standards of conduct are undermined, thereby increasing the possibility that violence could recur. Besides, the improved social status of many perpetrators deepens the feelings of gross injustice on the part of victims and survivors who have had to live for all these years in humiliating silence and powerlessness.

The power structures remain untouched in many areas—even with the end of the armed conflict, as in the case of many former military commissioners—raising the specter of renewed violence and fueling fears that repression could recur. From the victims' standpoint, justice modifies social relationships and the way in which power is wielded in society.

> *The government should really do justice. Also, it should be forced to remove those bad people, since that's its responsibility. Because if the people who did all the damage remain in their positions of responsibility, the repression could return.* Case 1271, Pueblo Chajul, Quiché, 1985.

However, contrary to the tendency to equate the victims' desire for justice with a desire for revenge, the testimonies do not contain demands for vengeance or the death penalty.

> *There shouldn't be vengeance, because vengeance causes the violations to start all over again—over a piece of land.* Case 7442, Plan de Sánchez, Baja Verapaz, 1982.

> *I hope that they seek laws to give some punishments. Because taking life— I don't think that works. What I say, punishment yes. But taking life—I think not. That makes us into murderers again.* Case 1274, Pueblo Chajul, Quiché, 1982.

Restoring the Meaning of Authority

Demands for justice include the struggle against both impunity and corruption, which often go hand in hand. The first step to ending both must be the dismissal of military or civilian officials who bear significant responsibility for the violence against the civilian population, including members of the military intelligence apparatus. Without changes in the leadership of these military structures, which bears a heavy responsibility for the atrocities committed, those responsible for the violence will continue to act with impunity. This is particularly true given the power these organizations have over society and over other government institutions, and the web of complicity they wove during the years of armed conflict. Such dismissals are also measures that can help people surmount their feelings of humiliation and injustice over the deaths of their loved ones.

We never want weapons again, we never want bombardments; no more massacres, no more abductions and murders, no more impunity; we don't want any more corruption. Dismiss the high-level military officers who are involved in these bloody acts, because thousands and thousands of victims gave their lives to demand their rights and defend what belonged to them and their families. Case 1885 (guerrilla murder of military commissioner), Cobán, Alta Verapaz, 1983.

During the conflict, altered power structures and the violence used against the population negated the meaning of authority as a force that serves the community, especially as it is understood by the Mayan culture. But political repression also changed the value of laws and norms governing social relationships. In order to safeguard the meaning of community-based authority, the justice usually applied by the authorities must now be turned toward the public officials who misused it.

[We need justice] to keep these violent acts from happening again, and so that the blessed authorities don't continue to commit this injustice. Because they had decided among themselves to finish off the workers, or rather the peasants. Case 1316, Aldea Parraxtut, Sacapulas, Quiché, 1983.

Thus, restoring the meaning of law means modifying the rules governing social relationships and restoring community relations that were ruptured by violence. While this perspective is very common among the survivors (social condemnation as a form of reparation), justice also includes an element of prevention without which the present and the future are imperiled.

I want there to be a law, a justice [system] that punishes the guilty, that punishes those who have done wrong. There should be a law that punishes so that these things don't happen again. Because if the things they have done—the violence that has disappeared our brothers—are left as they are, it means that the law doesn't exist, that justice doesn't exist. And so they'll keep doing it without any fear, without any care; they'll have free rein to do what they want. Case 5910 (forced disappearance), Sayaxché, Petén, 1988.

Putting an End to Impunity

This desire for justice is not naive by any means. Some people are very conscious of the difficulty of achieving justice under current conditions. The lack of political will and the army's power have made it clear to many that their desire for justice must be channeled through organized actions in order to become a reality.

> *I would say that it is going to depend on the people's effort to prosecute them in the short or long term, right? It's the only hope, unless perhaps one day it ends once and for all.* Case 7336 (murder), Patzún, Chimaltenango, 1984.

One of the perceived obstacles is an inefficient and corrupt judicial system. The demands for law enforcement in the context of the arbitrary methods of strong-arm governance require judicial reform and the removal of judges and prosecutors who are corrupt or have contributed to a situation in which wrong-doers can act with impunity.

Instead of public security models based on increasing social control and new methods of militarizing daily life, some people interviewed focused on the need for a new public security model in order to prevent renewed violence from the power elite.

> *The ideal would be that this authority be punished, because it doesn't do us any good to take them to court. Corruption in Guatemala gets worse every day, and whoever has the most money wins. If I have some, and I pay a good lawyer—even the person who is going to judge me—I am going to come out ahead. But if I don't have money, I won't be able to do this, and he is going to go free. There should be more authorities, more drastic, more competent. Because now they are getting more authorities, meaning more police, but all of that money is being wasted, because the police are the ones who are probably doing the things. The press is always saying that the police kill, steal cars.* Case 3077 (abduction and torture), Salamá, Baja Verapaz, 1982.

Justice for the Future

Justice is also relevant in terms of allowing those who committed atrocities to change their situation. Unless they acknowledge the facts and accept social censure, they will never have the chance to face their past, rebuild their identity, and reestablish their relationships with the victims and with society.

> *You have to think that if you have done something, it's better to be punished, depending on your crime; you should be punished and not killed. If you have made a big mistake, or have killed another, the law would be the one to investigate it.* Case 9524 (perpetrator), Huehuetenango, 1980-82.

Some people point out the importance of justice for the generations to come. Without a clear ethical sense of condemnation of the atrocities, violence can become a pattern of accustomed conduct with the attendant impact on youth and the future of society.

> *What we want is that the perpetrators, or those responsible, be prosecuted so that they can see what it's like, since they didn't take pity when they harmed our families. There should be legal justice. All of those responsible for the martyrs should be investigated, because they are happy and peaceful, with two or three houses, women, cars, stores.* Case 5339, Plan de Sánchez massacre, Rabinal, Baja Verapaz, 1982.

Where there are generic references to God in the testimonies (9 percent), justice is also frequently mentioned, meaning that usually they are not incompatible. However, some testimonies mention "God's justice," meaning a feeling of resignation or acceptance of the events. It is difficult to determine if this appeal to "divine justice" is distinguished from the desire for justice, if it constitutes a type of learned helplessness, or if it implies that the desire for justice at the present time has been subdued.

> *At least I want to see the bones. I think that he is where FAMDEGUA is doing the exhumations. I leave it to God. I'm not asking for justice.* Case 9925 (forced disappearance), El Chal, Petén, 1981.

> *We only have one God and our dignity. I want justice to be done to those responsible, because it isn't good to continue without law.* Case 0577 (murder), San Pedro Chicaj, Cahabón, Alta Verapaz, 1981.

References to forgiveness rarely figure in the testimonies. Most people demand first a public acknowledgment of the facts and the punishment of those responsible. Forgiveness as a voluntary attitude of reconciliation with the offenders is only accepted as a corollary to acknowledgment of the offense, justice, and social restitution.

> *I think that a call should be put out to the victims of this situation from many years back, not just since 1983 but many years before that, to help achieve justice. Because I am not going to remain silent....This business that I am going to forgive: I forgive when I see that some of them are behind bars, let that be perfectly clear. Not here, nor anywhere else, am I going to forgive so that everything stays like it is. It's impossible.* Case 2155 (forced disappearances), Tactic, Alta Verapaz, 1983.

CONFRONTING THE CAUSES

Social Change for Peace

A second large category of demands found in the testimonies has to do with social change. Many survivors are conscious of the fact that unless some of the causes of the conflict are addressed, and without a genuine willingness to fulfill commitments, a recurrence of the violence is quite possible. Three of the most critical social demands are demilitarization, land tenancy, and freedom to rebuild daily life.

Demilitarization of Daily Life

The first demand has to do with reducing the army's presence in the communities and generally modifying its relationship to the population.

> *For this we are seeking a solution, and the government also has to look for solutions for us, because its army comes to bother us wherever we are; they should pull it out. We don't want any more war.* Case 0717, Senococh, Uspantán, Quiché, 1988.

The testimonies frequently describe the power of weapons and the destruction they have inflicted on communities, whether through the military commissioner system earlier on, the subsequent guerrilla presence, or the fifteen years of militarized control by the civil patrols. The demand for demilitarization includes confiscating and destroying weapons, or eliminating the arms trade in communities.

> *We've already turned in our weapons (civil patrol), and we are getting used to living like before, when we managed without weapons. Our parents taught us to plant, not to carry weapons. I hope they don't arm the community again, because weapons are frightening.* Case 4687, Aldea Guantajau, Quiché, 1982.

For the people, demilitarization begins by dismantling military structures such as the military commissioners and the civil patrols. These structures completely altered community relations and values; weapons and army control had a direct influence on methods of governance.

> *In order to prevent the violent acts that occurred, and keep occurring, the first thing is that the authorities have to enforce the law. They should collect all the weapons that are circulating all over the place, the ones that have carried out the violence. The military commissioners should be removed, because they are the ones who have done so much damage to the Guatemalan people.* Case 6456 (murder), Morales, Izabal, 1968.

> *To prevent these violent acts from recurring, it is necessary to get rid of the civil patrols, the soldiers, members of the military who have committed so many massacres. They should sign the Peace Accords, and the Catholic church should continue to support the peace process.* Case 4789, Finca La Estrella massacre, Chajul, Quiché, 1981.

Forced recruitment was a constant threat to young people who were required—and often abducted—to join the army. This aspect of militarization has had an enormous impact on people's lives. Thus, the demand for demilitarization includes alleviating the pressure on young people and providing useful, community-based alternatives to obligatory military service. Postwar social reconstruction must reduce the army's presence in society and make progress toward a true demilitarization.

To keep this from happening again—I think that things happen by organizing ourselves, by raising our awareness. That time can return if we don't understand each other. But if we understand the need we have experienced as poor people, as Guatemalans, we think that this will not be the same perhaps. We agree to doing service, but in the community instead of in the army; they can be literacy teachers, health promoters. Case 2297, Aldea Buena Vista, Santa Ana Huista, Huehuetenango, 1981.

Changes in Local Power Structures

Demilitarization entails reforms of local power structures, including a reassessment of the role of civilian and traditional authorities. The demands for reconstruction and community participation in local power structures call for genuine recognition of the community's protagonist role and for participatory structures and systems.

To keep these episodes from happening again, we should work in peace, first with the family, and then with the community. Work with those still left in Guatemala, who didn't seek refuge outside the country; struggle to live happily, like before the violence. Know the rights of human beings, restore the integrity of civilian authority. And the government should promise to uphold the law and the Constitution. Case 0977, Santa María Tzejá massacre, Ixcán, Quiché, 1981.

Many people demand reforms that go beyond the formal system, to promote rejection of such war-imposed values as arbitrariness, authoritarianism, and social discrimination. This perspective is relevant for the future since new authoritarian power structures could emerge without a formal military structure. In some parts of the country, the civil patrols were recently converted into development committees, which threaten to become a new method of social control based on leveraging aid and development projects. They are examples of attempts to preserve the old structures under a different name.

What we want now is for someone to guide us, to lead us to the common good—right here in my village Najtilabaj—someone who encourages us to reject any deception. And for our children to enjoy a better life. What we want now is for them to take our petitions into account and not to be sub-jected to authoritarianism and to whatever their plans are. Case 10684 (murder), San Cristóbal Verapaz, Alta Verapaz, 1982.

Demobilization and Army Reforms

The three concrete demands for army reform are demobilization of the military units, officers, and soldiers most implicated in atrocities; dismantling of clandestine structures; and moral restitution for the victims. Reducing the army's coercive power over society and its dominance of government institutions requires removing and changing personnel. But it is also essential to replace the military hierarchy and power with democracy and with a society, government, and legal system capable of controlling the army. These reforms cannot be limited to the formal structure of the army and security forces, however. The intelligence apparatus and its network must be investigated and dismantled as clandestine repression centers. The continued existence of these parallel power structures are a threat to the future.

> *It depends on the soldiers. Many of them carried out the massacres because they had to; others were definitely abusive. The army leadership should be removed and new people put in so that there can be democracy and respect. It also seems wrong to me that the retired military officers have a salary, the people's money. They should work instead, like we peasants work.* Case 1280, Caserío Palob Massacre, Nebaj, Quiché, 1980.

For many victims, effective measures to demilitarize Guatemala include an expedient international supervisory presence. Many survivors and families have expectations of institutions, such as the Historical Clarification Commission (CEH) established by the Peace Accords, one of which is that they help formalize and shape the demands that have been articulated by the people.

> *No more weapons. What is needed is the immediate deactivation of the government's clandestine structures. And it is also necessary to bring it before the truth commission, and the eyes of the whole world, so that they can be witnesses to what is happening to us, the poor—the discrimination and the violation of our rights.* Case 568, Cobán, Alta Verapaz, 1981.

The Desire for Freedom

Aspirations of freedom are related to demands for an end to military control over daily life. People who were clustered into settlements such as model villages and subjected to total army control, or more commonly, those who experienced other forms of militarization such as civil patrols, want freedom of movement and trade, and the ability to reorganize their lives.

We don't want to be tied anymore, to be corralled. We want to live in freedom, we want to live in peace. Group testimony, San Lucas Chiacal, San Cristóbal Verapaz, Alta Verapaz.

The testimonies relate demands for freedom to the ability to express their identity and their culture. In part, this includes the freedom to observe their rituals and ceremonies, and to express their personal beliefs. But it also has to do with working conditions. For many people, the demand for better working conditions on the farms refers to wages and economic benefits, but also to changing a lifestyle in which they are subject to the bosses' orders. Behind these demands for greater freedom in labor conditions and modes of production is a vindication of their identity as peasants, rather than merely farmhands.

Addressing the Land Issue

Socioeconomic measures to defuse some of the root causes of the conflict must accompany measures for truth, justice, or demilitarization. From the perspective of many victims, the only way to put an end to violence is by resolving issues such as land tenancy and living conditions.

Well, for me, ending all the violence—let's say those who have power, those who use weapons, like the army—what I know is that all the killing comes from their weapons. Or the number of soldiers should be reduced. And in order to stop the violence, to end the problem once and for all, that will come when they distribute lands to the poor; after that, there will be no more violence or problems. Case 6629, Finca Sapalau, Cobán, Alta Verapaz, 1981.

Better land distribution is not only a form of restitution; it is, more important, a measure to prevent new problems and social conflicts.

EXPECTATIONS FOR PEACE

Expectations for the peace process include demands for improving the socioeconomic conditions of the poor, reducing social inequalities, and reforming government and political systems so that they represent the people's needs. Although the testimonies were compiled prior to the signing of the Peace Accords, some witnesses foresaw the danger that the peace process would be reduced to little more than a demobilization process, or a deactivation of the armed conflict, unless socioeconomic and legal reforms were included to address some of the root causes of poverty.

Demands Directed toward the URNG

Explicit demands have been made of the URNG. The relatives of people who were killed by the guerrillas, or whose deaths or current whereabouts remain unclear, have demanded public investigations into the incidents and acknowledgment of the memory of their family members. Given the strategic confusion built into armed operations during the eighties, the demands for clarification and the truth about murders allegedly committed by the guerrillas involve all of the different armed groups.

> *The family wants an investigation of the incident, of both the armed forces and the EGP, given that the latter never clarified or denied the communique that appeared. [And investigation of] the government armed forces, because the subsequent machine-gun attacks were identified; because it was a mode of action against people who helped the communities; and because it is the responsibility of the government to clarify the situation, which it never did.* Case 3338 (abduction and forced disappearance), Chiantla, Huehuetenango, 1981.

There are other explicit demands having to do with the guerrillas' treatment of the population. In rural areas particularly, their promises of social change or defense from the army were precluded by the way the war progressed and by perceived inconsistencies in the guerrillas' conduct. Some people who became involved in the war, or who saw in the guerrillas an opportunity to improve the situation, later felt abandoned when the guerrillas failed to react in times of severe crisis.

> *I wish to live in peace; that these acts of violence not be repeated for our children. We want the guerrillas to stop deceiving the people, because what they said wasn't true: they didn't defend us from the soldiers. All of the dead are innocent; they are the civilian population. But the guerrillas run away; they don't stop to face the army; instead, they leave the population to face the army. The army and the civil patrols murdered everyone. We don't want it to happen again. They should sign the Peace Accords because we poor people are the ones who suffer.* Case 2454 (murder and scorched earth), Chipal, San Juan Cotzal, Quiché, 1982.

> *The guerrillas should admit their mistakes. They should remember the flyers they distributed that said "the guerrillas are united with the people and will never be defeated"; that wasn't true. The army should admit its mistakes when it came, pretending to be civilians, to investigate and then punish with death. There was deception.* Case 8008, Los Angeles, Ixcán, Quiché, 1981.

The Eyes of the World; International Presence

Despite efforts by the government and army to discredit internationally the demands and accusations put forth by human rights groups, international awareness continues to be a deterrent and play a preventive role for victims and relatives.

The ability of victims and their support groups to pressure the government and its agencies into monitoring the accords concerning populations affected by the war (refugee return, for example) has corresponded to their ability to publicize their suffering beyond their own borders. The fact that the government is bound by international treaties, laws, and human rights instruments—and that it needs to restore economic ties to other countries—has contributed to this change. Despite the resistance from a large segment of the economic, political, and military sectors, international pressure and presence have supported people's expectations for peace and respect for human rights.

For this reason, testimonies concerning international presence frequently demand that international human rights groups remain in Guatemala to supervise compliance with the Peace Accords. The testimonies do not specifically evaluate this presence, but they describe its overall contribution to restoring social harmony and respect. International presence is highly regarded when its role clearly has been consistent with the community's previous experience, values, or expectations.

Thanks to those people who thought to create an authority to defend our values. We should support them, understand that they are defending what we had lost. Because of these authorities, we feel more enthusiastic. Now we have to take into account that we all have the same worth, educate our children, give them good advice, good ideas; not like those people were raised who got involved in that evil, destructive policy. They should be careful about how they live, about making something of themselves in this world. Case 2300 (forced disappearance), Nentón, Huehuetenango, 1982.

The Role of the Catholic Church

References to the Catholic church are found in the testimonies in conjunction with the search for truth and its role in human rights education. These statements may tend to be favorable toward the church, since the testimonies were compiled by people and institutions linked to it. Nonetheless, its institutional presence and the trust that many sectors of society place in it constitute a demand that it continue actively to defend the human rights of the people.

The struggle of the church, of all brothers and sisters, of all of humankind would be for this not to recur—for it not to happen again. Because we are people here on the earth God gave us. We are not animals, and according to the books of the Bible, God says that he gave us life and only he can take it away. Case 9513 (torture), Huehuetenango, Huehuetenango, 1981.

The people's expectations of the Guatemalan Catholic church represent a challenge. REMHI's testimonies offer material for reflection on the church's social activity, both in terms of its commitment to the people and its own vision as a powerful institution.

Well, I believe that our religion, the Catholic church, has a huge commitment with all of these cases of violence. In our religion, we are going to go back, not to the Old Testament, but to the Christ who wore a tunic, the Christ who said: "Even the birds have a place to lay their head and the Son of Man does not." If we have religion in our heart, sincerely, I think that we can overcome the economic powers and political powers. But today, our God is money, political power, economic power. I ask myself this question: if there is religion, why is our world like this? Case 5444 (murder), Guatemala City, 1979.

Giving people back their memory is one of these expectations. Some families and communities affected by the violence believe that the search for truth must not end with the publishing of a report. Instead, it must return to its source; it must promote—by producing materials, and so forth—the role of memory as an instrument of social reconstruction.

I feel relieved by giving my testimony because I have told what I have suffered. Thank you, all of you who have come to visit us, to receive our testimony. It allows us to unburden ourselves, because we are very oppressed. Thank God, this has helped us unburden ourselves. I hope you will give us a book so that it will remain as a history, so that our children will understand what we suffered. Case 7462, Aldea Chichupac Massacre, Baja Verapaz, 1982.

REPARATIONS[1]

We have to reunite and demand our rights. What I demand now is that the government pay me for damages. We make our living with our pigs, our chickens; we have no other business. The people also demand what they

---

[1] According to the United Nations Human Rights Commission, reparation must cover the totality of damages suffered by the victim. These include individual measures related to the *right to restitution*, which are oriented toward restoring the victim to a situation comparable to that which existed prior to the violations (employment, properties, repatriation, and so on); *indemnization measures* refer to economic compensation for harm suffered; *readaption measures* are understood as those covering expenses like legal assistance or health care. *General reparation measures* are symbolic acts such as public acknowledgment of government responsibility; official statements to restore the victims' dignity; commemorative ceremonies, monuments, and acts honoring the victims; and including in historical documents a faithful account of exceptionally gross violations committed. The right to reparation also contemplates *guarantees* that violations of people's rights will not continue. These guarantees include dismantling para-state armed groups; terminating exceptional measures, legislative or otherwise, that are conducive to violations; and instituting administrative or other measures affecting state agents who have been responsible for violations and atrocities.

have lost, because it's all we have to live on. The army wants to finish us off because it doesn't want us to get ahead. Our grandfathers said that it was the government's duty to help, but the bad governments took over and they didn't help us anymore. Case 3909, Aldea Xemal, Quiché, 1980.

Another demand has to do with proposed social restitution for survivors, exhumations of the victims, and measures for their collective memory.

Reparations cannot bring back life nor recover the enormous social and cultural losses. Nonetheless, the government has the obligation to take measures that help to compensate for some of the losses suffered by the victims and survivors of atrocities and crimes against humanity and that enable populations affected by the violence to live with dignity. Demands for reparations relating to the dignity of murder victims or the disappeared begin with formal acknowledgment of the incident. This is followed by elucidating the victim's fate, and is made concrete by finding the remains, exhuming them, and reburying them in keeping with religious and cultural, public and private rituals. The diverse forms of "reparation" demanded in survivors' testimonies have to do with economic compensation or development projects; scholarships and study programs; commemorative acts and monuments; and psychosocial care for victims and survivors.

To get rid of the sorrow we feel, perhaps there is a way, an encouraging word in order to get rid of this sorrow. Maybe there is a way to help us get rid of our problems caused by these enormous sorrows. Case 3907, Nebaj, Quiché, 1980.

The value of assistance must be evaluated from the standpoint of its practical benefits and its importance for people's dignity. Reparation measures must never be regarded as a substitute for the demands for truth and justice. Moreover, delivering assistance often can give rise to new problems and divisions among communities unless reparations are made based on explicit criteria.[2]

Ceremonies and burials in keeping with religious and cultural traditions are essential to the grieving process. Community participation can be an important indicator of the quality of the work and the accompaniment the communities demand. The reparation component of exhumations must include appropriate handling of the remains in keeping with cultural beliefs and practices, and the provision of clear information about the process.

The first thing we want is their support in giving a Christian burial to the brothers and sisters who are in that place—who are stuck in that forsaken place. And second, our community has been completely neglected by the

---

[2] Therefore, acts of reparation must include the participation of the affected population, its decision-making capability, and transparent criteria based on equity that guide each step of the different forms of reparation, whether of an economic or psychosocial nature.

government. We have no means of communication, no roads; we have noth-
ing recognized by the government; we are totally abandoned....When it
starts to be processed, we want the national and international authorities to
come and verify the facts. We want true justice. Case 560, Cobán, Alta
Verapaz, 1981.

But demands to investigate the fates of relatives, conduct exhumations, and
the like are also tied to the family's need to rebuild their lives. Despite their
conviction that the person is dead, many families face bureaucratic red tape (for
example, for inheritance purposes, property titles, or other legal matters) which
entails renewed efforts, added humiliation, and more expenses incurred from the
repression they suffered.

It would be good for us to tell the legal authorities to tell those from the
municipality to take them out, to erase [register as deceased] the names of
the dead [from the book of registered births], so that they go free and we
don't have any more problems. We want you to go to the authorities so that
they take out those names, and so that they recover the dead, recover the
bones of the dead. That is what we think. Case 10514, Sawachil Massacre,
Alta Verapaz, 1980.

The value of memory as a form of restitution goes beyond reconstructing the
facts. It represents a moral judgment that ethically repudiates the perpetrators.
Commemorations and ceremonies confer meaning and public acknowledgment
on the memory. Besides reconstructing the past, collective memory is valuable for
its element of social mobilization that helps survivors break their silence and
honor their relatives. These rituals and commemorations must not be merely a
recollection of pain but also a memory of solidarity.

Many family members reaffirm the value of collective memory, transmitted to
new generations as a part of their education. This is especially true for the Maya
people. They see the importance of spreading this memory through public acts,
publicizing the findings, designing educational materials, and engaging in community activities.

I hope that all of this is recorded so that the little children of today learn
about it some day and try to keep it from happening again. Fifteen years
ago we buried all of our dead, and it still has not been recognized as a
cemetery; but we know they are there, and that's how we want it. Case
11418 (murders), Caserío El Limonar, Jacaltenango, Huehuetenango, 1982.

Part Two

THE METHODOLOGY OF HORROR

Chapter Seven

THE INTELLIGENCE BEHIND THE VIOLENCE

THE INTELLIGENCE STRUCTURE

THE DYNAMICS OF VIOLENCE; THE ROLE OF THE INTELLIGENCE SERVICES

Guatemalan intelligence services played a pivotal role in the evolution of counterinsurgency policy. They comprise a complex network of military and police corps that permeated the social fabric (through agents, informers, and so forth), maintained their own hierarchies, and almost always enjoyed total autonomy of action. Military intelligence has played a key role in directing military operations, massacres, extrajudicial executions, forced disappearances, and torture. Throughout the armed conflict, intelligence officers and specialists were deeply involved in systematic human rights violations.

The internal structure and organization of the intelligence apparatus has changed over time, according to government policies, military dictates, and the evolution of the conflict. The intelligence apparatus is essentially a military structure, however, and its two most important agencies are *La 2,* as the Army Intelligence Directorate is known, and the *Archivo,* the intelligence division of the Presidential General Staff *(Estado Mayor Presidencial*—EMP). In addition, because of their efficiency and relative autonomy to conduct undercover operations, the Mobile Military Police (*Policía Militar Ambulante*—PMA) and the National Police's special unit, known over the years as BROE or *Comando Seis,* played important roles at different times. Military commissioners and the Civilian Self-defense Patrols (PAC) also formed part of the intelligence framework.

This intricate web of corps and institutions is directed by the "intelligence high command": the president of the Republic, the defense minister, the minister of the interior, the National Defense chief of staff, the director of the Army Intelligence Directorate (D-2), and the chiefs of the Presidential General Staff and the National Police. At a higher level, a more exclusive group has access to all intelligence and is charged with strategic decision-making. This group is essentially the Army High Command: the president, the defense minister, and the National Defense chief of staff.

THE NAME OF FEAR: *LA 2*

Popularly known as *La 2,* the Army Intelligence Directorate (D-2) is a division of the National Defense Staff (*Estado Mayor de la Defensa Nacional*—

EMDN).[1] Its scope of activity gradually increased during the sixties and seventies and reached its peak in the eighties. *La 2* figures prominently in the worst incidents of violence; its dossier is replete with disappearances, murders, abductions, and torture. It conducted extensive espionage and information-gathering operations by tapping telephones and operating a sophisticated computer network containing files on people, complete with their photographs, and information on their political and organizational affiliations.

Intelligence agents are a privileged group within the army structure. They have access to the best services, and they enjoy easy access to professional training that grooms them for administrative and policy-making posts in the government bureaucracy. By virtue of their direct contact with high-level officers and political leaders, they can obtain awards and advantages more readily than other officers. This privileged status is also reflected in the fact that intelligence agents have their own chain of command within the broader military structure.

> The G-2 [intelligence] officer of a military command operates freely and autonomously within his jurisdiction....The agent owes more allegiance to the Intelligence Directorate than to the military unit commander. In fact, even if he is a lower-ranking officer, the G-2 has the authority to impose his views on the commander (*elPeriódico*, August 11, 1997).

Agents working for *La 2*, operating under pseudonyms, have vehicles, communications equipment, and safe houses at their disposal. Its national command structure, and its mid- and low-level structures, are designed to operate from the shadows. It is directed by the National Defense Staff (*elPeriódico*, August 11, 1997). During the eighties, there were an estimated two thousand active-duty personnel in *La 2* (Simon 1987). Its key agents were assigned to command positions in the army, giving military intelligence control over a wide range of material, technical, and human resources to carry out its own operations.

In the late eighties and the first half of the nineties, military intelligence was used to direct much of the counterinsurgency policy, as well as to fight organized crime, drug trafficking, and common crime. Eventually commanders began using these structures for illicit activities such as car theft, kidnapping for ransom, and drug activity.

La 2 runs a network of confidential agents (*confidenciales*) whose intelligence and counterintelligence activities encompass government agencies, urban sectors (slum, middle-class, and residential neighborhoods) and rural areas. These are generally plainclothes agents. A code of silence or internal *compartmentalization* governs agents and informers.

> All personnel were subject to army laws and regulations....According to Article 35 of the Regulations for Specialists...they are required to be discreet,

---

[1] The National Defense Staff was previously known as the Army General Staff *(Estado Mayor General del Ejército*—EMGE).

refrain from divulging assigned orders and activities; the more sensitive their mission, the more faithfully must they maintain secrecy (*Crónica* magazine, August 20, 1993).

Operational coordination has existed between *La 2* and *Archivo*.[2] The December 10, 1985, abduction and murder of Eugenia Beatriz Barrios Marroquín (age 26) provides an example of the effective use of telephone espionage and its agile coordination with the clandestine apparatus, or death squads.

To carry out non-operational intelligence tasks, *La 2* organized a network of military commissioners and their auxiliaries and informers. The Mobile Military Police were tapped for investigations, information, and surveillance; the army's network of *confidenciales,* operating from a military command structure disguised as civilian, infiltrated different sectors of society.

La 2 personnel are organized into four sections: international intelligence, technical intelligence, analysis, and counterinsurgency. A fifth section is counterintelligence, which is charged with surveillance of its own agents, although during certain periods it took control of the entire military structure.

THE *ARCHIVO:* THE INTELLIGENCE DIVISION OF THE PRESIDENTIAL GENERAL STAFF (EMP)

The EMP's intelligence service was originally created with the official purpose of providing security to the president and his family. Soon, however, the military leadership assigned it tasks having to do with fraud in border areas through customs and migration. Finally, it was assigned political espionage functions.

Beginning in 1986 when a civilian president took office, the *Archivo*'s presidential advisory role afforded it greater renown and political influence. Nonetheless, from the start, the *Archivo* was part of the "inner circle" because of its proximity to power. General Héctor Gramajo described the EMP under General Romeo Lucas (1978-82) as follows:

> With hindsight, it is possible to see more clearly how the Presidential General Staff became a repository for speculation and complaints about army-related issues, a reflection of the moral decay of the officer cadres. This was aggravated by abuses within the president's inner circle, which organized parties for him at General Lucas' private farm, in the municipality of Sebol (Alta Verapaz), in the northern part of the national territory. On such occasions,

---

[2] The National Police have played a subordinate role in this coordination by merely receiving indications to *clean out* the surrounding areas prior to intelligence operations. Subsequently, when police investigators are of no further use, they may even be killed. This was the case of José Miguel Mérida Escobar, the National Police investigator in charge of the Myrna Mack investigation, who discovered the identity of one of the material authors of the crime, Sergeant Major Noel de Jesús Beteta Alvarez. Investigator Mérida was murdered in the street less than fifty meters from the Police General Headquarters on August 5, 1991.

discretionary use was made of helicopters from the army's meager air mobile flotilla (Gramajo 1995).

Throughout the armed conflict, the *Archivo* participated in the intelligence services' "division of labor" by focusing on urban insurgent structures. Nonetheless, *Archivo*'s substantial influence over the president and its independent financial, technical, and human resources enabled it to maintain a certain degree of autonomy from *La 2* and even from the EMP hierarchy. Originally known as *La Regional*,[3] the EMP's intelligence division was outfitted with highly sophisticated equipment for monitoring telecommunications and images (videos, photographs, television) and electronic espionage (electronic earphones, microphones). The United States provided this technical and advisory support following the 1963 coup d'état.

The *Archivo* was involved in organizing paramilitary groups and death squads such as *Jaguar Justiciero* (Avenging Jaguar). Various sources have estimated the size of *Archivo*'s staff at between twelve hundred and thirty-five hundred.[4]

THE CRIMINAL INVESTIGATIONS DEPARTMENT AND OTHER POLICE ENTITIES

The Criminal Investigations Department *(Departamento de Investigaciones Criminológicas*—DIC) is the intelligence division of the National Police. Despite several name changes over the past twenty years, its basic functions—political persecution rather than public safety—have remained constant since it was founded as a political police force under President Manuel Estrada Cabrera.[5]

The police also were involved in political repression. During the demonstrations *(jornadas)* of March and April 1962, the so-called Model Platoon made its debut, attacking demonstrators and wounding and detaining several people. This served to radicalize the protests, especially student demonstrations.[6]

Perhaps the paroxysm of that exercise, of the perversion of police functions, occurred under the recent authoritarian regimes which, beginning in 1963,

---

[3] *La Regional* was the name widely used to refer to the Government Telecommunications Office (*Oficina Gubernamental de Telecomunicaciones*) and later the Regional Telecommunications Police (*Policía Regional de Telecomunicaciones*).

[4] Washington Office on Latin America (1995) estimates that there are 3,000 civilian informers and 530 people working in the formal structure. The Guatemalan magazine *Crónica* puts the number of personnel at 300, multiplied by four, since "the small unit structure branches out from below, extending into society like the roots of a tree" (August 20, 1993).

[5] In the twenties it was known as the Judicial Police, the Judicial Guard, and the Judicial Department; in the sixties, the Detective Corps; in the eighties, the Department of Technical Investigations (*Departamento de Investigaciones Técnicas*—DIT); and, in the nineties, it became the Criminal Investigations Department (*Departamento de Investigaciones Criminológicas*—DIC).

[6] The Model Platoon was the precursor to other police shock units including the Antiriot Squad, the BROE, and the SWAT. The corps comprised an average of three hundred men over the course of its existence.

were dominated by civilian-military cliques; at that time the police were important tools of state terrorism in the context of the overall counter-insurgency strategy (Aguilera 1993).

In the capital city the Fourth Police Corps was most involved in illegal operations, in conjunction with the Detective Corps. Both were charged with conducting *social cleansing* operations. For such tasks they used personnel who usually had been discharged for breaches of discipline. So-called discretionary funds were used to pay them, the same funds commonly disbursed to pay informers. These discharged individuals (*rebajados*) also worked as body guards after being relieved from service.

Comando Seis, which formed part of the plainclothes police in the seventies,[7] was designed as an immediate reaction squad to conduct covert operations against urban guerrillas. *Comando Seis* directed the operation that resulted in the massacre at the Spanish Embassy in 1980.

THE MOBILE MILITARY POLICE (PMA)

The Mobile Military Police attached to the National Defense Ministry also developed its own intelligence capability. By the early eighties it enjoyed operational autonomy in Guatemala City and Escuintla. The PMA was staffed by two types of personnel: one conducted control and surveillance of the rural population, and the other provided security to private companies.

Created in June 1965, the PMA was initially staffed by former soldiers who kept order in peasant communities. However, they also performed a function less typical of military police, which was to fight crime and disturbances inside the military ranks.

Several documented cases, such as those of Maritza Urrutia and guerrilla commander Efraín Bámaca, include similar accusations that the PMA headquarters in Zone 6 of the capital in the first case, and the PMA headquarters in San Marcos in the latter, held prisoners in clandestine detention centers where psychological and physical torture sessions took place.

THE TREASURY GUARD

For its part, the Treasury Guard (*Guardia de Hacienda*), organized to track down contraband and illegal stills, eventually created its own intelligence center, the Special Services section, whose installations were used as clandestine jails.

---

[7] The command structure of these corps, in the seventies, included Donaldo Alvarez Ruiz, attorney and politician, as interior minister; General Germán Chupina Barahona, National Police director; Manuel de Jesús Valiente Téllez, a self-described colonel, as chief of the Detective Corps; and Pedro García Arredondo, who also identified himself as a colonel, as chief of *Comando Seis*.

The Treasury Guard is implicated in the White Van case (*la Panel Blanca*), as this was the type of vehicle it routinely used to commit human rights violations. Among its victims were former student leader Ana Elizabeth Paniagua and José Albino Grijalva.

INTELLIGENCE NETWORKS

Military intelligence has relied on a huge network of military commissioners and *confidenciales* (also known as *orejas*, literally "ears"). These are civilians, authorized to carry weapons, who collect information on people's movements and pass it along to the army base's intelligence section (S-2), either directly or through the civilian affairs section (S-5).[8] In the eighties, a mere accusation by a military commissioner was frequently all it took for the accused to be killed. Characterized as the army's eyes, ears, and arms, the military commissioners engaged in numerous actions against the civilian population. Its network comprised about twenty-eight thousand people, enough to cover each of the urban and rural population centers in the country.

The *orejas* were civilian networks created by *La 2* to maintain preemptive control over different sectors of society. There were different levels within the ranks of *orejas,* the first being those distinguished by their longstanding proximity to the army. This group received better training—during which its members conducted intelligence missions—are better paid, and work full time in the area of infiltration and espionage.

In the eighties the Civil Self-defense Patrols (PACs) joined the military intelligence network to meet the growing need for direct, mass control over the population. The civil patrols originated in 1981 as a civilian militia promoted by then-army chief of staff General Benedicto Lucas García. But in 1982, under the rule of General Efraín Ríos Montt, they became a permanent control apparatus and anti-guerrilla shock force.

DEATH SQUADS

Death squads appeared in 1966 as part of the army's first massive counteroffensive against guerrilla forces. They were conceived as the operational branch of intelligence and served primarily to threaten, torture, and execute political opposition figures. One of their main impacts was to spread psychological terror among the population.[9] In 1967 alone, more than five hundred people appeared on death

---

[8] The Intelligence Section (S-2) is the military intelligence structure operating in smaller cities and rural areas. Ordinarily, this section exists at local military bases, and in army patrols and platoons where it forms part of the officer staff structure (*plana mayor*).

[9] The counterinsurgency campaign of 1966 and 1967 left eight thousand people dead. Numerous corpses that had been thrown into the Motagua River were found with signs of severe torture. These events were widely covered by the press.

lists. These squads were noted for their strong anticommunist stance, which they used to legitimize their cause among certain social strata.

The first death squad, known as the White Hand (*la Mano Blanca*) surfaced in June 1966. Its logo was a hand representing its five civilian commanders, which included Raúl Lorenzana, Orantes Alfaro, and Nufio. The army provided financial and operational support, and the squads also received funds from wealthy individuals, especially residents of Antigua Guatemala.

Another squad, the Anticommunist Council of Guatemala (*Consejo Anticomunista de Guatemala*—CADEG), also emerged in 1966 and, in February 1967, the New Anticommunist Organization (*Nueva Organización Anticomunista*—NOA) appeared. Both of these squads were organized by the army and there were no civilians in their command structure. Later, squads emerged periodically as a vehicle for conveying threats. The Secret Anticommunist Army (*Ejército Secreto Anticomunista*—ESA) was resuscitated under the Lucas García government. In the late eighties and early nineties, new squads emerged including the Avenging Jaguar (*Jaguar Justiciero*), which threatened human rights activists in the capital and in other cities.[10]

STRATEGIES OF CONTROL: INTELLIGENCE IN ACTION

INTERNATIONAL SURVEILLANCE

The International Section of *La 2* was organized to track political emigration (through identity documents), and monitor international human rights entities such as those pertaining to the United Nations, the Organization of American States, and nongovernmental solidarity groups.[11]

Since the mid-sixties, International Intelligence has coordinated its activities with Central American and United States intelligence agencies through a command center set up in the Panama Canal Zone. This section has organized and supervised the foreign travel of undercover agents—usually to Mexico and Costa Rica, countries which received substantial political emigration during the eighties—and of former insurgent militants who were trained in personality-altering techniques and, having been convinced to become traitors, have worked for the

---

[10] More than twenty death squads have been identified, some of which made only brief appearances. These include *Acción Patriótica de Recuperación Institucional* (APRI), which operated in 1967; *Comité de Resistencia Anticomunista de Guatemala* (CRAG), 1967-68; *Frente Unido Anticomunista* (FUNA), 1967; *Frente de Resistencia Nacional* (FRN), 1967; *Movimiento por la Memoria de Mario Méndez Montenegro* (MPMMMM), 1967; and the *Movimiento Anticomunista de Guatemala* (MAG), 1967 (Aguilera Peralta and Romero Imery 1981).

[11] On one occasion the army publicly denounced URNG activists in those forums, particularly the activities of the representative of the guerrilla delegation in Europe, Jorge Rosal, and one of his collaborators of Dutch nationality.

intelligence services. The goal was to collect information, operational and otherwise, in order to maintain surveillance and abort the plans of the insurgency and political opposition.

TECHNOLOGY AT THE SERVICE OF VIOLENCE

The Technical Section handles sophisticated espionage equipment and information collection. Its equipment must be operated by specialized personnel trained by the intelligence services themselves or recruited from universities, banks, and corporations. According to *Crónica* magazine, Eduardo Suger Cofiño, a renowned physicist and mathematician, was recruited in the sixties to set up a computerized system to track the population. He was reportedly recruited by the army chief of staff, General Marco Antonio Espinoza,[12] who invited him to restructure the Defense Ministry's administrative personnel (*Crónica* magazine, May 30, 1997).

The Technical Section has a computer center, which was installed with U.S. army assistance during the government of Enrique Peralta Azurdia; it has been periodically upgraded to include the latest technology. In the eighties this computer center operated out of the old Military Academy building.

The government's wire-tapping capability increased notably during the Cerezo administration when Guatemalan military intelligence acquired a telephone digester, an electronic device capable of tapping up to five hundred lines. When triggered by certain preprogrammed words, this device activates a tape recorder and prints out the conversation almost simultaneously. The Guatemalan Telecommunications Company (GUATEL) developed the human and electronic capability to monitor international calls[13] and an undercover department of *Archivo*'s technical section operated from the GUATEL installations.

Another area of operations involved tampering with the mail of public figures, and political and opposition leaders. This was handled by *Archivo*'s Technical

---

[12] Espinoza, former chief of the Presidential General Staff (EMP), was indirectly accused in MINUGUA's preliminary report of May 20, 1997, of being responsible for the disappearance of Juan José Rodas, alias Mincho, a member of the guerrilla organization ORPA who had been involved in the kidnapping of Olga de Novella in August 1996. Espinoza, who is also a petroleum engineer, was invited by Suger to teach advanced mathematics at Francisco Marroquín University.

[13] GUATEL operated under the Defense Ministry during the Ríos Montt regime. Then-director Colonel Carlos Aníbal Menéndez Cabrera directed telephone espionage against political opposition figures and corrupt officials (Washington Office on Latin America 1982, 28). More recently, in June 1995, it was revealed that deputies of the governing party, *Partido de Avanzada Nacional* (PAN), had been spied upon through recordings of their telephone conversations. The tapes were made public—in order to denounce their contents—by then-deputy Juan Francisco Reyes López of the *Frente Republicano Guatemalteco* (FRG) party. Nonetheless, it was the *Archivo* that came under suspicion. Reyes López only acknowledged that the tapes had been sent anonymously to his office in the Congress (*Crónica* magazine, June 30, 1995).

Section, which set up an office at the central post office to intercept and open correspondence. On August 4, 1997, Juan José Orellana,[14] an *Archivo* agent hired as a discretionary employee by the Postal Service under orders from Colonel Juan Valencia Osorio,[15] was sentenced by a Guatemalan court to four years in prison (commutable) for the crime of tampering with private correspondence and documents.

SURVEILLANCE OF DAILY LIFE

The Analysis Section of *La 2* is charged with processing information and submitting periodic reports containing events, names, places, and relationships, outlining different scenarios, and making recommendations. Potential sources include agents, specialists, informers, newspapers and magazines, and electronically acquired information. An *agent* is usually a person who is trained, and paid, to conduct undercover operations, legal or otherwise. The agent may infiltrate political parties, labor unions, revolutionary organizations, or other associations. Agents carry out highly secretive tasks and are directed by the respective intelligence agency, which the agent may or may not belong to.

The *specialist*, in contrast, is an agent who operates more or less openly and holds an identity card (*carnet*) that does not necessarily indicate affiliation with the intelligence organization. The specialist may participate in operations and join irregular commandos. An *informer* is a known or anonymous individual who provides information to the intelligence organization but is not part of it.

Personnel recruitment may involve an open process through a selection office at the lower levels,[16] and a much more involved process at the specialized level.

---

[14] From June 7, 1990, to March 26, 1993, Orellana, whose title was postal inspector, sat in a discreet office on the second floor of the central post office and opened correspondence. President Jorge Serrano Elías, State Counsel Acisclo Valladares Molina, and then-Human Rights Ombudsman Ramiro de León Carpio were among the victims of this practice.

[15] Colonel Juan Valencia Osorio, together with General Edgar Godoy Gaitán and Lieutenant Colonel Juan Oliva Carrera are being prosecuted as the intellectual authors of the murder of Myrna Mack; there has been no progress in the case for several years. In 1990, Valencia was the *Archivo* chief, Godoy headed the EMP, and Oliva was the second in command of the *Archivo* (also known as the Public Security Department—DSP).

[16] When the Secretariat for Strategic Analysis was being created, advertisements offering jobs to university graduates in the social sciences fields were placed in the newspapers for several months during 1995. The positions were described in such a way that a number of leftist militants sent their resumés to the Secretariat thinking that it was some kind of private research institute. [*Note:* The Secretariat was originally set up under President de León Carpio as the army's response to criticism of the DSP. It was declared unconstitutional in 1994 and later authorized by executive decree in 1997. Ostensibly a civilian organization, it is controlled by army officers.]

ERADICATING THE ENEMY WITHIN

The Counterinsurgency Section of *La 2* basically consists of operational commandos whose objective is to block insurgent groups from carrying out their plans by *neutralizing* or eliminating alleged members. *Neutralization* can be defined as immobilization achieved by terrorizing the insurgent support base; abduction, detention, and torture to extract information from the victim and ultimately, secure his or her voluntary collaboration; and extrajudicial executions.

This section is divided into bureaus (*negociados*), each of which specializes in one of the insurgent groups: the Guerrilla Army of the Poor—EGP, Revolutionary Organization of the People in Arms—ORPA, the Rebel Armed Forces—FAR, and the Guatemalan Workers Party—PGT. Each command has its own leadership and resources (information, weapons, vehicles, funds, and personnel), which allow it a high degree of operational autonomy.

Chapter Eight

TARGETING THE PEOPLE

The army attempted actively to involve the population in the war as a means of furthering its strategy. To this end, it carried out targeted studies of the relationship between the people and the guerrillas in different areas, and it examined the sociocultural characteristics of the communities that could prove useful to its strategy of penetration and control. Although its discourse was replete with vague ideological references to international communism, the army was much more precise in designing its operational strategy. It used the combined expertise of military psychology and sociology to exploit social differences and the strength of community bonds, apart from ideological concerns.

The army did not maneuver the same way in every region. It adjusted its strategy vis-à-vis the civilian population based on whether the area was considered a "red zone" (under guerrilla control), a "pink zone" (guerrilla presence), or a "white zone" (no guerrilla presence). Its approach to the population followed a strategy specifically designed for each type of zone.

CONTROL OF HOSTILE POPULATIONS

The strategy designed for civilian populations in zones considered to be under guerrilla control included the following steps:

1. Make contact with the population.
2. Establish control over it.
3. Provide security for it.
4. Compile information on the guerrillas' local political organization.
5. Initiate socioeconomic reforms (Ejército de Guatemala 1983, 85).

Detentions were evaluated from the standpoint of their practical utility for obtaining information as well as their psychological impact on the population, taking into account the risk that those who collaborated would later be marked in the community. The following behavioral profile is described in the army's counterinsurgency manual; the goal is minimizing the adverse consequences that detentions might have on the community's trust:

115

1. You cannot expect them to change their attitude, nor speak freely upon being arrested.
2. Fear that subsequent detentions of others in the community will be linked to the information they provided.
3. The people know. An indirect method would be simultaneously to arrest a large number of unimportant suspects and, based on what they divulge, proceed to arrest the leadership of local clandestine guerrilla structures (Armed Political Organizations—OPA) (Ejército de Guatemala 1983, 94).

Mass detentions were used not only to collect information, however. They were also a means of forcibly gathering people into one place. This "concentration" model facilitated control of both people and territory.

INVOLVING THE PEOPLE IN THE WAR

In disputed territories, attempts to control the population centered on having a local leadership sympathetic to the army and directly involving the population in the guerrilla war.

As the army increased its control, some villages were organized into "model villages." The army tried to portray these publicly as its alternative for rural community development in conflictive zones. Both the timing of their organization (following massacres and "cleansing" operations) and their location (militarily strategic areas) were designed to use the civilian population for military actions (reinforce the rear guard, interrupt guerrilla routes, secure disputed territories, and so forth).

The civilian population was also included in war plans, as one more force to be taken into account. Its assigned missions were to participate in *tasks considered of public utility* and *internal security functions*. Some key missions were informing on people and making accusations; guard duty in strategic locations; participation in counter-propaganda activities; so-called self-defense activities, including patrols and fighting the guerrillas; and finally, assisting the army with information, guides, and transportation.

A STRATEGY AT THE VILLAGE LEVEL

They really treated us with contempt. They would repeat their advice, the way you do with a baby. They still despise us; we have no dignity. They definitely despise the indigenous people there—all of the poor. Now we are below them, because we have done wrong in their eyes, and they despise us. That's how they are with us now. TC Acamal, Alta Verapaz, 1986.

As part of its policy of controlling people and territory, the army implemented projects to militarize rural communities based on an exorbitant level of social control that affected nearly half a million Mayans. These projects included so-called strategic villages, model villages, and development poles. Between fifty thousand and sixty thousand people lived in model villages, representing between 12.5 and 20 percent of the highland population. Between 1982 and 1986, the army experimented with its own social reorganization model in these villages in order to establish absolute control over populations considered to be the social base of the guerrillas.

DEVELOPMENT POLES[1]

1. *Ixil Triangle Development Pole:* Municipality of Nebaj, Aldea Acul, Tzalbal, Juil-Chacalté, Río Azul, Pulaj, Xolcuay, Ojo de Agua, Santa Abelina, Bichibalá, Salquil-Palob Atzumbal, Juá-Ilom, Chel, Xemal/Xepatul, Chiché, San Felipe Chenlá and Xix; Municipalities of San Juan Cotzal, and Chajul.

2. *Playa Grande Development Pole:* Departmental jurisdiction of El Quiché: Xalbal, Cantabal, San José la 20, Efrata, Santa Clara, San Pablo, San Francisco, Trinitaria and adjoining villages. Alta Verapaz jurisdiction: Salacuín and border villages.

3. *Chacaj Development Pole:* The villages of Chacaj and Ojo de Agua. Municipality of Nentón.

4. *Chisec Development Pole:* Chisec, Setzí, Saguachil, Sesuchaj, Carolina, Setal, Semuy, Pecajbá, Santa Marta, Semococh, Las Palmas, El Tamarindo, Cubilhuitz, Secocpur, Sibisté, and Ticario (in the municipality of Chisec); and Acamal (in the municipality of Santa Cruz Verapaz).

Many other villages besides those usually recognized were established in areas disputed by the army and the guerrillas (in the Ixcán, for example: San Marcos; San Luis Ixcán and La Nueva Comunidad; Santa María Tzejá and Santiago Ixcán; Samaritano; and tentatively, Los Angeles) (Falla 1987).

---

[1] As described earlier, the only recognized development poles were (1) the Ixil area in the municipalities of Nebaj, San Juan Cotzal, and Chajul; (2) Playa Grande, in the departments of El Quiché and Alta Verapaz; (3) Chisec, Alta Verapaz, in the municipality of Chisec; and (4) Chacaj, in Nentón, Huehuetenango. However, various army publications also mention Yanahí, in the Petén department, and Yalihux, in Senahú, Alta Verapaz, as poles. Neither of these appear in Decree 65-84, but they are included in various official publications.

A DAY IN THE LIFE OF ACAMAL

4:30 Formation, raising the flag, singing hymns (national anthem, army anthem, and the "Macho Patroller"), yell anti-subversive slogans. Participation of women.
5:30 Breakfast (the basic diet consisted of three tortillas, a few beans for each meal, and occasionally a little rice).
6:00 Formation and ideological speech (fifteen minutes after breaking for breakfast, the people had to return to formation).
7:00 Talk on civil self-defense (men) by the army; talk on health or food preparation (women) by the Public Health Ministry.
8:00 Work.
12:00 Formation (the people returned to formation at noon, sang the hymn, and had the ideological reeducation talk).
13:00 Lunch.
13:15 Ideological reeducation talk.
14:00 Work.
18:00 Formation, sing hymns, lower the flag, and yell slogans. (The sergeant's trusted aide had the primary responsibility for taking the "news report" to the office at noon and at 18:00.)
19:00 Dinner.
19:15 Ideological reeducation talk.
21:00 End of the day.

THE CIVIL SELF-DEFENSE PATROLS: THE MILITARIZATION OF DAILY LIFE

A WAR STRATEGY

The Guatemalan army formed the Civilian Self-defense Patrols in late 1981 as part of the counterinsurgency strategy.[2] The main function of the PACs was to involve the communities in the army's anti-guerrilla offensive. The army realized that the insurgency enjoyed significant support from the civilian population. It

---

[2] Later they were officially called Voluntary Civil Defense Committees (*Comités Voluntarios de Defensa Civil*), although in decrees issued in 1986 (for example, Decree 26-86, the army's Organic Law) they are referred to as Civil Defense Committees (*Comités de Defensa Civil*—CDC) or simply Civil Defense. They are defined as a "spontaneous, non-military organization." For more information on the different types of civil patrols and their voluntary nature, see Procurador de los Derechos Humanos/Human Rights Ombudsman et al. 1994. For information on how the patrols operated under civilian governments, see Popkin 1996.

therefore intended to use civil patrols to seal off communities from potential guerrilla penetration as well as remove the guerrillas from areas where they had already established a presence.

The patrols began to operate under the government of Gen. Romeo Lucas García.[3] However, they were not legally established until April 1, 1982, under the National Plan for Security and Development *(Plan Nacional de Seguridad y Desarrollo)* of the military junta installed by the coup d'état and led by General Efraín Ríos Montt. Their existence was extended by Decree 19-86, at which time the Cerezo administration changed their name to Voluntary Civil Defense Committees.

There are no official figures on the number of men who belonged to the civil patrols. By 1982-83, they comprised approximately 900,000 peasants between the ages of fifteen and sixty years, representing nearly 80 percent of the male population in indigenous rural areas. Civil patrol membership fell to 500,000 under the Cerezo government (1986-90) and about 375,000 remained when the patrols were dissolved in 1995.

The civil patrols were a cost-effective system for sentry duty and repression that was not onerous for the army or government since they were unpaid and usually poorly armed. Moreover, they became a forced labor supply in many areas, particularly in the areas of provisions and infrastructure-building. In the war economy, the creation of the civil patrols also enabled the army to redistribute troops to other areas.

> *Those from Xococ (Rabinal) were the first to organize themselves for self-defense, into self-defense patrols. And at the end of 1981 they came, with the army, to oblige Río Negro to organize. If they didn't, they were all guerrillas.* Case 1118, Río Negro, Rabinal, Baja Verapaz, 1981.

While tapping into the civilian population had obvious advantages for the army, it was not without its complications. These included the tendency not to collaborate or the risk associated with arming a population over which the army had achieved little social or psychological control.[4] These issues were carefully evaluated in the course of strategic military planning. The following characteristics were essential to the self-defense system: "It must be desired and not imposed; look for early successes to create bonds and raise combat morale; it must be based on a profound understanding of the inhabitants, their concerns and difficulties, and those with the greatest proclivity should be chosen as leaders" (Ejército de Guatemala 1983, 97-98).

---

[3] Army Chief of Staff General Benedicto Lucas García made the first public statements referring to the civil patrols when he referred to the organization and training of peasant militias (*Prensa Libre*, November 18, 1981).

[4] In fact, according to *Manual de contrainsurgencia* (Ejército de Guatemala 1983), the civil patrol system is designed for "pink" areas rather than "red" ones; that is to say, it was meant for areas where the guerrilla presence was less significant.

TYPES OF CIVIL PATROL VIOLATIONS

In the testimonies compiled by REMHI, civil patrols were responsible for 12.76 percent of all incidents and military commissioners for 7.44 percent. Taken together, one of every five incidents reported can be attributed to these irregular government forces. Civil patrols participated in murders (3.4 percent of all violations), torture and other cruel treatment (2 percent), forced disappearance (1.82 percent), irregular detention (1.8 percent), and threats (1.18 percent). Civil patrols, together with military commissioners, are implicated in one in five cases of deaths resulting from the persecution of people seeking refuge in uninhabited areas (1.3 percent of the total number of documented violations).

The civil patrols are identified as the perpetrators in nearly one in five massacres (18.12 percent), while the military commissioners are identified in one in twenty (5.38 percent). Taken together, these irregular government forces were responsible for one out of every four collective murders.

Among the most aggressive civil patrols—those implicated in massacres and other gross human rights violations—were those from Xococ, Vegas de Santo Domingo, Patixlán, Chuaperol, Nimacabaj, Panacal, La Ceiba, and Pichec (Baja Verapaz); Pojom and Colotenango (Huehuetenango); and Chacalté (Quiché).

THE IMPOSITION AND FORMATION OF THE CIVIL PATROLS

In order to organize effectively and to incorporate people into the civil patrols, the army tried to build on previously existing community networks or structures that facilitated the recruitment and control of the population. Most of the time it focused on people who were leaders or held posts that lent themselves to the task, such as military commissioners, but it also worked through other community or production structures.

At the army's behest, the military commissioners were often responsible for organizing the civil patrols and supervising their activities. This afforded them much more power to intimidate and control than they had previously exercised. The power they wielded through their weapons and their ability to act with impunity had a lasting effect. Following the period of massacres and mass murders, the commissioners' role was to maintain military control in communities. They imposed their authority through the civil patrols, personal intimidation, and threats against social or political groups.

VOLUNTEERS BY FORCE

People were pressured to join the civil patrols through intimidation, accusations, and death threats against entire families. Threats were the primary means of involving the men in the community and, through them, establishing control over their families. The control of daily life made it very difficult for people to resist participating in the patrols.

We did it out of fear. We cooperated because whoever didn't cooperate would be punished. And besides that, they dug a huge ditch, there on the side of the road. We were afraid and had to do it, because where else [could we go]? And we were in their grasp, in their hands. Case 0542, Aldea Río Negro, Rabinal, Baja Verapaz, 1982.

As time passed, less inclined communities sought ways collectively to refuse to continue the patrol system. These efforts were most successful in areas the army considered less strategic. Despite people's resistance to the patrols, however, they continued to function in most areas up to the end of the armed conflict.

Many communities had no choice but to accept the organization of the civil patrols under threat that otherwise the army would eliminate them. In other cases, the patrols were presented to communities as a way of "redeeming" themselves with the army; in other words, a commitment to the army "proved" that they were not collaborating with the guerrillas. The civil patrol system forced the civilian population to take part in the war—on the army's side.[5]

If we didn't patrol, they said we were guerrillas. We were careful for this reason. Because we were afraid of the guerrillas and the soldiers. That's how we lived in 1982, 1983, 1984, until the patrols ended in 1994. Nentón Workshop, Huehuetenango, October 18, 1996.

The army also used other strategies to persuade people to join the civil patrols. Indoctrination techniques and civic action programs were among the psychological tactics aimed at encouraging conformity among the population.

Civic education is part of psychological action; it begins by providing thorough information about the security forces' chances of success in the countersubversion struggle. Any manner of harsh treatment should be avoided during instruction because it discourages the participation of individuals who are motivated and fit for combat. It is also important not to be too benevolent, because this will cause a relaxation of discipline (Ejército de Guatemala 1983, 99).

THE PATROL STRUCTURE

In order to carry out their assigned tasks, the civil patrols required a hierarchical structure that generally followed a military model: a patrol chief and platoons

---

[5] It must be recalled that the civil patrols were established concurrently with the scorched-earth policy implemented by the military regimes.

of patrollers, depending on local conditions and the number of members recruited. The patrol chiefs, or military commissioners in some cases, reported directly to army commanders.

The army allowed the population to choose the patrol chief in certain communities where there was no previously identified risk of leadership hostile to army presence. This participation helped to increase acceptance of the system and compliance with subsequent orders. Usually, however, the army or military commissioners selected the patrol chief from a trusted circle of people.

> They assigned me by name. "You are the commander. You have to carry the list. The number of the patrol first, your name, address, a PAC insignia on your sleeves. You have to carry the flag." Key Source 49, Santiago Atitlán, Sololá, 1982.

MILITARY TRAINING AND PATROLS

According to the army, the patrols required training to increase their effectiveness and, most important, to observe military discipline, since most of them had not even done their obligatory military service: "Instruction must include civic education and military training by the army" (Ejército de Guatemala 1983, 99). Physical training and military indoctrination were particularly stressed in communities that the army considered most conflictive due to greater guerrilla presence or proximity. In many places, those days of training became a collective practice session involving the entire community.

> There was marching there where we were. About a month of training every day or every three days. They made them climb across a rope. The soldiers weren't there; former soldiers were teaching the course. Everyone went, from fifteen year olds to old people. The old people would get hurt and the [instructors] didn't care. They had civic Monday, civic Tuesday, civic Wednesday, depending on the community. Men and women had to attend. Nentón Case, Huehuetenango, October 18, 1996.

Although the army had a vested interest in the patrol system and assigned tasks to patrollers, the population was not armed indiscriminately, probably because the army could not be sure of the communities' loyalty. Most of the time, the army provided a small, limited amount of weaponry. In other cases, the patrollers used hunting weapons, machetes, or sticks. Weapons distribution correlated with the level of discipline and loyalty to the army. This led to discrepancies even among the civil patrollers in a single community.

Civil patrols frequently accompanied army battalions on sweeps or during massacres. There were also cases in which they appeared to act with more autonomy; this was especially true in cases of civil patrols who acted aggressively toward other communities. On extremely rare occasions, the civil patrols acted on their own.

The patrollers from Xococ requested reinforcements from Cobán, and then the soldiers arrived. Case 0537, Agua Fría, Uspantán, Quiché, 1982.

Civil patrollers went out on sweeps and patrols looking for the guerrillas. The army also used them as guides, in part because of their familiarity with the terrain, but also as a form of defense against potential guerrilla attack. In most cases, civil patrollers were forced to go ahead of the soldiers and were the first to succumb to mines or ambushes.

Our strongest feeling about patrolling was fear, because of going out ahead of the army. The army never went first; the patrol always went as a lure. And we feared that there could be an attack at any moment. Nentón Workshop, Huehuetenango, October 18, 1996.

CAPTURES OF CIVILIANS

The civil patrols worked with the army to pursue and capture people fleeing in uninhabited areas; these often became mass round-ups, especially in the Ixil area and Alta Verapaz. They also carried out selective detentions in their communities. Another civil patrol activity was to search for alleged guerrilla collaborators whose names appeared on previously prepared lists. Such detentions were not limited to the alleged collaborators, however, but also included an element of exemplary terror: there were reports that people other than the ones being sought were detained and murdered (because their names were similar, they resisted detention, and so forth).

In many communities, the patrols would show up accompanied by neighbors who had fingered people in the community. The accusers often wore hoods, although in some cases there were visible signs that they had been cruelly tortured.

They lined them up. They took the list. There was a prayer from the Feast of the Agony. They left them in two pits, thirty-four men. Two who had been brought from the town began to dig the hole. They kept watch over them. They had the whole village covered. The thirty-two men who were catechists remained. Those were the men who began to work with the church. On January 18, 1982, a lot of soldiers and civilians arrived in Chirrum....The commander from Chirrum had the list. Case 7463, Chichupac, Rabinal, Baja Verapaz, 1982-83.

MASSACRES AND MURDERS

The civil patrols murdered many people in their own communities. According to the testimonies, most of these murders took place without prior indications that the victims were involved in guerrilla military operations. Some of the victims may have been members of the guerrilla infrastructure in place in many communities

(Local Irregular Forces—FIL). At the same time, however, the killings were indiscriminate; anyone considered suspicious was liable to be targeted. These incidents were characterized by a disproportionate use of force, which was used against victims who were completely defenseless and who were often killed in front of their families.

On the first of November, 1982, at 6:00 in the morning, the civil patrollers (from San Francisco farm, Santa Avelina, Pamaxán) surprised them where they were sleeping in a hiding place, and they all began to run away. When they were too tired to keep running through the forest, the patrollers caught up with them. They were killed right there, slashed with machetes—cut to pieces and left in the place where they were killed. The eldest daughter was tortured and raped, and they didn't kill her until twelve noon. Case 3931, San Pedro La Esperanza, Uspantán, Quiché, 1982.

CONTROL OVER PEOPLE'S MOVEMENTS

Another civil patrol function was to watch and monitor fellow community members. People could not move freely within their own communities, or travel to other places to work, trade, or visit relatives or friends. In order for them to do so, the commissioner or the patrol commander had to authorize the departure and issue a pass that had to be presented to the military authorities upon arrival at the destination.

We couldn't go into town anymore because they would be waiting for us and the civil patrollers kept track of us. When we went into the town, they demanded to see our personal identity documents. We couldn't go out in groups of two or three, because they would treat us as if we were guerrillas. Case 0544, Aldea Río Negro, Rabinal, Baja Verapaz, 1982.

THE SPOILS OF WAR

Civil patrollers plundered the communities they destroyed, stealing property, clothing, food, livestock, and so forth; this was especially true during massacres and military incursions. Sometimes this was done in depopulated villages whose inhabitants had already fled. In other cases, however, ritualistic plundering preceded and followed mass killings.

They took things, chickens, cows. Eight days after leaving, they took out [people's] things and set fire to them. They took coffee, sugar, beds, furniture; they had mules; they didn't leave a single saint standing. My daughter, whom they killed, didn't have any clothes left. They took twelve cows that had recently calved; they broke my cooking pot, my cane-cutting machine, and they burned down three houses. They began to take our new clothes, hens, cows. They ate near the clinic. They took my fattened cow. They skinned her, and the soldiers and civilians ate her. They cut down our corn, bananas, sugar cane. They took our cloth wraps, sashes, hoes, machetes. Case 7463, Chichupac, Rabinal, Baja Verapaz, 1982-83.

SOLIDARITY AND RESISTANCE

Despite the civil patrols' impact on communities, and the fact that many were implicated in serious human rights violations, there were also instances of mutual support and resistance among patrollers. These centered on avoiding the adverse consequences of being denounced, or sharing the burden of obligatory patrol duty through acts of solidarity, such as covering a sick patroller's rounds. Such actions were possible in areas where patrollers had not adopted the counterinsurgency ideology but patrolled in order to preserve their unity and forestall accusations against the community. Some patrollers helped families search for victims or used their positions to protect others from further danger.

The mother realized that her son (he was a patroller) hadn't arrived. She went to a group of patrollers on duty and said to them, "What have they done with my son? Where have they taken him?" Then one of them helped her look for him. One of the patrollers wanted to pick up the body, but it couldn't be done because he was dead, and they saw that his throat had been mutilated; they had beaten him. Case 362, Cantón Racaná, Santa María Chiquimula, Totonicapán, 1984.

There were also cases of patrollers who acted in defense of people in their community, even to the extent of confronting the soldiers or requesting the release of someone in detention.

The wife of the civil patrol commander gave us five pounds of corn to make some tortillas, since they were on their way to the detachment with some other men to speak on behalf of their detained compañeros. *When they arrived, the captain said, "Here come the rest of the guerrillas." They came close to dying. When they came in, Don Marcos Sical and his companions (patrollers) were the ones who were left in the community.* Case 3069, Chua Tiox Cheé, Concul, Rabinal, Baja Verapaz, 1981.

While these acts of solidarity were not common, they are examples of the adaptive strategies developed by communities as a form of self-protection. There were also cases of refusal to patrol or protests against obligatory civil patrol duty. Beginning in 1986, some of these initiatives in opposition to the civil patrols developed into an incipient social movement, the Council of Ethnic Communities Runujel Junam (CERJ). The CERJ grew stronger over time and, by the early nineties, had become the organized representation of an increasingly open rejection of the civil patrols, which led eventually to their dismantling in 1996.

Chapter Nine

THE METHODOLOGY OF HORROR

This chapter attempts to address the question of how such atrocities could have been committed in Guatemala. Exposing the methodology used will help to determine needed reforms of the army and state apparatus. This could lead to concrete measures to make the shared desire and demand of "Never again!" a reality. Some of these methods are analyzed based on testimonies compiled by the REMHI project of members of the army, the intelligence corps, and the civil patrols. Some data on guerrilla actions against the civilian population are also provided.

The impact of militarization on Guatemalan society reaches far beyond the end of the armed conflict and has significant consequences for the future in terms of how the security forces are trained, their ability to operate with impunity, education about violence, and the perpetuation of clandestine power structures.

FORCED RECRUITMENT

Throughout most of the armed conflict, the army used forced recruitment to fill its ranks.[1] Most soldiers are lower-class young people, and a high percentage of them are of Mayan origin. Since the time of the liberal revolution, however, virtually the entire officer corps is made up of ladinos (traditionally dominant, non-indigenous Guatemalans) trained in military academies and special forces schools.

Soldiers were kept under intense psychological pressure throughout their military training. From the moment that they were rounded up (the customary means of forced recruitment), soldiers were trained in a system designed to suppress their identity and premised on absolute submission, isolation from familiar social surroundings, and training in a system of values and customs that was completely devoid of any notion of human rights or international humanitarian law.

At that time they were grabbing people to do their service. Whoever did not serve was a guerrilla. "We'll kill you," they said. We said that, in that case,

---

[1] Twenty percent of rural youths were forced into two years of military service, during which time, in addition to military customs, they acquired other habits of a hygienic, linguistic, and social nature (alcohol consumption and prostitution, for example).

we better go. We were a group of about twenty from the village, and we decided to do our service. We came. It was the first battalion that showed up. Case 9524, Barillas, Sololá, Quiché, not dated.

Other young people who volunteered for military service also describe the contrast between their image of the army and security forces, and their experiences once they were on the inside.

Those of us who joined voluntarily went with a different mentality about what the army was, right? But when I began to see their methods, what it was they were really doing, I wanted to back out. But I said to myself, "If I get the hell out of here, these guys will kill me, because I have already seen a lot." Case 1871, (former intelligence agent of the G-2), different locations, 1981-84.

Despite the risk, many soldiers who were forcibly recruited refused to remain in the army. Desertion appears to have been commonplace, even though deserters who were recaptured were harshly punished.

SPECIAL FORCES

Intelligence corps and special forces used soldiers who had completed their military training and had combat experience. The selection process emphasized skills the army considered relevant to the counterinsurgency struggle; basically, those associated with controlling the population, along with an inclination toward absolute obedience.

Financial benefits did not result only from promotions; many members of the army and intelligence corps reaped the advantages of their positions of power. The coercive power associated with military credentials allowed the bearer to use accusations and denunciations in order to blackmail people and obtain personal favors.

Anibal Pérez and Pajuil joined La 2 or rather, they joined the army many years ago. They began as soldiers doing their military service. What happened is that they knew certain people: Pajuil was first; he knew several people and so they sponsored him to join La 2. They recommended him. Like I told you, a person gets ahead there if he has a sponsor or operates extremely well. Then he begins to advance and to move up. Key Source 80, former G-2, not dated.

AN EDUCATION IN VIOLENCE

We completed three months that they said were for study. They arrived at a firing range and sent us to grab about three hundred dogs. We grabbed them and they shut us in together. "Okay, listen, this is the meat that we are going to eat today." They took us to a firing range located below the university among the gullies, and they set us to kill those dogs. They filled a cauldron with blood, like a barrel. Each one of us had a disposable cup filled with blood and had to down it. Whoever didn't drink it was two-faced. They gave us each a cup of dog blood. They didn't serve us lunch that day in order to get us to eat that; our lunch was that cup of blood. During the meal they gave us dog stew. This is the reason many people deserted: they got sick. That was how they ended the course. Case 9524, Barillas, Sololá, Quiché, not dated.

There is a sociopolitical structure and methodology underlying torture, rape, or massacres; there is also a psychosocial framework for training, and a set of dominant values and organizational strategies that, in many cases, remains intact. This system largely explains the extreme destructiveness of the political repression, and it remains visible in current patterns of postwar violence.

FOSTERING VIOLENCE

In order to carry out its actions, the army developed a military training system based on forcible recruitment, trained obedience, strict control over groups, and complicity in atrocities.

During the training period, the army tried to instill in its soldiers an ideology that would serve as a frame of reference to justify their actions psychologically. The army fostered a sense of group unity and morale, and a preconditioned hostility toward anything that could be related to the guerrillas. In this context, the act of serving the army was in itself a direct asset for the good of the country. This portrayal of the conflict was designed to present the army as a victim. Poverty was blamed on guerrilla actions, and the mother country was glorified as a supreme entity that required unanimous cooperation to ward off the foreign threat of communism.

They put confusing ideas into your head there. For example, they tell you that, in Guatemala, "We can't allow ourselves to be conquered. Nothing to do with communism. Communism comes to take away lands and everything. It comes to exploit; it comes to do this and it comes to do that." They brainwash you; they brainwash you good, to see how the movement is. They say to them: "Look, you know that such and such." And the soldier gets indignant and says: "Yes, the ones who caused this are the guerrillas, and that's why Guatemala is poor." And you start to react, but why? Because they have already brainwashed you. "Look, you know that the guerrillas have come to do this." And they train you like that, all those things. So with a word they all become enemies of the people, of the whole country.

And when you are in training, you say, "That's true." Key Source 80, former intelligence officer of the G-2, not dated.

Violence was remunerated and became the group norm. Stories of how cruelty was rewarded with promotions and awards provide a stark illustration of the objectives of military training and methods.

One of the most important variables for promotion and enhancing one's status was not how well one followed orders, but rather the brutality with which they were carried out. The ability to kill, to take initiative during massacres, and to demonstrate cruelty in the course of operations were implicitly valued by the army and other security forces. Internal competition to ascend the ranks was an added incentive for agents and officers to become increasingly involved in repression. A perverse system was created in which disregard for human life was a prerequisite for promotion. This further demonstrates the level of involvement of officers and mid-level personnel, since those who failed to participate in these types of activities were not promoted.

COMPELLED OBEDIENCE

Failure to obey orders was met with harsh physical punishment, isolation in small cells, and other forms of degradation. These punishments were not limited to the transgressor, however; the entire group was often penalized for individual deviations from the norm. The "buddy system" was the method of choice to encourage members to police each other; it served as an internal monitoring system.

Let's say they told you to kill this person. You couldn't say, "I won't do it," because they had drilled into us that an order was to be obeyed without question. Case 1871 (former G-2), different locations, 1981-84.

For the repressive apparatus, the total compartmentalization of activities was an effective system; it minimized the risk of disobedience, which, in turn, increased conformity with the assigned duty and with the established hierarchy. For the military chiefs, focusing on one specific assignment encouraged conformity without raising the issue of individual ethics or esteem.

This system also allowed people to gradually increase their involvement in repression. This phenomenon, known in psychology as the "foot in the door" approach[2] was used deliberately and systematically not only to foster obedience,

---

[2] In Greece, as well as in the military training of SS officers in Nazi Germany, the military selected future torturers based on their deference and submission to authority. They first assigned the apprentice to guard prisoners and later to join arrest squads. This was followed by beating prisoners, observing torture sessions and, only then, directly engaging in torture. Step by step, an obedient individual became an agent of cruelty. Obedience bred acceptance (Staub 1989).

but also to increase acceptance of repressive acts. If a perpetrator began to feel too deeply implicated, or if discord arose among perpetrators, they risked death because, by that point, it was too late to backtrack.

> *In order to get points with the Office, they put you through tests that gradually eliminate people. They stain your hands with blood. This is important to make you loyal, since then you can't back out. Or, if you want out, they kill you. They order you to kill to implicate you, to test you. They give you a target.* Myrna Mack Foundation interview with Noel de Jesús Beteta Alvarez in the Centro Preventivo de la Zona 18, April 7, 1994.

As if these devices weren't enough, the army organized group reinforcement sessions to carry out explicit assignments emphasizing group loyalty—genuine blood pacts. This was an attempt to discourage any kind of dissent by emphasizing the negative repercussions for everyone involved; references were even made to other Latin American countries that were prosecuting military authorities involved in repression.

> *When the problem was going on in Argentina—when a soldier stood up in court to tell so and so to remember what he had done—they brought us together. And they showed us the videos and they got out news clippings from Argentina to say that we should never let this happen here in Guatemala. This was ten years ago. Why? Because of fear, I mean, they instruct and train people not to betray them. There are lots of officers' meetings to make sure no one talks. This is what they were instilling in people—so that their power wouldn't be weakened and so that we wouldn't turn on each other. And I think they were successful, because up until now this hasn't happened.* Key Source 80, former G-2, not dated.

ENFORCING COMPLICITY

In an attempt to force the complicity of young officers who might resist participating in atrocities, the army developed a system of operations designed to involve them from the outset. According to some testimonies, this discouraged guerrilla infiltration. The murder of drifters or alleged criminals became a kind of "social cleansing" that was frequently intertwined with counterinsurgency activities.

> *The psychological operations that they do to the people who work there compromise them so that they can't talk. They went there and pressured them and shut them up; they silenced them. If they don't buy their silence with money, they buy it with repression, with threats. This is what they did. They shut them up.* Key Source 80, former G-2, not dated.

The intelligence apparatus had all the characteristics of a mafia. There are numerous tales of personal favors—including abductions or disappearances stemming from family or sentimental problems—which were repaid with protection, promotions, or a returned favor. Anything could be accomplished through this system, as long as it was not detrimental to the internal power structure or, later on, to the army's attempts to gain legitimacy.

CONTEMPT FOR HUMAN LIFE: "THE STEP OF DEATH"

Becoming inured to suffering was the first step in training for violent acts. Contempt for life was not just a feature of military operations; it was also built into military training in the form of total disregard for the dignity and lives of the soldiers. This desensitization also involved celebrating and normalizing horror as if it were a festive occasion. The widespread atrocities of that period were also an integral part of military training.

> When I got there, they sent me to Senahú, because we were going to travel to the place on foot. So when I got there, I got out and I asked for the officers, and they weren't there, and the ones from La 2 weren't either. And they yelled to me, "Hurry or you're going to miss out on something good." And when I got there they only had one of the boys left, and they were cutting off his head. That is what I was missing. Key Source 80, former G-2, not dated.

Learning to kill was part of the training and methodology for military operations or abductions. In the lexicon of military instruction, it was referred to as "the step of death." Soldiers learned different methods of killing, how to organize mass killings, and how to conceal corpses.

> "Okay, today we are going to learn how to kill people." So you make some practice holes. This is how you make the practice holes, after you have studied the theory. But that is not the practice. You are going to go and kill your compañero. They just tell you, "Look, you grab like this, and kill like so, and you throw him away like this. But before killing him you turn him over." After you have learned the "step of death," you are taught firsthand how to kill. You calmly shoot him in the chest or the forehead—the coup de grâce—and then to the grave. So death is a step that we study. After that it's a matter of practice. Once you are in the place you will be assigned. They would torture one day, they would torture the next day, the third day, and then there was a rest period of a week or so. [The detained] were always fed, but only a little bit. So after a week we looked at what we could do next. The person there who gave orders to kill was the second section chief. The second section chief was the S-2 officer. He specifically gave orders

even to the point of killing someone, finishing someone off. Case 1741 (perpetrator), Izabal, 1980-83.

EXTENDING CONTROL

When the commander's expectations were not met by his subordinates, or when "specialists" got out of control or knew too much, they were killed. Over the years, many members of the intelligence services fell victim to their own colleagues.

Maybe you've been working for two or three years and the other guy for ten or twelve years. You are called in quietly, secretly: "That one, tonight we are going to finish him off because he isn't doing anything. We're going to get rid of him." They invite him for a Coca Cola or a drink and...that's it. Some of those from the special company are already dead, most of them are dead, because they went around singing, "I'm from the Intelligence Service, I am this..." And, they were yelling in the streets and drinking, getting involved with women. And sometimes they even had women who were also in the guerrillas, and these guys would give them a weapon. Case 1741 (perpetrator), Izabal, 1980-83.

The level of control over the lives of implicated agents and officers transcends their direct participation, and even their period of service in the security forces. It extends throughout the social network under army control, and it requires observing the code of silence in order to avoid being killed or having future employment opportunities blocked.

THE WAYS OF HORROR

The interrogator is not an anomaly, bloodthirsty or psychopathic, lacking in sensitivity (a widespread notion that comes from ignorance of the subject matter); above all, he is a unique resource, whose training in various fields of science, the arts, religion, customs, and so on, gives him access to the core inconsistencies and enable him to consciously delve into the complex inner world of what is inaptly termed "Human Being" (Ejército de Guatemala 1980).

MASSACRES: THE ANATOMY OF DESTRUCTION

Explaining the Unexplainable

The ones responsible are the army, the civil patrols, and the former military commissioner. Seventy-five army troops and one hundred civil pa-

trollers participated in these murders. They were caught on the path. They tortured them and bound them hand and foot with ropes. And as this was happening, the patrollers took off their clothes before killing them, leaving them naked there. They began to beat and torture them, and they threw them down right there on the path. The [neighboring people] left the bodies of those two "brothers" there on the path. They couldn't get them; they couldn't bury them. Because maybe they would be on the lookout near the victim for whoever went to get the body, and they would kill them too. Case 3243, Aldea Panamán, Buena Vista, Uspantán, Quiché, 1982.

As part of its counterinsurgency policy, the army routinely carried out collective murders of alleged collaborators (FIL[3]) in order to destroy the guerrillas and their infrastructure. Subsequently, particularly between 1980 and 1983, the army annihilated entire communities considered to be the guerrillas' social support base. Civilians militarized as civil patrollers and military commissioners participated in many of these massacres either under duress or as a result of their previous indoctrination.

Although these massacres will never be fully explained (Falla 1993, 46), the army offensive, the progression of massacres, and their internal structure, obeyed a certain logic.[4] They were not merely a spontaneous reaction by soldiers or officers. In order to isolate the guerrillas, the army launched a series of large-scale, indiscriminate massacres against their civilian support base. The army routed these civilians out of their hiding places in the hills and forests; it terrorized them; it laid siege to them to starve them out, after having burned their homes and stored crops, destroyed their household utensils, and stolen their belongings. In this way, people were forced to surrender and subsequently clustered into "special camps." This practice of massacres, pursuit, burning, and siege is known as the scorched-earth policy.

The guerrillas also carried out massacres against some population groups and occasionally against an entire community that either opposed them or had been drawn into the counterinsurgency struggle by the army.

---

[3] Local Irregular Forces (*Fuerzas Irregulares Locales*—FIL) were clandestine guerrilla organizations that served as an infrastructure and support base. They were known as Local Political-Military Organizations in the army's counterinsurgency lexicon.

[4] In 1980, General Tho, who for many years was South Vietnam's assistant chief of state for Armed Forces Operations, described South Vietnam's counterinsurgency policy as along the same lines as that implemented by the Guatemalan army: (1) Destroy the main enemy force and "eliminate the enemy infrastructure"; (2) use the strategic "clear and control" concept, since if a force was not kept in place to maintain control of the area, the Viet Cong could return and resume its activities; (3) later, put a development phase into place, similar to the model villages and development poles (Falla 1987).

THE MASSACRES
(Testimonies compiled by REMHI)

Among the testimonies compiled by the REMHI project, 29.9 percent include massacres, defined as "collective murders of three or more people" (1570 out of 5238 cases).

In this chapter, however, we have further narrowed the definition of massacre to "collective murders associated with community destruction" (422 massacres). A comparison with the other collective murders (massacres that were more selective in nature) yields similar results in terms of geographical distribution, date, and responsibility. The majority of the massacres examined (70 percent) occurred in 1981-82. An estimated total of 14,000 massacre victims, including dead and disappeared, is based on average numbers of victims, although the total may be as high as 18,000 victims.

Most of the recorded massacres took place in El Quiché Department (263), followed by Alta Verapaz (63), Huehuetenango (42), Baja Verapaz (16), El Petén (10), and Chimaltenango (9). There were also massacres in other departments (see the list of massacres below), and certainly, many other cases were never recorded. Data on the perpetrators demonstrate the key role massacres played in the overall counterinsurgency policy: the army is implicated in 90.52 percent of the massacres (acting alone in 55 percent of the cases and in conjunction with military commissioners and civil patrollers in the rest). Civil patrollers and military commissioners were involved in 35.54 percent of the cases (as the only force in 4.5 percent of these case and, in the remainder, acting with the army); guerrilla forces were responsible for 3.79 percent of the cases; and unknown forces for 1.18 percent.

Countless Deaths

> *They killed many people—pregnant women, old men, old women. No one saw exactly how many; everyone was too afraid to count.* Case 6021, Yoltán, San Mateo Ixtatán, Huehuetenango, 1981.

Most of the massacres resulted in many, even mass, deaths (31.21 percent involved more than twenty-one victims). Most massacres were indiscriminate in that the victims were of all ages and categories.[5] In the testimonies examined, most of the victims were men (there were male victims in 82 percent of massacres), although women were also included in the majority of massacres (62 percent). Some selective massacres only targeted men as most likely to be guerrilla collaborators.

---

[5] A breakdown by factors shows victims belonging to different population groups in most massacres.

The Time of Destruction

> *At first they said that the army didn't cause any harm. But once they saw that they actually destroyed the community, that they burned it down, and killed, and burned up whoever didn't protect themselves, many fled into the hills. That's how they saved themselves.* Case 2512, El Desengaño, Uspantán, Quiché, 1981.

Most of the massacres[6] were preceded by a deteriorating social climate, increased selective repression, and measures taken by the population to protect itself from the violence. Military persecution leading up to the massacres usually included murders and disappearances. Prior attacks by the guerrillas or civil patrollers are occasionally described.

In other words, the prevailing climate of repression and persecution was consistent with the aim to destroy community or cooperative leadership and eliminate the guerrilla presence. The facts reveal, in practice, a decision to annihilate certain communities.

> *The army was killing the people, and so they decided to collaborate with the guerrillas. The guerrillas advised the community. The people believed in them, and when the army realized this, it came to kill those in the community.* Case 4922, Aldea Xix, Chajul, Quiché, 1980.

Analysis shows that after October 1981 there are more testimonies describing increasingly indiscriminate massacres (a greater element of surprise; more instances of congregating the population into one place, separating people into groups, and pursuing them into the hills; a high percentage of female victims; widespread environmental destruction; and more cases of clandestine burial) than in the earlier stage. This suggests that, from that date on, massacres played a more important role, were increasingly premeditated, and included more community-

---

[6] For this analysis a team selected 165 massacres and indexed them, producing preliminary reports linking different testimonies about a single incident and creating a format for data analysis that included general variables, background information, modus operandi, victims, how the massacre was carried out, and aftermath. As with the indexing of the testimonies, *the absence of a particular variable does not mean that it was not actually present, but rather that it did not appear as such in the testimonies of the survivors; therefore, the frequency of a given variable may, in fact, be much higher.* Overall, the sample is representative of the proportions of large-scale violence compiled by REMHI for each department, with the exception of Alta Verapaz (the proportion is underestimated) and Baja Verapaz (the proportion is overestimated). The sample also produced higher values for guerrilla massacres (7 percent in the sample, compared to 3.4 percent of all massacres). However, since there were fewer of these cases, an analysis of a larger sample better illustrated the pattern of massacres attributed to the guerrillas. Several other testimonies of massacres compiled from the Ixcán, San Marcos, and Atitlán, which were not included in the sample, also appear in the text.

wide destruction, which coincided with a major army offensive that began in Chimaltenango and moved into broad swaths of the Highlands.[7]

The Onset of Death

The soldiers come for a certain period of time and they position themselves around the church, the highest place. They were keeping track of everything from there. They were waiting there with their weapons, as if they were waiting for animals to pass by. Case 1640, Sechaj, Los Pinares, Alta Verapaz, 1982.

Massacres frequently contained an element of surprise (52 percent). This suggests that surprise was part of a pre-determined modus operandi that included arriving at the most propitious time for rounding up the most people and taking control of the entire village. The controlled and calm atmosphere in which most massacres were carried out, combined with the lack of any allusions in the testimonies, indicate that the army did not meet with armed resistance from the communities.

In other cases, the fact that the population fled upon realizing what was happening may have helped prevent additional massacres. Following the massacres in Cuarto Pueblo and Piedras Blancas, for example, the army arrived in Mayalán (Ixcán, El Quiché) only to find it had been abandoned (REMHI, *La guerra en Ixcán* 1997).

We began to post lookouts to be ready for the army. Some of us were together when the army arrived and the soldiers began to fire their weapons and burn houses. They only killed one pregnant woman. And all of us fled into the hills. Case 8074, Mayalán, Ixcán, Quiché, 1980.

The practice of congregating the population appears in one in three testimonies concerning exemplary terror and is an example of an inordinately perverse form of deceit.

The soldiers came. They held a meeting. They said they were going to distribute toys. They gave dolls to some of the little kids, but not to all of them. Afterward they assembled all of us men, they lined us up, and they asked for our cédulas [identity documents]. Well, they gave out the gifts, and the soldiers had parked a tank in case anyone tried to flee. Case 7446, Chichupac, Baja Verapaz, 1982.

_____

[7] The first phase was a strategic offensive in Chimaltenango and southern El Quiché, which began in mid-November 1981 during the presidency of General Lucas. According to Aguilera, the Victoria 82 campaign consisted of a predominantly military, offensive phase against the main guerrilla fronts, their strategic forces, and their civilian support base (Aguilera Peralta, 1985).

Pursuing people as they fled into the hills appears third in order of frequency (17 percent) and demonstrates the practice of indiscriminately finishing off the population. Pursuit into the hills was part of the army's modus operandi in many areas, including Alta Verapaz, Ixcán, the Ixil region, and Huehuetenango. It was the central feature in some cases, however; during large-scale massacres in Chimaltenango and las Guacamayas, defenseless people were killed as they were fleeing.

The use of lists to search for people characterized more selective massacres of leaders or individuals accused of belonging to the guerrillas.

The army tells us that there are guerrillas among us and they have a list. They read the list, and we ask, "Who then?" And they mentioned the names and they harmed them. They took the detainees and they killed them. Case 1369, Tzununul, Sacapulas, Quiché, 1981.

One in six massacres analyzed occurred on a special day for the community involved. Whether it was market day, a holiday, or a religious ceremony, attacks were scheduled for special days in order to take advantage of the people coming together in order to maximize the impact. In some cases the choice of day was clearly symbolic (Christmas Day in Palob, Bijolom, and Quejchip, in the Nebaj area). This aspect, together with the concentration of the population and the army's evident control over the situation, demonstrates that the massacres were premeditated. The massacre of Cuarto Pueblo (Ixcán, El Quiché, 1982), for example, lasted for three days; it was not a reflex action during the course of combat. According to witnesses, the army was in constant radio contact with the base, and a helicopter provided air support to the operation. The chain of command reached the highest echelons: the massacre was the result of strategic plans and tactics in a campaign directed by officers and carried out by troops.

The helicopter came and flew over Cuarto Pueblo. At first, the people were frightened and left, but then the helicopter flew off and the people came back to the market. They didn't realize that the soldiers were approaching and surrounding the people. They had them congregated there for about two days. And the soldiers put wires red, red hot from the fire into them, stuck into their mouths and all the way down into their stomachs. They kicked others, not caring if it was a little child or a woman, or if she was pregnant. They didn't spare anyone there. Case 920, Cuarto Pueblo, Ixcán, Quiché, 1982.

The Path of the Massacres

In addition to torching and destroying homes, over half of the massacre cases examined include accounts of torture and mass atrocities (56 percent) and seizure of members of the population (52 percent).

The sizzling fat pours out, you see; how the poor women's fat pours out of them. It was like when it rains and the water runs into the ditches. That's how the fat pours out, pure water. "And what is that?" I thought, when I went in. It's pure fat pouring out of the poor women, running out like water. Case 6070, Petanac, Huehuetenango, 1982.

Destruction of nature (burning and destroying crops and livestock, 30 percent), and theft and looting (23 percent) are part of the utter destruction that elevate massacres to the level of scorched earth.

After all this, after they had already killed a lot of people, the commissioners from several hamlets surrounding Cahabón got together and, with the soldiers, went to gather up everything those people had: their machetes, their new clothes, new underwear, hoes, grinding stones, pails. Those commissioners got together and took everything that people used in their homes. Case 5931, Sechaj, Pinares, Alta Verapaz, 1982.

Burials in common graves, often dug by the victims themselves, are described in a significant percentage of testimonies (17 percent). Such clandestine burials were frequently used to hide the evidence of the murders. Sometimes, however, the army used other methods to conceal incidents.

They began to carry off the dead, and they went to dig a hole. They put them all in there, about seventy people with their feet and hands in the air. Well, that was that. They say that on the second day, the people went to get everyone, so sad. They tied them all up and they blindfolded them and they went to kill them in Armenia Lorena. I saw it. They were tortured, burned, shot. When night fell, they went to throw them under the bridges. They were all loaded into a truck, and two or three were thrown out at each bridge. They scattered them all along the route to Coatepeque. They were all killed unjustly. The people from Tiubuj died; they said there was a guerrilla cooperative there. Even now, who knows? I don't know. There was another massacre just like the one at Sacuchum Dolores in Armenia Lorena. Case 8649, Sacuchum Dolores, Tiubuj, San Marcos, 1982.

At other times the massacres occurred during large-scale ground operations supported by aerial bombardments of the areas. At least one out of every nine communities examined were bombed either before or after the massacres. The most heavily bombed areas were the communities in the Ixil region and Sacapulas in El Quiché, certain parts of Baja Verapaz (such as Las Vegas), and Huehuetenango.

It was when the army had taken all of the people from Palob, which would have been during the first massacre. Then all the people had to leave, more than three hundred people left to save their lives. But the army pursued

them and found them in the hills above the village. It found them there and
massacred most of the people. Case 7727, Palob, Nebaj, Quiché, 1982.

Some communities were treated particularly harshly, with unrelenting persecution and repeated massacres. At least one in nine massacres followed earlier
massacres in the same community. This pattern was particularly pronounced in
the Ixcán Grande cooperatives, against the Ixil population (in areas such as Palob,
Salquil, Xeucalbitz, Chel), and isolated areas of Uspantán, where people had
taken refuge.

Life after Death

Following a massacre, the people's most frequent reaction was to flee for their
lives (40 percent), either into the hills and forests, into exile, or to other communities.

But the army was killing us, who knows how many people they killed. So
we spent a year and a half living only in the hills. We couldn't go to our
fields because the army was on the lookout for us. The patrollers were there.
We couldn't come out of the hills; we often went hungry. Case 3624, Las
Guacamayas, Uspantán, Quiché, 1982.

In the testimonies analyzed, one in six villages where a massacre occurred was
razed.

They leveled the community. Those who survived left. They fled into the
hills. They didn't live there anymore, they abandoned everything. Some of
us were already there; it was nearly two years of suffering, of fleeing in the
hills, and seeing how to get a little corn—something to eat. We lived on the
run. Case 8341, Los Josefinos, Petén, 1982.

Another significant number of villages that were strategically located from the
army's standpoint remained under direct military control (22 percent). Most survivors hid in the hills and forests out of fear, and they were often pursued, captured, and relocated. Many others died as a result of army persecution that followed them into the hills.[8] Still others ultimately were able to find refuge in
inaccessible jungle or mountainous areas, where they established new community situations; this was the case in areas of Alta Verapaz, or the CPRs in the
Quiché and Petén departments.

The same thing happened to several groups besides ours: they captured
some and killed others. A total of fourteen were massacred, including sev-

---

[8] One in ten victims whose deaths are reported in the testimonies apparently died while
being pursued in the wilderness.

eral women. Those who were captured were congregated in the center of town and could only go to work nearby, always passing by the guard post. They count the tortillas, what time you leave, what time you come back. Case 0902, Santa María Tzejá, Ixcán, Quiché, 1982.

Survivors were often unable to return to their communities. There were others, however, who went back once the immediate danger had passed to find their family members, recover their belongings, or try to save people who had been left behind wounded. Thus, many of them, with trepidation and sorrow, witnessed firsthand the devastation of their lives.

That was where they finished those people off. There was a lot of smoke, and it stank. So we went to see. So many people were there among the rushes, on the riverbanks. Some still had some life in them, but we couldn't do anything for them because they were losing so much blood. Other people's hearts were still beating. Case 2295, Lajcholaj, San Rafael Independencia, Huehuetenango, 1981.

Guerrilla Massacres

Almost all of the guerrilla massacres occurred in 1982, when the communities were highly militarized by the civil patrol presence.[9] In many cases, victims report that these massacres were provoked by their refusal to collaborate with the guerrillas. In some cases (two out of twelve), the massacres were preceded by a civil patrol attack.

[It happened] because, the day before the massacre, the patrollers went to search for the guerrillas in the place where they were camped above the community of Panamán. The patrollers from the hamlet brought back knapsacks with documents, overalls, and bibles. Case 8741, Lancetillo, Uspantán, Quiché, 1982.

Techniques such as the use of informers, congregating the people in one place, separating them into groups, and orgies were not reported in massacres attributed to guerrilla forces. There are, moreover, no cases of obligatory participation, rapes, repeated massacres, or razed hamlets. There is less of a tendency toward mass flight, although this occurred in some cases (three out of twelve). Lists were used more frequently in the guerrilla massacres documented by REMHI (five out of twelve). These factors suggest a more selective use of collective murders, which differentiates these cases in a general sense from massacres designed to eliminate communities.

---

[9] Of the sixteen massacres attributed to the guerrillas, twelve were analyzed in this sample.

By the time Don Domingo realized it, they were already near the house, and he grabbed his daughter and ran from the house together with his wife. They had already gotten about hundred meters away from the house when they fired their guns and set the house on fire. Case 8749, Rosario Monte María, Quiché, 1982.

At the first cross, that's where they killed them (the thirty-two). They didn't grab just anyone, but they had a list and followed the list. And whoever wasn't on the list, well, they weren't going to take that person. He'd be scared stiff, but they'd leave him there. Case 4700, La Estancia, Santa Cruz del Quiché, Quiché, 1980.

Most victims were men, although the killings were occasionally indiscriminate. Women were among the victims in half of the guerrilla massacres and, less frequently, the deaths of children or the elderly are reported.

They got to Santos's house looking for her husband (Benigno Coc Ixim), because he was the patrol chief. They didn't find him at home. This armed group opened fire and killed his mother and four of Benigno's brothers. After that, this armed group continued to carry out its massacres of other families. Case 0703, Lancetillo, Uspantán, Quiché, 1982.

The most indiscriminate guerrilla massacre occurred in Chacalté, where between sixty and one hundred people were killed.[10]

They spoke Ixil, and they had their faces covered with black bandanas. They were wearing green clothing, and they carried weapons, knapsacks, and some large weapons. Some of them were women. Case 4262, Chacalté, Chajul, Quiché, 1982.

He was patrolling with ten other men in a place called Balama, where the auxiliary courthouse was located. The guerrillas came and shot him in the forehead. Don Diego tried to run—he hid in the church—and that was where they killed him. There were many dead people in the church. A lot of blood was being spilt. Case 4277, Chacalté, Chajul, Quiché, 1982.

The victims also denounce atrocities and razing of houses in five of the massacres. There are fewer instances of destruction of nature (two), theft (one), and burning of corpses (two).

Francisco was shot at the guard post. They crushed Ana's head with a club, and Domingo Guzmán. Case 4264, Chacalté, Chajul, Quiché, 1982.

---

[10] During its exhumation, the Anthropological Forensic Team of the Archdiocesan Human Rights Office (ODHAG) found the remains of at least seventy-five skeletons in two pits.

These massacres led to increased civilian collaboration with the army and strengthened the civil patrols. In some cases, however, the same communities experienced subsequent massacres at the army's hands (as occurred in Chacalté in 1985).

So all the people here started to collaborate with the army. Case 8800, Lancetillo, Uspantán, Quiché, 1982.

They had to organize the civil patrols, and they had to merge into a single community. They couldn't live apart anymore because they were being killed. They had to support each other. Case 8734, Rosario Monte María, Quiché, 1982.

===

LIST OF MASSACRES

A total of 410 massacres were tabulated based on the original analysis of the testimonies. Additional massacres were documented as this report was being written. Therefore, the list below includes more massacres than those described in the analysis. The dates that appear below are the ones most frequently cited in the testimonies, taking into account that people are sometimes unable to recall such information exactly.

Key:

Ar = Army
Pol = Police
MC = Military Commissioner
PAC = Civil Patrol
G = Guerrilla
DS = Death Squad
In dates: 0 = month or year unknown

PLACE	DATE	FORCE
1 GUATEMALA (city), GUATEMALA (dept), GUATEMALA	1-80	Ar,Pol
2 RABINAL (city), RABINAL (munic.), BAJA VERAPAZ	9-81	Ar,Pol,MC,PAC
3 PICHEC (village), RABINAL, BAJA VERAPAZ	1-82	Ar,Pol,MC,PAC
4 CHIXIM (hamlet), CHUATEGUA (village), RABINAL, BAJA VERAPAZ	7-82	Ar
5 CHICHUPAC (hamlet), XEABAJ (village), RABINAL, BAJA VERAPAZ	1-82	Ar,Pol,PAC
6 PLAN DE SANCHEZ (hamlet), RAXJUT (village), RABINAL, BAJA VERAPAZ	7-82	Ar,Pol,MC,PAC
7 VEGAS SANTO DOMINGO (village), RABINAL, BAJA VERAPAZ	11-81	Ar,Pol,MC,PAC
8 XOCOC (village), RABINAL, BAJA VERAPAZ	2-82	Ar,MC,PAC
9 BUENA VISTA (hamlet), XOCOC (village), RABINAL, BAJA VERAPAZ	4-82	Ar,Pol,MC,PAC
10 CHIRRUM (village), RABINAL, BAJA VERAPAZ	1-82	Ar,Pol,PAC
11 RIO NEGRO (village), RABINAL, BAJA VERAPAZ	2-82	Ar,MC,PAC

12	LOS ENCUENTROS (hamlet), RIO NEGRO (village), RABINAL, BAJA VERAPAZ	4-82	Ar,PAC
13	PANACAL (village), RABINAL, BAJA VERAPAZ	9-81	Ar,PAC
14	LAGUNA CHISAJKAP (hamlet), CUBULCO (villa), CUBULCO, BAJA VERAPAZ	2-82	Ar,PAC
15	SUTUN (village), CUBULCO, BAJA VERAPAZ	11-81	Ar,PAC
16	RANCHO BEJUCO (hamlet), PACOC (village), EL CHOL, BAJA VERAPAZ	7-82	Ar,MC,PAC
17	EL APAZOTE (village), EL CHOL, BAJA VERAPAZ	8-82	Ar,MC,PAC
18	ROCJA PASACUC (hamlet), COBAN (city), COBAN, ALTA VERAPAZ	9-81	Ar,PAC
19	SAN JOSE RIO NEGRO (farm), COBAN (city), COBAN, ALTA VERAPAZ	1-81	Ar,MC,PAC
20	EL PETATE (farm), COBAN (city), COBAN, ALTA VERAPAZ	0-80	Ar,PAC
21	SACAAL (village), COBAN, ALTA VERAPAZ	0-82	Ar
22	SANIMTACA (farm), COBAN, ALTA VERAPAZ	6-83	Ar
23	SACACHE (farm), COBAN, ALTA VERAPAZ	0-82	Ar
24	SACOMUN (farm), COBAN, ALTA VERAPAZ	7-80	Ar
25	SACHAL (farm), COBAN, ALTA VERAPAZ	0-81	Ar,PAC
26	CHAMA (farm), COBAN, ALTA VERAPAZ	0-81	Ar,PAC
27	SALQUIL (farm), COBAN, ALTA VERAPAZ	0-82	Ar
28	CRUZ RAXMAX (farm), COBAN, ALTA VERAPAZ	0-82	Ar
29	EL PAIZAN (farm), COBAN, ALTA VERAPAZ	0-80	Ar,MC,PAC
30	COOPERATIVA SAMAC (farm), COBAN, ALTA VERAPAZ	6-83	Ar,MC,PAC
31	CHIQUIGÜITAL (village), SANTA CRUZ VERAPAZ, ALTA VERAPAZ	10-81	Ar
32	PAMBACH (hamlet), CHIQUIGÜITAL (village), SANTA CRUZ VERAPAZ, ALTA VERAPAZ	6-82	Ar
33	SAN CRISTOBAL VERAPAZ (municipio), ALTA VERAPAZ	0-82	Ar
34	LAS PACAYAS (village), SAN CRISTOBAL VERAPAZ, ALTA VERAPAZ	3-79	Ar
35	EL CONGUITO (hamlet), LAS PACAYAS (village), SAN CRISTOBAL VERAPAZ, ALTA VERAPAZ	0-81	??
36	NAJTILABAJ (village), SAN CRISTOBAL VERAPAZ, ALTA VERAPAZ	0-82	Ar
37	CHIRREXQUICHE (hamlet), NAJTILABAJ (village), SAN CRISTOBAL VERAPAZ, ALTA VERAPAZ	12-82	Ar,PAC
38	CHITUJ (hamlet), NAJTILABAJ (village), SAN CRISTOBAL VERAPAZ, ALTA VERAPAZ	3-82	Ar,PAC
39	CHITUJ (hamlet), NAJTILABAJ (village), SAN CRISTOBAL VERAPAZ, ALTA VERAPAZ	11-82	Ar,PAC
40	SAN LUCAS CHIACAL (village), SAN CRISTOBAL VERAPAZ, ALTA VERAPAZ	6-83	Ar,PAC
41	SAN LUCAS CHAAL (village), SAN CRISTOBAL VERAPAZ, ALTA VERAPAZ	0-80	Ar
42	SANTA INES CHICAR (farm), SAN CRISTOBAL VERAPAZ, ALTA VERAPAZ	0-80	Ar
43	SANTA INES CHICAR (farm), SAN CRISTOBAL VERAPAZ, ALTA VERAPAZ	0-81	Ar
44	KATALJI (village), SAN CRISTOBAL VERAPAZ, ALTA VERAPAZ	0-80	Ar
45	SAN ISIDRO (village), SAN CRISTOBAL VERAPAZ, ALTA VERAPAZ	0-80	Ar
46	SANIMTAKAJ (village), SAN CRISTOBAL VERAPAZ, ALTA VERAPAZ	0-80	??
47	TAQUINCO (hamlet), CAHABONCITO (village), PANZOS, ALTA VERAPAZ	2-0	Ar
48	PANZOS (village), PANZOS (town), ALTA VERAPAZ	5-78	Ar,MC,DS
49	YALIJUX (hamlet), SENAHU (town), SENAHU, ALTA VERAPAZ	0-80	Ar,MC
50	OXLAJUJA (TRECE AGUAS) (farm), SENAHU, ALTA VERAPAZ	0-78	Ar
51	SEMUY (hamlet), SETOC (village), SAN PEDRO CARCHA, ALTA VERAPAZ	0-80	Ar,PAC
52	SEMUY (hamlet), SETOC (village), SAN PEDRO CARCHA, ALTA VERAPAZ	0-82	Ar,PAC
53	SAIJA (farm), SETOC (village), SAN PEDRO CARCHA, ALTA VERAPAZ	0-80	Ar,MC
54	GANCHO CAOBA (farm), SETOC (village), SAN PEDRO CARCHA, ALTA VERAPAZ	0-83	Ar
55	CHIQUISIS (hamlet), CHIRREQUIM (village), SAN PEDRO CARCHA, ALTA VERAPAZ	6-82	MC,PAC
56	RAXRRUJA (hamlet), YALMACHAC (village), SAN PEDRO CARCHA, ALTA VERAPAZ	1-82	Ar
57	CAHABON (town), CAJABON, ALTA VERAPAZ	8-82	Ar,MC
58	CHICHAJ (hamlet), CAHABON (town), CAJABON, ALTA VERAPAZ	3-80	MC
59	SALAMTUN (farm), CAHABON (town), CAJABON, ALTA VERAPAZ	0-0	MC
60	CHI KA'HA (farm), CAHABON (town), CAJABON, ALTA VERAPAZ	0-0	MC

61	CHAJBELEN (village), CAJABON, ALTA VERAPAZ	8-82	Ar,MC
62	SACTA (hamlet), CHAJBELEN (village), CAJABON, ALTA VERAPAZ	0-80	Ar
63	CHIMOXAN (hamlet), CHAJBELEN (village), CAJABON, ALTA VERAPAZ	10-82	MC,PAC
64	CHIMOXAN (hamlet), CHAJBELEN (village), CAJABON, ALTA VERAPAZ	10-82	Ar,MC,PAC
65	SEGUAMO (hamlet), CHAJBELEN (village), CAJABON, ALTA VERAPAZ	9-82	Ar,MC,PAC
66	PINARES (hamlet), CANTZUM (village), CAJABON, ALTA VERAPAZ	4-80	Ar,MC,PAC
67	SEBALAMTE (hamlet), MARICHAJ (village), CAJABON, ALTA VERAPAZ	5-80	MC,PAC
68	SETZAPEC (village), CAJABON, ALTA VERAPAZ	6-81	Ar
69	SETZAPEC (village), CAJABON, ALTA VERAPAZ	6-82	Ar,MC
70	TZIBALPEC (farm), CAJABON, ALTA VERAPAZ	0-82	Ar,MC
71	CHISEC (town), CHISEC, ALTA VERAPAZ	1-82	Ar
72	CHISEC (town), CHISEC, ALTA VERAPAZ	2-82	Ar,PAC
73	SAWACHIL (hamlet), CHISEC (town), CHISEC, ALTA VERAPAZ	8-81	Ar
74	SETZI (hamlet), CHISEC (town), CHISEC, ALTA VERAPAZ	8-82	Ar
75	PECAJBA (hamlet), CHISEC (town), CHISEC, ALTA VERAPAZ	0-82	Ar,PAC
76	LAS RUINAS (hamlet), CHISEC (town), CHISEC, ALTA VERAPAZ	0-82	Ar,PAC
77	SAN MIGUEL SECHOCHOCH (farm), CHISEC (town), CHISEC, ALTA VERAPAZ	3-82	G
78	XAMAN (farm), CHISEC, ALTA VERAPAZ	10-95	Ar
79	SEAMAY (hamlet), REBELQUICHE (village), CHISEC, ALTA VERAPAZ	9-81	Ar
80	SEMANZANA (hamlet), CHAHAL (town), CHAHAL, ALTA VERAPAZ	0-82	Ar
81	SAN MARCOS (farm), EL ESTOR, IZABAL	0-82	Ar
82	CAULOTES (village), CAMOTAN, CHIQUIMULA	12-81	Ar,MC
83	SACALA (hamlet), LAS LOMAS (village), SAN MARTIN JILOTEPEQUE, CHIMALTENANGO	0-0	Ar
84	EL MOLINO (village), SAN MARTIN JILOTEPEQUE, CHIMALTENANGO	0-81	Ar
85	CHUABAJITO (hamlet), PATZAJ (village), SAN MARTIN JILOTEPEQUE, CHIMALTENANGO	0-80	Ar,MC
86	SAN JOSE LAS CANOAS (farm), SAN MARTIN JILOTEPEQUE, CHIMALTENANGO	0-83	Ar
87	RETIRO LAS CANOAS (farm), SAN MARTIN JILOTEPEQUE, CHIMALTENANGO	8-82	Ar,DS
88	SANTA ANITA LAS CANOAS (farm), SAN MARTIN JILOTEPEQUE, CHIMALTENANGO	5-88	Ar,MC
89	PATZAJ (village), COMALAPA, CHIMALTENANGO	0-81	Ar
90	XIQUIN SANAI (village), COMALAPA, CHIMALTENANGO	0-82	Ar
91	SAN DIEGO CHIMACHOY (village), SAN ANDRES ITZAPA, CHIMALTENANGO	10-82	Ar,MC
92	LA VICTORIA (village), OSTUNCALCO, QUETZALTENANGO	0-81	Ar
93	TUICUBNIBE (PARAJE) (farm), CONCEPCION CHIQUIRICHAPA, QUETZALTENANGO	8-84	Ar
94	BARRANCA DE GALVEZ (village), SAN MARCOS, SAN MARCOS	8-84	Ar
95	EL TABLERO (village), SAN PEDRO SACATEPEQUEZ, SAN MARCOS	1-82	Ar
96	SACUCHUM (village), SAN PEDRO SACATEPEQUEZ, SAN MARCOS	0-82	Ar
97	TOJCUTO (village), TAJUMULCO, SAN MARCOS	2-0	Ar
98	BULLAJ (village), TAJUMULCO, SAN MARCOS	6-81	Ar,PAC
99	TOTANA (village), TAJUMULCO, SAN MARCOS	1-81	Ar
100	TOTANA (village), TAJUMULCO, SAN MARCOS	2-0	Ar,MC
101	VILLA NUEVA (village), TAJUMULCO, SAN MARCOS	2-0	Ar
102	LAGUNA ESCONDIDA (farm), IXCAHUIN (canton) (village), NUEVO PROGRESO, SAN MARCOS	6-83	Ar
103	EL TUMBADOR (town), EL TUMBADOR, SAN MARCOS	0-81	Ar
104	EL RETIRO (village), EL TUMBADOR, SAN MARCOS	0-81	Ar
105	TUIBUU (village), TOCACHE (village), SAN PABLO, SAN MARCOS	0-82	Ar
106	SAN NICOLAS (village), CHIANTLA, HUEHUETENANGO	4-82	Ar,PAC
107	MIXLAJ (village), CHIANTLA, HUEHUETENANGO	0-81	Ar
108	TZALA (hamlet), NENTON (town), NENTON, HUEHUETENANGO	7-82	Ar
109	YALAMBOJOCH (village), NENTON, HUEHUETENANGO	1-82	Ar

110	SAN FRANCISCO (hamlet), YALAMBOJOCH (village), NENTON, HUEHUETENANGO	6-82	Ar
111	NUBILA ENTRE 2 RIOS (farm), NENTON, HUEHUETENANGO	6-82	Ar,PAC
112	CATARINA (village), JACALTENANGO, HUEHUETENANGO	1-81	Ar
113	LIMONAR (hamlet), LA LAGUNA (village), JACALTENANGO, HUEHUETENANGO	1-82	Ar
114	TZISBAJ (village), JACALTENANGO, HUEHUETENANGO	9-82	Ar
115	LA LIBERTAD (town), LA LIBERTAD, HUEHUETENANGO	0-81	Ar
116	SAN MIGUEL ACATAN (town), SAN MIGUEL ACATAN, HUEHUETENANGO	0-0	G
117	JOM (hamlet), CHENICHAM (village), SAN MIGUEL ACATAN, HUEHUETENANGO	0-79	Ar
118	COYA (village), SAN MIGUEL ACATAN, HUEHUETENANGO	6-81	Ar
119	COYA (village), SAN MIGUEL ACATAN, HUEHUETENANGO	9-81	Ar
120	EL MUL (hamlet), COYA (village), SAN MIGUEL ACATAN, HUEHUETENANGO	10-81	Ar
121	IXLAHUITZ (hamlet), COYA (village), SAN MIGUEL ACATAN, HUEHUETENANGO	7-81	Ar
122	XOCOL (hamlet), CHIMBAN (village), SAN MIGUEL ACATAN, HUEHUETENANGO	2-0	Ar
123	SAN RAFAEL LA INDEPENDE (town), SAN RAFAEL LA INDEPENDENCIA, HUEHUETENANGO	7-82	Ar,PAC
124	LA JCHOLAJ (village), SAN RAFAEL LA INDEPENDENCIA, HUEHUETENANGO	2-81	Ar
125	SAN MATEO IXTATAN (town), SAN MATEO IXTATAN, HUEHUETENANGO	5-81	Ar
126	NACAPOXLAC (hamlet), SAN MATEO IXTATAN (town), SAN MATEO IXTATAN, HUEHUETENANGO	7-82	Ar
127	PETANAC (hamlet), GUAISNA (village), SAN MATEO IXTATAN, HUEHUETENANGO	7-82	Ar
128	CONCEPCION (town), CONCEPCION, HUEHUETENANGO	6-79	Ar
129	JOLOMHUITZ (village), SAN JUAN IXCOY, HUEHUETENANGO	10-81	Ar
130	SAN SEBASTIAN COATAN (town), SAN SEBASTIAN COATAN, HUEHUETENANGO	7-82	MC
131	SAN JOSE PUEBLO NUEVO (hamlet), SAN SEBASTIAN COATAN (town) SAN SEBASTIAN COATAN, HUEHUETENANGO	0-81	Ar
132	LOS ANGELES (farm), BARILLAS (town), BARILLAS, HUEHUETENANGO	5-82	Ar
133	XOXLAC (village), BARILLAS, HUEHUETENANGO	6-81	Ar
134	XOXLAC (village), BARILLAS, HUEHUETENANGO	5-81	Ar
135	NUCA (village), BARILLAS, HUEHUETENANGO	6-82	Ar
136	CANANA (hamlet), NUCA (village), BARILLAS, HUEHUETENANGO	7-82	Ar
137	CANANA (hamlet), NUCA (village), BARILLAS, HUEHUETENANGO	7-82	Ar
138	EL QUETZAL (village), BARILLAS, HUEHUETENANGO	2-82	Ar
139	PUENTE ALTO (hamlet), EL QUETZAL (village), BARILLAS, HUEHUETENANGO	6-81	Ar
140	YOLHUITZ (hamlet), JOLOMTAJ (village), BARILLAS, HUEHUETENANGO	6-82	Ar
141	MONTE BELLO MOMONLAC (village), BARILLAS, HUEHUETENANGO	6-82	Ar
142	CENTINELA (village), BARILLAS, HUEHUETENANGO	0-82	Ar
143	XENAXICUL (village), AGUACATAN, HUEHUETENANGO	0-81	Ar
144	LAS MAJADAS (village), AGUACATAN, HUEHUETENANGO	4-80	Ar
145	BUENA VISTA (village), SANTA ANA HUISTA, HUEHUETENANGO	1-81	Ar
146	COYEGUAL (village), SANTA ANA HUISTA, HUEHUETENANGO	0-80	Ar,MC,PAC
147	CUMBRE DEL PAPAL (PARAJE) (village), IXTAHUACAN, HUEHUETENANGO	0-82	Ar
148	SANTA CRUZ DEL QUICHE (city), SANTA CRUZ DEL QUICHE, QUICHE	7-82	??
149	PAMESABAL (hamlet), SANTA CRUZ DEL QUICHE (city), SANTA CRUZ DEL QUICHE, QUICHE	1-80	Ar
150	PACHOJ (hamlet), SANTA ROSA CHUJUYUB (village), SANTA CRUZ DEL QUICHE, QUICHE	7-81	Pol
151	CUCABAJ (hamlet), SAN SEBASTIAN LEMOA (village), SANTA CRUZ DEL QUICHE, QUICHE	12-81	Ar,PAC
152	CUCABAJ (hamlet), SAN SEBASTIAN LEMOA (village), SANTA CRUZ DEL QUICHE, QUICHE	8-81	Ar,PAC
153	CUCABAJ (hamlet), SAN SEBASTIAN LEMOA (village), SANTA CRUZ DEL QUICHE, QUICHE	0-80	Ar
154	CHICABRACAN (hamlet), SAN SEBASTIAN LEMOA (village), SANTA CRUZ DEL QUICHE, QUICHE	8-81	Ar
155	CHICABRACAN (hamlet), SAN SEBASTIAN LEMOA (village), SANTA CRUZ DEL QUICHE, QUICHE	7-80	Ar,PAC
156	CHICABRACAN (hamlet), SAN SEBASTIAN LEMOA (village), SANTA CRUZ DEL QUICHE, QUICHE	12-81	Ar,PAC
157	CHICABRACAN (hamlet), SAN SEBASTIAN LEMOA (village), SANTA CRUZ DEL QUICHE, QUICHE	8-81	Ar,MC,PAC

158 CANTON PACHO (hamlet), SAN SEBASTIAN LEMOA (village), SANTA CRUZ DEL QUICHE, QUICHE   0-81   PAC

159 EL CARMEN CHITATUL (village), SANTA CRUZ DEL QUICHE, QUICHE   4-81   Ar

160 CHUACAMAN (hamlet), EL CARMEN CHITATUL (village), SANTA CRUZ DEL QUICHE, QUICHE   12-82   G

161 LA ESTANCIA (village), SANTA CRUZ DEL QUICHE, QUICHE   4-80   Ar,MC,PAC,DS

162 LA ESTANCIA (village), SANTA CRUZ DEL QUICHE, QUICHE   8-81   G

163 LA ESTANCIA (village), SANTA CRUZ DEL QUICHE, QUICHE   8-81   Ar,MC,PAC

164 SUALCHOJ (hamlet), LA ESTANCIA (village), SANTA CRUZ DEL QUICHE, QUICHE   0-82   Ar

165 CHAJBAL (village), SANTA CRUZ DEL QUICHE, QUICHE   6-81   Ar

166 CHAJBAL (village), SANTA CRUZ DEL QUICHE, QUICHE   11-81   Ar,Pol

167 XESIC (village), SANTA CRUZ DEL QUICHE, QUICHE   0-81   G

168 XESIC (village), SANTA CRUZ DEL QUICHE, QUICHE   0-81   Ar

169 XESIC (village), SANTA CRUZ DEL QUICHE, QUICHE   7-82   Ar

170 XESIC (village), SANTA CRUZ DEL QUICHE, QUICHE   4-82   Ar,PAC

171 CHICHE (town), CHICHE, QUICHE   5-81   Ar

172 CHICHE (town), CHICHE, QUICHE   5-79   Ar

173 CARRIZAL (hamlet), CHICHE (town), CHICHE, QUICHE   0-82   Ar,PAC

174 CARRIZAL (hamlet), CHICHE (town), CHICHE, QUICHE   0-82   Ar,PAC

175 CHUPOJ (hamlet), CHICHE (town), CHICHE, QUICHE   0-82   Ar,PAC

176 TULULCHE (village), CHICHE, QUICHE   0-85   Ar

177 AGUA TIBIA (hamlet), CHINIQUE (town), CHINIQUE, QUICHE   0-0   Ar,PAC

178 XIMBAXUC (hamlet), CHINIQUE (town), CHINIQUE, QUICHE   0-0   PAC

179 LA PUERTA (hamlet), CHINIQUE (town), CHINIQUE, QUICHE   0-82   Ar,PAC

180 TAPEZQUILLO (hamlet), CHINIQUE (town), CHINIQUE, QUICHE   0-0   Ar,PAC

181 CANTON CUCABAJ (hamlet), LA PUERTA (village), CHINIQUE, QUICHE   7-81   Ar

182 ZACUALPA (town), ZACUALPA, QUICHE   0-82   Ar,PAC

183 ZACUALPA (town), ZACUALPA, QUICHE   0-80   Ar

184 PIEDRAS BLANCAS (hamlet), ZACUALPA (town), ZACUALPA, QUICHE   0-82   Ar

185 CHIXOCOL (village), ZACUALPA, QUICHE   0-82   Ar

186 SAN ANTONIO SINACHE (village), ZACUALPA, QUICHE   0-82   Ar,PAC

187 SAN ANTONIO SINACHE (village), ZACUALPA, QUICHE   5-82   Ar

188 CHAJUL (town), CHAJUL, QUICHE   5-80   Ar

189 CHAJUL (town), CHAJUL, QUICHE   11-81   Ar

190 CHAJUL (town), CHAJUL, QUICHE   9-79   Ar

191 TZITZE (hamlet), CHAJUL (town), CHAJUL, QUICHE   2-0   Ar

192 POI (hamlet), CHAJUL (town), CHAJUL, QUICHE   1-81   Ar

193 ILOM (village), CHAJUL, QUICHE   2-82   Ar,PAC

194 CHEL (village), CHAJUL, QUICHE   2-81   Ar

195 CHEL (village), CHAJUL, QUICHE   1-81   Ar,PAC

196 CHEL (village), CHAJUL, QUICHE   0-83   Ar,PAC

197 CHEL (village), CHAJUL, QUICHE   2-80   Ar

198 AMACHEL (hamlet), CHEL (village), CHAJUL, QUICHE   2-82   Ar,PAC

199 JUA (hamlet), CHEL (village), CHAJUL, QUICHE   2-80   Ar

200 XESAYI (hamlet), CHEL (village), CHAJUL, QUICHE   2-82   Ar

201 VIALA (farm), CHEL (village), CHAJUL, QUICHE   3-82   Ar

202 XEMAL (village), CHAJUL, QUICHE   2-80   Ar

203 PAL (hamlet), XEMAL (village), CHAJUL, QUICHE   2-82   Ar,PAC

204 BIJUM (hamlet), XEMAL (village), CHAJUL, QUICHE   2-81   Ar

205 XOLCUAY (village), CHAJUL, QUICHE   3-82   Ar,PAC

206 XIX (village), CHAJUL, QUICHE   1-82   Ar,PAC

207	XIX (village), CHAJUL, QUICHE	2-82	Ar,PAC
208	CHACALTE (village), CHAJUL, QUICHE	2-85	Ar,PAC
209	CHACALTE (village), CHAJUL, QUICHE	6-82	G
210	JUIL (hamlet), CHACALTE (village), CHAJUL, QUICHE	3-81	Ar,PAC
211	KAJCHIXLAJ (village), CHAJUL, QUICHE	5-81	Ar
212	LA ESTRELLA (farm), CHAJUL, QUICHE	2-82	Ar,PAC
213	COBADONGA (farm), CHAJUL, QUICHE	3-80	Ar
214	IXLAJ (village), CHAJUL, QUICHE	3-80	Ar
215	XECHULULTZE (village), CHAJUL, QUICHE	2-80	Ar
216	SIBANA (village), CHAJUL, QUICHE	0-80	Ar
217	BISIQUICHUM (village), CHAJUL, QUICHE	0-84	Ar
218	LA PERLA (farm), CHAJUL, QUICHE	0-0	Ar
219	CPR SIERRA (farm), CHAJUL, QUICHE	0-84	Ar
220	CPR SIERRA (farm), CHAJUL, QUICHE	2-83	Ar
221	CPR SIERRA (farm), CHAJUL, QUICHE	0-88	Ar
222	XOLJA (hamlet), CHAJUL, QUICHE	3-82	Ar
223	BATZUL (village), CHAJUL, QUICHE	1-81	Ar
224	BATZUL (village), CHAJUL, QUICHE	5-82	G
225	CHICHICASTENANGO (villa), CHICHICASTENANGO, QUICHE	0-82	Ar
226	CHUPOL (hamlet), CHICHICASTENANGO (villa), CHICHICASTENANGO, QUICHE	7-80	Ar
227	CHUPOL (hamlet), CHICHICASTENANGO (villa), CHICHICASTENANGO, QUICHE	12-81	Ar
228	PATZIBAL (hamlet), CHICHICASTENANGO (villa), CHICHICASTENANGO, QUICHE	6-83	MC,PAC
229	CHUABAJ (hamlet), CHICHICASTENANGO (villa), CHICHICASTENANGO, QUICHE	0-82	Ar,PAC
230	CHUJULIMUL (hamlet), CHICHICASTENANGO (villa), CHICHICASTENANGO, QUICHE	0-81	Ar
231	SEMEJA (hamlet), CHICHICASTENANGO (villa), CHICHICASTENANGO, QUICHE	0-82	Ar
232	CAMANCHAJ (hamlet), CHICHICASTENANGO (villa), CHICHICASTENANGO, QUICHE	0-80	Ar
233	CHICUA (hamlet), CHICHICASTENANGO (villa), CHICHICASTENANGO, QUICHE	0-80	Ar
234	CANTON CHOCOJOM (hamlet), CHICHICASTENANGO (villa), CHICHICASTENANGO, QUICHE	0-83	PAC
235	PATZITE (town), PATZITE, QUICHE	9-81	G
236	SAN ANTONIO ILOTENANGO (town), SAN ANTONIO ILOTENANGO, QUICHE	0-0	Ar
237	CHUICHOP (hamlet), SAN ANTONIO ILOTENANGO (town), SAN ANTONIO ILOTENANGO, QUI	12-81	Ar
238	XOLJUYUB (hamlet), SAN PEDRO JOCOPILAS (town), SAN PEDRO JOCOPILAS, QUICHE	0-0	Ar
239	CHITUCUR (hamlet), SAN PEDRO JOCOPILAS (town), SAN PEDRO JOCOPILAS, QUICHE	0-0	Ar
240	CUNEN (town), CUNEN, QUICHE	1-81	Ar,MC,PAC
241	CHIMANZANA (village), CUNEN, QUICHE	0-81	Ar,MC
242	CHIMANZANA (village), CUNEN, QUICHE	1-82	Ar,MC
243	CHUTUJ (hamlet), CHIMANZANA (village), CUNEN, QUICHE	1-82	Ar
244	SAN JUAN COTZAL (munic.), QUICHE	2-82	Ar,PAC
245	SAN JUAN COTZAL (town), SAN JUAN COTZAL, QUICHE	8-82	Ar
246	SAN JUAN COTZAL (town), SAN JUAN COTZAL, QUICHE	7-80	Ar
247	TIOMAC (hamlet), SAN JUAN COTZAL (town), SAN JUAN COTZAL, QUICHE	5-83	G
248	CHAMUL (farm), SAN JUAN COTZAL (town), SAN JUAN COTZAL, QUICHE	7-80	Ar
249	CANCAN (hamlet), ASICH (village), SAN JUAN COTZAL, QUICHE	1-82	Ar
250	BIBITZ (hamlet), ASICH (village), SAN JUAN COTZAL, QUICHE	2-81	Ar
251	CAJIXAY (village), SAN JUAN COTZAL, QUICHE	1-82	Ar,PAC
252	CHISIS (village), SAN JUAN COTZAL, QUICHE	1-82	Ar,PAC
253	CHICHEL (village), SAN JUAN COTZAL, QUICHE	5-82	G
254	XEPUTUL (village), SAN JUAN COTZAL, QUICHE	0-82	Ar
255	CHIPAL (village), SAN JUAN COTZAL, QUICHE	1-82	Ar,MC,PAC

256	SAN FRANCISCO (farm), SAN JUAN COTZAL, QUICHE	5-81	Ar,Pol
257	SAN FRANCISCO (farm), SAN JUAN COTZAL, QUICHE	4-83	Ar,PAC
258	SANTA AVELINA (farm), SAN JUAN COTZAL, QUICHE	10-81	Ar
259	SANTA AVELINA (farm), SAN JUAN COTZAL, QUICHE	0-79	G
260	CHINIMAQUIN (farm), SAN JUAN COTZAL, QUICHE	1-82	Ar,MC,PAC
261	JAUVENTAU (hamlet), SAN BARTOLO (town), SAN JUAN COTZAL, QUICHE	1-82	Ar,PAC
262	BUENOS AIRES (farm), SAN JUAN COTZAL, QUICHE	0-0	Ar
263	JOYABAJ (villa), JOYABAJ, QUICHE	0-81	MC,PAC
264	CHORRAXAJ (hamlet), JOYABAJ (villa), JOYABAJ, QUICHE	1-81	MC,PAC
265	CHORRAXAJ (hamlet), JOYABAJ (villa), JOYABAJ, QUICHE	0-82	Ar
266	XEABAJ (hamlet), JOYABAJ (villa), JOYABAJ, QUICHE	0-82	PAC
267	PATZULA (hamlet), JOYABAJ (villa), JOYABAJ, QUICHE	1-82	Ar,PAC
268	PERICON (hamlet), PACHALIB (village), JOYABAJ, QUICHE	11-81	PAC
269	PIEDRAS BLANCAS (farm), JOYABAJ, QUICHE	0-0	Ar
270	PAXTUT (hamlet), JOYABAJ, QUICHE	11-81	PAC
271	XECAX (hamlet), NENTON (town), NEBAJ, QUICHE	2-81	Ar
272	SALQUIL (village), NEBAJ, QUICHE	8-82	Ar,PAC
273	SALQUIL (village), NEBAJ, QUICHE	0-91	Ar
274	PALOB (hamlet), SALQUIL (village), NEBAJ, QUICHE	0-81	Ar,PAC
275	PALOB (hamlet), SALQUIL (village), NEBAJ, QUICHE	10-82	Ar
276	PARRAMOS (hamlet), SALQUIL (village), NEBAJ, QUICHE	5-82	Ar
277	XEIPUM (hamlet), SALQUIL (village), NEBAJ, QUICHE	12-81	Ar,PAC
278	BIJOLOM (hamlet), SALQUIL (village), NEBAJ, QUICHE	0-84	Ar
279	BIJOLOM (hamlet), SALQUIL (village), NEBAJ, QUICHE	4-82	Ar
280	VIVITZ (hamlet), SALQUIL (village), NEBAJ, QUICHE	0-82	Ar
281	JALAVITZ (hamlet), SALQUIL (village), NEBAJ, QUICHE	0-82	Ar,PAC
282	TZALBAL (village), NEBAJ, QUICHE	4-82	Ar
283	TZALBAL (village), NEBAJ, QUICHE	5-82	Ar
284	CANAQUIL (hamlet), TZALBAL (village), NEBAJ, QUICHE	3-82	Ar,PAC
285	XOLOCHE (hamlet), TZALBAL (village), NEBAJ, QUICHE	0-83	Ar
286	BIPECBALAM (hamlet), TZALBAL (village), NEBAJ, QUICHE	0-82	Ar
287	XECOCO (hamlet), TZALBAL (village), NEBAJ, QUICHE	5-83	PAC
288	CHABUC (MICROREGION OF XOLOCHE (hamlet), TZALBAL (village), NEBAJ, QUICHE	5-82	Ar,PAC
289	CHABUC (MICROREGION OF XOLOCHE) (hamlet), TZALBAL (village), NEBAJ, QUICHE	0-80	Ar
290	CHABUC (MICROREGION OF XOLOCHE) (hamlet), TZALBAL (village), NEBAJ, QUICHE	9-83	Ar
291	ACUL (village), NEBAJ, QUICHE	4-82	Ar,PAC
292	ACUL (village), NEBAJ, QUICHE	0-82	Ar
293	XEXOCOM (hamlet), ACUL (village), NEBAJ, QUICHE	1-84	Ar
294	PULAY (village), NEBAJ, QUICHE	0-79	Ar
295	COCOB (hamlet), PULAY (village), NEBAJ, QUICHE	2-80	Ar
296	PEXLA (hamlet), PULAY (village), NEBAJ, QUICHE	2-80	Ar,PAC
297	XONCA (village), NEBAJ, QUICHE	2-82	Ar,PAC
298	SUMAL (village), NEBAJ, QUICHE	4-83	Ar
299	SUMAL (village), NEBAJ, QUICHE	5-85	Ar,PAC
300	SUMAL (village), NEBAJ, QUICHE	8-82	Ar,PAC
301	BICTOZ (hamlet), SUMAL (village), NEBAJ, QUICHE	0-82	Ar,PAC
302	XEUCALBITZ (hamlet), SUMAL (village), NEBAJ, QUICHE	4-85	Ar,PAC
303	SANTA MARTA (village), NEBAJ, QUICHE	0-81	Ar
304	CHUATUJ (village), NEBAJ, QUICHE	8-82	Ar

305	CHUATUJ (village), NEBAJ, QUICHE	10-81	Ar,PAC
306	CHUATUJ (village), NEBAJ, QUICHE	0-84	Ar
307	CHORTIZ (hamlet), CHUATUJ (village), NEBAJ, QUICHE	7-82	Ar,MC,PAC
308	BICALAMA (village), NEBAJ, QUICHE	2-83	Ar,PAC
309	BICALAMA (village), NEBAJ, QUICHE	7-84	Ar,PAC
310	BICALAMA (village), NEBAJ, QUICHE	0-82	Ar
311	BICALAMA (village), NEBAJ, QUICHE	10-81	Ar
312	IXTUPIL (village), NEBAJ, QUICHE	0-81	Ar,PAC
313	SACSIGUAN (village), NEBAJ, QUICHE	4-82	Ar,PAC
314	SACSIGUAN (village), NEBAJ, QUICHE	0-0	Ar
315	SUMAL CHIQUITO (village), NEBAJ, QUICHE	0-0	Ar
316	NEBAJ (town), NEBAJ, QUICHE	2-80	Ar
317	NEBAJ (town), NEBAJ, QUICHE	8-82	Ar,PAC
318	BISAN (hamlet), NEBAJ (town), NEBAJ, QUICHE	6-82	??
319	RAMAS CHIQUITAS (farm), NEBAJ, QUICHE	0-82	Ar,PAC
320	SAN ANDRES SAJCABAJA (munic.), QUICHE	0-0	Ar,MC
321	CHILIL (cas.), CHINANTON (village), SAN ANDRES SAJCABAJA, QUICHE	0-0	Ar,MC,PAC
322	USPANTAN (town), QUICHE	0-80	Ar,MC,PAC
323	USPANTAN (town), USPANTAN, QUICHE	0-82	Ar
324	CARACOL (hamlet), USPANTAN (town), USPANTAN, QUICHE	8-81	Ar,PAC
325	EL DESENGANO (hamlet), USPANTAN (town), USPANTAN, QUICHE	3-81	Ar,Pol,MC,PAC
326	MACALAJAU (hamlet), USPANTAN (town), USPANTAN, QUICHE	2-82	Ar,PAC
327	AGUA FRIA (hamlet), USPANTAN (town), USPANTAN, QUICHE	3-82	Ar,PAC
328	LAGUNA DANTA (hamlet), EL PINAL (village), USPANTAN, QUICHE	9-81	Ar
329	LANCETILLO (village), USPANTAN, QUICHE	9-82	G
330	PANAMAN (hamlet), LANCETILLO (village), USPANTAN, QUICHE	4-82	Ar,MC,PAC
331	LAS GUACAMAYAS (village), USPANTAN, QUICHE	4-80	Ar,PAC
332	LA TAÑA (village), USPANTAN, QUICHE	3-82	G
333	CRUZCHUT/CRUZCHIP (farm), USPANTAN, QUICHE	0-0	Ar
334	SARAGUATE (farm), USPANTAN, QUICHE	5-81	Ar,PAC
335	SACAPULAS (munic.), QUICHE	3-82	Ar,PAC
336	SACAPULAS (munic.), QUICHE	5-82	Ar,MC,PAC
337	RIO BLANCO (village), SACAPULAS, QUICHE	4-80	Ar
338	RIO BLANCO (village), SACAPULAS, QUICHE	8-82	Ar,PAC
339	TZUNUNUL (village), SACAPULAS, QUICHE	9-81	Ar
340	TZUNUNUL (village), SACAPULAS, QUICHE	3-82	Ar
341	TZUNUNUL (village), SACAPULAS, QUICHE	2-82	??
342	GUANTAJAU (village), SACAPULAS, QUICHE	5-82	Ar
343	GUANTAJAU (village), SACAPULAS, QUICHE	12-81	Ar
344	GUANTAJAU (village), SACAPULAS, QUICHE	3-82	DS
345	PARRAXTUT (village), SACAPULAS, QUICHE	3-80	Ar,MC,PAC
346	PARRAXTUT (village), SACAPULAS, QUICHE	1-82	Ar
347	PARRAXTUT (village), SACAPULAS, QUICHE	1-81	Ar,PAC
348	PARRAXTUT (village), SACAPULAS, QUICHE	3-82	Ar,MC,PAC
349	SALINAS MAGDALENA (village), SACAPULAS, QUICHE	4-83	Ar,MC,PAC
350	SALINAS MAGDALENA (village), SACAPULAS, QUICHE	8-82	G
351	SALINAS MAGDALENA (village), SACAPULAS, QUICHE	2-81	Ar
352	TIERRA CALIENTE (village), SACAPULAS, QUICHE	3-82	Ar
353	TIERRA CALIENTE (village), SACAPULAS, QUICHE	2-82	Ar

354	TIERRA CALIENTE (village), SACAPULAS, QUICHE	2-82	Ar,MC,PAC
355	TIERRA CALIENTE (village), SACAPULAS, QUICHE	2-82	Ar
356	TIERRA COLORADA (village), SACAPULAS, QUICHE	2-82	Ar
357	CANTON SIANCHOJ (village), SAN BARTOLOME, QUICHE	12-81	Ar,MC,PAC
358	ROSARIO MONTE MARIA (village), CHICAMAN, QUICHE	10-82	G
359	LLANO GRANDE (village), CHICAMAN, QUICHE	0-82	Ar,PAC
360	IXCAN (municipality), QUICHE	2-81	Ar
361	SAN PABLO (village), MICROREGION 1 (farm), IXCAN, QUICHE	3-82	Ar
362	EL QUETZAL (village), MICROREGION 1 (farm), IXCAN, QUICHE	2-82	Ar
363	SAN ALFONSO (village), MICROREGION 1 (farm), IXCAN, QUICHE	3-81	Ar
364	VICTORIA 20 DE ENERO (village), MICROREGION 1 (farm), IXCAN, QUICHE	2-82	Ar
365	SAN LUCAS LA 12 (village), MICROREGION 1 (farm), IXCAN, QUICHE	3-81	Ar
366	SANTO TOMAS IXCAN (village), MICROREGION 1, IXCAN, QUICHE	2-82	Ar
367	LA TRINITARIA (village), MICROREGION 1 (farm), IXCAN, QUICHE	2-82	Ar
368	SAACTE 1 (village), MICROREGION 2 (farm), IXCAN, QUICHE	0-81	Ar,PAC
369	ZONA REINA (farm), MICROREGION 2 (farm), IXCAN, QUICHE	0-82	Ar
370	SANTA MARIA TZEJA (village), MICROREGION 3 (farm), IXCAN, QUICHE	2-82	Ar
371	SANTA MARIA TZEJA (village), MICROREGION 3 (farm), IXCAN, QUICHE	6-82	Ar
372	SANTA MARIA DOLORES (village), MICROREGION 3, IXCAN, QUICHE	0-81	Ar,PAC
373	SANTA MARIA DOLORES (village), MICROREGION 3, IXCAN, QUICHE	2-81	Ar,MC
374	KAIBIL BALAM (village), MICROREGION 3 (farm), IXCAN, QUICHE	1-82	Ar
375	KAIBIL BALAM (village), MICROREGION 3 (farm), IXCAN, QUICHE	4-82	Ar
376	SANTIAGO IXCAN (village), MICROREGION 3 (farm), IXCAN, QUICHE	0-82	Ar
377	SAN JUAN IXCAN (village), MICROREGION 3 (farm), IXCAN, QUICHE	5-82	Ar
378	SAN JUAN IXCAN (village), MICROREGION 3 (farm), IXCAN, QUICHE	9-82	Ar
379	SAN JUAN IXCAN (village), MICROREGION 3 (farm), IXCAN, QUICHE	0-83	Ar
380	SAN JUAN IXCAN (village), MICROREGION 3 (farm), IXCAN, QUICHE	0-83	Ar
381	SAN JUAN IXCAN (village), MICROREGION 3 (farm), IXCAN, QUICHE	6-82	Ar,PAC
382	SAN JUAN IXCAN (village), MICROREGION 3 (farm), IXCAN, QUICHE	5-82	Ar
383	SAN JUAN IXCAN (village), MICROREGION 3 (farm), IXCAN, QUICHE	4-82	Ar,MC
384	NUEVA ESPERANZA (village), MICROREGION 4 (farm), IXCAN, QUICHE	9-82	Ar
385	PIEDRAS BLANCAS (village), MICROREGION 4 (farm), IXCAN, QUICHE	1-82	Ar,PAC
386	CHACTELA (SAN JUAN CHACTELA) (village), MICROREGION 6 (farm), IXCAN, QUICHE	0-80	Ar
387	CANIJA (village), MICROREGION 6 (farm), IXCAN, QUICHE	2-82	Ar,MC,PAC
388	SENOCOCH (village), MICROREGION 6 (farm), IXCAN, QUICHE	6-88	Ar,PAC
389	ASUNCION (village), MICROREGION 6 (farm), IXCAN, QUICHE	2-82	Ar
390	XALBAL (village), MICROREGION 7 (farm), IXCAN, QUICHE	2-82	Ar
391	XALBAL (village), MICROREGION 7 (farm), IXCAN, QUICHE	12-82	G
392	XALBAL (village), MICROREGION 7 (farm), IXCAN, QUICHE	6-81	Ar
393	XALBAL (village), MICROREGION 7 (farm), IXCAN, QUICHE	1-83	Ar
394	XALBAL (village), MICROREGION 7 (farm), IXCAN, QUICHE	0-84	Ar
395	XALBAL (village), MICROREGION 7 (farm), IXCAN, QUICHE	0-84	Ar
396	MAYALAN (village), MICROREGION 7 (farm), IXCAN, QUICHE	6-82	Ar
397	MAYALAN (village), MICROREGION 7 (farm), IXCAN, QUICHE	7-83	Ar
398	CENTRO 1 (CENTRO BELEN)(1ER. C) (village), MICROREGION 7 (farm), IXCAN, QUICHE	0-82	Ar
399	CUARTO PUEBLO-LA UNION-SELVA R (village), MICROREGION 7 (farm), IXCAN, QUICHE	2-82	Ar
400	CUARTO PUEBLO-LA UNION-SELVA R (village), MICROREGION 7 (farm), IXCAN, QUICHE	2-81	Ar
401	CUARTO PUEBLO-LA UNION-SELVA R (village), MICROREGION 7 (farm), IXCAN, QUICHE	8-82	Ar
402	CUARTO PUEBLO-LA UNION-SELVA R (village), MICROREGION 7 (farm), IXCAN, QUICHE	3-82	Ar

403	PUEBLO NUEVO/TERCER PUEBLO (village), MICROREGION 7 (farm), IXCAN, QUICHE	12-82	Ar
404	PUEBLO NUEVO/TERCER PUEBLO (village), MICROREGION 7 (farm), IXCAN, QUICHE	3-82	Ar
405	IXTAHUACAN CHIQUITO (village), MICROREGION 7 (farm), IXCAN, QUICHE	0-82	Ar
406	CPR IXCAN (farm), IXCAN, QUICHE	12-84	Ar
407	ZUNIL (farm), IXCAN, QUICHE	7-83	Ar
408	ZUNIL (farm), IXCAN, QUICHE	8-85	Ar
409	CHINATZEJA (village), IXCAN, QUICHE	2-0	Ar
410	CHAILA (farm), IXCAN, QUICHE	0-82	Ar
411	TRES AGUADAS (COMUNIDAD) (farm), FLORES, PETEN	4-81	ArMC
412	JOSEFINOS (farm), LA LIBERTAD, PETEN	2-82	ArPAC
413	LAS 2 RR (PARCELAMIENTO) (village), LA LIBERTAD, PETEN	12-82	ArMC
414	LA PITA (hamlet), SANTA ANA, PETEN	12-82	ArMC
415	EL MANGO (village), SANTA ANA, PETEN	0-81	ArPAC
416	PITO REAL (hamlet), DOLORES (village), DOLORES, PETEN	8-81	Ar
417	EL QUETZALITO (COMMUNITY) (village), DOLORES, PETEN	0-82	Ar
418	RANCHO SAN MARTIN (Farm) (village), DOLORES, PETEN	2-82	Ar
419	SUBIN (farm), SAYAXCHE (town), SAYAXCHE, PETEN	0-0	Ar
420	PALESTINA (village), POPTUN, PETEN	0-82	Ar
421	LA HAMACA (REFUGEE CAMP), CHIAPAS, MEXICO	0-85	ArPAC
422	EL CHUPADERO (REFUGEE CAMP), CHIAPAS, MEXICO	0-84	ArPAC

THE ANGUISH OF TORTURE

Torture is described in conjunction with massacres and detentions. Besides seeking information, the purpose of torture is to destroy the victims' identity and either eliminate them or make them into accomplices to repression against their own neighbors and associates. In Guatemala, the social aspects of the use of torture represent an assault on the collective identity. In rural areas, torture sessions frequently were held in public, in front of relatives and neighbors, as a form of exemplary terror.

One in five testimonies compiled by REMHI includes accounts of torture. Torture accounts for 12.64 percent of the total acts of violence recorded. Many torture victims were subsequently killed. In the testimonies collected, 30 percent of all murder victims appeared with signs of torture. For decades (and not including war-related incidents), the appearance of tortured corpses was part of waking up every morning, whether reading the newspapers or traveling footpaths and roadways. Many of these corpses were later buried anonymously.

According to our data, most torture victims were men (90 percent). These cases do not include rape, however, which was a specific form of torture used against women. One in six massacre cases analyzed in the testimonies describe sexual assaults.

Torture was frequently used during massacres. Witnesses report the following atrocities, listed from greater to lesser frequency: mutilations (18 percent), beatings (17 percent), rape (16 percent), harsh detention conditions (12 percent), preparing their own graves (6 percent), followed by other forms of torment.

[Handwritten annotations in top margin: "EXTREME CRUELTY was the principal cause of death. it was not enough to simply eliminate — the Army sought to instill FEAR in those that remained"]

[Handwritten annotation top right: "TORTURE as a combat strategy"]

Overall, extreme cruelty was the principal cause of death during massacres (three out of five cases), compared to victims killed by firearms, bombings, or other explosives.

Government military and paramilitary forces are reported to be responsible for 87.38 percent of the torture cases; another 6.92 percent are attributed to the guerrillas; and those responsible for the remaining cases are unknown.

While the guerrillas did not use torture as a combat strategy, the testimonies report instances of cruelty toward people accused of being military commissioners, civil patrollers, or alleged army collaborators in the early eighties. The cases compiled (6.92 percent of the total) describe cruel acts such as death threats, blows, and injuries inflicted with sharp instruments during murders.

[Handwritten annotation left margin: "THIS WAS NOT TRUE OF the guerrilla groups"]

[Handwritten annotation bottom: "(correction: the guerrillas did use torture but not as a combat strategy like the military)"]

ONE STORY OUT OF MANY

Yolanda Aguilar Urízar was kidnapped and tortured in October 1979. Her father, a prominent Christian Democrat, and her brother had died years before, on August 3, 1975, in a deliberately provoked car accident. That attack had actually been directed against her mother, América Yolanda Urízar, who was working at the time with the Legal Office of the National Workers Central [*Central Nacional de Trabajadores*—CNT]; she was forcibly disappeared years later.

In the first room where I was, there was a chair where, for the first time, I realized that they were going to torture me. And I got there, and of course they stripped me, right? Then one came and they immediately put on the radio, because it made sense so that no one would hear the screams. Once I was naked, they put on the radio, and a nineteen- or twenty-year-old boy came in, with light-colored eyes, blond, who could have come out of any private school, right? And he told me: "Look, we don't want to hurt you, and I want us to talk, and I want you to tell me everything you know. Because, as you can imagine, some of those compañeros are really bad and so, if you don't tell me—he is going to have to treat you badly. So I want us to be friends, I want you to tell me everything you know...."

That was when the rape happened. And I remember clearly that about twenty men raped me, because I have bits of memory, let's say, that Valiente Téllez* was there; this Mr. Arredondo** was there. And the only thing I remember is that while one was having relations with me, right, others were masturbating. Some other ones were rubbing me, right? They put their hands on my breasts. I lost consciousness several times. That was when they hit me. They slapped my face and others put cigarettes on my breasts, and each time I started to come around, I saw a different man on top of me. And I remember when I *could no longer feel that that someone was with me. I was in a pool of urine, semen, I guess blood too. It was truly humiliating, incredibly humiliating....*

They took me to a sink full of filth. You could see mold, fungus; there was a horrible smell besides, and I remember that they put [my head] in there once or twice. The feeling of suffocation is one of the most terrible things, you know. Every time you want to breathe, you fill up with shit, so you do everything possible not to breathe, but you can't....In that same room they used what they call the gamezán*** *hood on me....*

Then they took me to another door, and there were planks along the top of that doorway. Have you seen the crucifixion? Well here, very nearly, was Jesus Christ; there was a man, there was half of a man—the most horrendous thing I have ever seen—a man totally disfigured. He already had worms, he had no teeth, no hair, his face was disfigured, he was hanging, I mean, by his hands.

Right then, someone from the Judicial arrived. He was carrying a tiny scythe, a small one, like for cutting coffee. It was red hot, and he grabbed the penis and cut it off. That guy let out a scream that I have never forgotten, a terrible scream, so horrifying that for many years I remembered that scream. He died. Later there was a cassette of Spanish music that had a scream almost like it, and I guess I fainted.

Leaving the Country

To end this chapter, let's say that all my papers were prepared for me to leave, and I left on January 31, 1980, the day the Spanish Embassy was burned. I found out later what had happened at the Spanish Embassy. From then on, I was in Mexico, Cuba, and Nicaragua. I completed my recovery in Cuba, because the medical system there is fabulous, and the atmosphere of peace and security helped a lot. I went back to Nicaragua. Case 5447, Guatemala City, 1979.

*Manuel de Jesús Valiente Téllez, chief of the Judicial Police. **Pedro García Arredondo, chief of *Comando Seis*. ***A hood lined with a chemical irritant—TRANS.

THREATS

Threats were often used against people considered counterinsurgency targets. They were usually directed against an individual or his or her family. Threats were conveyed publicly, if necessary, to politically neutralize the person. They frequently included accusations of belonging to the guerrillas. In other cases, the aim was to paralyze an individual or break up a group through threats of abduction or attack. Threats were sometimes delivered anonymously, or their authors concealed their identity by issuing the threat under the name of one of the death squads. There were cases in which an entire organization or community was threatened.

Lists frequently circulated during the sixties, sometimes accompanied by photographs. Posters were pasted up featuring enlarged photographs of social leaders and guerrillas, offering rewards for information about the whereabouts of the latter. In the seventies, such lists were included in public notices signed by death squads such as the Secret Anticommunist Army (ESA), the New Anticommunist Organization (NOA), and the White Hand *(la Mano Blanca)*; these would give the people listed between twenty-four hours and one week to leave the country.

DATA ON THREATS AND THE RELATED CATEGORY OF ATTACKS

The REMHI project recorded a total of 1,577 incidents of threats with a total of 7,378 victims. Some responsibility was also assigned to the insurgent forces, who were implicated in three hundred cases of this type of violation, comprising 19.02 percent of all cases.

The analysis yields comparable findings when cases of massacre survivors, who are by definition considered victims of an attack or assault, are included in the general category of attacks. Three percent of the attacks attributed to guerrilla forces, particularly robberies or burning down of facilities, targeted groups or institutions.

Government agents were responsible for 71 percent of threats reported in the testimonies; more than 19 percent were attributed to the guerrillas; and 9.35 percent to unknown agents. An analysis by victim rather than by case, however, reveals a pattern of indiscriminate army attacks on the population, since these account for nine out of every ten attack victims (88 percent).

Threats against Popular Movement Advisors

Attorneys Marta Gloria de la Vega and Enrique Torres provided legal assistance to various labor unions, including those of the Coca Cola plant, Acricasa, Minas S.A. (Ixtahuacán), Cordelería La Rápida, Exguapagra, and the National Workers Central (CNT). From 1976 on, they were subjected to threats, including telephone calls and people watching their house. At the time, the Coca Cola union[11] had grown more powerful.

We had already been threatened by the owners' attorney, Héctor Mayora Dawe, to the effect that they were against the union and that if the workers organized, blood was going to flow. Before the attack, we had also been offered a lot of money. [They said that] before the union was formed they spent $300,000 on advertising and, since its formation, they were spending $400,000; therefore, they were offering us the $100,000 difference to stop

_____

[11] Coca Cola, Inc., sells the Guatemalan franchise to Embotelladora Guatemalteca, S.A.

offering legal counsel to the unions. In 1976 we received several telephone threats at the office and at home. The threats increased in 1977....They were saying that there were plots available in such and such a cemetery, and that they were ready for us.

One day the two attorneys were attacked. Afterward, they remained in Guatemala, until they were forced to leave the country in 1978:

On the periférico *[bypass] near Channel 3, I saw a big van coming. It pulled up beside our car and bumped into it once, then rammed it at higher speed. It pushed us like that three times; we hit sideways. My whole face on the right side was crushed, my chin and head, and I had a broken leg. The gear shift broke Enrique's leg in six places. He was hospitalized for three months. Some people helped us out of the car. Afterward, a car stopped with three men in civilian clothes in it. One of them said: "We're going to take them." I began to scream, and I said they were taking us to disappear us. Fortunately, the people stopped them from doing it. We later learned that the vehicle that had pushed us was registered for the use of the interior minister, Donaldo Alvarez Ruiz. Case 0602, Guatemala City, 1977.*

The threats continued, since the lawyers remained in the country working with the unions. Several unionists had been killed and assaulted, but in 1978 *"the manager of Coca Cola, Alfonso Riege Banash, began to talk about the order in which we would be killed."* The situation deteriorated and finally, after *"living like rats for two months,"* they decided to leave the country.

ABDUCTION PROCEDURES

The training curriculum (also referred to as "the course" or "training process") for intelligence agents included techniques for carrying out clandestine operations and abductions. Intelligence agents specialized in the logistics of abductions, the division of labor among different members of the group; and coordinating rapid, clandestine strikes.

That Intelligence Service program gives the courses. How you are going to get into a house; you have go in looking carefully because you don't know if there is a weapon inside. Because when you are going to abduct someone, you proceed directly to the abduction and "blum!" to the car and, "fuii," he disappeared and he's gone. Case 1741 (perpetrator), Izabal, 1980-83.

Intelligence officers were always responsible for selecting people for abduction. Abductions were organized events governed by a series of administrative procedures; responsibilities were delegated and information was compartmentalized. *Especialistas* were usually the material authors of a well-planned system.

PLANNING AN ABDUCTION

It happened in 1983, I don't remember the month. The abduction took place at 2:00 in the afternoon, in broad daylight. I don't remember his name. They just said, "Look, that's him." They don't tell you the name, they just point the person out. Not until you are going to take him, to kill him, that's when you find out who it is that's behind bars.

"Abducted' means that you take someone unexpectedly during the night— detained—the G-2 rarely detains, it only abducts, so that no one knows who did it. Unexpectedly at night they take the person, naked, without a nightshirt or underwear. You break down the door and take the person, and you shove him into the car and goodbye. Then you leave and that's it. Case 1741 (perpetrator), Izabal, 1980-83.

Victims of abduction frequently disappeared. According to the testimonies, six out of ten people abducted have still not reappeared. A minority of victims reappeared alive (14 percent). One out of every three abduction victims was found dead, often bearing signs of torture. Many illegal (or irregular) detentions, which are not included in these figures, may also be considered abductions (10 percent of the cases compiled). This illustrates the frequency with which abductions were used to intimidate or eliminate victims.

SHORT-TERM ABDUCTION OR DETENTION

Intelligence organizations used brutal tactics like short-term abduction or detention for propaganda purposes and, unlike cases of forced disappearance, the victim was not killed.

If the purpose of the abduction was to induce collaboration, torture and threats were used to elicit information and break the victims' spirit. Accordingly, the treatment received varied depending on whether the victim agreed to collaborate. Victims who agreed to the offer were immediately treated more humanely and received good food, clothing, and cigarettes. During the next stage, the captors manipulated their victims' emotions in order to achieve psychological control over them. The victim was required to contact his or her family, for which the captors supervised temporary departures from the detention center. The captors would also give money to the family if it was having financial troubles. This served a dual purpose: on the one hand, there was the threat that the victim's family would be detained and killed. On the other was the threat that the detainee would be killed, even as the family became financially dependent on the intelligence services. The goal was to extend the detention center's influence, and the effects of psychological torture, to the entire family group. The technique was so effective that the intelligence apparatus came to rely on it heavily.

Staged Confessions: Publicity

Maritza Urrutia, a thirty-three-year-old Guatemalan teacher, was abducted on July 22, 1992, by a Presidential General Staff (EMP) commando. She was subsequently detained for one week at a Mobile Military Police (PMA) station in Guatemala City. She was abducted because of her affiliation with the Guerrilla Army of the Poor (EGP). From the outset, her captors' behavior, and the treatment she received, focused on breaking down her resistance and eliciting information. But her detention was also a publicity stunt to discredit the guerrillas and enhance the government's credibility at a time when the latter was facing accusations of human rights violations in the United Nations Human Rights Commission in Geneva.

Torture

Maritza was subjected to various forms of torture: she was interrogated repeatedly while in a weakened state and sometimes videotaped. She was psychologically manipulated by her captors; she was drugged during interrogations; she was humiliated and attacked in intimate ways; she was exposed to constant noise and light, and deprived of sleep; her life and the life of her four-year-old son were threatened. Throughout her detention, except when she was being videotaped, she was forced to wear a hood made from newspaper over her face. She was handcuffed the entire time. And finally, she was continually pressured to admit publicly her affiliation with the EGP and request amnesty.

> *"Your son is fine. Someone is taking care of him. He is eating cookies. He's fine," he told me. I was terrified and extremely worried about my little son. I thought I was going to have a nervous breakdown from the worry. They showed me horrible photographs of dead bodies. The corpses had been tortured and mutilated. The photographs were horrific, and they completely unnerved me. They told me the same thing could happen to me if I didn't cooperate with them.*
>
> *They took me to a public telephone, and they made me call my parents to tell them not to worry about me. Afterward, the interrogation lasted until 4:00 A.M. I was extremely nervous, exhausted, and afraid. They brought a portable radio to the room and turned it up full blast. They left the light on, and I was handcuffed to the bed, alternating hands, and I always had to keep the newspaper hood over my head.*
>
> *The interrogation lasted for hours. Around 5:00 P.M. the light-skinned man said they were going to bring another man who would not treat me so kindly. I was exhausted and nervous, and I was shaking a lot, and I yelled for them to please not bring the other man. I started to beg them not to hurt me. I told them I would cooperate.*
>
> *He said they wanted me to go to Geneva to speak in favor of the government before the United Nations Human Rights Commission. I was to thank the many people who had taken an interest in me, like General Carlos Arana Osorio, the defense minister, General García Samayoa, and others. I had to*

[handwritten margin note: TORTURE as propaganda. A way to instill fear in others and force their cooperation]

say that I went to Mexico in 1986, that my husband was a member of the EGP, and that I had worked for the organization. They wanted me to give the names of certain people, say that I was sorry to have caused my family so much worry, but that I wanted to leave the EGP organization, and that I had gone away for a time to "legalize" my situation. I was to ask forgiveness of the organization and say that I wanted to leave it in order to end this struggle that had caused so much harm to my country. I was to end my statement by asking the army for amnesty and protection for myself.

Even as they were torturing her, her captors tried to keep up her physical appearance; they eventually gave her a day and a half of rest after the first videotapes did not come out well. They bought her makeup and toiletries for the sessions, which took place over several days.

I put on a lot of makeup. I did it so that if people who knew me saw the video, they would realize that something was wrong and that I hadn't made the tape voluntarily.

From that time on, her captivity consisted of endless taping sessions with variations of the message: (1) add a part in which she also would thank the Archdiocesan Human Rights Office and the U.S. Embassy; (2) then, add a part where she would thank Otto Peralta, president of the Association of University Students (AEU) of San Carlos University, and take out the part where she thanks the military; (3) eliminate the reference to amnesty and gratitude to the army and, again, refer to Otto Peralta and the history department of the university, and add a part where she asks her comrades to abandon the struggle.

"When you say in the video that you don't want to belong to the organization anymore, you have to say it like you really mean it. It seems like it troubles you to leave the organization, like what you're saying isn't true," he would say. They told me I should smile when I spoke.

The light-skinned man[12] took me to the telephone. He told me to call Teleprensa first. I said, "I'm Maritza Urrutia. I would like you to include in your program tonight a video that some friends of mine delivered to you." Then we called Notisiete [News Seven] and I said the same thing.

The light-skinned man gave me detailed instructions. They were the conditions for my freedom: request amnesty; hold a press conference in which I tell the defense minister that I want to cooperate with the army, that perhaps I could go to Geneva and speak at the United Nations on the army's behalf.

The next day she was taken to a meeting with the state attorney, Acisclo Valladares, who expedited the amnesty process, even changing the dates she had

---

[12] In a subsequent investigation, the "light-skinned man" was identified as Captain Edy Ovalle Vargas. This was confirmed by a key witness who participated in the operation.

belonged to the organization to facilitate her request (it should have been prior to 1988). At no time did he ask where she had been for the past week, whether she had been involuntarily detained, or how she had been treated. Neither Valladares, nor the judge who granted her amnesty, asked if she had been forced into it or commented on her deteriorated physical condition a week into her kidnapping.

Despite the fact that she was still threatened and under surveillance, Maritza Urrutia decided not to follow her captors' instructions. On September 30, 1992, she testified in Washington, D.C., before the Inter-American Human Rights Commission of the OAS.

> *I feel fortunate to have survived this trial. I have the good fortune to be alive. I cannot help but think of the many other Guatemalans who have not been so lucky....*
>
> *For the thousands of people who have been disappeared, tortured, and murdered by the Guatemalan army, for the political convictions for which I was kidnapped, for all the Guatemalans who mobilized to secure my release, members of the academic community, religious sectors, displaced persons, human rights activists, parents, brothers and sisters, relatives, and other loved ones; for the international figures and institutions who pressured the government for my release; for the future of my son and of all Guatemalan children; and, for myself, I made the decision to continue to denounce the outrages that the army has committed with impunity for the past thirty years.* ODHAG case 001, Guatemala, 1992.

FORCED DISAPPEARANCES: A SMOKE SCREEN

Forced disappearance has been one of the barbaric, selective methods most frequently used by Guatemalan intelligence. It was used on a mass scale during certain periods of the armed conflict. Forced disappearance accounts for one out of every five cases reported in the testimonies. Most of these victims were seized suddenly during a covert action and were never heard from again. Forced disappearance gives rise to tremendous uncertainty over the fate of the victims and their physical and psychological well-being, and it causes protracted suffering for the families.

THE DATA

Forced disappearances were among the most frequently reported incidents, after individual and collective murders; they accounted for one out of every five cases recorded. The testimonies compiled by the REMHI project confirm 3,893 victims of forced disappearance. In REMHI's testimonies, the army and paramilitary forces were responsible for seven out of every ten forced disappearances (guerrillas or unknown perpetrators accounted for the rest). Besides the army, police units and military commissioners with ties to military intelligence played a significant role (forced disappearance accounts for one in four incidents attributed to the police and military commissioners respectively).

Despite unmistakable evidence of military and police involvement, and the total impunity with which they acted, the government and army have consistently denied having any control over, or responsibility for, forced disappearances. To date, the absence of official investigations has impeded attempts to search for the disappeared.

Covert actions and the initial uncertainty surrounding these incidents enabled intelligence agencies to delay public reaction and camouflage state responsibility. This also provided the captors with more opportunities to break down the detained-disappeared person's resistance. Disappearance had additional objectives, such as spreading terror and paralyzing the victim's social circle. In most of the cases involving intelligence corps, attempts were made to cover up any evidence to preclude investigations and ensure the perpetrators' ability to act with impunity, to escape punishment.

WIPING OUT LIFE: THE FORCED DISAPPEARANCE OF A FAMILY

Adriana Portillo lived with her family in Jutiapa. Her brother, Carlos Alfredo Portillo Hernandez, a member of the guerrilla army ORPA, perished in July 1981 when the army bombed a guerrilla safe house in Zone 14 in Guatemala City. Two months later, six members of her immediate family were abducted and disappeared: her two daughters, Rosaura, ten, and Glenda, nine; her seventy-year-old father, Adrián Portillo; her stepmother, Rosa de Portillo; her little sister, Alma Argentina Portillo, age eighteen months; and a sister-in-law, Edilsa Guadalupe Alvarez, eighteen. This took place in Zones 1 and 11 of the capital. According to the report, a police commando was responsible for these incidents.

On Friday, September 11, 1981, at about 9:00 A.M., a group of heavily armed men in civilian dress, riding in a white four-wheel-drive Cherokee Jeep with polarized windows and no license plates, arrived at the office where my father worked. After interrogating him, they took him away and we never found out anything more about him. My brother, Antonio, who witnessed my father's capture, went to warn my stepmother. But upon arriving at the house, he witnessed another military operation in progress,

> *including several vehicles without license plates, army jeeps, and police patrol cars.*
>
> *My stepmother, my sister-in-law, my baby sister, and my two daughters were in the house, located at Second Avenue 1-57, in Zone 11 of the capital. Eyewitnesses saw the women and girls, crying and begging for help, pushed into one of the police cars.*
>
> *We got to my father's house and we were immediately surrounded by members of the National Police, the Mobile Military Police, the army, and the Judicial Police. They were all heavily armed, and they pointed their weapons at us while they interrogated us. We didn't have any idea what was happening. They told us to go in if we wanted to see them. We refused to go in. When we realized what was happening, we started to hurry away from the house, and the men began to pursue us. But there was a taxi driver nearby who had probably seen everything. He started the car, opened the door for us to get in, and we left.*
>
> *We never reported this for fear of reprisals. We were too afraid to talk about what had happened. In December 1981, we left Guatemala.* Case 5021 and 5022, Guatemala City, September 11, 1981.

EXECUTIONS: "DOING SOMEONE IN"

Assassination was a criminal act that was frequently used, particularly by the intelligence services, to eliminate people previously selected because of their political activities. Since assassinations were carried out in covert operations, there were no written orders; members of the commando were referred to by pseudonyms, and the vehicles and weapons used were not registered to avoid being traced.

In general, the head of intelligence in a given zone ordered an extrajudicial execution, in certain cases after consulting with the highest echelons of military intelligence. If complications were anticipated, these actions were coordinated with other security forces, even to the extent of previously notifying the National Police that they should "clear out" an area and refrain from interfering with the commando's actions.

The methodology included surveillance of the individual for several days or weeks in order to become familiar with his or her movements. In general, the method of killing, the day, or escape alternatives were left up to the specialist responsible for the abduction or murder. The plans had to take into account the need to simulate a case of common crime or make identification difficult (for example, acting under cover of darkness); to choose an opportune moment (no witnesses); and to ensure that the person would not be merely wounded. Numerous assassinations of leaders and intellectuals, including anthropologist Myrna Mack, followed this pattern.

[handwritten margin notes: Assassinations were secretive, were made to look like a common crime. Unlike (it seems) torture and short-term abduction the Army didn't want people to know they committed the assassinations]

This type of assassination mission doesn't happen all that often. It depends on the situation; but during that period, there was a lot of work. I think that I probably had about thirty assassination missions, and those were just mine. There were also the other people in the group, so the count was twenty times thirty. There were some six hundred a year, just from that office (EMP). In the case of Myrna, they passed me the file. I analyzed and studied it, and I began to follow her. These kinds of missions take no longer than two weeks, from the time you start observing until the moment of execution. We don't make any report until the mission has been completed. Once that mission was completed, I shredded the file. I burned it, and I never mentioned the subject again to anyone in the office. All of my reports were made orally to the chief, Juan Valencia Osorio. That was also where the method of killing her came from, so people would consider it a common crime. Afterward, they tried to eliminate me, and they even had armed men watching my house and going around asking for me. I am convinced that Juan Valencia Osorio ordered my death. (Myrna Mack Foundation interview with Noel de Jesús Beteta Alvarez in the "Centro Preventivo" in Zone 18, April 7, 1994.)

INFILTRATION

The information that intelligence agencies amassed about insurgent forces and social organizations enabled them to pursue a strategy of active infiltration during certain periods of the armed conflict. The initial process was multilayered. Social organizations that encompassed strong, organized movements, or guerrilla front groups such as those cultivated at San Carlos University and in certain labor unions, were more vulnerable to infiltration because they were so accessible.

Infiltration enabled military intelligence to design plans for the selective neutralization of insurgent leadership, and even to establish internal balances of power that were favorable to army strategies.

THE DEADLY DECEPTION
The Students' Case of 1989

In August 1989, several student leaders of the University Students' Association (AEU) were abducted and disappeared or killed in Guatemala City. In this way, attempts to reorganize the student movement, which had been virtually dismantled, were again struck down by counterinsurgency actions. Initial suspicions of infiltration by military intelligence (EMP) were later confirmed in several testimonies.

In September 1987, student leaders from different academic departments and student groups were invited to student training conferences to be held in December of that year. These conferences were sponsored by several organizations, including the United Representation of Guatemalan Opposition (RUOG), the Mexico office of the World University Service, and the Guatemalan Human Rights Commission (CDHG).[13]

A group of students that had been contacted to travel to Mexico was invited to attend a Student Encounter organized in Puebla. They contacted Willy Ligorría, then-president of the Association of Law Students (AED) and member of the Social Democratic Party (PSD), and Silvia Azurdia Utrera. Apparently the student conference was a joint decision by the different organizations of the URNG, although certain student leaders were discouraged from participating directly as members of URNG organizations. Willy Ligorría, with three others (from the agronomy school), went to the event along with other student leaders.

A student who later conducted an investigation of Ligorría reported that he had strong ties to an armed "gang" from Zone 18; it had long been suspected that the army had organized these gangs. Several factors contributed to the suspicions against Ligorría: he was always accompanied by three or four alleged "law students" who had never registered at the Law School; he would cultivate certain leaders by inviting them to the movies and expensive restaurants; he wore expensive clothing; and he squandered money. At the same time, however, Ligorría maintained a revolutionary discourse, was a member of ORPA, and was in contact with Danilo Rodríguez (the FAR delegate to the URNG's grassroots work).

Following the investigation, the decision was made to expel Ligorría from the AEU's executive committee; also contributing to this decision was his misappropriation of funds from the Huelga de Dolores (Strike of Sorrows) Committee, his direct involvement in embezzling AEU funds and, finally, his usurpation of the position of Secretary General of the AEU (by acting in that capacity on different occasions and signing international documents, which was confirmed by a rubber stamp found in his possession at the time of the investigation). The AEU already suspected that he was affiliated with army intelligence (G-2). After Ligorría's departure, the threats began, the pamphlet bombs, and an explosive was thrown at the house of a member of the AEU directorate.

The threats escalated in 1989, some of them signed by death squads such as *La Dolorosa* (Our Lady of Sorrows), the Avenging Jaguar, or the Secret Anticommunist Army (ESA), leaving everyone terrified. But the situation reached a climax in August 1989. By then, Ligorría was no longer part of the AEU's executive committee and, although he continued to have personal relation-

---

[13] REMHI, *Insurgencia and Contrainsurgencia, su choque en la Universidad de San Carlos y el Movimiento Estudiantil* (1997).

ships with members of student organizations, he no longer did so from within the AEU. Nonetheless, he continued to maintain a high profile and a combative, and even intimidating, posture. Marco Tulio Montenegro, nicknamed the Monster, who was a good friend of Ligorría's, was still active in the AEU at the time.

On August 21, AEU member Iván Ernesto González was detained and disappeared. The following day Carlos Contreras Conde, the head of the University Student Movement (MEU), was abducted near the university. On the same day, Hugo Leonel Gramajo was abducted in front of the INAP headquarters and taken away in a red pickup with foreign license plates. On August 23, Víctor Hugo Rodríguez Jaramillo and Silvia Azurdia Utrera, MEU founders, were kidnapped and violently forced into two cars that had cut off their escape. That same day, the AEU called a press conference to denounce the incidents:

That afternoon, we announced that we were in permanent session. Mario de León left the press conference and, at 19:45 hours, he was detained at a National Police checkpoint on Petapa Avenue. He was taken, with his pickup and all, inside a trailer truck (according to eyewitnesses who wished to remain anonymous) and his whereabouts were never discovered.

Aarón Ubaldo Ochoa was disappeared the following day. During a meeting to discuss the students' response, Willy Ligorría called a student leader aside to tell him that he knew where Hugo Gramajo and Aarón Ochoa were being held and that, if he wanted, he (Ligorría) could take him to the missing students. A few days later he spoke again to this leader and asked him to get him an appointment with the Unitary Commission of the Masses (CMU/URNG). In September, student activists Carlos Chutá Camey, Carlos Humberto Cabrera, and Carlos Palencia were abducted; they were found dead shortly thereafter.

Willy spoke at several university meetings following the murder of the AEU students. He participated in demonstrations and was applauded by some. On Saturday, September 15, at 2:15 P.M. he left for Panama with Marco Tulio Montenegro and Byron Milián Vicente. Marco Tulio returned to the country on November 11 to join the AEU, but by then everyone was suspicious of him. A short time later he was stabbed to death with a bayonet-like weapon. According to Willy, he had been with him the whole night at the Ritz Continental Hotel. It was rumored that it had been an EGP action, but they were the ones who did it, military intelligence....
One morning, Willy arrived at EMP headquarters and was warmly received at the door. Shortly afterward, he emerged as the Chief of Investigations of the Public Ministry. Key Source 13, Guatemala City, 1989.

TORTURE METHODS AND TRAINING

Torture is intended to humiliate the person physically and/or psychologically. Interrogations, pressure, and torture of detainees were part of the training courses and practicums given to intelligence service members. Techniques were standardized and accompanied by manuals, internal regulations, and so forth (for example, the army's *Manual de interrogatorio*). This is indicative of a defined, institution-wide approach that was not dependent on the officers in charge or their individual styles.

Procedures include techniques to confuse and manipulate detainees, to lead them to incriminate themselves, and to obtain information and accusations against others. Abducted individuals were routinely tortured with electric shocks, blows, and asphyxiation, among other techniques. Mutilations were used once the decision had been made to kill the detainee. Most people who were tortured were subsequently murdered and their bodies disposed of in clandestine cemeteries.

> This is his service, that of torturing with electric currents, with blows, clubs, and all, kicks, or the hood lined with lime. Torture is so they'll tell the truth, if it's true, if what is said is affirmative or negative....The answers are studied, from the first day to the last....If after eight or ten days of being interrogated there is no change, that person is freed. But once someone feels that they are being pressured by the torture, everything changes. And that one says, "Yes, it's true, yes, I'm going to tell you the truth, but don't hit me anymore, no more." Then yes... Case 1741 (perpetrator), Izabal, 1980-83.

People's inability to withstand suffering was taken as confirmation of the accusations against them. Even though many victims probably denounced others or admitted to the accusations against them, this did nothing more than confirm their guilt, and the need to kill them, in the eyes of their executioners. Some were able to survive. A few others were freed—under surveillance—after agreeing to collaborate with the security apparatus by accusing other people, neighbors, friends, of belonging to the guerrillas. Finally, in a few exceptional cases, some victims were freed following outside intercessions with high-level military commanders, political pressure, and so forth.

At the start of the internal conflict, torture culminated in the extrajudicial execution of the victim. Cruelly mutilated corpses appeared on the roads on the outskirts of major cities, particularly the capital. By the eighties, however, experiments by Argentinean advisors refocused the objectives of torture. The first warning a captive received from his captors was, "He who cooperates, lives, he who doesn't, dies." And the principle held. Some detentions ended up being short-term abductions, after which the individuals were freed with the idea that they would continue to collaborate; others were coerced into betrayal by torture and were partially integrated into military operations as sources of information. Still others were psychologically transformed into direct agents of repression.

INDUCED BETRAYAL

One of the purposes of torture is to convert the person being tortured into a collaborator. When exposed to extreme suffering, people can give names or information, real or otherwise, in an attempt to relieve their pain. Detainees face the dilemma of whether to protect their individual identity (by capitulating to their captors' demands) or their social identity (by not divulging information that compromises others). In circumstances of threat or extreme suffering from torture, either response has profoundly negative repercussions for that person.

Military intelligence also made use of internal divisions, power struggles, or personal dissatisfaction, which may have been discovered through infiltration, to induce betrayal. In the nineties, a double escape that led to the public disclosure that Efraín Bámaca (aka Comandante Everardo of the ORPA) was alive made it possible to identify three distinct reactions to torture and induced betrayal. After months of detention, two detainees who belonged to ORPA escaped (there were three who could have done so, but one decided not to participate in the plan). Once free, one of the escapees took action against his captors by denouncing the existence of clandestine jails in the San Marcos military zone, where Bámaca was still being held. The other opted to remain silent.

SILENCED VOICES: THE UNRECOGNIZED PRISONERS OF WAR

On March 8, 1991, Santiago Cabrera, a member of ORPA's Luis Ixmatá Front, was detained in San Marcos by members of the G-2 and transferred to the Santo Domingo Military Base (San Pablo). His testimony describes the use of torture to force prisoners to cooperate, as well as the existence of prisoners detained by the army and used as collaborators, whom the army denied holding.

THE CAPTURE AND TORTURE OF EFRAÍN BÁMACA

The initial torture

They began to hit me with a concrete block. The ones who hit me were the same ones who had detained me: Lieutenant Colonel and Intelligence Chief Héctor René Pérez Solares; G-2 specialist, Margarito Sarceño Medrano; the captain in command of the San Pablo base; the chief of military commissioners of San Pablo, G-2 member, Emilio Escobar. Afterward they sent Karina to tell me, "Carlos [a pseudonym], tell the truth, because of you, they are hitting me more." And she was crying. They were forcing her to say that.

Inducing collaboration

Three people from the G-2 came in with "Augusto," who was a former URNG combatant from my own Luis Ixmatá Front. Augusto was captured in Decem-

ber 1989, together with another combatant who went by the pseudonym "Alfredo," who disappeared in 1990. Later Augusto would tell me that he was shackled to a bed for five months and tortured. He showed me scars on his legs from electric shocks. The army had also forced him to kill two captured civilians in cold blood. I was present later when he asked to be discharged from the army. Colonel Julio Alpírez told him that if he wanted his discharge, they'd give it to him, but it would be a "permanent" discharge (death).

In Military Zone 18 in San Marcos, a G-2 specialist known as "Gualip" interrogated me. He kept me shackled to a bed with my feet bound. I could only go out occasionally: the army would take me out to point out caches or identify dead or detained people. I spent five months like that.

Seeking conversion

Afterward a new phase began. They began to test me, to see if they had broken me psychologically with the pressure and torture I had undergone. Now they only shackled me at night and only by one hand. The new head of the G-2, Jesús Efraín Loarca Aguirre, let me out to do exercises. I was pale, and he wanted to take pictures of me for propaganda, to show I was an army volunteer and that I regretted the time I spent with the guerrillas....I decided that the only way to escape from there was to act like a model prisoner, obedient and respectful. In that way, I looked for the right moment to make my escape.

Little by little, they gave me tasks to do. I realized that the army had a new, special strategy for us as prisoners of war. Before, when they captured our compañeros, they tortured them and always killed them. Now they kept some of us alive in order to break us psychologically and get military information out of us. They also wanted to force us to work with them in the intelligence section.

The torture of Efraín Bámaca

Everardo (Efraín Bámaca) had been my commander, and I wanted to see him. I saw Everardo with my own eyes in Santa Ana Berlín. He was lying on a metal cot, with his hands shackled and his feet bound with a rope[14]; he was interrogated day and night. They wanted to break Everardo's spirit.

---

[14] Another testimony collected by the REMHI project corroborates Bámaca's capture, uninjured, his detention in the Santa Ana Berlín military zone, how he was used to point out caches containing supplies, arms, and so forth, and patrols. According to this testimony, he was later murdered

by a new specialist by the last name of Carrillo, so that he could practice. The military specialists who killed Bámaca are José Víctor Cordero Cardona, alias Yegua, and Rodolfo Hernández Marroquín. His body was buried in one place and his head in another (this technique is used so that when the body is discovered, the person cannot be identified) on the outskirts of the Santa Ana Berlín Detachment in Coatepeque, at the edge of some cane fields below Santa Lucía Cotzumalguapa (ODHAG Case 002, Guatemala, 1995).

On July 18, they took Everardo to a secret room in the army infirmary. Before being transferred to the infirmary, he had said that, before arriving in San Marcos, he had been in the Quetzaltenango Military Zone in June. They were interrogating him there, and he sounded to me as if he were drowsy or drugged. His entire body was very swollen. He was blindfolded. One or two days later I saw Everardo again. He was dressed in a soldier's uniform and I couldn't see his arm or leg. But his body wasn't swollen anymore. He was also speaking normally again. That was the last time I saw Commander Everardo. I left the base for a few days, and when I came back he wasn't there.

The escape

I escaped into Mexico on December 22, 1992. Since the G-2 members trusted me after so much time, they gave me six days of leave to be with my family. I took advantage of the opportunity to leave the country once and for all and denounce the whole situation of prisoners of war, including Everardo. Certified Testimony given by Santiago Cabrera at the United States Department of State, November 30, 1994.

CHARACTER TRANSFORMATION: TAKING ON THE OPPRESSOR'S IDENTITY

The ultimate goal of torture is to alter the detainee's personality through psychological torments designed to remove any notion of time and space. Torturers are divided into the "bad guys" and the "the good guys." Prisoners often becomes dependent on the latter, thereby becoming more susceptible to the pressures, demands, and values of their torturers. This "modification" process, sometimes termed *brainwashing,* can engender a gradual, progressive metamorphosis. The process includes friendliness, torture, teaching, and propaganda: instruction in a new ideology.

Jorge Herrera, a former FAR and PGT militant from San Carlos University, was detained five years after his brother was disappeared from EMAUS [a retreat center in Escuintla] with a group of union members. He opted to collaborate with military intelligence. He helped to convert other captured insurgents, including a CAVISA union activist who was also a PGT militant. Herrera became an intelligence advisor. And, when it became impossible for Pellecer to remain in the EMP after Jorge Serrano's failed coup attempt in June 1993, Herrera was called upon to replace him as an intelligence advisor in the EMP. From that time on, he played a key role as a presidential intelligence agent, negotiating with the business sector and newspaper executives under the Ramiro de León administration (Myrna Mack Foundation).

FROM JESUIT TO MURDERER: THE CASE OF PELLECER FAENA

On June 8, 1981, Jesuit priest Luis Eduardo Pellecer Faena was violently abducted in Guatemala City. Witnesses assert that Pellecer was wounded during his capture. When intelligence chief Colonel Francisco Ortega Menaldo of *La 2* found out about the detention, he asked to take over the case.

Ortega Menaldo was interested in applying his knowledge of psychological torture to convert the priest. He took it as a personal challenge. Some officers viewed him with suspicion, distrusting such sophisticated methods. The escape of Toj Medrano (CUC leader) from Army General Headquarters after having collaborated with the army—which cost General Oscar Humberto Mejía Víctores his job—had made us distrustful of those methods, even though they were still used. Key Source 1098, Guatemala City, not dated.

Months later, on the afternoon of September 30, the presidential public relations secretary, Carlos Toledo Vielman, held a press conference in which Pellecer Faena spoke at length about his Jesuit training, his membership in an intellectual elite of the Society of Jesus, and his work with the Delegates of the Word in El Salvador and Nicaragua. He denounced the way these movements were used, like other Catholic institutions (such as Cáritas and the Colegio Belga), to promote the insurgent cause. He confessed that he had been an EGP militant since 1980, and that he had worked with former Jesuit Enrique Corral on the EGP's National Propaganda Commission and the Community Coordinator [*Coordinadora de Pobladores*]. He asserted that his disappearance had actually been a "self-kidnapping."

Pellecer's startling declarations had a strong impact on the Catholic church. The tension between the church and the government had grown since 1980. Two priests had been killed in just two years. The diocese of Quiché had been closed down, and Bishop Juan Gerardi was banned from entering the country. A month before Pellecer Faena reappeared, the army had denounced the involvement of priests in the guerrillas and the use of Catholic high schools as "centers of Marxist indoctrination."

The Society of Jesus and other social groups responded publicly that Pellecer had been cruelly tortured until he "snapped." An analysis of the tape of the press conference led to the conclusion that his physical appearance was dramatically altered. He had gained an inordinate amount of weight, and his teeth had changed the shape of his face. The sources interviewed were consistent in saying that military intelligence had approached three dental surgeons to do reconstructive surgery on the detainee. They were later killed, the first two for refusing to cooperate, and the third after he had finished the job.

The EGP issued a press release saying that Pellecer Faena was not a militant but rather a "collaborator" of that organization. Military intelligence exploited the "Pellecer case" to the greatest extent possible. He was taken to several countries to give presentations to military intelligence commanders and, for the next twelve years, he was an influential advisor to the intelligence services. He was assigned to the Presidential General Staff (EMP), where he remained close to Ortega Menaldo until President Jorge Serrano's failed coup d'état in May-June 1993.

Pellecer was a brilliant guy. He amazed us with his knowledge and incredible reasoning ability. He became our teacher.... We owed a lot of our successes against subversion to him, even in a personal sense, in our training. At those times his presence was critical for fine-tuning our plans and incorporating disciplines that had never even occurred to us. Key Source 1098, Guatemala, not dated.

CLANDESTINE PRISONS

According to firsthand testimonies collected, army intelligence maintained secret houses that functioned as clandestine detention centers for interrogation and torture. Very few people held in such locations escaped death after having been brutally tortured.

Psychological techniques were applied to force the cooperation of detainees thought to possess additional information. According to the testimonies gathered, most detainees were held for periods of weeks or months. Some information has been obtained about cases of protracted detention for up to two years, but none longer than that.

They tortured them on the edge of the lake where the specialists had taken them. They took charge, they interrogated and beat them, they tortured their feet, their hands, and put hoods on them. They beat them about the head, the chest. They beat them in the chest area; they tortured them. They also used electric shocks on their ears, using a battery current, a running car, to give them electric shocks. And they tortured them also by cutting off their fingers, but that was at the end. Case 1741 (perpetrator), Izabal, 1980-81.

PSYCHOSEXUAL CONTROL OVER THE TROOPS

Rape and Humiliation of Women

The rape of women was a systematic practice during military operations in rural areas and detentions of suspected guerrilla supporters in the cities. Many perpetrators viewed rape as something natural, and of little significance, in the course of violence against women and communities. This *normalization* of violence was used as a form of psychosexual control over soldiers, in which women were considered part of the "spoils of war."

Violence against civilians considered "friendly," however, was severely punished because it ran counter to the army's strategy of creating settlements and working together with the civilian population. Therefore, violence was not indiscriminate; rather, it relied on a cost-benefit analysis in function of the army's principal objective, which was to induce the civilian population to collaborate.

SEX AFTER A MASSACRE: FROM PSYCHOSEXUAL CONTROL TO AN INITIATION RITE

Tell the girls to give us a show. Right there, where they had massacred those guys, they put down some mats and an oil lamp by the other one. They lit it.... We had a tape player there, and he explained the idea to the girls, and they began to dance; they stripped one by one. But there was a variation: each soldier also had to dance and strip with them.

So the lieutenant grabbed his hat, and placed it in the center. He got out a ten quetzal bill and said, "Guys, put up as much as you want, and I'm going to tell one of the girls who's up for making love in front of everyone." She came out wrapped in a towel, kind of embarrassed, the poor thing. She came out and, well, the guy who had paid to be with her, well, there he was with all his manhood showing. But when he saw the situation like it was, well, he made a fool of himself. And we all started to laugh and suddenly he became impotent and couldn't do anything. And the girl was all embarrassed, lying there. It seems she had never done anything like that....

Then all the guys, well they got all excited because it's something that really makes an impression on you. It really affects you, right? And I've got to tell you that the night was a success with the girls. It made us laugh when a soldier got with one, and after a few minutes with her, "the next guy, lieutenant," and another and another. So all seventy had a turn, right, and some went two or three times. But the upshot is that the guys—we all were able to relieve our tension and our needs.

But one thing I didn't agree with. Some soldiers there were sick; they had gonorrhea, syphilis. So he ordered them to go last, when we had all had a turn.
Case 1871 (former G-2), various locations, 1981-84.

PREPARING THE MASSACRES

A process of material and psychological preparation preceded most of the massacres. Decisions about razing hamlets usually were planned with great care.

Preparing such operations required a perpetual state of psychological pressure, permanent alert, and an immediate reaction capability on the part of the troops.

Carrying out massacres also required an enormous amount of "work," which had to be well set up: detaining and separating the people into groups, interrogation and torture, preparing pits, flammable materials for burning different sites, food preparation, and so on. Massacres were not spontaneous reactions, nor were they bursts of disorderly violence. To the contrary, they were the product of a carefully designed process to organize and carry out the task of repression.

> There were different groups. One group of assassins they called Alpha. There were four groups: one for security; one that went in to search the houses in case there was something there; another group in charge of killing; and the other to aid anyone who was wounded. Each group had its mission. Case 9524, Barrillas, Sololá, Quiché, not dated.

Besides teaching obedience and training in the techniques described, the army took advantage of other stimuli, such as the desire to plunder, which largely guided the soldiers' behavior. In this way the troops were ready and willing to destroy indiscriminately, particularly in places where they encountered no resistance.

This behavior, which was officially sanctioned by the army, was based on regarding people with contempt: "They are shit; they don't deserve to live because they support subversion." Extreme contempt is evident in the way the killing and razing took place. The army often used people's silence as evidence that they were guerrillas: "We have to finish them all off, because those people don't say anything when we ask them questions." Contempt, then, was the inverse of defeat, and the act of committing a massacre sealed the feeling of victory. According to many testimonies, the initiative behind the massacres came from higher levels. But witnesses also described the insensitivity of the soldiers who carried out the massacres: "*It made them laugh.*"

PREPARING A MASSACRE

1. Keep up constant pressure
We were going to sleep when suddenly, at around ten o'clock at night, the sound of trucks. But not to do one of those jobs. Instead, right away they told us to get up, grab our backpacks, and get up on the trucks, because there was another assignment.

2. Messages of perpetual threat
What we found when we arrived was actually some sort of carpentry shop. But since they, the officers, would exaggerate in order to impress us and frighten

us; and they minimized the things we did so that we wouldn't feel them all at once, we took comfort in the fact that we were following orders.

3. Exemplary terror: progressive desensitization

We were stopped on the path and the lieutenant said that we weren't going to keep hauling those prisoners, that he was going to kill them right there. That was when he ordered us to kill them, but since we weren't supposed to shoot— so that they wouldn't know we were there—he ordered us to decapitate them all. They didn't bury them; they just left them dumped there instead. And that was something that made a strong impression on me, because I had never actually seen how a person was decapitated before.

4. Freedom to reap the benefits

I remember on that occasion they ordered us to destroy everything: to burn the beds and bed covers, the dishes. The best part was that we had free rein and, heck, we each had a chicken for breakfast, lunch, and dinner....We all lived the high life.

5. Modified behavioral standards

First, he informed us that we were going to participate in an operation. The files of the general headquarters of the Guerrilla Army of the Poor had been discovered, and they had identified the areas that they [the EGP] controlled. We were going to rout them out of there. We had to be careful because everyone there was an enemy and a guerrilla. We were going to clear out the area and kill everyone. And if anyone refused to obey the order, or protested what was going to be done, that person would join the group that was going to be executed.

6. Division of labor and setting up the infrastructure

There were weeds and some trees there. A specialist who was giving the orders told us to begin to excavate the grave, right? But I never liked to participate in those sorts of things when I was there, like in the executions, because I don't like it; I wasn't a supporter of that policy. I knew it was bad; I didn't like it, and besides being an evangelical, I had that which was bad and I didn't like the task. So, I decided to involve myself in digging the ditch. We made the ditch, a ditch 1.10 meters deep by 1 meter wide, and a few meters long.
Case 1871 (former G-2), various locations, 1981-84.

CONCEALING INFAMY: CLANDESTINE CEMETERIES

In order to cover up its mass murders, the army dug pits and common graves to bury the bodies of the dead. According to the testimonies, one method used systematically was to pour something flammable over the bodies and set them on fire. This complicated the identification process and eliminated much of the potential evidence. In some cases, the people were not quite dead. Corpse mutilation and the burning of the remains were means of ensuring that there would be no survivors.

> *A clandestine cemetery where thirty or forty people were put into each hole. There was no way around it; we had to cut them off at the knees so that they would all fit down in the hole...and we threw gasoline on them. That flame shot up ten or fifteen meters high, that high, the gasoline. And those moans coming from inside the fire, they cried and screamed.* Case 1741 (perpetrator), Izabal, 1980-83.

There are numerous clandestine cemeteries located in areas where massacres and murders were carried out. According to the testimonies, many other cemeteries are located on the grounds of military zones and bases that were used as clandestine detention centers.

Conclusions

FROM THE MEMORY
OF ATROCITIES
TO THE VIOLENCE OF TODAY

What are the potential consequences of the training, methodology, and infrastructure of violence in Guatemala? How might they jeopardize the future in the context of post-conflict reconstruction?

IN SEARCH OF AN EXPLANATION

Attempts to arrive at a definitive explanation for horror often encounter two contradictory tendencies: general resignation in light of the "innate evil of humanity," or the view that participation in atrocities can be attributed to some type of psychological disorder. Neither of these explanations corresponds to reality.

The first instance fails to take into account the importance of the structures that made systematic human rights violations possible; these are found in war strategies and methods that targeted the civilian population. Further, studies on the psychological state of many perpetrators, including the cruelest violators of the Nazi regime, did not find evidence of a pathological personality; rather, they were people who could be considered "normal."[1] Although certain personality traits, such as authoritarian tendencies, might facilitate such participation, this does not imply that such individuals have "psycho-pathological problems" that explain their individual responsibility for these actions.

Nonetheless, there were individual variations: some soldiers deserted, other people actively resisted recruitment or participation in civil patrols. In some cases, obedience was a way of saving a person's life; in many others, however, people voluntarily participated in actions against the civilian population.

---

[1] In COLAT, *Así buscamos rehacernos* (Brussels, 1987). Most research has shown that the inclination to obey orders, even to the point of causing pain and suffering to others, is common in the general population, if there is an underlying system conducive to this type of behavior.

175

VIOLENCE IN THE POSTWAR PERIOD

The large number of people deformed by [or educated in] violence through the civil patrols and the practice of forced recruitment indicates the danger that militarization will have long-term repercussions. Militarization has influenced value systems and behavioral patterns and enabled perpetrators to acquire expertise and perpetuate power networks.

For the groups most heavily involved in violence against others, the loss of values includes devaluing human life and seeing violence as a normal way of dominating others or resolving conflicts. Some of these effects may also permeate civil society as a consequence of the impunity that has accompanied the violence.

In the absence of concrete measures to counteract this situation—compounded by pervasive impunity and the profound economic problems assailing many sectors of society—the war's legacy is already apparent in new forms of social violence.

Finally, the horror carried out over all these years has led to the consolidation of clandestine networks that operate in the individual or collective interests of powerful groups. In the postwar context, these networks have organized into criminal gangs whose objective is personal enrichment through drug trafficking, kidnapping, automobile theft, and so forth. Many of these organized gangs continue to use the methods described in this chapter. These groups cannot be considered in isolation from traditional power structures, including the army. It is, therefore, the government's responsibility to dismantle them.

THE STRUGGLE TO RECLAIM MEMORY

As in our discussion of victims, the memory of atrocities likewise is an important aspect of violence prevention. Versions that justify what happened not only attempt to exonerate the authors, but also, in effect, justify the ideology and methods underlying the use of horror. Without public acknowledgment and social censure of the guilty, the perpetrators may ultimately be strengthened in their positions.

The perpetuation of power structures imposed through violence has significant repercussions for the future. History contains many examples of different approaches to the social task of reconstructing a distorted memory. These approaches range from rationalizing atrocities to blaming the victims. Official versions of events frequently invoke the need to "turn the page of history in order to rebuild society." Besides, denial of the past, or a standardized memory, helps those responsible for crimes keep their self-image intact.

This intentional distortion of memory is an example of social fraud and one more humiliation for the victims. It also has long-term ramifications for society, such as the installation of democracies with military oversight, as has occurred in other Latin American countries that lived through military dictatorships; the proliferation of right-wing or racist movements in Europe; political leaders who were previously involved in fascism or Stalinist repression reconstituted into neo-nationalists; and, the gradual transformation of the instigators of the war into "champions of peace." All of these scenarios illustrate the risk that past and present atrocities could be repeated (Páez and Basabe 1993, 6:7-34).

Memory has a clear preventive function. Preventing a recurrence of tragedy is largely dependent on dismantling the structures that made such horror possible.

Part Three

THE HISTORICAL CONTEXT

Chapter Ten

BACKGROUND

FROM BARRIOS TO PONCE VAIDES

Prior to the liberal reform of 1871, political and economic power in Guatemala remained concentrated in the hands of families descended from the *conquistadores* or Spanish colonial administrators. When his movement triumphed, General Miguel García Granados issued a manifesto, on May 8, 1871, pledging to legally reform the state in order to prevent excesses of personal power and provide a legal framework for land ownership that would benefit powerful coffee growers. It was actually General Justo Rufino Barrios who introduced liberal reforms, while donning the mantle of a personal dictatorship.

These reforms combined technological advances and new military theories—such as the organization of a professional army—with the suppression of communal and ecclesial land rights and the introduction of forced labor. Indigenous communities located in coffee expansion regions were the hardest hit, especially in the *bocacosta* region of Quetzaltenango, San Marcos, and Alta Verapaz.

Until that time, indigenous peoples enjoyed relative independence because of their possession of communal lands. By failing to recognize the emphyteutic census [land census] instituted by the conservatives in the nineteenth century (weakening, although not totally abolishing, indigenous land rights) plantation owners were able to acquire lands they rented from the communities.

In addition to the land issue, liberalism addressed the issue of forced labor. In 1877, the Regulation of Day Laborers (*Reglamento de Jornaleros*) was enacted, and the Vagrancy Law (*Ley contra la Vagancia*) was enacted in 1878, requiring indigenous people to work 100 to 150 days per year on the coffee plantations. As a result, labor was cheap; men earned one *real* per day, and women half that. Each year, some 100,000 indigenous people descended from the highlands to the *bocacosta* region to work the harvest. That period marked the beginning of numerous indigenous uprisings against political chiefs, financial backers, and plantation owners. The guerrilla war fought by the indigenous people of Momostenango was one of the major revolts, as were the attempted uprising of the Quichés in 1877, and the 1898 San Juan Ixcoy rebellion. Ladino militias quashed these revolts and then proceeded to seize indigenous lands.

When José María Reina Barrios took power in 1893, he revoked the forced labor law of 1877. However, indigenous people who failed to pay their exemption from service or show that they had performed three months of labor on a coffee, sugar, cacao, or banana plantation were legally required to serve in the *Zapadores* (Engineers) Battalion, which carried out government projects.

THE MILITARIZATION OF RURAL AREAS

The liberal governments drew from the colonial experience by requiring peasants to form militias. As in the colonial period, they were concerned because there were population groups dispersed throughout remote areas far from the capital city. Besides, an efficient, decentralized coercive force was needed to ensure an adequate labor force.

One of the principal tasks assigned the plantation owners, therefore, was to represent the political authorities, and they were invested with military, as well as civil and police powers. The reserve militias were made up of recruits between the ages of fifteen and fifty. Plantation owners or their agents had to circulate a list every Sunday. The workers were required to form squads subordinated to the boss, as if the latter were a military commander.

Militarization of the plantations included punishments of forced labor to build the coffee-growing infrastructure. A month of labor with the feared *Zapadores* Battalion was synonymous with abuse and, in many cases, death. Women and children were in charge of the fields when the men were absent, having been mobilized for different jobs. Faced with such protracted penalties, many people fled in desperation.

The rise of the new economic groups did not occur without friction. In 1898, an uprising backed by western coffee growers, commanded by the political chiefs of San Marcos and El Quiché departments, attempted to prevent Reina Barrios's reelection. When the plot failed, Interior Minister Manuel Estrada Cabrera retaliated by ordering the public execution of two prominent businessmen from Quetzaltenango: Juan Aparicio and Sinforoso Aguilar. When Reina Barrios was assassinated, Estrada Cabrera took over the presidency (1898-1920), transforming the Liberal party from an elite of professionals and public officials into an organization built on liberal middle-class circles.

Under Estrada Cabrera, coffee agroexporters, including the Herrera, Klee, Alejos, Falla, and Cofiño families, gained strength. The same was true of industrial families, such as the Castillos, the Novellas, and the Herreras, and financiers such as the Aguirres, the Saravias, the Castillos, and the Matheu Sinibaldi families. In 1901, the government signed a pact with United Fruit Company for banana production. The franchise issued in 1904 for the construction of the Puerto Barrios-El Rancho-Guatemala City railway included fifteen hundred *caballerías* [1 *caballería* = 110.355 acres—TRANS.] of land and exemption from export taxes for thirty-five years. Until 1920, the United States provided 70 percent of Guatemalan imports and controlled 80 percent of its exports.

Indigenous rebellions continued throughout this period. In 1905, the uprising of Totonicapán occurred. At the same time, however, associations of artisans and workers flourished. By 1919, thirty-six new worker or artisan associations had emerged.

In 1920, a conspiracy led by plantation owners and business sectors displaced from power since 1871 surfaced. Manuel Cobos Batres emerged as the leader of the protest, together with Bishop José Piñol y Batres. The Workers League (*Liga Obrera*), led by Silverio Ortiz, had been founded the year before, as had the Unionist Party (*Partido Unionista*), which advocated a parliamentary system, fiscal reforms, and Central American integration. Working-class militias formed in the midst of the 1920 protest movement, and an insurrection developed that claimed seventeen hundred lives. Estrada Cabrera was overthrown, and the government of sugar producer and banker Carlos Herrera Luna took power (1920-21). Herrera recognized certain advances in the area of cooperatives and individual rights but used the Demonstration Regulation (*Reglamento de Manifestaciones*) to curtail protests. The Guatemalan Railway Workers Union (*Unión Ferrocarrilera de Guatemala*) was particularly noted for its militancy during this period.

In 1921, a triumvirate led by General José María Orellana (1921-26) overthrew Herrera. Orellana renewed negotiations with the Bond & Share Electric Company. He also introduced the quetzal as the national currency, on a par with the dollar, which constituted a de facto devaluation in favor of the coffee producers. In 1924, United Fruit signed a rental contract encompassing all uncultivated lands located in the Motagua River basin, spanning sixty-two miles. In 1926, the Central Bank of Guatemala was founded as the only institution authorized to issue the quetzal. The government opened the National Labor Department and backed several worker-protection laws although, in 1922, it suppressed a Quiché Indian uprising.

Jorge Ubico Castañeda was elected president in 1931; formerly the political chief of Verapaz, he had ties to influential families such as the Castañedas, the Urruelas, the Herreras, the Doriós, the Klees, and the Saravias. Like Estrada Cabrera, Ubico presided over a lengthy, autocratic administration. In the early thirties, Guatemala suffered the effects of the international economic depression. Although Ubico could not continue to devalue the currency, he gained the support of coffee growers by maintaining social order in rural areas through an obligatory public-works program. In 1934, the government settled land-development debts in an attempt to assist less competitive entrepreneurs in their attempts to hire manual labor and to address the pressures created by the extreme indebtedness of the workers and the acute fiscal crisis. This enabled an indigenous minority to participate in trade by relocating throughout the country. These indigenous groups broke away from their *zahorinesy* cultural background [shamans] and became part of a religious conversion movement that facilitated the penetration of the Catholic and Protestant churches in the highlands beginning in the thirties and forties (Falla 1992).

Ubico replaced ladino mayors with his own administrators while retaining indigenous auxiliary mayors. He transferred the newly established Labor Department, which was under the Ministry of Economy, to the General Directorate of Police (*Dirección General de Policía*). And he used the army to implement his policies: the army forced peasants to build roads and stretch telegraph wires across the nation. Moreover, the Ubico government brutally persecuted its adversaries. When it uncovered a plot against the government in 1934, it decimated those involved. Ubico was famous for the "flight law" (*ley fuga*), under which prisoners were killed during supposed escape attempts. In June 1944, amid widespread protest, he was obliged to turn power over to a military triumvirate headed by General Federico Ponce Vaides, who governed for 108 days.

THE MILITARY COMMISSIONERS

President Ubico established the military commissioners as local army representatives in a July 9, 1938, executive decision. The commissioners filled the chronic vacuum created by the lack of public administration in the countryside. Their duties, which were unpaid and lasted indefinitely, included army recruitment, apprehension of criminals, and issuing citations and summonses. From the start, the commissioners acquired tremendous influence through their ability to negotiate who would be required to serve in the army. Their role would change dramatically with the onset of armed conflict, particularly in eastern Guatemala.

Meanwhile, inter-ethnic conflicts escalated. Local disputes between indigenous and ladino residents of Patzicía, Chimaltenango, fueled by General Ponce's promise of land to the former, quickly spread to the national political scene. This culminated in the massacre of Cakchiquel Indians after they rose up against the ladinos (and killed between sixteen and nineteen). The army's intervention on October 21, 1944, left more than forty Indians dead. During the next few days, however, paramilitary groups from Zaragoza joined an "Indian hunt" that left a toll of between four hundred and six hundred victims.

Faced with a conspiracy by political and military leaders and a popular uprising in the capital, the Ponce Vaides regime, vestiges of Ubicoism, fell on October 20, 1944, bringing another chapter of Guatemalan history to a close.

THE OCTOBER REVOLUTION

During the period of the October Revolution (1944-54), the middle class (army officers, professionals, business people, and artisans) assumed the administration of government and political institutions. The new order was based on a participatory system that supported government reforms (the right to vote, municipal autonomy); the government bureaucracy swelled and intellectuals were increasingly involved in policy-making. There were thirty registered political parties, including the United Front of Arevalist Parties, which supported the drafting of the 1945 Constitution.

President Juan José Arévalo (1945-51) espoused a liberal model of state intervention—a variation on U.S. President Franklin D. Roosevelt's New Deal, which he described as "spiritual socialism" to distinguish it from Marxist materialistic socialism. His economic policies bolstered small-scale industry and fostered the emergence of small-scale farmers. He also promoted cotton and rangeland stock farming, both of which required large tracts of land and a new type of salaried agricultural labor. The business sector also grew, stimulated by high prices for exports and increased internal buying power.

Organizations of entrepreneurs and workers multiplied during this period. In 1948, the General Confederation of Guatemalan Workers (*Confederación General de Trabajadores Guatemaltecos*—CGTG), under the leadership of Víctor Manuel Gutiérrez, was legally incorporated, and eventually reached a strength of ninety thousand members. Simultaneously, the National Peasant Confederation of Guatemala (*Confederación Nacional Campesina de Guatemala*—CNCG), headed by Leonardo Castillo Flores, was expanding in the countryside. By 1949, ninety-two unions had been legally incorporated.

Soon, however, conservative groups began to conspire against the Arévalo administration. Colonel Francisco Javier Arana and Jacobo Arbenz had emerged as the leaders positioned to replace Arévalo in 1951. But Arana planned to accelerate the process. In July 1949, with the backing of some plantation owners, Arana presented Arévalo with an ultimatum: he demanded that Arévalo cede his power to the army and finish his term as a civilian figurehead for the military regime. The president asked for time and, together with Arbenz and other loyal officers, tried to arrest Arana. Apprehended alone, Arana resisted and was killed in a shootout. When the news reached the capital, Arana supporters rebelled, but the unions and loyal army units quashed the uprising. Nonetheless, political tensions deepened during the rest of Arévalo's term.

Colonel Jacobo Arbenz won the 1950 elections as a candidate of the Popular Liberating Front (*Frente Popular Libertador*—FPL), which represented the middle classes. Arbenz began to study the agrarian situation. The Agricultural Census of 1950 revealed that 99.1 percent of farms were small holdings accounting for only 14 percent of the land; 0.1 percent of holdings occupied 41 percent of the land surface included in the census; 40 percent of farms were owned by twenty-three families; fifty-four farms took up 19 percent of the land; and there were approximately 250,000 landless peasants.

Like Arévalo, Arbenz tried to involve the business sector in addressing this issue. In 1951, he created a commission made up of three businessmen to study the situation of national farms. In 1952, Congress approved Decree 900, or the Agrarian Reform Law, mandating the expropriation of farms not under cultivation, which would be turned over to peasants through Local Agrarian Committees (*Comités Agrarios Locales*). The expropriated owners would be reimbursed with twenty-five-year government bonds at a 3 percent annual interest rate. Some

100,000 peasant families became beneficiaries of the law during the eighteen months it was in force; expropriated lands were worth U.S.$8.5 million, and 101 national farms were affected.

Beneficiaries committed abuses during the implementation of the Agrarian Reform Law. Thirty farms were needlessly invaded when they could have been readily obtained through legal means. In some parts of eastern Guatemala, the CNCG misapplied the Leasing Law (*Ley de Arrendamientos*) solely to benefit its own members. At the same time, however, plantation owners unleashed a wave of violence.

The AGA spearheaded the opposition to agrarian reform, a struggle in which the Aycinena Arrivillaga family played a prominent role. The anticommunist political opposition, which had developed during the Arévalo administration, began to gain impetus. On March 19, 1952, a rebellion occurred in Salamá with the participation of Juan Córdoba Cerna and the Committee of Anticommunist University Students (*Comité de Estudiantes Universitarios Anticomunistas*) directed by Mario Sandoval Alarcón. In addition, landowners organized Committees to Defend the Land and Civic Unions that set out to kill agrarian leaders, despite the fact that the agrarian reform had benefited the prosperous entrepreneurs of Retalhuleu, Escuintla, and Coatepeque.

DECREE 900 IN SAN MARTÍN JILOTEPEQUE

The following farms were affected in San Martín Jilotepeque: La Merced, Canajal de Medina, Rosario Canajal, and Los Magueyes. The latter two functioned with a typical peasant labor-for-land arrangement (*finca de mozos*): in exchange for the right to grow subsistence crops on these farms, the peasants had to provide seasonal labor on the owners' other farms on the southern coast. This farming system (often using dormant lands) was designed at the turn of the century. Carlos Herrera Luna bought Rosario Canajal farm in 1911 for use as a *finca de mozos*. There are no entries in the Land Registry (*Registro de Propiedad Inmueble*) regarding how it may have been affected by Decree 900, and the files on the agrarian reform implementation were destroyed. Therefore, these events can only be reconstructed through oral history.

The *fincas de mozos* owned by the Herrera family spanned a strip of land from San Juan Sacatepéquez to Joyabaj, El Quiché, and extended to other, more remote, municipalities such as San Juan Cotzal. The reversal of the agrarian reform turned San Martín into a focal point of intense social conflict for the next three decades. Despite spending on infrastructure for services after the 1976 earthquake, the main issues of control over land and recognition of indigenous authority were left unresolved; these issues only began to be addressed after the outbreak of armed conflict in that region in 1980-81.

The United States government played a critical role with respect to Decree 900. The United Fruit Company filed suit alleging the unconstitutionality of the Agrarian Reform Law. Distrustful of the justices, the government dismissed the court, leading its own administration into an institutional crisis.

In 1953, Dwight Eisenhower became president of the United States, John Foster Dulles was named secretary of state, and Joseph McCarthy entered the Senate. At the same time, the influence of the Central Intelligence Agency (CIA) had grown in the wake of the successful operation that overthrew the Iranian regime. U.S. Ambassador John Peurifoy, who arrived in Guatemala that same year, was the point person for U.S. policy. During his first meeting with President Arbenz, the ambassador demanded the expulsion of all communists from the government.

The business sector and anticommunist groups quickly joined the anti-government crusade. The Chamber of Commerce and Industry (*Cámara de Comercio e Industria*) joined an international campaign against the regime. The CIA's "Operation Success" was launched in October. On December 24, the Tegucigalpa Plan was ratified, unifying the National Liberation Movement. In May 1954, with the conspiracy already in its advanced stages, the United States signed military aid pacts with Honduras and Nicaragua, whence it was already preparing to launch a military invasion of Guatemala.

THE PROTAGONISM OF THE CATHOLIC CHURCH

Amid these political changes, the church was entering a new phase. Assaults by liberal governments had weakened the traditional power of the clergy. The shortage of priests (in 1940 there were 126 priests for every three million inhabitants) compelled lay people to take charge of maintaining the faith in their communities.

Archbishop Mariano Rossell y Arellano (1939-64) sought to restore the church's power and prestige in society and increase its influence over government policies and political leaders. The church needed to establish itself at the top of the social pyramid in order to re-create a propitious climate for preaching the gospel in Guatemala and bringing Christianity to the rest of society.

Anticommunism was rampant in the church of the fifties. It was a second dogma in the applied theology of much of the church hierarchy. For Archbishop Rossell, the anticommunist struggle was a crusade. On April 4, 1954, the archbishop published a pastoral letter calling on the population to rise up. His "Pastoral Letter on the Advance of Communism in Guatemala" stated, "Obeying the mandates of the Church, which command us to fight and defeat the efforts of communism, we must once more raise our voices in warning....These words wish to direct Catholics in a just, national, and honorable crusade against communism."

One year earlier, Rossell had organized the National Pilgrimage of the Image of Christ in Esquipulas, in which a replica of the image, which figures prominently in popular religion, was passed from village to village to lead the crusade against communism—in other words, against the Arbenz government. "The presence of the Blessed Christ accomplished more against communism than if a hundred missionaries, millions of books, and hundreds of Catholic radio hours had directed the anticommunist campaign" (Bendaña 1996).

In return, the 1956 Constitution recognized the church as a legally incorporated entity with the right to own property. It also permitted religious education in the public education system and backed the founding of the Catholic University. Moreover, it opened the door for missionaries and religious orders to enter the country, something which Rossell had misgivings about. Between 1950 and 1959, the number of priests grew from 132 to 346, most of whom were foreigners.

Subsequently, Rossell withdrew his unconditional support of the liberationists, especially after Castillo Armas was assassinated in 1957. In his message dated October 15, 1954, which received less attention than his earlier letter, he proclaimed:

> The future president must purge the government of all those who exploit the proletariat, who now are to blame for the inordinate increase in the cost of living, who now are the direct plunderers of the peasants' salaries, who now are the gainsayers of needed social assistance. The exploiters are more communist than the Soviet leaders, because the latter create communists at heart, and the former create communists of opportunity....It is more important to invest funds in social justice than in roads and public works....The main thing is to have a people free of communism because they are free of misery and injustice....

THE 1954 COUP D'ETAT

In the early morning hours of June 17, 1954, four columns of three hundred armed men converged from various points along the Honduran border and entered Guatemalan territory through Esquipulas. Their purpose was to overthrow the government of Jacobo Arbenz.

The liberationists were able to accomplish their goal because the army leadership did not want to fight; it joined the conspiracy against Arbenz, and demoralization permeated its ranks. On June 24, the rebels took the city of Chiquimula. Once there, they announced the creation of the Provisional Government of Guatemala, headed by Lieutenant Colonel Carlos Castillo Armas, commander-in-chief of the National Liberation Army, which was the armed branch of a broader movement. In a radio broadcast three days later, Arbenz announced his resignation as president, and on July 3, a junta of five army officers led by Castillo Armas took control of the government.

José Bernabé Linares, chief of the secret police under Ubico, returned to Guatemala with the new government. The National Committee to Defend against

Communism *(Comité Nacional de Defensa contra El Comunismo)* was founded and the Preventive Criminal Law against Communism (*Ley Preventiva Penal contra el Comunismo*) was enacted. The committee was authorized to order the detention of any person. During the months following the fall of Arbenz, twelve thousand people were arrested, and two thousand labor and political leaders went into exile.

The committee was responsible for making a list of all individuals who had participated in communist activities in any form. Anyone who appeared on the list was automatically presumed to be extremely dangerous. People detained by order of the committee had no right to habeas corpus, and inclusion on the list barred people from government office or employment. The list grew until it included every government adversary and critic. By December 21, 1954, there were seventy-two thousand people on the committee's list.

Chapter Eleven

THE ARMED CONFLICT IN THE SIXTIES

THE NOVEMBER 13 REVOLT

In 1960, the army was experiencing internal differences. Certain officers had become involved in the corruption instigated by Ydígoras. At the same time, many field officers were displeased and indignant over the training of the Cuban Anti-Castro force at Helvetia farm in Retalhuleu, owned by Roberto Alejos. They also viewed the unrest in the streets as an indication of the general deterioration and unpopularity of the government.

Divergent military currents had been forming for quite some time. The largest of these, which called itself the Company of Children of Jesus, comprised army officers who were interested in debating the political and economic situation in the country. Another group of officers from army general headquarters was led by Colonel Carlos Paz Tejada, a retired officer who was more left-leaning politically. The third group included officers who, as cadets, had participated in the events of August 2.[1]

The November 13 revolt was organized in several dispersed army bases, which initially hampered coordination. The insurrectionists were united by the signing of a petition for the removal of the Defense Minister. Major Rafael Sesam Pereira, who had participated in the battle of Gualán against the 1954 liberationists, was one of the instigators of the revolt. Another was Captain Arturo Chur del Cid, who had been detained at the General Headquarters since October under suspicion of plotting against Ydígoras.

The plans were modified on November 12 with the discharge of Herrera Martínez and Captain César Augusto Silva Girón, who had defended the Gualán Plaza in 1954 and was sentenced and imprisoned by liberationist war tribunals. That same day, the decision was made to launch the revolt by taking over army general headquarters. Of the fifty-five officers committed to participating that morning, only five showed up, among them Lieutenant Colonel Augusto Loarca and Majors Sesam Pereira and Chicas Lemus (Cox 1995).

The rebels searched for Colonel Paz Tejada, who remained in hiding, to take command, but they were unsuccessful. Amid the confusion, they were ordered to move to Zacapa, where they would be reinforced by the Puerto Barrios military

---

[1] On August 2, 1954, a group of cadets attacked cells at Roosevelt Hospital, where hundreds of liberationists were camped out, and neutralized them (Cox 1995).

base. At about 5:00 A.M., Colonel Eduardo Llerena Müller took the Puerto Barrios base without bloodshed.

The so-called November 13 Manifesto—which was not originally drafted as such—alluded to "total political and economic chaos," and maintained that "only the army can cooperate effectively with the people" to get rid of "the reactionaries and their allies, members of the army who unlawfully retain power and enrich themselves at the expense of the people." It called for the "installation of a regime of social justice in which riches pertain to those who work and not to the exploiters, those who starve the people, and the gringo imperialists."

As Second Lieutenant Luis Trejo Esquivel prepared to take the Zacapa base, coordination broke down in Jutiapa and El Quiché. The chief of army reserves in Totonicapán had infiltrated the plotters and denounced them to Ydígoras. The Quetzaltenango base, which was crucial to the operation's success, remained loyal to the government, thereby isolating the Puerto Barrios and Zacapa bases.

Ydígoras succeeded in neutralizing the air force, which appeared to be involved in the plot, by showing the pilots a total of one million U.S. dollars in (forged) checks issued by Fidel Castro and payable to the rebellious officers. The air force did not join the rebellion, but it also refused to act against the insurrectionists. The United States Embassy then offered to let the airborne fleet stationed at Guatemala's southern coast attack Cuba. This force comprised seventy-six planes of different types, mostly B-26 and C-46 bombers. This fleet alone was vastly superior to every other Central American air force (Cox 1995).

On the afternoon of November 17, operational forces commanded by Colonel Enrique Peralta Azurdia occupied the Puerto Barrios base without resistance, thereby ending the "rash attempt." The revolt was put down in less than one week. Many of those involved, mostly soldiers, surrendered to government troops. Most went into hiding, however, and others dispersed into Honduras, El Salvador, and Mexico.

Although nearly half of the officer corps sympathized with the rebels' cause, when the moment of truth arrived, they remained loyal to their superiors. Unlike 1954, in this case officers fulfilled their "military duty." What was lacking, moreover, was a unifying figure who could bring cohesion to an extremely diverse group of disgruntled officers. From that time on, "revolutionary convictions were no longer an army concern and they came to be emblematic of the guerrillas" (Cox 1995).

Some seventy officers, sergeants, and rank and file went into exile. Forty-five of these continued to plot from Honduras, making contact with political parties such as the Revolutionary Party (PR), the National Democratic Movement (MDN), and the Christian Democrats (DC). The politicians were hatching their own schemes and asked the former army members not to act alone, since they believed a coup d'état by another army faction was imminent.

But the months of conversations with the political parties dragged on and nothing happened. Meanwhile, other events intervened. On April 29, an altercation broke out between some of the *trecistas* (participants in the November 13, 1960, uprising) and members of the judicial police; it was, in fact, the first armed clash of the new period. The police and military noose continued to tighten and, in July, one of the group's leaders, Lieutenant Alejandro de León Aragón, was killed in an exchange of gunfire with the security forces. The rebels forged a relationship with the PGT on that same day.

THE INCIPIENT GUERRILLA MOVEMENT

THE *TRECISTAS*

The grassroots protests of March and April 1962 failed to achieve their purpose, but the government was also unable to dismantle the opposition movement. The army, whose most conservative sector had achieved internal hegemony and cohesion, became the pillar of the regime. These events also had an impact on the clandestine groups, the PGT and the *trecistas*, although this time the grassroots explosion and the military crisis did not coincide.

The *trecistas*, led by Lieutenant Colonel Augusto Loarca, Lieutenant Marco Antonio Yon Sosa, and Second Lieutenants Luis Augusto Turcios Lima and Luis Trejo Esquivel, among others, took action in the midst of political turmoil. On January 24, 1962, in a main downtown thoroughfare in the capital, they killed the chief of the Department of the Judicial Police, Ranulfo González Ovalle (aka "Seven Liters") whom they held mainly responsible for the death of Lieutenant Alejandro de León Aragón. Two weeks later, on February 6, this group—composed mostly of young former officers, sergeants, and soldiers—founded the Insurrectional Front Alejandro de León Aragón–13 de Noviembre. Immediately afterward, they moved to the northeastern part of the country to take over the Zacapa military base.

The rebels divided into three guerrilla units commanded by Yon Sosa, Trejo Esquivel, and former lieutenant Julio Bolaños San Juan. The initial plan was for the three columns to carry out various armed actions and later reunite near Teculután, Zacapa. Only Yon Sosa's column made it to the assigned meeting place, as army harassment of the other columns forced them to disperse.

Having failed to attack the Zacapa military base—where they expected their old comrades-in-arms to join them—and with the army in pursuit, the rebels were forced to return to Guatemala City to regroup. In the capital they took over Radio International and read a document entitled "Who We Are, What We Want, and What We Are Fighting for." They formed the Marco Antonio Gutiérrez commandos, commanded by Turcios, and carried out acts of sabotage during the March and April street demonstrations.

SPOTLIGHT ON CONCUÁ

On March 14, the government issued a press release announcing that on the previous day a group of agitators had clashed with a military patrol at a location between Concuá and Granados, in Baja Verapaz department. According to the release, thirteen guerrillas perished during the battle, and Rodrigo Asturias Amado, son of writer Miguel Angel Asturias, was taken prisoner.

The PGT and the Revolutionary Democratic Unity Party (*Partido de Unidad Revolucionaria Democrática*—PURD) jointly trained a guerrilla group that it called the 20 de Octubre Guerrilla Front (or Detachment) commanded by Colonel Carlos Paz Tejada. This group issued a manifesto entitled "Rebellion Is the Only Path! No More Ydígoras!" and ensconced itself in the hills of Baja Verapaz. The army wiped out this group of twenty-three men in a surprise ambush. They had made several fatal mistakes: they were unfamiliar with the terrain, were poorly trained, ignored security measures, and lacked social support (PGT 1962).

FAR (REBEL ARMED FORCES)

In May 1962, a large group of university and secondary school students were forming a new organization called the Movimiento Revolucionario 12 de Abril (MR-12 de Abril) (the name recalled the date that three law students had been murdered).

The PGT, meanwhile, asserted that the situation in the country was propitious for armed struggle. In January 1962, the PGT had sent several militants to Cuba for military training: Edgar Ibarra, Alejandro Sancho, Ricardo Miranda, and "Judith." Twenty young people from the Patriotic Youth Workers (JPT), an affiliate of the PGT, had also recently arrived there with Cuban government scholarships to study at the university. Within a short time, however, they too sought military training as guerrillas; included in this group were Monterroso, Ricardo Ibarra, Julio César Macías, Rodolfo Payeras, Tristán Gómez, Carlos López, Luis Rivas, Mario Lemus, Plinio Castillo, and José María Ortiz Vides. Several of this group would become part of the future guerrilla forces and a few, such as Julio César Macías, José María Ortiz Vides, and Mario Lemus, would become guerrilla commanders.

In September, a delegation of the MR-13 de Noviembre arrived in Havana and visited former president Arbenz to propose that he lead the guerrilla movement once it had attained a degree of stability.

According to Yon Sosa, the plan to launch a guerrilla war gained impetus after his return to Guatemala in early December 1962. That was when the work of installing three guerrilla fronts, which would operate in San Marcos, Zacapa, and in the mountains of Izabal, officially began (Yon Sosa 1968). Prior to December, contacts between the MR-13 de Noviembre and the PGT were still mired in mutual reservations and suspicions, and the Cubans asked each party for its appraisal of the other.

At the end of December, the PGT sponsored a meeting among the leaders of the MR-13 de Noviembre, the Movimiento-20 de Octubre (M-20 de Octubre, armed branch of the communists), and the MR-12 de Abril; thus the FAR was founded. At that meeting Marco Antonio Yon Sosa, Luis Trejo Esquivel, and Luis Turcios Lima represented the MR-13 de Noviembre; Mario Silva Jonama, Carlos René Valle, and Joaquín Noval represented the M-20 de Octubre; and students Horacio Flores, Roberto Lobo Dubón, and probably Guillermo Paz

Cárcamo attended on behalf of the MR-12 de Abril. Yon Sosa was named commander-in-chief of the FAR.

The three fronts (or "foci," as Yon Sosa referred to them) that had been agreed upon in the plan of action to launch the guerrilla war began to take shape. Each front would have a military commander assisted by a political captain.

But the army detected the Izabal camp, forcing the guerrilla leaders to retreat deeper into the mountains and commence military operations. That was how, as Yon Sosa points out, the guerrilla struggle was hastily launched in Guatemala in early 1963.

The second front, commanded by Luis Trejo Esquivel, tried to set up camp in La Granadilla mountain in Zacapa. The third front, which would have been commanded by Luis Augusto Turcios, had to establish itself in Sierra de las Minas, Zacapa. On October 29, 1963, Turcios's unit adopted the name Guerrilla Edgar Ibarra (GEI) in honor of the leader of the student group FUEGO who had been killed in a skirmish just days before. This column began its ascent from Lake Izabal up the Sierra de las Minas, heading for the massif in the direction of Zacapa. Shortly before, in the capital, the police had discovered a support house for the future guerrillas containing maps, plans, and lists of collaborators.

The modus operandi of this early incarnation of the FAR did not follow the "deploy and detonate" formula of the Guevarist focal point approach. The amalgam of former soldiers, university students, and some peasants and workers conferred a distinct character on each group. Impending political events in the rest of the country, however, would abruptly raise the profile of the guerrilla phenomenon.

THE 1963 COUP D'ETAT

In January 1963, the defense minister, Colonel Enrique Peralta Azurdia, vetoed Arévalo as a presidential candidate. Nonetheless, on March 28, Arévalo made a surprise appearance before the Guatemalan press. On March 31, Peralta himself, backed by fifteen other colonels from the principal army commands, overthrew Ydígoras and took over the government in a bloodless coup d'état. The first proclamation of the coup plotters opened by stating "that the Republic is on the verge of an internal conflict as a result of ongoing subversion fostered by procommunist sectors, and communist infiltration has been increasing at an alarming rate with every day that passes."

For the first time the army as an institution took over the government. According to the *Miami Herald* (December 24, 1966), the decision to overthrow Ydígoras emanated from a meeting in late 1962 between President John Kennedy and his political advisors, as well as CIA Director Richard Hellman, and U.S. Ambassador to Guatemala John O. Bell. In contrast, Colonel Peralta Azurdia asserts in his memoirs that the military coup had been carefully planned over two years at the initiative of a group of officers led by him, and that the United States Embassy had no prior knowledge of the action. In any event, Washington had no objections to

Peralta Azurdia, and the relationship between the two countries remained unchanged.

The triple alliance of opposition parties (PR-MLN-DC) backed the coup in public declarations by their respective leaders, Mario Méndez Montenegro, Mario Sandoval Alarcón, and Salvador Hernández Villalobos. Various business sectors, including the Chamber of Commerce, the Coffee Exporters Association (*Asociación Nacional del Café*—ANACAFE) and the National Association of Sugar Cane Producers (*Asociación Nacional de Cañeros*) also declared their support.

The army governed between 1963 and 1966, based on a Fundamental Governmental Charter and by decree, while constitutional guarantees were suspended. In essence, the military regime derogated the 1956 Constitution, dissolved the Congress, suspended the legal status of Ydígoras' party and his ally, the MDN, and issued Decree 9 entitled "Defense of Democratic Institutions." Another law, Decree 1, established that all crimes against government security would be prosecuted by military courts. The distribution of "communist literature" was punishable by two years in prison; the manufacture of explosives, five years; membership in the communist party, ten years; and terrorism, fifteen years. Any person involved in an act of terrorism that resulted in injury or death would be executed. This decree was enforced quite arbitrarily and was used to persecute anyone who organized workers or joined unions.

The new chief of state also introduced a corrective economic policy to counteract the corruption of the Ydígoras administration. The government's official discourse embraced the development-based approach espoused by international agencies and the industrialization model based on the notion of a Central American Common Market. The government also introduced a policy of economic oversight and regulation.

In April, the new government issued the Labor Charter, which contained guarantees similar to those contemplated in the 1956 Constitution. Peralta Azurdia established a minimum wage, required employers to pay the Christmas bonus, and instituted an income tax, which affected less than 1 percent of the population. Although Guatemala was the last Latin American country to institute this tax, both the AGA and the Coordinating Committee of Agricultural, Commercial, Industrial, and Financial Associations (CACIF) opposed such measures.

THE MENDEZ MONTENEGRO GOVERNMENT

PR candidate Julio César Méndez Montenegro won the March 6, 1966, elections. Because he failed to win a simple majority, however, Congress had to elect the president through "secondary elections." This was an early indication of the weakness of the new government.

However, the candidacy of Méndez Montenegro, a prominent attorney and university professor, and the PR's slogan about what the "third government of the revolution" would accomplish, had raised public expectations. For the FAR, which had announced a unilateral cease-fire at the prospect of serious democratic reforms, this created a dilemma in terms of the validity of armed struggle.

It was at that time, in fact, that the viability of a negotiated solution to the conflict was first discussed. But army raids against guerrilla leaders four days before the elections made it clear that Peralta Azurdia and the military zone commanders had opted for a military solution to the armed conflict. This would have tragic consequences for society in the years that followed.

THE CASE OF THE 28

The capture, torture, and subsequent murder of leaders and members of the PGT, the FAR, and the MR-13 de Noviembre, which occurred March 3-5, 1966, marked the beginning of an escalation of violence that would continue throughout the second half of the sixties. Although these forced disappearances were recorded in history as the "Case of the 28" (the number given by the guerrillas), in fact no fewer than thirty-two people were detained and summarily executed, some of whom never appeared in the reports.

None of the writs of habeas corpus filed produced results. On May 3-4, a FAR commando kidnapped the vice-president of the Congress, the president of the Supreme Court of Justice, and the government secretary of information. The FAR issued an ultimatum for the presentation of the disappeared individuals (not their release) and listed the places where they were allegedly being held: the Treasury Police prison, the National Police prison, certain military bases, and a Judicial Police prison.

Prior to this raid, only the guerrillas' peasant supporters in the east had experienced systematic political terror. From that time onward, leftist leaders would suffer the same persecution. In the prevailing atmosphere the army was sending an unmistakable message to the political parties: the war against the guerrillas is to the death. A week earlier the PGT and the FAR had decided to support Méndez Montenegro. After the elections the contact between the president and the FAR continued, but without results. The PR's dilemma was as follows: negotiate with the FAR or put up with pressure from the army and the Democratic Institutional Party (PID). The message the recently elected leaders were receiving was that if they leaned toward negotiations, power would not be handed over to them.

In mid-July, two former agents asserted that "the 28 had been murdered long before, some of them at the order of Colonel Rafael Arriaga Bosque" (appointed defense minister by Méndez Montenegro) (_El Gráfico_, July 19, 1966). After being tortured and murdered, the bodies of the detainees were taken in plastic bags to the airport in Guatemala City. From there it is presumed that they were thrown into the Pacific Ocean. The case provoked tremendous public indignation.

Relatives of "the 28" filed a complaint against former Judicial Police chiefs Alberto Barrios and José María Moreira; former National Police director, Luis

González Salaverría; and the former director and former third commander of the Treasury Police, Colonel Luis Coronado Urrutia and Captain Justo Rodríguez, respectively. Although government, Congress, Supreme Court, and the army promised to investigate the multiple crime, the perpetrators were never punished.

On April 28, the Constituent Assembly, which was on the verge of dissolving, decreed an unusual amnesty for "all members of the government army and police forces...who, after July 3, 1954, carried out, in order to repress or prevent subversive activities of any nature, activities tending to attack, harm, or destroy the government system upon which the institutional life of the nation has been based, and activities related to same." The government was acknowledging that it had used repression to defend the government model established in 1954.

THE PACT WITH THE ARMY

On May 4, 1966, Méndez Montenegro signed a pact with the army that, besides solving the PR's problem regarding negotiations with the FAR, also granted the army autonomy to implement a military plan against the guerrillas. By the time the Congress had settled the election of the new leader, the pact had been signed.

Through this pact, "The Army of Guatemala guarantees the turnover of Public Power to *Licenciados* Julio César Méndez Montenegro and Clemente Marroquín Rojas...and further guarantees that said individuals will remain in their positions throughout their constitutional term. The guarantees contemplated in this clause are subject to observance of the conditions set forth in this document."

The conditions were the following:

1. Strict compliance with Articles 27, 49 (second paragraph), and 64 of the Constitution, which stipulate that "all communist actions and those against the existing democracy are punishable."

2. Guarantees protecting all of the assets held by civilian and military officials under the Peralta Azurdia government (the amnesty had excluded the protection of assets obtained irregularly through political vendettas or counterinsurgency actions.

3. Guarantee of the full autonomy of the army (for example, the defense minister and the army chief of staff were appointed based on candidates proposed by the Army High Command itself).

Several years later, Méndez Montenegro would assert that his only promise was to agree that the appointment of the army leadership would be based on a list drawn up by the army (Aguilera and Romero 1981). In contrast, shortly after the agreements were signed and while they still remained secret, Clemente Marroquín wrote in *La Hora*:

We are giving warning that the military government will be reluctant to turn power over to the PR and that it will possibly demand many conditions, including that the army structure or development not be touched. This is to say that there will be a military state within a civilian state (April 15, 1966).

The signing of the pact was a milestone in civilian-military relations. It was not the first time that the military had ensured its autonomy prior to accepting a civilian government, nor would it be the last. But the fact that a civilian president signed a secret pact with the army command lent impetus to the creation of a formidable hidden force that would place its stamp on the implementation of national security policy. This set the stage for the emergence of certain clandestine state structures of political terror that would ultimately sabotage the justice system and the government's own role as arbiter of conflicts.

ARMY REORGANIZATION

While the military regime had relied on the traditional forms of repression, marked changes in the army structure were taking place during this new period, with meddling by the United States. The size of the army doubled, and special counterinsurgency units were created within the regular army structure. The Mobile Military Police (PMA) was formed, especially in rural areas, and the National Police and the army were united under a single command structure. A modern communications network was set up, which extended throughout Central America. And, the presidential security agency (the Governmental Telecommunications Office) was established to coordinate police and military intelligence resources.

After 1963, United States military aid primarily served to strengthen specialized counterinsurgency units, which were conceived as permanent auxiliary forces within the regular army. The aid was channeled through the Military Assistance Program (MAP), whose significance had grown after the 1960 military rebellion. MAP presided over training in counter-guerrilla techniques, small-unit tactical operations, and containing rebellions. Weapons were replaced, and army communications and transport were upgraded. Guatemalans were trained by advisors, mobile teams, and military training schools in Panama and the United States.

This initiative focused on four brigades: Mariscal Zavala and Guardia de Honor in Guatemala City, the General Manuel Lisandro Barillas Brigade in Quetzaltenango, and the Captain General Rafael Carrera Brigade in Zacapa. The latter two were located in areas that, at that time, were guerrilla strongholds.

At the end of this period, the principal differences in the army had to do more with organization than with equipment or training: eight thousand men had been added to the regular army, together with more than one thousand mobile military police, and nine thousand military commissioners. The army acquired the capacity to organize an intelligence and a rural control apparatus, two key components of a counterinsurgency war.

The army was not interested in competition, and it therefore boycotted plans to strengthen the National Police and its intelligence apparatus. Ultimately, U.S. assistance for civilian security forces began to be deemphasized, leaving the latter under military control. The presidential intelligence apparatus maintained its communications network with the U.S. base in Panama and with its counterparts in other Central American countries. The army tried to remove this agency from the Presidential Palace to keep the heads of government from using it for their own political ends. But *La Regional*, as it was widely known, controlled by the military presidents of the seventies, remained the strategic branch of the Executive and carried out a campaign of political terror in conjunction with the other military intelligence agencies.

PARAMILITARY GROUPS

Paramilitary organization and actions played a key role in counterinsurgency policy in the sixties. The military commissioners' auxiliary role in regular army operations was the determinant factor in the defeat of the guerrillas. The commissioners, described by the Méndez government's defense minister Rafael Arriaga Bosque as the "eyes and ears of the army," were trained, armed, and put in charge of local security in order to destroy the guerrilla infrastructure. They also gathered intelligence, passing along information about insurgent presence, political organizers, and foreigners, and participated in military operations alongside the army. From approximately 1964 to 1968, the number of commissioners jumped from a total of three hundred countrywide to thirty times that number. Although their presence was greatest in conflictive areas of eastern Guatemala, the commissioners constituted an immense public control network that was present in every city, town, village, hamlet, and farm.

The commissioners' local political power broadened. Decree 283 of October 27, 1964, granted them the right to bear arms without a license—the same right was extended to plantation owners and their administrators—making them the equivalent of salaried security agents. Nine thousand commissioners were named in 1965, including plantation owners, industrialists, body guards, and university affiliates. They were distributed throughout the country, although 971 commissioners were mobilized in Jutiapa alone, the equivalent of one out of every fifty men in that department. The identity document carried by the commissioners gave them unlimited authority to detain and interrogate suspects, and they lost no time in committing abuses against the population.

In addition to the commissioner system, the army expanded its operational capacity using clandestine groups known as death squads, which operated in urban and rural areas. MLN leader Mario Sandoval Alarcón claimed that these groups were sponsored by army general headquarters, under the command of Colonel Rafael Arriaga Bosque, and that other high-level military officials were involved, including Manuel Sosa Avila and Colonel Carlos Arana Osorio, commander of the Zacapa military base. The death squads "were army members who passed themselves off as civilians," although there were "also organizations that operated parallel to the army, with MLN support," according to the influential liberationist. The White Hand was one of the squads directed by Army General Headquarters. The NOA, which belonged to the second category, was steered by the MLN through its leader Raúl Lorenzana, while other civilian sectors (such as conservative plantation owners) organized its funding and logistics. Besides these groups, the police force organized its own death squad.

Death squad activities broadened the army's political scope of action against the guerrillas: they facilitated clandestine assaults on insurgent organizations and leaders, enriched the army's intelligence capability, and allowed the army greater freedom and legitimacy to further its strategic positions. Government minister Héctor Mansilla Pinto insisted that the violence experienced during those years was the result of "internal strife between the extremes."

The policy of terror left no room for legal remedies. Habeas corpus, often a lifesaving measure for detainees and victims of abduction, no longer functioned. The criminal justice system, in other words, the government's right to sanction, was prostrated before a de facto system in which state power guaranteed that perpetrators could act with impunity. An uncontrollable escalation of terror had begun in Guatemala.

It is difficult to establish the number of victims during this period; estimates range as high as 20,000. Some sources estimated 8,000 deaths between 1966 and 1968 (Jonas 1991). In its 1968 report to the United Nations Human Rights Commission, the Committee for the Defense of Human Rights (a group of families of victims with links to San Carlos University) provided the names and circumstances of death of 719 people, and the abductions of 252 more, all of which occurred between July 1966 and October 1968 as a result of death squad activities.

ESCALATING VIOLENCE

Between July and October 1966, the first one hundred days of the Méndez Montenegro government, the political situation remained at an impasse. It appeared that the civilian government was assuming a more tolerant posture. The FAR, meanwhile, refrained from attacking army bases and troops, limiting itself to armed propagandistic activities during occupations of communities. The guerrillas seemed to be easing up.

But tensions soon flared. In July, an amnesty covering the period from 1960 on had been decreed on behalf of the guerrillas. The president called on the insurgents to return to civilian life, warning that they would otherwise be crushed. The PR backed this position. Guerrilla leaders Bernardo Alvarado Monzón (PGT) and Luis Turcios Lima (FAR) declared a unilateral cease-fire that would remain in effect if the civilian government removed all liberationists from positions of authority and reined in the army. Colonel Arriaga Bosque said that the army was remaining alert and respected the Constitution. Everything appeared to be at a standstill until, on October 2, Turcios Lima died in a mysterious traffic accident; the next day, the army launched an offensive in the eastern part of the country.

The guerrilla structure, comprising some three hundred combatants and approximately five thousand supporters, was torn down between October 1966 and August 1967 (Figueroa 1996). In March 1967, Guatemalan poet Otto René Castillo and Nora Paiz, exhausted after a long trek, were captured; they were subsequently tortured and murdered. One hundred men were killed just outside Río Hondo, Zacapa, where, to this day, their bodies remain buried in a clandestine cemetery.

THE DECLINE OF THE GUERRILLAS

Turcios's death was pivotal for the FAR. On October 10, the PGT's Political Commission announced the decision to appoint "César Montes" as the new FAR commander. Montes had to move from the mountains to the city, leaving "Camilo Sánchez" in charge of the Edgar Ibarra Front (FGEI). It was Sánchez and "Pablo Monsanto" who decided to take the town of San Agustín Acasaguastlán, El Progreso, an event that received extensive publicity. But the army offensive launched on October 3, one day after Turcios's death, was already underway.

After taking San Agustín, the guerrillas lost contact and were dispersed into small patrols. The first group to succumb to the army offensive was commanded by "La Chancha." Symbolically, the army recovered the same Browning 30mm rifle that the guerrillas had previously captured during one of their most successful operations, the ambush at Sunzapote, Río Hondo, Zacapa. The army stepped up its operations in Zacapa, Chiquimula, and Puerto Barrios. Between October 1966 and May 1967, the FGEI was wiped out. Mario Botzoc, a charismatic student leader and FAR member, was killed in March, and urban resistance chief Arnaldo Vásquez Rivera was killed in April.

Camilo Sánchez assigned Carlos López to take fifteen guerrilla fighters to Sierra de las Minas. When the latter were unable to make contact, they demobilized, but the majority were captured in the process. When Montes learned of Sánchez's order, he requested an explanation, signaling a rift within the guerrilla movement.

A group of one hundred guerrillas (although the core group consisted of only about forty) had remained in Cuba to receive military training. This group had tried unsuccessfully to keep Turcios from leaving. A plan that would affect the entire continent was being devised in Cuba. Ricardo Ramírez, a confidant of Fidel Castro, was involved. The plan was to establish three focal points of conflict in Latin America (Bolivia, Venezuela, and Guatemala) in order to provoke a military crisis comparable to Vietnam.

But the plan to ignite the Americas quickly floundered. Ché Guevara died in the Bolivian jungle in October. The Venezuelan guerrilla landing was detected, and ongoing U.S. Navy patrols in the Caribbean impeded the mobilization of the Guatemalan insurgent group still in Cuba. By then, it had become clear to the Cubans that the FAR had collapsed.

The offensive operations pursued the guerrillas in the capital, where the army relied heavily on death squads. The PGT regrouped and decided against joining the battle. However, in January 1968, Rogelia Cruz was captured; her corpse, bearing evidence of rape and torture, was found on the southern coast. Leonardo Castillo Johnson, her partner and a prominent PGT leader, was enraged and unleashed a wave of military actions in the capital that resulted, over a few hours, in the deaths of a group of U.S. military advisors, an attack on Manuel Villacorta Vielman, the death of Alfonso Alejos, and a grenade attack against army general headquarters. This chain reaction culminated in Castillo Johnson's own death on Martí Street, as he was trying to elude fierce police pursuit. Educator Rafael Tishler, also a member of the PGT's Central Committee, was captured at the end of the month, and six bodies were later found in an alleged safe house.

Confined to the capital, "Camilo Sánchez" kept up constant military actions. But he was captured early one August morning in Zone 11 of Guatemala City. In a rescue attempt, a guerrilla commando tried to kidnap U.S. Ambassador Gordon Mein, killing the diplomat in the process. The FAR carried out Camilo's plan of concentrating in the Petén and, in January 1969, adopted the rallying cry "Everything for the Front" (*todo para el frente*). From February to April, twenty-four select FAR guerrillas tried to establish their area of operations, but they underestimated the difficulty of the terrain and were lost. In the capital, new classes of guerrillas, graduating from secondary schools (Aqueche, Normal, and Central), kept the FAR structures alive.

In 1970, the guerrillas once again had to confront the issue of elections. The PGT called on people to refrain from voting or to invalidate their vote. The FAR, in contrast, decided to encourage the public to vote for General Carlos Arana Osorio, the military commander who had brought about the guerrillas' defeat in the east, in order to polarize society and hasten the shift toward armed struggle.

In February 1970, Monsanto and Percy Jacobs kidnapped Foreign Affairs Minister Alberto Fuentes Mohr, thereby securing the release of fellow FAR member Vicente Girón Calvillo, who had been apprehended by the security forces. Two weeks later, the FAR kidnapped Sean Holly, the U.S. Embassy's labor attaché, and demanded the release of two other militants. Two weeks later, German Ambassador Karl Von Spretti was kidnapped; the guerrillas tried to exchange him for fifteen other detainees. This time, however, the government hardened its stance. It denied that it was holding the detainees, even as the security forces tightened security around the diplomatic corps, thereby preventing the guerrillas' next move: the kidnapping of the Israeli ambassador. In April, the FAR negotiated a ransom with the German government for the release of its ambassador, but before the agreed-upon amount of U.S. $700,000 could be delivered, Von Spretti's murdered corpse was found.

Serious disagreements soon erupted within the FAR, and between July and August, a major schism occurred. Percy Jacobs (responsible for the Gordon Mein kidnapping attempt), "Sustos," and Arévalo Bocaletti broke with Pablo Monsanto, whom they blamed for the failure to establish a guerrilla presence in the Petén. Monsanto maintained that control of funds was at the heart of the dispute. The dissidents headed for El Salvador and later settled in Mexico. They tried to establish a presence there but were detected by the security forces. The three former guerrillas were found assassinated in Guatemala's San Marcos department. And Landa Castañeda, a former FAR member implicated in the Von Spretti murder, was killed in El Salvador.

Arana was elected president on July 1, 1970, and, in January 1971, he unleashed a brutal wave of terror. He decreed a state of siege, closed off all access to the city, and conducted a house-to-house search. Political leader Adolfo Mijangos López was killed during that period, and Alfonso Bauer Paiz was attacked. The PGT, which was in the process of rebuilding its youth organization (JPT), was hard hit. The army hunted down the communists' intellectual leadership, who supposedly had designed a military plan. Fifteen militants were detained before the security forces finally zeroed in on their target: Marco Antonio Leoni. The young militant and PGT military chief was detained on 18th Street in Zone 1 of the capital.

The FAR was on the defensive in the capital city, although it continued to carry out punishing attacks such as the murder of journalist Isidoro Zarco of the Guatemalan daily *Prensa Libre*. The Cuba group, which had broken off relations with the FAR in 1969, decided to form another organization. The MR-13 de Noviembre was mortally wounded, having been bled of its cadres over the preceding years, when Yon Sosa undertook to rebuild it. He carried out a couple of insignificant military actions in the capital together with "El Indio" Hernández and "Coche" Vides. He then tried to contact the group from Cuba, which at that time was arriving in Chiapas, but he was detained by the Mexican army together with indigenous guerrilla leader Socorro Sical. Although Yon Sosa identified himself with his military rank, and turned over his weapon and money to the man who would one day be known as General Casillas, his life was not spared. The MR-13 de Noviembre ceased to exist following the death of Yon Sosa. Its surviving leaders were killed in the ensuing years, Luis Molina Loza in 1971 and Thelma Gracioso in 1973.

Despite ongoing political persecution, the grassroots movement reemerged during the state of siege. This inspired a tactical realignment of the PGT, which shifted its emphasis to social groups, leaving the military strategies on the back burner. But on September 28, 1972, the police detained six founding members of the party at a meeting house: Bernardo Alvarado Monzón, Carlos Alvarado Jerez, Mario Silva Jonama, Carlos René Valle y Valle, Carlos Hernández, and Hugo Barrios Klee. The house manager, Fantina Hernández, was also taken. The PGT would never recover from the blow. In December 1974, its new secretary, Huberto Alvarado, was murdered, thus ending the cycle of war of the sixties.

THE CATHOLIC CHURCH

The Catholic church of the sixties was absorbed by its own expansion. Nonetheless, there were indications even then of changes that would have a profound impact on the church in this decade. In 1959, Pope John XXIII announced the ecumenical council that would be held in four sessions from 1962 to 1965 and concluded by Pope Paul VI. The Second Vatican Council had a pastoral focus, meaning that it emphasized the content and method of the gospel message in contemporary society. It introduced the "return and recovery of the holy scripture" as a source of theological reflection as well as the definition of church as "people of God." The church was reconciling itself with the world of contemporary Europe.

As the Latin American church endeavored to interpret Vatican II in Medellín (1968), it systematically turned to the social sciences to devise a rational explanation for the structural causes of poverty; it underscored accompaniment of the poor, a renewed spirit of community in local parishes, a united pastoral effort, and the struggle for peace and justice. In the case of Guatemala,

> the principles of Liberation Theology were unknown to most pastoral agents who had been trained in anti-communist church settings and pre–Vatican II theological concepts. Later, it was extremely difficult for them to embark systematically on a new theological course of study given the heavy demands of their pastoral duties. The reality, the faith experience and practice of the poor would be the fountain from which pastoral agents would drink their spirituality and commitment...(although) the Medellín documents would serve as their reference and the source of inspiration for their actions (REMHI, *Presencia y acción de la Iglesia en el conflicto armado,* 1997).

Two issues were uppermost in the bishops' minds during those years, judging from their joint letters: land tenure and political violence, which intensified under Méndez Montenegro. The Guatemalan Bishops' Conference (CEG), founded in 1964, issued its first statement on violence in a May 9, 1967, message that still stopped short of attributing responsibility.

The presence of foreign clergy that had begun during the previous decade remained strong, and the church continued its decentralization process with the creation of several new dioceses. The number of priests grew from 346 in 1959 to 608 in 1970. The Maryknoll Fathers began their work in Huehuetenango; the Missionaries of the Sacred Heart went to El Quiché; the Missionaries of the Immaculate Heart of Mary settled in Escuintla; and the Dominicans went to Alta and Baja Verapaz. The Franciscans, the Carmelites, the Capuchins, the Jesuits, and the Spanish Institute of Foreign Missions (IEME), were involved in other areas and activities throughout the country. Different orders of women religious also began their missionary work in many parishes. The Guatemalan Religious Conference (CONFREGUA) was founded in June 1961 and would have a significant impact on the church's evolution over the next three decades.

There were three distinct currents among the clergy: the sacramentalists, the movement-based group, and the developmentalists. The sacramentalist view of pastoral care emphasized administering the sacraments; the movement-based group worked primarily through Catholic lay organizations such as the Christian Studies Program (*Cursillo Cristiano*) and the Christian Family Movement (*Movimiento Familiar Cristiano*). The developmentalist current sought to address people's immediate needs through cooperativism, peasant leagues, pro-improvement committees, and the construction of schools and basic infrastructure. This last group occasionally provided short-term assistance through Cáritas and Catholic Relief Services.

In many hamlets and villages members of Rural Catholic Action (*Acción Católica Rural*) were the ones who responded to the offer of developmentalist pastoral care. These were usually peasants who had attained a slightly higher economic and social status than the majority of the population and were taking part in a "green revolution" produced by the introduction of chemical fertilizers. Alternatively, they were businessmen who targeted peasants with superior buying power. The Christian Democratic Party (which was founded in 1956 by Catholics close to Bishop Rossell), carrying the developmentalist standard, influenced and politicized cooperatives, peasant leagues, and Catholic Action. In opposition, the indigenous religious leadership (*cofradías*) opted to support the MLN and the PID. But by that time the Melville Fathers, Maryknoll priests who had arrived in the country in 1957 and had been organizing youth groups, had decided to support the armed struggle.

Beginning in 1965, the Jesuits and the Maryknollers had organized social-skills-training courses in rural areas. Advanced students, priests, and women religious participated in these courses. The Cráter project (a Maryknoll project that put well-to-do students in touch with impoverished communities) grew out of these courses.

These were the years of the U.S. government's Alliance for Progress, as well as the huge agricultural expansion efforts in northern Huehuetenango and El Quiché (Ixcán and the Zona Reina). The cooperative movement peaked and new crops were introduced in El Quiché, Huehuetenango, San Marcos, Sololá, and the Petén. The government Agrarian Reform Institute (INTA) turned the colonization of the Ixcán Grande area (El Quiché) over to the Maryknoll Fathers, and it progressed significantly due to the work of Father William Woods.

Besides agricultural projects, religious orders were involved in health and education. They created radiophonic schools to promote literacy, with the support of church radio stations: Radio Chortí in Jocotán, Radio Mam in Cabricán, Radio Nahualá, Radio Atitlán in Santiago Atitlán, Radio Colomba, Radio Quiché, and later, Radio Tezulutlán in Cobán. Many parishes opened health clinics, while religious groups worked with local health promoters. The Association of Community Health Services (ASECSA) was formed at the initiative of clergy and religious orders. Thus, by the end of the 1960s, the church had made its mark nationally as an institution committed to the social development of rural peasants and disadvantaged populations.

Chapter Twelve

THE MILITARY GOVERNMENTS OF THE SEVENTIES

THE MILITARY PROJECT

Beginning with General Carlos Arana Osorio's administration (1970-74), the army took over the government with a development plan for the medium term, which would have to be sustained through electoral fraud given the internal weakness of political alliances representing conflicting economic interests. Thus, a new cycle of economic growth began that, as in the early sixties, offered greater opportunities for business circles. The army tolerated a certain degree of grassroots activism in an effort to allay social unrest, particularly between 1974 and 1978. However, given the futility of achieving genuine reforms through the established channels, this activism rapidly shifted toward a new insurgent movement that began to challenge the system and, following the 1979 triumph of the Sandinista Revolution, to seek reforms through insurrection.

The industrial sector, which still enjoyed the protectionist advantages established in the context of the Central American Common Market (even though this sector was by then functioning as a junior partner to the transnational groups), became increasingly intolerant of the labor movement.

New export opportunities offered by the international market, increased productivity resulting from the introduction and rapid spread of fertilizers in the sixties, and expanded agricultural frontiers due to colonization raised the value of lands cultivated by indigenous populations, which had previously been considered of marginal value. Large-scale agricultural entrepreneurs, or army officers turned entrepreneurs, began to seize communal lands. Numerous small- and medium-scale entrepreneurs followed closely on their heels (especially ladinos from the east or from middle-class urban enclaves around the country), attempting to take possession of lands that had suddenly become valuable.

THE ARANA GOVERNMENT

General Arana formed a coalition government with the National Liberation Movement (MLN) and the Democratic Institutional Party (PID), notwithstanding serious differences between the two parties over economic policy. Both parties, however, agreed on the need to support a strong, military-run government that would put an end to guerrilla activities once and for all.

This alliance of two separate currents within the business sector was short-lived. Although the MLN-PID coalition took 74 percent of the municipalities in the 1972 elections, Arana distanced himself from the MLN in 1973 and proceeded to eliminate the principal leaders of *la Mano Blanca*, which was regarded as the MLN death squad (Handy 1984). The alliance was reestablished, however, in time for the 1974 elections.

POLITICAL TERROR

The objective of political violence was to crush the guerrilla infrastructure in the capital where, in 1970-71, the FAR in particular had carried out several noteworthy operations. A climate of terror also pervaded urban areas throughout the country.

Selective repression claimed numerous victims. Christian democratic deputy Adolfo Mijangos López was assassinated on January 14, 1971. Peasant leader Tereso de Jesús Oliva was killed a week later, on January 20. Julio Camey Herrera, a professor at San Carlos University, also lost his life during this period, and attorney Alfonso Bauer Paiz was shot at. Mijangos, Camey, and Bauer were members of a committee investigating a government contract with the Exploraciones y Explotaciones Mineras de Izabal, S.A. corporation, a mining company that operated in Izabal, mining nickel, copper, iron, and other minerals for export. In September, the PGT's Political Commission was apprehended. And, in October, student leader Manuel Cordero Quezada was murdered, sparking a protest campaign led by the Front against Violence (*Frente Contra La Violencia*). Many of these crimes were attributed to death squads such as *la Mano Blanca*, *Ojo por Ojo* (Eye for an Eye), and NOA.[1] In May 1973, a land takeover by indigenous communities from Sansirisay, El Progreso, was bloodily suppressed by then-army chief of staff Efraín Ríos Montt.

POWER ALLIANCES

In order to create a powerful economic bloc inside the business sector, General Arana used his contacts with Cuban exiles to forge alliances with emergent groups—protegés of President Richard Nixon—in the southern United States. He also explored common interests with the Somoza group of Nicaragua. Several families who had lost their traditional financial power joined the Aranista plan. Finally, numerous army commanders and officers received lands that were being colonized in the Petén through a public enterprise for development known as the *Fomento y Desarrollo del Petén*—FYDEP.

This alliance led to disputes with other business circles such as that led by the Castillo and Novella families. These disagreements were reflected in the MLN-PID alliance, as the MLN tended to be closer to the traditional interests

---

[1] *New York Times*, June 13, 1971.

of entrepreneurial families and the PID identified more closely with the military project. The old plantation owners were against the economic protagonism of the generals, and differences among the military leadership reverberated in the political parties. The Skinner Klee and García Granados families joined the army in nickel and petroleum extraction ventures and financial affairs through the Santander Bank. In 1971, entrepreneur Manuel Ayau founded Francisco Marroquín University to educate a new elite and reduce the interventionist influence of the AID-funded Central American Business Administration Institute (INCAE).

In 1973, agricultural sectors dissatisfied with the power of the General Association of Growers (AGA) formed the Agro Chamber in an effort to unite the numerous associations springing up all over the country. New sectors, such as poultry breeders and cardamom farmers, created their own associations. By the end of this period conflicts had arisen between different economic subgroups (meat and dairy farmers, cotton and textile producers, wheat and bread producers, cane and cattle farmers), which sought government intervention to solve their conflicts in the marketplace.

Competing economic interests ultimately fractured the political bloc that Arana had built and weakened the constituency of his successor, General Kjell Laugerud García.

THE LAUGERUD GOVERNMENT

Elections were held on March 5, 1974, and in a secondary vote in the Congress, General Kjell Laugerud, Arana's former defense minister, was elected president. The opposition, which had backed General Efraín Ríos Montt's candidacy in a broad alliance led by the Christian Democrats and encompassing social democrats and communists, denounced the elections as fraudulent. The MLN-PID coalition remained fragile after Arana imposed Laugerud's candidacy and the MLN chose its own leader, Mario Sandoval, as vice-president. This coalition would dissolve a year later, after failing to reach an agreement on control of the Congress.

In February 1976, after the earthquake in Guatemala, the MLN and PID clashed once more, this time over control of the National Reconstruction Committee (CRN). Nonetheless, the post-earthquake period was one of significant economic growth, which, as engineered by the government, particularly benefited PID and Aranist politicians and businessmen, excluding the MLN. But medium-term investment plans required a continuity of political leadership that extended beyond the electoral period. Thus, a new PID-PR-Aranist alliance was forged for the 1978 elections. Its slate included General Romeo Lucas, Laugerud's defense minister and administrator of the northern roadway connector project, and Francisco Villagrán Kramer, an international lawyer and member of the Revolutionary Party.

GRASSROOTS STRUGGLE

Land-tenancy problems set the stage for the emergence of the Committee of Peasant Unity (CUC), which published its first communiqué in the Guatemalan daily *El Gráfico* on November 19, 1978. The year before, a secretly organized indigenous group from the highlands and the southern coast had participated in the traditional May 1 demonstration. This group went on to participate in the October 20 commemorative march in preparation for a major demonstration in support of the miners of Ixtahuacán in November (Arias 1985).

The labor and urban grassroots movement gained impetus between 1976 and 1978. During the Laugerud government, 119 strikes and work stoppages took place involving more than 100,000 workers and resulting in over one million workdays lost. These events ranged from spontaneous confrontations accompanied by clashes with the security forces to mass mobilizations with national impact.

The National Committee of Labor Unity (CNUS), which had begun to operate by 1976, proposed joint actions with students and urban slum dwellers from lower-class neighborhoods. In March 1977 the National Workers Central (CNT) and the Latin American Workers Central (CLAT) split, an event that would contribute significantly to the radicalization of the CNT. The Organized Front of Unions in Amatitlán (FOSA) was founded in April, and in December the Emergency Committee of Public Employees (CETE) was organized.

Labor struggles peaked in 1978. Workers won better wages in several corporations. At the same time various public employee sectors added their demands, and the movement's struggles became increasingly cohesive and united, eventually encompassing religious, student, and urban sectors. More than 100,000 people mobilized for the May 29 protest of the Panzós massacre.

OTHER TRENDS

AN INTOLERANT BUSINESS SECTOR

Despite a recent upward trend in the economy (with more than 7 percent growth of the Gross Domestic Product in 1977 and 1978), business groups failed to open channels of consultation with the workers that would temper the expectations raised by this economic prosperity. Cotton growers and new entrepreneurs who had joined government ventures were the most prosperous, although the industrial sector continued to enjoy the protectionist advantages created by the Central American Common Market. These new groups were extremely intolerant of labor demands. Their intolerance ultimately led some entrepreneurs to forge alliances with the army in order to violently crush labor leadership and organizations.

RENEWED LAND SEIZURES

Land reappraisals launched a new round of seizures (a scaled-down version of those that accompanied the Liberal Reform), which, by the mid-seventies, had developed into a sharp increase in violence against peasant communities, surpassing even the violence unleashed against beneficiaries of the agrarian reform of the fifties. This cycle of land seizures became the backdrop for many of the violent incidents that occurred between 1980 and 1982.

THE DETERIORATION OF THE ELECTORAL SYSTEM

The army had to resort to electoral fraud in order to sustain its investment plan, given the internal weakness of political alliances built on opposing forces in the business sector. Therefore, beginning with the election of General Carlos Arana in 1970, the same pattern of succession, in which the defense minister became the presidential candidate with a guarantee of victory, was repeated. All of this took place under a veneer of formal electoral proceedings as provided by the 1965 Constitution.

THE RISE OF THE INDIGENOUS MOVEMENT

The 1976 earthquake was a true trial by fire for indigenous communities and regional centers. Overnight they were forced by circumstances to assume political and social responsibilities and address the enormous needs generated by the catastrophe. They had few resources available to them, in addition to being cut off from the departmental capital and Guatemala City, in some cases for several weeks.

In contrast to the old leaders appointed by external political authorities, the community elected new leaders with concrete job descriptions. The central government, overwhelmed by the scope of the disaster, tolerated the fact that the communities were taking the initiative and were virtually transforming themselves into local authorities that negotiated directly with international assistance agencies channeling relief.

EVOLUTION OF THE NEW GUERRILLA MOVEMENT

By 1976 the guerrilla struggle had been successfully reorganized in several parts of the country. The Revolutionary Organization of the People in Arms (ORPA) was finalizing its war preparations in San Marcos. The Rebel Armed Forces (FAR) was engaged in an internal debate that would lead it to adopt a strategy based on guerrilla fronts. A third group, the Guerrilla Army of the Poor (EGP), was advancing a new type of guerrilla warfare, even as the army launched the first counterinsurgency operation against EGP forces in northern El Quiché. When Lucas took power, the EGP was particularly active.

THE EVOLUTION OF COUNTERINSURGENCY

The army had spent the seventies shaping and refining a counterinsurgency strategy based on more than a decade of experience in anti-guerrilla warfare. Civic action was elevated and incorporated into the Army General Staff headquarters; intelligence and counterintelligence policy was designed for the medium term, although the presidency directly controlled the intelligence apparatus, as had been the case under the Liberal dictatorships. Intelligence work was premised on the notion that the counterinsurgency struggle would be cyclical in Guatemalan history. Therefore, it was geared toward striking at organizations in their early stages or reorganization phases, acting without haste and with a focus on information collection.

Moreover, several tactical innovations were introduced that would be used extensively in the course of the anti-guerrilla campaigns of 1980-81. The army chose the Israeli Galil rifle as the best weapon for anti-guerrilla warfare in the mountains and equipped itself with Bell helicopters, combat-fitted Pilatus aircraft, and Israeli Aravá cargo planes. This was accomplished with international assistance, which arrived this time from Israel, Taiwan, and Argentina, rather than directly from the United States.

THE LUCAS ERA

General Romeo Lucas García was chosen in elections decried as fraudulent, in which only 15 percent of the eligible population participated. His government was characterized by increasingly acute contradictions that had been building up throughout the seventies, since the Arana regime.

The trends observed during the Lucas administration marked it as a period of extreme violence and escalating political conflicts. In 1979, 1,371 political murders and abductions were recorded; there were 2,264 cases in 1980, and 3,426 cases in 1981 (Figueroa 1991). It was as if a series of political distortions that had been simmering during the earlier periods suddenly exploded. Those years are engraved in the memory of the Guatemalan people as the blackest period of their history: "the Lucas period." In a tragic progression, the country hurtled into the spiral of violence that would mark the following decade.

CONSPICUOUS CRIMES

President Lucas took power in July 1978. Between July and October the political space that had broadened under the previous regime narrowed abruptly. The initial attacks were launched in the aftermath of grassroots protests against the hike in urban transport fares; lists of people condemned to death were circulated, signaling the beginning of a new wave of repression. During the second half of 1978, five hundred corpses were found, two hundred of which showed signs of torture (Amnesty International 1980).

The wave of state-sponsored terror that began in 1978 included two distinct periods. The first, which lasted until approximately 1980, focused on destroying the grassroots movement. It therefore sought to eliminate unions, movements of urban residents, and high school and university student associations. The open, legal struggles that peaked in the protests of October 1978 were met with terror, which destroyed the progress made by the grassroots movement during the seventies (Figueroa 1991).

It is likely that the decision to resort once again to state terror was confirmed during protests against public transportation fare increases in October 1978. As these protests were suppressed, forty people died, three hundred were wounded, and fifteen hundred were detained. But other crimes were a continuation of the violence unleashed during the final months of the outgoing government. Such was the case of the murder of Father Hermógenes López, priest of the San José Pinula parish, on June 30, just hours after Lucas García took office. This murder marked the beginning of the escalation of violence against the Catholic church. Another example is the June 29 murder of CNT leader José Alberto Alvarado, which was a prelude to the impending violence against labor leaders. Repression in rural areas was intimately linked to land seizures and army counterinsurgency operations.

Among the most representative cases of violence in 1978 were the murder of Oliverio Castañeda de León, secretary general of the University Students' Association (AEU), perpetrated on October 20 in broad daylight in downtown Guatemala City, and the murders of attorneys Santiago López Aguilar and Jesús Marroquín, and Coca Cola union leader Pedro Quevedo. The violence mounted throughout 1979. The two most prominent leaders of the social democratic opposition were killed. On January 25, Alberto Fuentes Mohr, the head of the Social Democratic Party was murdered, as was Manuel Colom Argueta, a FUR leader, on March 22. Both killings took place in broad daylight in downtown Guatemala City during a conspicuous operation that even featured helicopter backup.

The wave of repression extended through 1980, taking on massive proportions that ultimately dismantled the increasingly radicalized urban labor organizations. In one significant case, on May 1 (Labor Day), thirty-two people were kidnapped in Parque Centenario in the capital. During Labor Day commemorative events, the CNUS called for the "overthrow of the Lucas regime and the installation of a revolutionary, democratic, and popular government." Shortly thereafter, on June 21, twenty-seven CNT leaders were abducted. On August 24, the Mobile Military Police abducted and forcibly disappeared seventeen CNT leaders and union advisors from the Incasa, Cidasa, and Kern factories in Emaús, Palín, in the department of Escuintla. These blows virtually decapitated a significant portion of the labor movement that, just a few years before, had extricated itself from the tutelage of the Christian Democrats. In 1980, a total of 110 labor leaders were murdered.

On January 31, 1980, the police burned thirty-nine people alive in the Spanish Embassy. Selective murder campaigns targeting rural community leaders commenced during the second half of that year, as peasant organizations became increasingly radicalized. In July, the army launched an offensive in the Ixil region by wiping out the village of Cocop, in Nebaj. On August 20, the army gunned down sixty men in the village square in San Juan Cotzal following a guerrilla attack on the army base.

The year came to a violent conclusion with the abductions of journalist Irma Flaquer and poet Alaíde Foppa in the capital. Repression persisted into 1981, targeting other sectors such as students (particularly the leadership of two leftist student groups from San Carlos University, the Robin García Revolutionary Student Front [FERG] and *FRENTE*) and the Catholic church, to the extreme that the diocese of Quiché was forced to shut down temporarily.

THE COUNTERINSURGENCY OFFENSIVES

Beginning with the massacres in the Ixil region, the army launched an extensive counterinsurgency offensive designed and conducted by the Army General Staff, which circumvented the interests and intrigues that paralyzed the Defense Ministry and most high-level commanders. It is possible to reconstruct the logic of that bloodbath by mapping out chronologically the bloody events that took place between January 1981 and March 1982.

The first three months of 1981 were characterized by an army offensive in response to armed actions by guerrilla forces in northeastern Chimaltenango and southern El Quiché departments. This was the first offensive that yielded a horrendous number [thousands] of victims. It appears that military zone commanders directed these first military campaigns against specific communities chosen for their affinity to the guerrillas. From June onward, these operations were planned and executed directly by the Army General Staff. Nonetheless, this initial campaign against the population of Chimaltenango was only a prelude to the real offensive that would begin on October 1.

A similar situation could be observed in the departments of Alta and Baja Verapaz, where isolated incidents of violence appeared to be random and, therefore, were presumed to be part of the routine repression carried out by the respective military zone.

The massacres continued and became increasingly dramatic. It was not until June, however, that the Army General Staff, commanded by General Benedicto Lucas García, the president's brother, launched an intensive anti-guerrilla offensive characterized by a coherent military strategy.

The offensive began with a campaign to dismantle the guerrillas' rear guard in the capital using operational intelligence units directed by the Presidential

General Staff (EMP). These units initially targeted specific militants or installations in isolated attacks geared toward acquiring more information. Then, on July 8, 1981, these units launched a campaign that combined military objectives with information collection and psychological operations. These operational units, which were highly compartmentalized and commanded from the highest levels (the army chief of staff), began an intensive campaign of propaganda and psychological warfare. They cast their nets wide and made use of information from private enterprise and government agencies. They started out with the Population and Housing Census of 1980 and, after a city-wide sweep, proceeded to demolish guerrilla safe houses, especially those belonging to ORPA and the EGP.

The offensive against ORPA began on July 9, 1981, with an assault on a residence in Vista Hermosa. On July 10, the army destroyed another guerrilla compound in Colonia El Carmen in the southern part of the city. Then, on July 18, the army destroyed the house where the EGP had sworn in its first unit in the city. On July 19 the army dismantled an ORPA safe house in Zone 14, killing ORPA leader Commander "Antonio." An EGP house was discovered on August 13 in Zone 11, and still another in Santa María Cauqué, replete with military equipment and a kidnapped businessman. The army killed approximately fifty guerrillas during this six-week campaign.

The army kept up the pressure on San Marcos, El Quiché, El Petén, and Alta Verapaz to preclude cooperation between organizations or between fronts within an organization. On October 1, 1981, it launched a massive offensive against the Augusto César Sandino Front (FACS). Months before, in July, this front had carried out a series of spectacular actions in the central highland region with tremendous support from the population, and a number of activists from the capital had recently taken refuge there.

In the same theater of operations directed by General Benedicto Lucas, the army deployed an advance post overnight between Tecpán and Los Encuentros and immediately began to raze every hamlet in the proximity of the Pan-American Highway. Thus, the massacres multiplied in proportion to the level of affiliation with the guerrillas, based on the wealth of information that had been amassed by the army. The only guerrilla response, meanwhile, involved sporadic attempts to harass the army by the FIL and one platoon of a permanent guerrilla unit.

The campaign covered 1,560 square miles, affecting thirty-six municipalities and three departmental capitals in the departments of Chimaltenango, Sololá, El Quiché, and Sacatepéquez. Five brigades were involved, with two thousand men from the three branches of the military, commanded by the army chief of staff. The latter created the Joint Operations Command to bring all branches, forces, and services under a unified chain of command. Forces from the military zones in Guatemala City, Cobán, Salamá, and Huehuetenango participated in the campaign, as well as the army advance posts in Santa Cruz del Quiché and Santiago Atitlán. The army also diversified and decentralized the rear guard, which no longer answered to the capital. The brigades' central command was installed in La Alameda School in Chimaltenango, bypassing Defense Ministry oversight.

The offensive featured highly mobile and diverse operations. The tactic was to retain the initiative, respond aggressively to attacks, and engage the enemy, rather than seek control of territory. Surprise attacks were emphasized; plans were not previously disclosed. The army also carried out operations to surround guerrilla forces for "hammer and anvil" strikes. For this they used natural barriers, such as the Motagua River, and tactical encirclement consisting of maneuvers to attract guerrilla units, fix their location, surround and eliminate them.

Despite the military complexity of this operation, the operational phase (not including the preparatory phase) began in November and lasted only three weeks. But this first offensive hit the civilian population the hardest because the guerrillas had only begun to establish themselves in the zone of operations and had deployed only a few platoons of regular fighters. The strategic significance for the army lay not in disabling guerrilla combat units, but in permanently cutting off the central highlands as a natural corridor between remote mountainous areas and the capital.

In addition to the civilian victims of this offensive, the army continued to concentrate on eliminating guerrilla support bases in combat zones or other areas where the guerrillas were known to be particularly strong. To this end, the two-pronged approach of individual murders and collective crimes continued in other areas of the country. They were directed by an increasingly centralized command structure under the Army General Staff but were carried out under the operational responsibility of the military zone commander, who placed his own unique imprint on the wave of repression that washed over each region.

Later, during the first months of 1982, the army offensive targeted the northwestern highlands and Alta and Baja Verapaz departments. The army pursued successive targets, using the civil patrols to maintain pressure on areas that had already succumbed to its control. In January 1982, the army launched a campaign against ORPA in San Marcos, where the massacre in the village of Sacuchum, San Pedro Sacatepéquez, occurred. One thousand soldiers surrounded the village on January 1 and proceeded to kill forty-seven people. The El Tablero massacre happened during the same period, following a five-hour battle between the guerrillas and approximately fifteen hundred soldiers from Santa Ana Berlín and San Marcos.

CHANGING AND UNCERTAIN TIMES

The tragic sequence of criminal acts related here occurred in an extremely complex context in which evolving social phenomena—such as an increasingly active indigenous-peasant movement and the expectations raised by the prospect of revolutionary change—came face to face with the decline of "showcase democracy," corruption, and the excessive ambitions of groups within the government bureaucracy and the business sector.

The international panorama was particularly bleak for General Lucas's government. Moreover, it is important to take into account a factor that rarely surfaces in analyses of those times: the Soviet Union's and Cuba's perception of a weakened United States government, which, in a more complicated strategic context, led both countries to guide and support revolutionary movements in support of their objectives of taking power.

As it turned out, their appraisal of the situation was overly optimistic, especially after Republican candidate Ronald Reagan won the November 1980 presidential elections in the United States. Powerful sectors in Guatemala took immediate note of this event. One significant example was the December visit of Roberto Alejos and Manuel Ayau to president-elect Reagan to discuss the new administration's policies for Guatemala. The Guatemalan businessmen had given U.S.$2,000,000 to Reagan's campaign (Escoto and Marroquín 1992).

This did not immediately help to clarify the international panorama, however, which hovered between the "triumphalist" stance of those who failed to perceive the changes in motion, and the uncertainty of those who felt they were receiving mixed signals. Since 1977 the Guatemalan army's relationship with the United States had been ambivalent. At that time the Carter administration had suspended military aid to Guatemala in response to reports of human rights violations as well as pressure from the British government due to Guatemala's attempts to claim Belize. In any event, the Lucas administration decided to pay the international price, as evidenced by the Spanish Embassy massacre.

In 1981, significant events at the international level exacerbated tensions. In August, Washington issued its first travel advisory for Guatemala. A few months later—in the midst of the guerrilla offensive and the army counteroffensive commanded by Benedicto Lucas—Great Britain recognized Belize's independence in a move that further isolated the Guatemalan government. Also during that year U.S. foreign policy began to regain the initiative and moved to take control of the Central American political crisis. Since December 1980, moreover, the Guatemalan army had evidence that the guerrilla organizations were unifying their tactical positions with assistance from the Cuban and Sandinista (Nicaraguan) governments. The insurgents were organizing the so-called Tripartite, which was a precursor to what would, in February 1982, become the URNG.

But it was not until 1982 that the regime's sanguine view of international changes was shaken up in the aftermath of the August 1981 Franco-Mexican communiqué calling for a negotiated solution to the Salvadoran conflict and officially recognizing the Salvadoran political and military opposition alliance known as the FMLN-FDR. Only then did the army comprehend that the international and regional situation could become a source of considerable pressure regarding the conduct of the internal conflict, and that it should make concessions on matters that would free it of international diplomatic pressure. Significantly, the army refused to participate directly in the Reagan administration's regional military plans. By then, the Guatemalan military had already designed a strategy of its own.

THE COUNTERINSURGENCY STRATEGY

The counterinsurgency effort centered on dismantling democratic and urban grassroots organizations and containing outbursts of peasant revolt. Intermingled with these goals, however, were the interests of the military group in control of the government bureaucracy and its counterparts in private enterprise. One of the most notorious cases was that of Colonel Héctor Montalbán and his family, who supervised and authorized loans for public administration projects via the Presidential General Staff (Key Source 132, Guatemala, the eighties).

While the guerrilla war struck hard at the business sector through kidnapping, extortion, and murder, the army-entrepreneur alliance broadened into direct collaboration on military operations. During the months prior to May 1980, a group of businessmen joined forces with the Army General Staff to organize the "Thousand Day Plan." This was a mammoth anticommunist campaign designed to create a climate that would justify the impending escalation of brutal repression.

It is worth mentioning that besides completely dismantling the legal political opposition, the labor movement, and other grassroots organizations, this joint effort's principal achievement was the harsh blows dealt to the EGP's Luis Turcios Lima Front on the southern coast, which was the agroexport sector's main area of interest. Thus, by mid-1980, the army had crushed the guerrilla front operating on the southern coast, annihilating approximately eighty members of its core leadership, without touching the rest of the civilian population.

In the early stages of selective repression the army utilized military commissioners, informers, and local authorities, many of whom had personal economic interests in lands belonging to indigenous groups. With the onset of selective repression in rural areas, many agricultural entrepreneurs serving as military commissioners, or running their own security groups, worked with the army to eliminate the peasant leadership, particularly in areas of conflict.

This policy of selective repression, in which the interests and priorities of the groups in power were intertwined, also provoked discord within the army, particularly as the guerrilla forces advanced. Therefore, when the EGP killed army chief of staff General Cancinos in 1980, most high-level commanders and officers believed that it was an internal settling of accounts (Gramajo 1995), since the previous murders of Colom Argueta and Fuentes Mohr had been widely attributed to Cancinos. Similarly, when Julio Segura, secretary of Economic Planning and presidential hopeful of one army faction, was killed in September 1980, rumors of an impending coup d'état abounded.

Precisely at that juncture, however, the army strategic command was reorganized. The Army General Staff rearranged the security and intelligence services, including D-2 and *La Regional*, which would later be known as *Archivo*. Colonels Francisco Ortega Menaldo and Manuel Antonio Callejas y Callejas, the latter Lucas's chief of *La Regional*, played key roles in this process. According to REMHI's testimonies, this group of officers, which also included José Luis Fernández Ligorría, was implicated in violence linked to common crime and administrative corruption under Lucas and was directly responsible for counterinsurgency operations in Guatemala City in 1981.

The army carried out a multifaceted strategy in the capital. Initially, it targeted the grassroots leadership, relying heavily on National Police director, General Germán Chupina Barahona, and his subordinates, Manuel de Jesús Valiente Téllez and Pedro García Arredondo. But it was not until 1981 that the army designed and executed a repressive campaign that actually had a strategic counterinsurgency focus: to destroy the revolutionary leadership in the city and, at the same time, demolish the logistical infrastructure that was rapidly being installed in anticipation of a major guerrilla offensive.

The army then attacked various guerrilla fronts based on a strategic priority. This strategy enabled the army to avoid dispersing, which was what the guerrilla tactics were aiming for, and to concentrate its attacks in calibrated offensives against different guerrilla fronts. Although it made sure to sustain the pressure on ORPA and FAR fronts, its offensives were primarily directed against major EGP strongholds.

This strategic realignment created tensions within the military hierarchy. Certain mid-level officers privately complained that superior officers were involved in embezzlement related to arms purchases. According to information from disgruntled officers, during the first trimester of 1981 the guerrillas had killed twenty-three officers and 250 soldiers. Moreover, in September of that year, Vice-president Francisco Villagrán Kramer resigned, thereby reducing the viability of the government program that sought to ensure its continuity through the 1982 elections.

In fact, part of the officer corps had reached a critical juncture in terms of the survival of the established order; this is reflected in a 1987 quotation from one of the protagonists of the period, Colonel Terraza Pinot:

> In...July 1981, the terrorists were planning to declare part of the national soil "liberated territory" so that its members would qualify as a belligerent force, which would give them access to international fora and recognition by the main countries of the totalitarian bloc....Their early actions were focused on: eliminating local authority by murdering, abducting, and disappearing auxiliary mayors, municipal mayors, and military commissioners, and burning down twenty-five municipal buildings; sabotaging the national economy by burning down farms, assaults, murders, and crop destruction; and, destroying roads.

So it was that, in the final months of the Lucas administration, the Army General Staff designed a counterinsurgency strategy that would attain its full effect after the March 23, 1982, coup d'état.

"SCORCHED EARTH"

The army's strategic offensive against indigenous highland areas strategic for the EGP began in FACS's area of operations. On the second anniversary of the

Sandinista triumph, this front carried out actions illustrative of the magnitude of the situation reigning in that zone. On July 19, FACS directed its social bases to block the Pan-American highway by knocking down trees and placing other obstacles along sixty-two miles of roadway. The scope of such actions left no doubt about the population's considerable involvement with the guerrillas.

From the first moment of the offensive, the army attacked the civilian population. It closed the road between Tecpán and Los Encuentros for an entire day while troops systematically burned down the surrounding homes. Meanwhile, the EGP's military force in the zone (one combat platoon and the Local Irregular Forces) made sporadic attempts to harass the army.

What the army found on the ground ultimately confirmed the massive involvement of the civilian population. For example, it verified that in a period of no more than two weeks, numerous traps had been laid, consisting of pits at least nine feet deep with sharps stakes set into them. Under EGP guidance the people had hastily built these traps as a self-defense mechanism; the tactic ultimately failed, however, since the army, unhampered by enemy harassment, easily detected the recently dug up earth.

Shortly after launching its punishing actions in the zone (the massacres had not yet occurred), the army, apparently with little enthusiasm, ordered the population to report to military posts to obtain identity documents. To accomplish this, the army made ample use of Emeterio Toj Medrano, a CUC founder and well-known local leader, whom it was holding at the time. Toj Medrano spoke in his native Kiché from a helicopter, directing people to go to the Chupol army post to receive the document and reiterating that they had nothing to fear from the army. Some went, but most did not.

The military offensive in southern El Quiché was rapidly advancing. The army penetrated further into the area, choosing to attack populations that lacked means to defend themselves. There are many examples that demonstrate that the army was not interested in pursuing or destroying the meager guerrilla fighting force active in the region, which, in turn, made few attempts to confront the army. Instead, the army razed homes and crops and expelled tens of thousands of peasants, condemning them to wander in the hills and forests struggling to survive. The massacres began shortly afterward.

At first glance the repression seemed totally indiscriminate, and in the sense that it targeted children, the elderly, women, and men with no distinction, it was. But a more careful analysis reveals that, while some villages were razed, others were punished in a more perfunctory manner. In still others the army gave speeches, warned and threatened, but refrained from massacring or destroying the village. This clearly demonstrates that the army had very precise intelligence, because its actions were proportionate to the population's relationship with the insurgency.

Army repression radically altered the correlation of forces in the area through forced displacement, but also because of the existence of sympathetic groups that had receded from view when the guerrillas took over. With official support, these groups joined in the repression with particular malice. Joining these groups were some people who rapidly changed allegiances and others who had no alternative.

At least in this area, these groups were the foundation for what would later become the PACs.

Statements by Benedicto Lucas to the effect that government officials had completely abandoned the countryside were the prelude to a coup d'état that he did not lead. His perspectives, however, elucidate how different officers became aware of the prevailing circumstances of poverty and neglect, government inefficiency, and a corrupt and politicized army. The confluence of these factors, compounded by international isolation, led more than a few officers to conclude that the guerrillas could win, despite the fact that the army offensive—little more than a leisurely stroll from a military view—had been a grisly holocaust for people living in so-called conflictive areas.

The army offensive caused the phenomenon of internal displacement. People streamed into the hills and forests with nowhere to go and nowhere to plant. They wandered, subsisting as best they could. This human drama cemented the army's territorial recovery and left the guerrillas with the daunting task of responding to the displaced population's need for protection and subsistence.

After the army had subdued the population living in the EGP's central highland stronghold, it proceeded to the northwest and the Verapaz region. It operated by concentrating its forces on successive targets without slackening the pressure on areas where it had already severed the links between the population and the insurgents. It left behind a troop presence in recovered areas, which was reinforced with rapidly organized civil patrols. By organizing the patrols, the army achieved one of its primary strategic objectives: to create a local authority loyal and subordinate to the army.

THE INSURGENTS' STRATEGY

The imminent takeover of power was the perspective that inspired the guerrillas, especially the EGP, the most active organization from 1981 on. Beginning in 1976, the EGP had embarked on a rapid escalation of military actions while ORPA, and later the FAR, were organizing their respective fronts in the northeast and northwest. By 1978 the guerrillas had adopted the notion of a "Popular Revolutionary Struggle" (_Guerra Revolucionaria Popular_) and were able to amass a formidable support base.

When the EGP's first regular military force penetrated southern El Quiché, a large percentage of the population was waiting for it. Far from a repeat of the earlier cycle of winning people over and organizing them, the EGP's political cadres and combatants were increasingly astonished by their overwhelming reception and the speed with which the population organized itself based on the guerrilla-proposed model. The organizing that had taken place in the seventies, with the substantial involvement of certain sectors of the Catholic church, had something to do with this.

During the second half of 1978 there was a marked escalation of guerrilla violence. In 1979 guerrilla warfare spread throughout the country with the emergence of new groups that attacked the agroindustrial sector. The EGP reasoned that it was sufficiently well established and decided to proceed to "all-out guerrilla warfare," meaning an offensive against enemy economic and military forces. It called for grassroots organization in support of the armed struggle, an alliance with democratic forces, unification of revolutionary forces, and international recognition. According to guerrilla commander "Rolando Morán," the idea was to attack local authorities and execute enemy cadres, but not to engage in structured military operations.

The EGP front Comandante Ernesto "Ché" Guevara was founded in Huehuetenango in mid-1979. On June 9, 1980, the EGP killed General Cancinos. In August, the FAR kidnapped the vice-minister of foreign affairs, Alfonso Alonso Lima, releasing him after the government published an EGP manifesto. On September 18 ORPA emerged publicly for the first time when it occupied Mujulia farm in Quetzaltenango. On October 7 a unit of the EGP's Otto René Castillo Front kidnapped Jorge Raúl García Granados, the son of a powerful businessman. That same month FAR kidnapped Elizabeth Lippmann, the daughter of a San Marcos rancher. However, the Ixil region in northern El Quiché was the site of more overt irregular warfare.

By 1980 the war had spread throughout most of the country, giving the impression that the army was not in control of the situation. Guerrilla activity intensified in the capital, with prominent attacks on high-level army officers. In rural areas the guerrillas quickly proceeded to more aggressive armed propaganda methods, including the occupation of towns and villages, taking over roadways, and, increasingly, engaging the army in combat. In the Ixil region the EGP organized a regular guerrilla unit ("19 de enero") and attempted to occupy and destroy fixed army installations. This provoked an immediate reaction from the army, which pinpointed that region as the area where the EGP was most likely to declare a "liberated zone."

The EGP also tried to establish guerrilla fronts in other parts of the country, taking advantage of the spontaneous uprising of indigenous peasants. But the insurgents were facing an overwhelming force that impeded them from pursuing a genuine military strategy. According to "Commander Benedicto," or Mario Payeras, who was deeply involved in the events, in the first half of 1980 alone,

> a guerrilla patrol was just beginning to establish itself along the Pixcayá River, the border between the departments of Guatemala and Chimaltenango, initially settling in the area of Cruz Blanca; within weeks, the guerrilla patrol had penetrated populated villages south of San Martín Jilotepeque and Comalapa, secretly organizing their support bases.

In Huehuetenango, the southern coast, and the *bocacosta* regions, the fronts were also in their preparatory stages.

"THE PEOPLE'S WAR"

Some indigenous populations began to collaborate actively in major military operations. When guerrillas occupied the towns of Chichicastenango and Sololá, the people cut telegraph wires and used nails, barricades, fallen trees, and other objects to block the roadways for dozens of miles in both directions in an effort to impede the army's overland access to the occupied areas. Once the occupation was over, the people thronged to Los Encuentros to give the participants a heroes' welcome, distributing tamales and *chuchitos,* playing marimbas, and shouting the victory cry "Hasta la victoria siempre." They organized a public party that stopped traffic for several hours (Arias 1985).

Guerrilla triumphalism reached its peak in 1981. The population organized spontaneously in various parts of the highlands where guerrilla organizations or the CUC had not yet arrived. One of the drawbacks to this was that certain regional CUC leaders, who for various reasons had separated or distanced themselves from the organization, proceeded to capitalize on this spontaneity and use the revolutionary fervor for their own ends. Overnight these regional peasant leaders became "commanders of guerrilla fronts," with no prior training or ties to the insurgent groups. This stance provoked fierce army repression in those areas, which hit the civilian population particularly hard. It also fueled the disloyalty of the leaders, who set themselves up as local political bosses and began to act like gangsters: raping women, assaulting people, and using funds channeled by international solidarity organizations for their own personal gain (Arias 1985).

Perhaps one of the most sinister aspects of the guerrilla offensive was the "destruction of local authority" campaign, which resulted in the murder of many rural inhabitants. Some of these were indeed collaborating with the army or paramilitary groups, given that in 1978 the MLN had won many municipalities. In September alone the EGP claimed responsibility for the deaths of ninety-seven army collaborators in different parts of the country.

In late 1981 the guerrilla support base comprised an estimated 276,000 people operating in sixteen out of the twenty-two departments nationwide. When the army launched its counteroffensive, however, there was no coordination with the other guerrilla organizations, which did not share the EGP's strategic vision. The army successively amassed its troops against each guerrilla organization. The EGP and ORPA, the two strongest organizations militarily, failed to articulate a coherent response.

THE POOR AGAINST THE RICH

The process of organizing the civil patrols demonstrated the limitations of the insurgent effort. The precipitous uprising of rural and indigenous populations gave a false impression of homogeneity. Even during the most euphoric moments, however, there were significant core groups of people, overshadowed by insurgent hegemony, who were waiting for their chance to change sides.

The EGP, in an attempt to simplify its message and make it more accessible, created and spread the notion of the struggle between rich and poor. The rural indigenous population did not perceive the rich as unknown powerful businessmen from the capital. Moreover, the rural indigenous were far from being a so-cially, economically, and culturally homogeneous group. There were myriad con-flicts among indigenous groups; socially and geographically speaking, these con-flicts took the form of disputes between villages, hamlets, and urban areas.

Besides these conflicts, several EGP fronts advocated the execution of military commissioners. At that time, the commissioners did not yet have a history of repression; they were peasants like the others and, naturally, had many family ties. Moreover, the EGP launched occupations of the county seats in some areas, including the zone where FACS operated. The guerrillas directed the burning down of municipal buildings, which had a detrimental impact on significant sec-tors of the population. To make matters worse, the situation got out of control during some occupations. The population—armed with axes and machetes—spontaneously joined the guerrilla units and proceeded to loot businesses; in the case of Joyabaj, the insurgents dynamited the population's water supply.

Less frequently, the armed population or certain insurgent military chiefs took advantage of the situation to settle personal accounts. Some of these cases were not just personal but involved reprisals against other villages, which led to kill-ings and forced recruitment. A situation that was out of control, coupled with the proliferation of armed people, led the general population to take weapons from whatever source was offering them, which worked to the army's advantage. All of this further dispersed the guerrilla military forces, making it impossible for them to consider a strike of any magnitude against the army.

THE VICTIMS

Military combat left the grassroots movement totally exposed. Following their accustomed methods, different grassroots organizations maintained a growing opposition as the Lucas government took office.

In 1981, while the labor unions remained shattered by the repression, the Janu-ary 31 Popular Front (*Frente Popular 31 de enero*—FP31) emerged, made up of grassroots sectors that strongly supported the guerrilla struggle. Significantly, the May 1 Labor Day March was not held that year. Repression of the popular move-ment had already left it disabled, and many activists felt there was no alternative but to go into exile or join the armed struggle.

This repressive campaign, coupled with the escalating guerrilla offensive that the army appeared unable to contain, fueled a rapid radicalization of grassroots organizations and indigenous communities. On February 14, 1981, the CUC assembled the indigenous leadership in the Iximché ruins and issued the docu-ment "The Indigenous Peoples of Guatemala to the World," also known as the "Declaration of Iximché," which called on indigenous communities to rebel. This rebellion was channeled into the guerrilla ranks, as occurred in Baja Verapaz. The first clashes between inhabitants of Río Negro and the army took place in March over the flooding of the Chixoy dam. Several CUC militants in Rabinal later contacted the EGP, requesting the formation of an armed group in the municipality. Soon thereafter, brutal repression was unleashed against the most active sectors in Rabinal, while the guerrilla unit had barely begun to operate. The triumphalist fervor of the moment led the vast majority of CUC militants to dissolve their own organizations and join the guerrillas.

THE CATHOLIC CHURCH

During the seventies the Catholic church worked intensively to form and strengthen Christian base communities, especially in rural areas. In various dioceses and parishes, and under different names (bible study circles, family of God, Catholic Action groups, catechism groups, and celebrations of the word), these communities became forums for consciousness-raising.

TRAINING CENTERS

Centers to train Christian leaders (catechists, delegates of the word, coordinators, faith promoters) multiplied during this period. The Peasant Training Center in Quetzaltenango, Emaús House in Escuintla, the *Campo de Dios* and the Apostolic Center in Izabal, the Center for Integrated Development in Huehuetenango, the Training Center in San Pedro Sacatepéquez, San Marcos, and the Center San Benito in Cobán were among those founded at that time.

Priests and women religious worked tirelessly in those centers, supported by bishops who viewed them as a way of spreading the gospel and building Christian communities.

One project that acquired national importance was the Social Promoters' Training Program (*Centro de Adiestramiento de Promotores Sociales*—CAPS), sponsored by Rafael Landívar University. The program created hundreds of experiential laboratories, trained peasant leaders, and encouraged social organization and community involvement.

The Catholic church was also concerned about the indigenous communities during those years. In 1971 Bishop Juan Gerardi promoted an Indigenous Pastors' Encounter in La Verapaz diocese, which was replicated in several other places in the west. Indigenous priests, together with foreigners, translated and distributed the Bible in Mayan languages. In Chimaltenango, the Kaqchiquel Missionary Program (*Programa Misionero Kaqchiquel*—PROMIKA) was founded in a joint effort by the Diocese of San Francisco (California) and the Diocese of Sololá. Most important, these programs promoted youth literacy in the Kaqchiquel language. Future indigenous leaders and intellectuals came out of these programs.

POLITICAL POLARIZATION

The close relationship between the Christian Democrats and Catholic Action, and their joint support of reform programs, reached a crisis point in the mid-seventies, brought on by the oil crisis, the rising cost of chemical fertilizers, and the expectations dashed in 1975 when the Christian Democratic presidential candidate General Ríos Montt was robbed of his victory. Catholic Action members, disillusioned by the Christian Democrat's non-confrontational stance, became increasingly radicalized and sought alternatives for political action.

In 1975 and 1976, military operations had already claimed their first victims from among Catholic Action members in the Ixil area and the northern part of the Quiché diocese. Between November 1976 and December 1977, 143 Catholic Action leaders and catechists in the Ixil and Ixcán regions of El Quiché were abducted and murdered.

There is no question that a sector of the Catholic church, inspired by liberation theology, played a crucial role in the cresting revolutionary movement in the late seventies. Indigenous Guatemala of that period seemed to offer the necessary space and ingredients for a convergence between Guevara's messianism and the faith of the grassroots, the likes of which had not been seen during the preceding decade (Le Bot 1995).

Relationships between parish leaders and their followers did not follow a single pattern or direction in the step from social movement to armed struggle. That is not to say that there weren't cases in which they were unified around the issue. Religion was a key intermediary in the relationship between guerrilla groups led by professional revolutionaries and indigenous communities. And it enabled the guerrillas to make a qualitative leap forward from 1976 on.

Nonetheless, other observers point out that, apart from economic demands, respect for human dignity was the area of the progressive church's discourse that most resonated among the indigenous population. This was a reflection of the strong sense of social awareness that was taking shape inside the Catholic church. This was especially true in the early seventies, after the Jesuits founded the Center for Investigation and Social Action (CIAS) in Zone 5 of the capital. The Center coordinated Jesuit initiatives in the capital and southern El Quiché and Chimaltenango with the efforts of clergy in Corazón de María in northern El Quiché and the work of Belgian and Swiss priests on the southern coast. This movement was evolving toward the formation of the CUC on the southern coast and in the highlands.

Most of the reflection processes taking place in rural areas in the seventies occurred in a religious setting. The church had the most extensive communications network available, which enabled it to reach even the remotest areas, and religion was a central feature in the lives of indigenous people.

In the aftermath of the Spanish Embassy massacre hundreds of Christians decided to join the guerrilla organizations, as did a group of priests who had participated in the consciousness-raising process described earlier.

Brutal repression of the Catholic church was a catalyst for this radicalization. The campaign of selective repression against the church was particularly bloody in 1980. On May 1, Conrado de la Cruz, parish priest of Tiquisate, was murdered; on May 12 it was Father Walter Voodeckers, parish priest of Santa Lucía Cotzumalguapa. In November, the government denied Juan Gerardi, the president of the

Guatemalan Bishops' Conference and bishop of El Quiché, permission to enter the country. Months before, in July, the church hierarchy had decided to close the diocese of El Quiché.

Repression against the church continued unabated in 1981. On May 14, Father Carlos Gálvez Galindo of the Tecpán, Chimaltenango, parish, was killed. On June 8, Jesuit priest and EGP collaborator Luis Eduardo Pellecer Faena was detained. Franciscan priest Tulio Maruzo was shot in Quiriguá, Izabal, on July 1. The corpses of two lay missionaries were discovered on July 25: Raúl Joseph Leger (Canadian) and Angel Martínez Rodrigo (Spanish). On July 27, Father Francisco Stanley Rother (United States) was murdered in the parish house of Santiago Atitlán, Sololá. Evangelical pastor Félix Moxón Chutá was also killed in July. And, on August 2, Spanish Jesuit Carlos Pérez Alonzo was abducted in Guatemala City.

The situation remained unchanged during the first months of 1982. On January 2, Father Horacio Benedetti of San Antonio Suchitepéquez parish was shot and wounded. Two days later, Fathers Pablo Schildermans and Roberto Paredes Calderón were abducted in Nueva Concepción, Escuintla; they were released three days later. On January 5, Father Venancio Aguilar Villanueva was murdered. Sister Victoria de la Roca, of the Order of Bethlehem, was disappeared on January 6 in Esquipulas, Chiquimula. And on January 19, Belgian cleric Sergio Berten was also disappeared. Guatemalan Dominican priest Carlos Ramiro Morales López, leader of the MRP-Ixim guerrilla group, was killed in the capital on January 20. On February 13, La Salle brother James Alfred Miller was killed in Huehuetenango. This seemed to be a preamble for the following period, which would approximate all-out religious warfare, although men and women religious would no longer be murdered.

LUCAS'S DEMISE

The PID-PR-Aranista alliance that brought Lucas to power was rapidly disintegrating. Lucas's triumph was, in itself, a clear indication of the fragility of electoral politics, which could not be counteracted by the "democratic opening" that allowed the registration of new parties in an attempt to restore legitimacy and end the political hegemony of the four traditional parties.

The presidential race began in 1981 in an openly tense climate, in which the constituted authority was seriously discredited. In September, General Aníbal Guevara, Lucas's defense minister, had launched his campaign, backed by the PR, the PID, and the FUN; he chose former mayor of Guatemala City and Arana-affiliate Ramiro Ponce Monroy as his running mate. Once again, the formula to maintain the status quo in order to safeguard the business objectives of the military hierarchy and its business counterparts was in place. But by then, this group was isolated from the business and military mainstream. Gustavo Anzueto Vielman entered the presidential race for the Nationalist Authentic Central (CAN), supported by General Arana and professionals Ernesto Berger and Danilo Parrinello.

Former finance minister Colonel Hugo Tulio Búcaro also announced his candidacy and claimed the support of Lucas.

Independent of the state security apparatus, the Army General Staff had put the finishing touches on its own counterinsurgency program, which did not include the government-business alliance forged two years before. Therefore, when General Aníbal Guevara was handed the presidency in apparently fraudulent elections, the army decided, in the midst of an undeniable institutional crisis, to break with the formal system. On March 23, 1982, it launched a coup d'état that would permit it to conclude its counterinsurgency offensive and redefine the government framework according to this strategy.

Chapter Thirteen

THE RIOS MONTT GOVERNMENT

A TURNING POINT IN HISTORY

General Aníbal Guevara was declared the victor of the March 7, 1982, presidential elections. However, on March 23, 950 army members carried out a coup d'état, installing a triumvirate headed by General Efraín Ríos Montt, and composed of General Horacio Maldonado Schaad (commander of the Honor Guard Brigade and an MLN ally) and Colonel Francisco Luis Gordillo (commander of the Izabal and Quetzaltenango Brigades in 1981). The Christian Democrats and the MLN immediately lent their support to the new regime. The crucial factor behind the coup was the profound crisis within the military-business alliance that had dominated political life throughout the seventies.

The military government immediately suspended the Constitution and issued the Fundamental Statute of Government (*Estatuto Fundamental de Gobierno*, Decree 24-82). It also terminated fifty public officials accused of corruption. On April 5, the Army Special Staff (*Estado Mayor Especial del Ejército*) presented a National Plan for Security and Development to the Council of Ministers. On June 9 General Ríos Montt relieved the other triumvirate members of their duties and declared himself president of the Republic. Ríos Montt surrounded himself with an advisory junta composed of six young army officers out of the thirteen who had supported the coup. He decreed the Political Organizations Law, which accorded the traditional parties a status of "committees of parties in formation" (political associations aspiring to be registered as political parties). Thirty-two new political parties were founded between 1982 and 1985 as a result of this measure.

By then, massacres of populations suspected of collaborating with the guerrillas were already underway in rural areas, and the new regime was in the process of establishing a legal framework in which to operate. On April 15, Decree 9-82 was effected, prohibiting the dissemination of news about political violence. On June 1 the military government issued an amnesty decree for political crimes. On June 16, by governmental agreement (31-82), the president appointed 324 municipal mayors at the recommendation of the respective military zone. On July 1 the regime declared a state of siege (Decree 44-82) and authorized former soldiers to join their local military zone. The Council of State was installed on September 15 as a consultative body comprising politicians, technocrats, and certain public figures designated by the government.

THE NEW COUNTERINSURGENCY

The young army officers who supported the Ríos Montt coup displaced the army hierarchy loyal to General Lucas García, officers of the Presidential General Staff (EMP), and various members of the military intelligence community known as *La Cofradía* (The Brotherhood). In March 1983 the Army General Staff was reorganized by Decree 28-83 and became the National Defense Staff (EMDN), with an inspector general, a vice–chief of staff, and five directorates: personnel (D-1), intelligence (D-2), operations (D-3), logistics (D-4), and civil affairs (D-5). These measures also displaced army graduating classes that were reaching the final stages of their military careers, leaving their future uncertain; this would be a factor in the rapid deterioration of the Ríos Montt government. Nonetheless, this military team was able to implement a comprehensive antisubversion strategy that combined military, political, psychosocial and anthropological components.

Throughout 1982 the army waged Campaign Plan Victoria 82 against guerrilla fronts in the north and northwestern regions, deploying two-thirds of its force. The offensive, which primarily targeted the civilian population (mostly indigenous-peasant), dismantled the guerrilla support base, claimed tens of thousands of victims, and caused enormous internal displacement. Although the insurgent strategic forces were not damaged significantly, the destruction of their support base obliged them to retreat to the areas where they had originally surfaced.

The army's later offensives against the remaining guerrilla fronts were less successful. In conjunction with the initial campaign, however, they restored government control and authority throughout most of the national territory (Aguilera 1985). It was an all-out effort, socially and geographically engineered "with the aim of qualitatively altering the characteristics that make the mountain [regions] the most propitious strategic venue for the accumulation of forces." It was an attempt to destroy the linchpin of the insurgent strategy (Payeras 1986).

The offensives were extraordinarily brutal in their attempts to eradicate the enemy and its support bases. In Annex H of the Campaign Plan Victoria 82, the army states:

Subversion exists, because a small group of people supported it, and a large number of people tolerated it, either out of fear or because there are causes that give rise to it. The war has to be fought on all fronts....The mind of the population is the main objective.

The military strategy tried to impede

the subversives' access to the population which constituted its base of Political and Social Support; to rescue members of the Irregular Local Forces (FIL), neutralizing or eliminating those who refuse to return to normal life;

annihilate the Local Clandestine Committees [CCL]; and eliminate the Permanent Military Units (UPM) (Ejército de Guatemala 1982).

The tactic was described as follows:

Deceive them: subversion must be fought with its own methods and techniques (there must be an ongoing disinformation plan); find them: the biggest problem is always locating the guerrilla military units since remaining hidden is an integral part of their fighting strategy (use local intelligence and saturate the area with patrols); attack them: when you have succeeded in locating a guerrilla force, maintain contact at all costs and inform immediately so that the superior unit can back up the operation and successfully annihilate the pinpointed enemy; destroy them: the mission is to destroy the guerrilla forces. Territorial control is a means of fulfilling the mission, but never the purpose or final objective.

The strategy reflected in the campaign plans, in addition to counterinsurgency operations, included others that affected the civilian population, including:

• Military presence throughout the country "to ensure the security and trust of the population." New military zones were created in every department; military jurisdictions coincided with administrative jurisdictions within an overall framework of regionalization.

• "Protect production centers" to prevent the sabotage of cotton and sugarcane plantations during the harvest.

• Control over seasonal workers who migrate from the highlands to the southern coast.

• Joint direction of military and psychological operations.

One of the themes that the army would later adopt was the need to "drain the sea" in order to safeguard the survival of the state. But the tactics employed contradicted this discourse by considering the inhabitants of vast areas as military targets. The following text illustrates this point:

The terrorist organizations have based their military strategy on the premise that "the sea is to the fish what the population is to the guerrillas." The terrorist criminals hoist their banner of taking the land from the rich and offering it to the poor, that of the ladinos to the indigenous; this is compounded by the beliefs of certain priests influenced by liberation theology. The situation was such that entire population groups took up arms and many went into the hills, deceived, hoping for change, and with the idea that their lives would be better once the revolutionary war was won. Time passed and the people were so deeply involved in subversion that they could no longer return to their places of origin (Ejército de Guatemala 1990).

THE MILITARY OFFENSIVES OF 1982-1983

THE IXIL REGION

Perhaps the most strategically significant offensive, from the army's standpoint, took place in the Ixil area. In 1980, the EGP had established its first regular military unit (known as January 19) in the area; circumstances were such that the guerrillas could potentially declare a liberated zone and demand international recognition as a belligerent force in an internal conflict. Recognizing the strategic importance of this region, the army reinforced the Huehuetenango and El Quiché military zones and maintained its units in a permanent offensive campaign.

But the population's overwhelming affinity to the guerrilla cause raised fears of an unexpected uprising. Therefore, the army used the first months of 1981 to burn remote villages, located far from the county seats. In April, it organized the first civil patrols in Uspantán. The patrols would eventually extend along the natural border between the Quiché and Ixil areas formed by the Río Negro, and into the ladino areas of Huehuetenango (Chiantla and Barillas), in a deliberate attempt to use ethnic discord for counterinsurgency purposes.

The army—which in 1981 had deployed a brigade under the command of its post in Nebaj, one company each in Chajul, Cotzal, Nebaj, two platoons on the La Perla and La Taña farms, and one each in San Francisco and La Panchita, the most remote areas in the region—immediately attacked the populations most supportive of the guerrillas, using the scorched-earth technique against the communities located near guerrilla enclaves.

Thus, in September, there were massacres in Xeucalbitz and Sumal, Nebaj, in which thirty-five people were killed and everything was burned to the ground. Gerónimo Pérez, the first bilingual teacher, was killed in Sumal Chiquito and then decapitated. The survivors set out on foot for Sumal Grande. That same month, the army massacred ten indigenous people in Tzalbal, twenty more in Palop, and razed the village of Río Azul. On October 24, 1981, sixty army rangers entered Palop and Kekchip and burned the houses. The people fled into the hills.

At precisely the same moment, the guerrillas were in the throes of a severe crisis:

Groups of members of the National Directorate [DN], which had formed variously in the mountains, the cities, or outside the country, operated as autonomous nuclei of the DN, without centralization, without coordination, often without information flowing among them. In February 1982, one nucleus of the Directorate formed by the commander-in-chief and leaders of the Ché Guevara and Ho Chi Minh Fronts convened a meeting of the DN in the mountains. From June to September 1982, "Comandante Benedicto" (Mario Payeras) convened an extended meeting of the National

Directorate of the EGP. The DN group in the mountains did not recognize the latter meeting. One of the agreements made during Benedicto's meeting was that "Camilo" and "Milton" would carry the agreements to other parts of the country along with a substantial amount of military equipment for the northern fronts. The EGP directorate was not reestablished until November 1982 (EGP 1984).

Therefore, much of the guerrilla response to the military offensives took the form of harassment and sporadic ambushes, mainly defensive or containment actions. The ambitious attacks of the preceding year were not repeated.

TXACAL TZE (CHACALTE)
A Guerrilla Massacre

Implementation

The final instructions were given in Secoch, on the morning of June 13, 1982. At noon, the troops mobilized and, using trails and observing strict security measures, they advanced to an area two hours from Txacal Tzé. They slept there. At three o'clock in the morning on June 14, they were ordered to move on. They were distributed according to platoons and units. By five o'clock in the morning, all means of access to the village had been closed off. By that time, everyone knew what they were about to do. The order was: everyone over ten years old had to die. It was believed that there were lots of weapons stockpiled in the village and that even the children were armed. The people were surprised by the first shots. The guerrillas said to them, "If you tell us where the weapons are, we'll spare your lives." At first the people responded belligerently with sticks, machetes, and rocks. But they were frightened when they heard the shots. During one moment when the shots were silenced, a woman left her house. The guerrillas told her, "Behave yourself and we won't do anything to you." The woman was carrying a knife, and she attacked a guerrilla. So the guerrillas tortured her, kicked her, burned her with cigarettes, and raped her. They killed her in the end. Patricio and Iván were the ones who raped her. An old man of eighty came and said, "Don't kill me." The guerrillas said, "Okay," but as the old man approached they tossed a grenade at him. The guerrillas kicked him, they beat him with their rifle butts, and they finally carved him into pieces. They burned a house with a man inside it, saying that he was a "reactionary" chief and had weapons in his house. The slogan was "Don't shoot, strike with pure machetes, boys...." They burned all the houses. There was a school in the middle of the village that had been transformed into a sort of fortification. As the attack developed, the people with more and better weapons began to take up positions inside the school; that's where the *"reactionaries" gathered. The guerrillas tried to approach it, but they were attacked. That was where most of the guerrilla casualties happened. The commanders decided to regroup and redeploy. Then they decided to tear down the roof of the school, which was solid, with big rocks. Once they had torn a hole in the roof, they threw grenades and explosives inside, and the shots could no longer be heard. One young woman said to a guerrilla, "Don't kill me and I'll be your woman." The guerrilla hit her on the head and killed her. The ones who were the most euphoric and drunken were the irregular forces (FIL), who were saying, "You don't play around with the guerrillas; you have to respect the revolution." The guerrillas confiscated twenty hand grenades, three mines; they did not find combat weapons, although there were 12- and 22-caliber rifles. There were no more than twenty-five or thirty weapons. It seems that they did find one M-1 rifle in the depot. The attack lasted about four hours. It ended at around nine o'clock in the morning. One guerrilla who had participated and did not want to give his name confessed that he counted 125 dead. Nothing remained in the village. The FIL burned the houses and took all the good clothing. They took the cattle, the corn, and divided it up.*

The aftermath of the massacre

There was no representation of the National Directorate of the EGP at the guerrilla front. The EGP was immersed in one of its worst crises. In January 1982, "Milton" and "Carlos" (Fernando Hoyos) had left the front. "Carlos" returned in March for a brief visit and died in July, before the massacre. Most members of the Directorate were in Mexico or in meetings.

No one was sanctioned by the Directorate. During the first few days, there was a kind of collective euphoria in the front, which was shared by the civilian population and military units. There was a sense that they had settled a longstanding score. In August, a week-long assembly was held. The need for carrying out that massacre and its consequences were discussed. Rafael Sigüenza said that it was butchery and could not be justified. But a pact was made there not to tell anyone what had happened and to make no amends. Everyone became dumb. There were people, not many, who dared to say, "They went too far," and to question efforts to justify the massacre. During the following days, some guerrillas began to feel conflicted about what had happened, and there were persistent misgivings about whether it had been the right thing to do. Key Sources 110, 091, 220, and 096, Txacal Tzé, 1982.

CLEARING OUT THE BORDER AREA

Huehuetenango

Within its strategy of taking over the government, the guerrillas attempted to cut off this department completely in 1981. The EGP's National Directorate was located there, and the zone's natural corridors connected it to the Ixcán and Ixil regions.

Thus, in 1981, Huehuetenango became the center of operations of the Ché Guevara Front, which was particularly well established in the municipalities of San Miguel Acatán and San Rafael la Independencia. The EGP launched a campaign to "eliminate the enemy's local power structure," killing numerous army collaborators before proceeding to direct harassment of military units. Also during this period the EGP received substantial support, some large-scale or collective, from border communities. In the rest of the department, however, extreme right-wing groups such as the MLN had many followers.

The EGP's offensive campaign lasted throughout the Ríos Montt government. In fact, it was in Huehuetenango that the guerrillas carried out their major offensives and later engaged the army directly. On June 2, 1982, the EGP confirmed that it had deprived twenty-seven of thirty-one municipalities in Huehuetenango of electricity, telephone and telegraph service, and radio contact, and sixteen municipalities were cut off by land from the departmental capital.

But in mid-June the army announced a counterinsurgency operation in northern Huehuetenango using three thousand soldiers and fourteen helicopters. This counteroffensive began in July but failed to defuse the guerrilla actions, despite an enormous toll in human lives. On July 13, in the midst of this offensive, Jesuit Fernando Hoyos ("Carlos"), a member of the EGP's National Directorate, died on the banks of the San Juan River. Later the guerrillas moved their general headquarters to the Ixcán jungle, and the guerrilla theater of combat operations focused on the area demarcated by the Ixcán and Xalbal rivers (particularly around Cuache hill).

The Ixcán

Following the March 23 coup d'état, the military zones of Cobán and Huehuetenango were added as points of army penetration into the Ixcán region in the department of El Quiché. These points intersected at Playa Grande. "The offensive was intended to force the EGP to retreat in precisely the same place where it had made its entrance eleven years before" (Falla 1987).

The army established its stronghold in Playa Grande, whence it coordinated operations, including reinforcements arriving from the capital, Petén, Huehuetenango, Cobán, and the east. They trained the "butchers" there, military intelligence specialists who became known for their cruelty during the massacres. Playa Grande, first a military base and later a military zone, was also a control center to monitor the population entering and leaving that side of the Ixcán. Numerous testimonies compiled by REMHI refer to the strict monitoring of provisions and transportation.

At that moment, the guerrillas still refused to acknowledge just how hard they had been hit. In February and March they maintained that "the guerrilla war [was] advancing unhindered" (EGP, *Informador guerrillero*, 1982). A URNG situation report about 1982 asserted that the "[army's] final offensive and Operation Victoria 82 have been an utter failure." Although it acknowledged that the army "had almost exclusively attacked the civilian population," it considered that the moment was "particularly favorable for taking our struggle all the way to victory, which is assured, which is within the scope of our capabilities" (EGP documents, no. 20).

OFFENSIVES IN THE CENTRAL CORRIDOR

The central highland (or populated highland) area was, in fact, the first affected by the army offensive designed by the Army General Staff using the new counterinsurgency model. Most of its operational paradigms would be used in the following offensives that took place under the Ríos Montt government.

The military theater comprised Chimaltenango department, part of Sacatepéquez, western Baja Verapaz, southern El Quiché, and northeastern Sololá. The EGP's Augusto César Sandino Front (FACS)—which had a strong presence in the zone—also carried out some military operations in Totonicapán.

Although this analysis looks at the Baja Verapaz area separately, it should be remembered that this entire geographical region constituted a single strategic unit; it was a belt that linked the remote northern fronts—where the guerrillas were planning to establish their "liberated territories"—to the capital city.

In February-March 1981, the army launched its first military campaign against central Chimaltenango, during which fifteen hundred peasants lost their lives. It subsequently pursued a campaign of selective murders or massacres against communities that supported, or sympathized with, the insurgent forces.

By then, the stash of weapons with which the insurgency would have armed this population had already been lost during the army offensives in the capital. In September-October, the EGP and ORPA joined forces to control the highlands of El Quiché, Sololá, and Chimaltenango, in order to block the route from the capital to the indigenous areas. But this plan was permanently neutralized when army chief of staff General Benedicto Lucas directed the occupation of Chupol, the most strategic location in the region, and announced the rescue of three thousand families that had been abducted by the guerrillas.

Sololá

For the EGP, Sololá and Totonicapán were part of the area that reinforced southern El Quiché, all along the Pan-American highway. Some of the population became involved in community organizing and institutions through the work of the Catholic church, catechists, and CUC members; this was particularly true in Argueta and Santiago Atitlán in 1980. Their principal demand was for land.

In addition to the EGP, various other groups converged in Sololá. Beginning in late 1979, ORPA established camps in Paraxot and Chuimango (the *bocacosta* region of Sololá) and in the skirts of the Atitlán volcano. Also active in the areas was the MRP-Ixim, which also carried out selective recruitment in Totonicapán and Quetzaltenango.

> *The Ixim flourished, but when the EGP came along political space began to close, to the point that the last report we received from a person in Chaquijyá was that the EGP had killed all of the Ixim combatants.* Key Source 207, Sololá, the 1980s.

The guerrillas' most noteworthy action was the takeover of the departmental capital of Sololá on October 28, 1981, the feast of Saint Simon, which was led by "Diego" (Julio Iboy).

> *The taking of Sololá had two objectives: to seize the weapons from the Reserves Command—which was sacked—and expand EGP influence in the region.* Key Source 199, Sololá, the 1980s.

The guerrillas cut off the electricity and, at five o'clock in the afternoon, launched their attack. During the day, the Local Irregular Forces had mobilized to reach the town and melted into a crowd attending a religious ceremony. Four agents died in an attack on the police station, and the rest surrendered. The EGP forces gathered up all the arms before freeing their captives. The governor, together with a member of the municipal corporation, died in a shootout in the middle of the street.

After the army had taken over Chupol and its environs, it installed several bases in the region: in Pixabaj and Guineales in 1982; in El Encanto-Pujujil in 1983; in Panajachel and Santa Clara la Laguna. Violence reigned. On March 19 the army killed three members of a single family in Chaquijyá and took their bodies to the Los Encuentros base. On June 11, 1982, the army killed eleven people in Caserío Buena Esperanza. For their part, in March 1982, the guerrillas murdered seven men—all of whom had families—in Los Encuentros, accusing them of collaborating with the army. And in September of that same year the EGP killed sixteen residents of Pujujil I, Chuacruz.

INTER-ETHNIC AND POWER RELATIONS IN THE GUERRILLAS

The complexity of inter-ethnic relations came to the fore in the midst of the armed conflict.

It could be that the Kaqchikel people did not want the Quiché people directing their structures, while the latter were more individually inclined to join the struggle full time. The Kaqchikel people are more community-oriented, tradi-

tional, and maintain stronger ties to family and the land. Not all parents allowed their sons to participate in the war effort full time, because they were needed to help work the land. Key Source 199, Sololá, the 1980s.

Indigenous-ladino relations were another facet of the problem:

Ladinos are a minority in Sololá, and usually live in the city and work in the public sector. When Sololá was taken, most of those who arrived were indigenous people. This led to comments from the ladinos to the effect that "all the Indians are guerrillas." Key Source, Sololá, the 1980s.

The guerrilla leadership was not exempt from these stereotypes:

The takeover of Sololá was nearly suspended because of disputes during the preparatory phase over who would lead it. We indigenous people were against having the city people come and tell us how to do it, even though they were from the National Directorate. This was our concern; our leaders, who were familiar with the terrain, should command us. It was worked out in the end, but there were some very tense moments. A similar thing happened in the Ixil area. It got to the point that an Ixil commander proposed an indigenous uprising inside the guerrilla ranks in response to the lack of sensitivity on the part of the ladinos in the Directorate; particularly because they were leading us into catastrophe with a high cost in human lives, particularly indigenous lives. This commander was dissuaded. We decided it wasn't the right moment, because at that time, yes,…we could get stuck between two fires: the army and the ladino guerrilla forces. Key Source 217, former combatant, the 1980s.

El Quiché

Throughout 1982 guerrilla actions continued to pervade virtually the entire department. The army responded with large-scale massacres of rural communities, especially in the central part of the department, for which it often relied on civil patrols from neighboring communities. This campaign was noted for a string of massacres in villages surrounding municipalities such as San Pedro Jocopilas, and for exemplary and selective murders in the departmental capitals of El Quiché and Chichicastenango. The following abbreviated tally corresponds only to January through March 1982:

• On January 5, three hundred people were killed during the San Bartolo Jacaltenango massacre, with the participation of civil patrollers from San Pedro Jocopilas (among them Chús Barrios, Mincho Girón, and Ernesto Girón, who had reportedly stolen lands from residents of San Bartolo);

• On January 22, in Cantón Chiticun, San Pedro Jocopilas, forty soldiers burned nineteen women and children alive;

• On January 23, army soldiers raped and murdered three teenaged girls in Cantón San Pablo, San Pedro Jocopilas;

• On March 6, the army killed two hundred people in Zacualpa, according to a March 11 report by the Guatemalan daily *Prensa Libre*;

• On March 29, four peasants were murdered in Santa Cruz del Quiché.

ALTA AND BAJA VERAPAZ

The EGP's Marco Antonio Yon Sosa Front (MAYS), founded in 1981, and the Augusto César Sandino Front (FACS) operated in the northern departments of Alta and Baja Verapaz, particularly in the southwestern areas. The EGP regarded both departments, especially the southwest, as a strategic logistical enclave because of their central location between the Augusto César Sandino Front (Chimaltenango), the Ho Chi Minh Front (Quiché-Alta Verapaz), and the FAR's Panzós Heróico Front (eastern Alta Verapaz and Izabal departments). The formation of MAYS and intense guerrilla activity for several months in 1981 and 1982 can be attributed to an effort to scatter the army forces—which already had launched their first offensive against FACS—and to the insurgent plan of "all-out guerrilla warfare."

Despite a few previous attacks, the real onset of guerrilla actions in the northern region occurred on September 12, 1981. On that day the EGP detonated several explosives in the city of Cobán (Alta Verapaz), destroying the Military Reserves Command headquarters, and in Salamá (Baja Verapaz) razing the departmental government building. The guerrillas also blocked transit between Mixco Viejo and Granados, and between Granados and El Chol, Salamá, and Rabinal. It was not until late 1981, after the emergence of MAYS, that the massacres began to be more open, with the systematic involvement of civil patrollers.

After the offensive of late 1981 in southern Quiché and northern Chimaltenango along the Pan-American highway, the army turned its attention, in January 1982, to the Chuacús Mountains and, later, to the Cuchumatanes Mountains. The army sent Presidential Guard units to these areas and simultaneously launched a series of machine-gun attacks "in a ring" around villages of Alta Verapaz. Meanwhile, MAYS stepped up its actions until August, when all of its activity ceased abruptly.

The army concentrated on eliminating all means of support for the guerrillas in the communities of Rabinal, Río Negro, and San Cristóbal Verapaz, the most strategic areas from the insurgents' standpoint. Thus, between September 1981 and August 1983, between 4,000 and 5,000 people were killed in the municipality of Rabinal, out of a total of 22,733 inhabitants (EAFG 1995).

General Ríos Montt issued an order to chop down all the trees within 165 feet of both sides of the main roadways to prevent the guerrillas from ambushing military convoys. In 1983, civil patrollers from San Cristóbal, Tactic, and Chamá began sorties to "hunt down" the people that were hiding in the hills and forests. Patrollers from Salaqwín, who were connected to the Playa Grande Military Zone, were particularly notorious for their hunting expeditions. The army established three places where the population would be congregated: Salaqwín, Las Conchas, and El Rosario farm.

San Marcos

During this period, human rights violations against the population in zones influenced by ORPA did not reach the same proportions as in EGP areas. This was due both to ORPA's style, which was secretive and detached from the "grassroots organizations," and to the fact that the army's strategic priority at the time was neutralizing the EGP. Nonetheless, there were a number of massacres and bombardments in San Marcos, which had a tremendous impact on the social fabric of the communities: these incidents occurred in Sacuchum Dolores and El Tablero (San Pedro Sacatepéquez), and Xolhuitz, Bulaj, and Montecristo (Tajumulco), among other places. Moreover, relations between peasants and plantation owners in the zone had always been extremely tense, leading rural landowners routinely to request army support and protection. According to testimonies from people living in the communities, during the conflict it was common practice for certain military chiefs to receive monthly payments to take particular care of certain farms, and army posts were set up on some haciendas.

El Petén

When the fighting intensified, beginning in 1981, the army had already begun to repress cooperatives, small hamlets, villages, and farm plots where a FAR presence was detected. The army gradually turned up the pressure on populations that potentially supported the guerrillas, in actions ranging from isolated murders—like the appearance, on March 14, 1979, of the corpse of Samuel Sucul, a peasant leader from San Luis Petén—to large-scale operations. In 1980, the first massacre was carried out in the village of El Limón (Santa Ana), and the practice spread. During May, June, and July 1981, the army focused on El Petén, where it carried out massacres and forced the population to flee into Mexico. In early 1982 the army organized the civil patrols, particularly in the county seats.

This pressure remained constant through the final months of the Lucas administration. Ríos Montt's ascension to power and the spread of the scorched-earth policy had devastating effects on El Petén, including massacres in the villages of Palestina, Josefinos, and Macanché in March and April 1982.

THE CAPITAL AND THE COAST

Repression became increasingly selective, mainly targeting the FAR and the PGT, whose infrastructure in the capital had not yet been attacked. The disappearances of fifteen high-school student activists from the FERG, three USAC labor leaders, and labor advisor Yolanda Urízar were among the more prominent actions.

The coast was a strategic disputed area, where all of the guerrilla organizations converged, and where the army concentrated a great deal of its firepower. Prior to the farm laborers' strike in February 1980, military bases had already been established in Palín (one) and Masagua (three). In 1982, additional bases were installed in Sipacate, La Gomera, La Democracia, and Tiquisate. Civil patrols were organized in all of these locations. However, the Santa Lucía Cotzumalguapa military zone is identified as the source of the harshest repression.

Extremely severe repression followed the 1980 strike. It began on the plantations with the killing or forced disappearance of farmhands living there full time. The unions were also attacked; for example, the Madre Tierra and Santa Ana Workers Unions were completely decimated (Key Source 017, Escuintla, the 1980s). Plantation owners also hired private security forces, mostly comprised of Mobile Military Police agents (PMA).

QUETZALTENANGO

Under Ríos Montt, the army was behind the reorganization of municipal authority. It hand picked the mayors, taking care that they were leaders in their communities. After these authorities took office, the army promoted the formation of civil patrols. Groups of six patrollers led search missions to pursue the guerrillas in forests and ravines. The army escalated the terror to counteract the population's probable sympathy with the guerrillas. In Coatepeque, the army paraded alleged guerrilla prisoners, naked and bearing signs of torture, in the public square, at the same time warning the population about the consequences of collaborating with the insurgency. In Santa Lucía la Reforma, army detainees were also tortured in front of the local population. Their bodies would later appear abandoned on the roadsides.

The army also conducted operations in communities and along the roadways, where it stopped buses and vans and searched the passengers, checking them against lists of people who were accused of collaborating with rebel groups. The soldiers occasionally were accompanied by hooded men who pointed out alleged guerrillas.

THE CHURCH TARGETED

When Ríos Montt came to power, the persecution of priests decreased at the same time that Catholic Action activists and catechists were bloodily repressed. In December, in the village of Tabil de la Santa Cruz del Quiché, the army forced civil patrollers to kill five Catholic Action activists. On December 4 soldiers went to the village of Santabal, San Pedro Jocopilas, looking for four Catholic Action activists and, when they could not be found, killed six women instead.

After Ríos Montt (an elder of the Church of the Word) took power, the offensive against the Catholic church changed its tactics. The pope's March 1983 visit to Guatemala was welcomed with six executions and presidential insults to the highest Catholic authority. In April, acts of sabotage marred Holy Week celebrations. Finally, on June 7, the Bishops' Conference condemned the regime in its pastoral letter, "Confirmed in Faith."

The arrival of Ríos Montt and the boom of neo-Pentecostal sects had explicit connotations for the counterinsurgency campaign. For example, following Ríos Montt's coup d'état, the Church of the Word (*Iglesia del Verbo*) began to be active in the Ixil area; this is the Guatemalan affiliate of the Fundamentalist Church Gospel Outreach, based in Eureka, California. The Church of the Word channeled the aid by creating the Foundation to Assist the Indigenous People (FUNDAPI), which has produced and distributed written information since January 1983.

Among the church elders involved in this program were Harris Whitbeck, missionary of the Word and an army officer, who specialized in counterinsurgency warfare; Alfredo Kalschmidt, delegate from Alta Verapaz from his headquarters in Chisec; Jesse Camey, head of the Program of Aid to Conflictive Areas (PAAC); Rolando Lavidalle Guzmán, public relations representative and PAAC liaison with the secretary of social welfare; Ray Elliot Jr, PAAC representative in Nebaj; George Hughes, responsible for the construction of air strips in the Ixil area.

SEARCHING AMONG THE ASHES

The following are accounts of La Verapaz Bishop Gerardo Flores's visits to parishes in his diocese from May 10-17, 1982:

Villages in some parishes (Rabinal, Chisec, Raxruha, San Cristóbal) are completely abandoned. Others contain a large number of widows and orphans; there are no men or young people. In some cases, churches and convents were destroyed (Cobán, San Cristóbal). Others live in a state of almost unbearable tension, because public accusations have been made that "they are all guerrillas." Pastoral work is paralyzed. Several parishes (Salamá, Rabinal, Calvario Cobán, San Cristóbal) have lost many of their catechists or delegates; they have either been killed, or forced into hiding or into ceasing their activities. In several villages Catholics have had to bury their bibles, hymnals, and religious icons.

Other parishes, or parts of their communities (Panzós, Senahú, La Tinta, Telemán, Tamahú, Purulhá, Cubulco, Chamelco, San Marcos Cobán), have not experienced large-scale violence but live in an atmosphere of fear, tension, and distrust caused by abductions, threats, accusations, rumors, bans, and restrictions on religious activities, or by the imposition of civil patrols, which has alienated catechists and discouraged the community.

However, still other parishes have experienced very little violence and remain calm (San Jerónimo, Catedral Cobán, Boloncó, Chahal, Las Casas, Tucurú). They are going about their activities normally, including visits to villages, seminars, meetings, and celebrations. This is also true of some parishes which report that calm has been restored (Raxruhá, Campur) or that violent incidents have occurred only during recent weeks (Tactic, Carchá).

Attacks are no longer aimed at priests and nuns, but rather catechists, who are more vulnerable: "All of the catechists are with the guerrillas." The revolutionary organizations try to infiltrate meetings and celebrations and manipulate them politically. In La Tinta and Telemán, there has been an unrestrained increase in the number of catechists: "Sometimes we place our trust in them without knowing who they are." It is said that spiritualism and witchcraft are on the rise and that the communities attend celebrations if a musical group is playing.

Evangelical sects

• Their influence is very strong in Polochic; for example, in Tamahú two catechists left taking all of their people with them.

• In Chahal, they frequently conduct home visits, and five catechists have become evangelical Christians.

• In Boloncó, the aggressive tactics used by the Protestants cause many to convert.

• In Cobán, certain evangelical women invite "prominent" Catholic women to charismatic meetings.

The situation is aggravated when conflicts of a political nature are combined with religious tensions. For example, in El Cruce, in Playa Grande, Catholics have a lot of problems, while Evangelicals are left in peace. The Protestants often escape repression (Rabinal) or are the ones provoking the problem in the first place, either by making false accusations or by obtaining public posts (like commissioners) in order to dominate the Catholic majority (Cobán). An extreme example of this is Salaqwim (Cobán), where the commissioner used his power to win followers: he gave a military service certificate only to those who worship at the Church of the Nazarene. He is responsible for the death of a catechist and the abduction of a group of ten people. They have also required a new identity card that states the person's religion.

Chapter Fourteen

THE MEJIA VICTORES GOVERNMENT

On August 8, 1983, Ríos Montt was overthrown in a coup d'état that installed his defense minister, General Oscar Humberto Mejía Víctores, as chief of state. The mutiny encountered little resistance. The Presidential Guard resisted, with a toll of five dead and thirty wounded, and a group of young officers issued a radio communiqué blaming Mejía Víctores for the repression of the preceding seventeen months.

The coup proclamation began by naming General Mario López Fuentes as army chief of staff; it also named the commanders of major military zones and garrisons throughout the country. This group would jointly dominate the political life of the country through the so-called Council of Commanders. The new military regime hastened to form a predominantly civilian government: Fernando Andrade Díaz-Durán, an influential political conservative and financier close to generals Rodolfo Lobos Zamora and Héctor Nuila Hub, was a key figure during the political transition. In fact, the coup did not signify a break with the process begun in 1982 but instead represented a less radical approach. Nonetheless, it was still unable to escape clashes with the business sector and political parties, and the peril of political instability.

In the aftermath of the most acute phase of counterinsurgency in the countryside, the rural infrastructure was partially destroyed, production was in a state of disarray, and hundreds of thousands of victims required emergency assistance programs that the government was not in a position to provide. The model village and development pole system did not even cover the basic subsistence needs of the people confined in those programs. Moreover, the international assistance that could be leveraged—by gaining control over World Food Program funds or AID rural development assistance, for example—proved insufficient.

With the 1983 coup d'état, an army priority was to restore internal stability, which had been jarred by the "young officers" behind the March 23, 1982, coup. Once the Mejía Víctores government was in power, it immediately turned its attention to refocusing the process of institutional government reform.

Chapter Fifteen

THE CEREZO GOVERNMENT

THE TRANSITION, 1986-1987

The Christian Democrats won the 1985 elections with 67 percent of the vote. During his campaign, presidential candidate Vinicio Cerezo was circumspect in his handling of the military issue. He frequently referred to "the violence of the past," but was careful to avoid explicit statements against the army. However, under pressure from the Mutual Support Group (GAM), he promised to form a commission to determine the fate of the disappeared. He also promised to hold a village-by-village referendum regarding the future of the civil patrols. He vowed that the "Interinstitutional Coordinators," which had militarized and decentralized public administration at the departmental, municipal, and village level, would be transferred to civilian control. He promised to take control of Military Intelligence (D-2) and the Presidential General Staff (EMP) by assigning people he trusted to those entities. He also announced that he would dissolve the National Police's Technical Investigations Department (DIT), created under Ríos Montt and accused of involvement in human rights violations.

During the election campaign, the parties uniformly rejected the idea of agrarian or fiscal reform and, with the exception of the Christian Democrats, they all criticized the military government's fiscal measures and backed a neo-liberal economic policy. Prior to the elections, the most modern segments of the business sector were confident of a possible Christian Democratic victory. They expressed their conviction that the Christian Democratic leadership shared their views on the business sector's role in the country's economic development by asserting that "no one will kill the goose that lays the golden eggs." Of course, this was true of certain segments of the business sector, but they were the ones who had played a prominent role in unifying and defining its goals. The rest appeared more united around concrete policies that could be adopted rather than in the political ability of the Christian Democrats to bring about the anticipated economic growth.

Some members of the business sector regarded the 1985 elections as a barometer of the prospects for medium- and long-term stability, and as a tool to evaluate the possibility that their economic proposals would be accepted as part of a new social consensus. Their support (for democracy) was expressed in the traditional way through campaign contributions to political parties. Moreover, in a conscious attempt to improve their own image and restore their leadership role in civil society, some business associations embarked on "civic education" projects concerning the Constitution and the electoral process. Members of the business sector shared a deep-seated aversion to political parties and the vast majority of their leaders.

CONCERTACIÓN[1]

The relationship between the Christian Democrats and the army had developed over the months leading up to 1985 elections through a National Dialogue convened by the military regime. After Cerezo's victory, the relationship deepened. Also during that period, the security forces used pressure and threats to limit the scope of any reforms that the new president might consider introducing.

Thus, on December 12, the same day that Cerezo announced that he would dissolve the DIT, Beatriz Barrios Marroquín, a teacher who had already been abducted once and was arranging her departure from the country through the Canadian Embassy, was brutally tortured and killed. This crime, which was protested by the diplomatic community, represented a challenge to Cerezo's pledge to put an end to the ability to operate with impunity.

On January 3, 1986, prior to taking office, Cerezo met with the Council of Commanders to introduce his cabinet (Gramajo 1995). For the position of defense minister, he had selected General Jaime Hernández Mendez, a military officer who had played a critical role in the coup d'état that brought down Ríos Montt and who only had one year of military service left before retiring from active duty. For the position of army chief of staff, he had selected General Héctor Alejandro Gramajo, an officer with ties to army currents that espoused the "development theory."[2]

Cerezo had met Gramajo when the latter was a military attaché assigned to Washington, D.C. Gramajo, in turn, had chosen Colonel Manuel Antonio Callejas as his vice–chief of staff. Callejas was the leader of the military intelligence clique known as *La Cofradía*, but he had been loyal to Gramajo throughout his military career. Cerezo named Colonel Roberto Mata Gálvez as chief of the Presidential General Staff (EMP), another "developmentalist" officer who had held important posts during the counterinsurgency campaign; at the same time, however, José Edgar Rolando Solís, a military intelligence officer and *Cofradía* member, was selected to be the vice–chief of the EMP. General Edgar Augusto Godoy Gaitán, who had held administrative and army staff positions under General Lucas, was named director of military intelligence (D-2).

---

[1] *Concertación* in the Latin American context refers to a process of dialogue and consultation with a view toward agreeing on a course of action or a joint position—Trans.

[2] Various currents within the army adapted ECLAC's development model—which promoted social spending and community organization as the path to overcoming poverty—to its security policy; in other words, security and development to ensure national stability.

Gramajo was not the most highly qualified officer for the position of army chief of staff; and the appointment of Jaime Hernández Mendez, a key player in the 1983 coup, as minister—despite the fact that he was just one year away from retirement—was an acknowledgment of the power elite installed in 1983.

The army officers best known for their developmentalist views in the National Reconstruction Committee (CRN) were promoted to posts in the army chief of staff's office or the government. The new roles of the chiefs of the presidential and vice-presidential staffs enabled them quickly to establish control over public activities and over the offices of the president and vice-president.

At the same time, the military regime acted to secure its future from a legal standpoint. On January 10, 1986, alone, sixteen decrees were promulgated, out of a total of forty during that period. The most widely known were Decree 8-86, which granted amnesty for all political and related common crimes committed from 1982 to 1986; and Decree 25-86, which modified, once again, the Army Organic Law. Other important but less well-known decrees enacted as part of this package were Decree 43-86, establishing the National Security Council, and other decrees granting hereditary lifetime pensions to officials of the military regime and modifying the system governing military assets. The civil patrols were legally recognized as "Civil Defense Committees"; the Ministry of Urban and Rural Development was established; and a contract was approved with a French company SGS for export oversight.

Three days after the new president took office, the Council of Commanders met with the incoming army high command to hear the army chief of staff explain his new policies (Gramajo 1995). During that meeting, Gramajo emphasized professionalism and the apolitical nature of the institution, and presented his Campaign Plan Consolidation 86. He warned that corruption would not be tolerated and spoke of a "centralized doctrine" on security matters.[3]

One of the purposes of Campaign Plan Consolidation 86 was to rearticulate a comprehensive security doctrine: National Stability. "In Guatemala, the continuation of the war using diverse methods" became the catchphrase used even by the president to summarize this new concept. In terms of methods, Gramajo asserts that they proposed to involve civilian and even international entities to attend to the civilian population affected by the armed conflict. He was referring particularly to the United Nations High Commissioner for Refugees, the creation of the Special Committee for Attention to Refugees (CEAR), and the Ministry of Development, as well as the transfer of the Interinstitutional Coordinators to recently elected civilian governors. At the same time, it was announced that the Civilian Self-defense Patrols, now called Voluntary Committees, would not be expanded during 1986.

---

[3] Since the seventies, the army had applied a "centralized decision and de-centralized execution" doctrine, which left the selection of victims or arbitrary application of repressive measures in the hands of mid-level commanders. Gramajo's emphasis on "centralized doctrine" may well refer to greater control of repressive activities.

Nonetheless, during the early months of the new administration, the military issue did not appear to be a priority for the president; he concentrated instead on negotiating an economic and social reorganization program that would satisfy the concerns of the developmentalist sector within the army.

THE INITIAL AGREEMENTS

In June, the president announced in a press conference that he was developing a concept of national security in keeping with the new democracy. During the same period, the press office of the United States Embassy distributed a speech that the U.S. Assistant Secretary of State, Elliot Abrams, had given at the Inter-American Defense College: "Today we learn a new lesson; in addition to the link between security and development there is a second link, between security and democracy." Several weeks later, the newly designated National Police chief, Colonel Julio Caballeros, acknowledged that there was coordination between the police and the army, given that it was "the first line of defense against subversion."

The president sided with the army in response to pressure groups who were demanding an accounting of the violence and prosecution and punishment of those responsible; this had a tremendous public impact. Cerezo also supported the army as it developed its war plans. In 1986, service support units were the priority: the Military Hospital was fully equipped and transport units were completed. The United States supplied most of the assistance to resupply the army.

Throughout 1986 the army limited its operations to what Gramajo would refer to as "Reconnaissance in Force": rapid incursions into guerrilla-controlled zones, concentrating large numbers of troops in small areas to minimize casualties. These campaigns, which took place in April and May and again from October to December, did not prevent guerrilla operations from reaching their 1985 levels between the first and second half of 1986. Financial difficulties appeared to limit the army's offensive capability. Nonetheless, a large number of civilians were captured during these military operations, according to press accounts from late 1986.

The civilian government's collaboration with the army was most apparent in its treatment of populations displaced by the war. In April, displaced people began to return home and requested the protection of the Catholic church in Izabal and La Verapaz. In both places the army abducted and killed some of the returnees, while the president turned a deaf ear to the church's protests (Mack 1989).

The second area of government *concertación* with the army's position was President Cerezo's refusal to engage the guerrillas in a dialogue process. Initially, in statements made by Commander "Pablo Monsanto," the URNG offered a "grace period" to avoid distracting the government from fulfilling its campaign promises. In May, the URNG presented a comprehensive proposal for purging and reorganizing the security forces. The president responded in his Army Day speech by warning that the only possible dialogue was through acceding to the government amnesty.

In October, the URNG published an "Open Letter" proposing a dialogue at the highest levels. In November 1986, according to Gramajo, the guerrillas approached the Spanish Embassy to propose talks, which were approved by the army high command. But by the end of the year the guerrillas evidently felt "let down" by the expectations raised by Cerezo and had resumed their normal military operations.

In terms of previous agreements with the business sector, the Christian Democratic government was organized around party politics, although individuals clearly interested in strengthening ties with the business sector were named to key posts; for example, Federico Linares, with ties to the Castillo family, was named president of the Bank of Guatemala.

The first negotiation between the government and the business sector produced the Economic Stabilization Plan, in which entrepreneurs offered to support certain populist measures with a special export tax in exchange for matching payments.

The Economic and Social Adjustment Program (PRES) went into effect on May 1. This program allocated one million quetzales for the creation of 400,000 new jobs; it increased cash holdings to cut back on short-term credit and adjusted interest rates for inflation; it established a 30 percent across-the-board export tax reduction. It also retained a managed foreign exchange market but established three exchange rates that enabled agroexporters to receive foreign currency at a 2.5:1 ratio, thus compensating for the additional tariffs.

The business sector appeared generally satisfied with this overall negotiation— which proceeded more smoothly than their previous experiences with the military regime. Nonetheless, it reserved the right to criticize the Christian Democrats' "nationalizing" tendencies and to pressure for a reduced public sector (paid ad in the *Prensa Libre*, March 21, 1986).

Although the first two years of the Christian Democratic government produced a favorable economic balance, the business sector was the only beneficiary, since the populist or "progressive" aspects of the Economic and Social Adjustment Program never materialized, despite an increase in the public budget. The government, however, utilized only 30 percent of funds allocated for social spending due to financial burdens imposed by the Bank of Guatemala.

THE TENSIONS BEGIN

The government soon reacted to this situation by changing the course of its policy in 1987, prompting, in turn, a reaction from the business sector. On March 19, the president published his "Memorandum to All Guatemalans," which outlined his 1987 National Reorganization Plan (PRN). This plan included extensive structural reforms to repay the government's "social debt" to its people.

That same month the government also announced a campaign to relinquish national farms, and UNAGRO called for the removal of Agriculture Minister Rodolfo Estrada. In response, the government began to examine the possibility of tax reform, adjusting the tax base, creating a separate value-added tax, and raising taxes on certain imports. The president began a two-point negotiation with the private sector: tax reform, and the government role in the economy. At the same time, he requested 100 million quetzales from CACIF to ward off a fiscal deficit.

The government had also undergone internal changes. Rodolfo Paiz replaced other members of the economic cabinet and prepared his tax-reform package independently of the negotiations. The resulting political tensions led to the resignation of Federico Linares, president of the Bank of Guatemala.

Also in March, the Department of Administrative Oversight of the Presidency (DECAP) was created by governmental decree. It was headed by Colonel Hugo Morán Carranza, who had previously been involved in monitoring tax evasion by certain entrepreneurs from his position at the Finance Ministry. This was the backdrop for the first major public clash between the government and the highest echelons of the business sector: the business strikes of 1987, which brought the *concertación* stage to a close and ushered the business sector's new shock force into the public scene.

RUMBLING IN THE BARRACKS

According to Gramajo, the first military protests were against the "vindictive spirit" of civilian officials who had entered government service with an anti-army attitude.

In May of 1987 some observers noted the danger that a "clique" of high-level commanders too close to the president might be formed, which would destroy the institutional calm achieved by Mejía Víctores.

The "developmentalist" policy gave rise to criticism in military circles: it was paralyzed by bureaucratic inefficiency, pressures from the business sector, and differences between the Development Ministry (headed by René de León Schlotter) and other government agencies, including the office of the vice-president (under Roberto Carpio Nicolle).

The army continued to prioritize its Civilian Affairs Section, to the point that, in 1986, the Army Staff published its doctrinal paper. At the end of that year, the Civil Affairs Section circulated a document entitled "Analysis of the Causal Factors that Render the Government's Overall Strategy Unworkable."

The war on corruption announced by the president during his first months in office also generated distrust and suspicion in the army ranks, since allusions to "past corruption" could well refer to the army. Moreover, the foreign-policy approach of "active neutrality," announced at the meeting of Central American presidents in Esquipulas, caused confusion in the ranks, because, at the time, the defense minister was also the president of the Central American Defense Council.

The new civilian government's security policy also made the army ranks uneasy. The dismantling of the DIT did not appear to be a serious problem for the security apparatus, which rechanneled the department's most important elements into the recently created Special Narcotics Investigations Brigade (BIEN). It also represented progress in the area of legal protections. Judges were only able to review data from the files of the former DIT through certificates issued by the police.

In any event, the security priorities in this first year seemed to focus on upgrading methods and structures, and updating the data base. The psychological campaign against the Mutual Support Group was the most significant program during this period, together with certain cases of violence in the countryside that were indicative of the commanders' failure to adhere to the "centralized doctrine."

THE POWER OF THE NEW RIGHT-WING BUSINESS ELITE

As the new government took over, new groups also took control of corporate decision-making at precisely the same moment that the regional and international economic and political balance seemed favorable for the growth and consolidation of the Guatemalan business sector. The economic sectors that benefited from the government's fiscal policies immediately rebounded. Thus, during 1987, nontraditional exports rose, as did sugar and cotton production, due to favorable internal market prices established during negotiations with the minister of economy; coffee production also increased because its exportation was legalized.

Industrial output and basic grain production also increased, stimulated by the deregulated price ceilings. The construction sector grew by 20 percent, according to CACIF, and tourism revenues tripled their 1986 values. CACIF announced capital repatriation in the amount of U.S.$200 million and nontraditional exports rose by 53 percent. Finally, the financial sector had become increasingly consolidated; in 1987 the three largest banks monopolized 39 percent of financial transactions, compared to 23 percent in 1983.

All of these were factors in the organized business sector's increasingly aggressive anti-government stance. In March 1986, the National Cotton Council and UNAGRO opposed the proposed diversification of designated cotton-growing areas, which were mostly idle. But in 1987, when Juan Luis Bosch and Víctor Suárez joined the Board of Trade, and Edgar Heinemann the Chamber of Commerce, the business sector further hardened its position. On September 11, CACIF convened the first nationwide half-day business stoppage.

Juan Carlos Simons, MLN deputy, linking the new taxes to the dialogue with the guerrillas that had taken place in Madrid, asserted that "the army is divided." Defense Minister Gramajo voiced his opposition to the "destabilizing right-wing" that wanted the army to do its "dirty work." The battle against the taxes was ultimately lost by the businessmen, and the taxes were approved. But during the struggle, unmanageable forces had broken loose within the business sector; they would soon jeopardize the difficult commitments associated with structural transition.

A NO-WIN BATTLE

Selective repression of the grassroots movement did not end with the installation of a civilian government. On May 15, pastor Nicolás Chuy Cumes was killed, and, on June 2, the Mutual Support Group reported that 120 people had been forcibly disappeared during the first six months of the year. The situation did not improve in 1987. The murders and disappearances of labor unionists, professionals, and students continued; by way of illustration, four physicians were killed in the capital in April alone.

In most cases the repression appeared to be counterinsurgency related. However, on March 20, 1987, President Cerezo rationalized these attacks as the work of common criminals, affirming that, "to date, no political or labor leader has been attacked."

Repression was most intense in rural areas where the URNG had stepped up its military pressure; this was especially true in Suchitepéquez, San Marcos, and Quetzaltenango. A string of murders occurred in response to actions by groups of people demanding land and to ORPA's ongoing presence in the area. In Izabal, where union struggles had taken place, and in the east and the southern coast, where the guerrilla presence was expanding, repression was very much in evidence, especially in Chiquimula.

In 1986 the army continued to concentrate its counterinsurgency actions in the Ixil region. In September the army launched its "Year-end Offensive" to round up the population remaining in areas with guerrilla presence. Following this military campaign, General Gramajo declared that ninety families a week were seeking army protection in the Ixil area, and the rapid construction of model villages began. Overall, the army reported that in 1987 it had "recovered" two thousand displaced persons out of an estimated seven thousand.

When Gramajo became defense minister, a new army strategy began to emerge. This strategy would be sidelined following the May 1989 coup attempt, further weakened when Gramajo stepped down in May 1990, and ultimately replaced by the new government in 1991. Nonetheless, Gramajo's policy encompassed army personnel and cadres who would reemerge in May 1993 to lead the negotiations concerning the army's future from 1994 until their conclusion.

The most striking aspect of 1986 was the process through which the civilian government adapted to the army's conditions; in 1987 the dominant theme was the discourse of the new military team, which would face its first challenge in the form of the May 1988 coup attempt. The two pivotal factors during that period were the formation of a new group in the highest echelons of the army and its relationship with that other power center, the business sector.

During this period the civilian government still enjoyed a considerable margin of trust, within what would be known as "a supervised democracy." Repressive actions were essentially subordinated to military objectives, although the initial symptoms of autonomous patterns of repression had already begun to surface.

THE POWER OF *EL SINDICATO*[4]

Although a corporate spirit and group privileges united the army against outside pressures and challenges, the exclusive and competitive nature of the military career fostered the emergence of internal allegiances. The intense growth of the army command structures in the early eighties, during the harshest period of counterinsurgency war, created even greater pressure in this regard. In fact, under the new Army Organic Law, a large number of colonels would have to retire, having just turned fifty, without having had the opportunity to reach the High Command.

Moreover, from the time General Gramajo began to promote a group of officers loyal to his plan, others who felt they had been shunted aside began to agitate for the "historic rights" of the twenty-eight colonels comprising the Council of Commanders that had supported the August 1983 coup d'état.

Gramajo tried to give *El Sindicato* a personalized focus that revolved around his leadership. Efforts to update military doctrine through the development of a National Stability Thesis followed in this direction. By all indicators, one factor that helped Gramajo solidify his influence was that the army leadership was disconcerted by having to coexist with a civilian government. However, it is true that, from the outset, he encountered rival leadership and currents of thought that clung to the old system.

His first move was to assure that General Manuel Callejas y Callejas, the ranking officer in *La Cofradía*, would be appointed army chief of staff. But he also had to promote other officers who were openly hostile to his policy course. These included Generals Pablo Nuila (named director of the Military Studies Center [CEM], José Luis Díaz Muñoz (assigned to the Mariscal Zavala Military Brigade), Julio César Ruano (director of the Mobile Military Police), and Colonel Byron Disrael Lima, the director of intelligence in 1985 (named commander of the Poptún Military Zone in Petén), all of whom rose and fell in the army ranks during this period.

---

[4] The term *El Sindicato* (the Union) was coined by *La Cofradía* to refer to a group of army officers involved in intelligence activities under Lucas García, who were among those supporting the army's reformist current that backed the 1982 coup d'état. Officers belonging to *El Sindicato* were particularly influenced by the theories of low-intensity warfare and development as conceived by the United States army (those theories came back into style during the war with the Nicaraguan Sandinistas). In contrast, officers in *La Cofradía* were from the "Taiwan school"; in other words, they were more interested in applying social-control mechanisms and security-related intelligence. But ideology aside, the complicity born of government intelligence work appeared to be the strongest tie among members of *La Cofradía*, while *El Sindicato* members defined themselves by their "nonparticipation" in that work.

General Gramajo organized his personal work team in the Defense Ministry and situated loyal officers in other government agencies. This group (composed of officers of different ranks) designed the new military strategy in the areas of internal security, international relations, and internal army policy. Gramajo himself insinuates that this group was quite powerful in matters such as talks with the URNG, international negotiations on human rights issues, and the limits of the "centralized doctrine" of internal security, all directly related to the ministry's policy.

NATIONAL STABILITY DOCTRINE

The new National Stability policy announced by President Vinicio Cerezo in June 1986 was refined by General Gramajo in 1987 and 1988. The army's role was quite explicitly defined as the "guarantor of the survival of the State." "We must be the moral reserve of the nation," warned Gramajo. He defined the central dilemma of this initiative as an attempt to answer the question: "Is the army anticommunist or pro-democracy?" Civilian government was understood as a vehicle for the continuity of his overall counterinsurgency strategy, and he recommended "maintaining security as the foundation of national stability."

At the same time, Gramajo tried to convey his new military thinking to other sectors of society. The so-called "Business Forum: 27 Years of Struggle for Freedom" was the most relevant initiative. In 1988, the National Defense Staff published "The Thesis of National Stability," in which the concept of "internal security" is described as follows:

> The entirety of actions carried out by the State, in the context of national security and within the bounds of the country, with the aim of destroying or neutralizing antagonisms or pressures, of any origin, form, or nature, that oppose or potentially oppose the attainment and maintenance of national objectives.

The new concept of National Stability and the way in which it was introduced both within and outside the army soon led to a groundswell of opposition inside the armed institution that would culminate in the attempted coup of 1988.

THE YEAR-END OFFENSIVE

Campaign Plan Fortitude 87 included an "outward" component that began in September when the army assembled special units and troops from various military zones to carry out the so-called Year-end Offensive against the EGP and ORPA.

In March, the army organized a massive recruitment campaign among unemployed workers on the southern coast called Friendship 87. In April, it attracted attention by using several Chinook helicopters donated by the U.S. Southern Command to transfer troops to reinforce the Playa Grande military zone. One month later, the army launched incursions against guerrilla fronts in the Ixil area, which were accompanied by the mass recruitment of civil patrollers.

The Year-end Offensive in northern Guatemala mobilized approximately thirty-five hundred troops, in a combination of battalions from each military zone, joined by special forces troops. The centralized command of the Kaibil Balam Task Force, led by Colonel Jaime Rabanales, helped coordinate operations to hone in on precise targets, which in turn allowed the army to install patrols in advance posts in areas formerly controlled by the guerrilla forces.

However, the Year-end Offensive had the greatest impact on the displaced population rather than on guerrilla military units, which suffered few casualties. The plans were further complicated by the fact that, in November, the U.S. Congress failed to approve an aid request for U.S.$10 million.

In January 1988, Gramajo announced his Campaign Plan Unity 88, which aimed to "transform the military advantage into a political advantage and impede guerrilla contact with the [civilian] population." The Task Force was dissolved, and the responsibility for the offensive fell to special forces units of paratroopers, Honor Guard troops, and rangers, who were to defend the advance posts that had been installed in 1987. Meanwhile, the regular troops assigned to the military zones turned their attention to the control of the displaced population.

In February 1988, ORPA launched a military offensive in Patzún, an area formerly devoid of any particular guerrilla activity; the FAR, meanwhile, stepped up its takeover of villages and roadways in the Petén. For its part, the EGP concentrated on expanding its guerrilla fronts southward—in the direction that the Year-end Offensive had come in—and rebuilding its logistical networks so that they functioned independently of the civilian population.

ACTIVE NEUTRALITY

In early 1987, Cerezo described "active neutrality" to his coreligionists as follows: "Our threat is in the mountains, not in Nicaragua. The regional conflict must be handled in a manner that benefits our internal situation." Until that moment, the civilian government's foreign policy was nothing more than a continuation of that of the military regimes. Months later, when the Central American presidents signed the peace plan proposed by Costa Rican President Oscar Arias, the Guatemalan government began to lose control of the situation.

Gramajo had established relationships in Washington, D.C., through the office of liberal attorney Paul Reichler, who had also worked as a consultant for the Sandinista government in Nicaragua. The Foreign Affairs Ministry had been turned over to Christian Democratic "strongman" Alfonso Cabrera, who brought in people close to the army, such as Ariel Rivera and Antonio Arenales Forno, and sent others, such as José Luis Chea and Francisco Villagrán Jr., to Geneva and Washington, D.C.

Although a Verification Commission was created to monitor compliance with peace agreements, Cerezo was confident that his mediation on the Sandinista issue would neutralize any pressure from the guerrilla groups. Otherwise, the government confined itself to formal compliance with the agreements by issuing a new amnesty decree in November (which it used for propaganda purposes during the Year-end Offensive), establishing the National Reconciliation Commission (CNR), and meeting with the URNG in Madrid in October.

For its part, the URNG notably increased activities on the political-diplomatic front. In 1988 the URNG reiterated its proposals for a cease-fire, the creation of demilitarized zones, and a political dialogue with the government. Its political initiatives centered on institutions such as the Catholic church, the CNR, and President Arias of Costa Rica, who had offered their services as mediators.

The army adopted a defensive posture toward these initiatives, invoking the letter of the Constitution of 1985 to justify its strategy of "not recognizing the subversives as any kind of belligerent force in an internal armed conflict." The army high command communicated this position to the National Reconciliation Commission in a February 1988 meeting. In any event, the army succeeded in keeping the Guatemalan internal conflict off the Central American peace process agenda in 1987 and 1988.

THE "MESSAGE SYSTEM" AND OTHER METHODS

Army repression took on two forms during this period: one was tied to the progress of the war; and the other was aimed at intimidating grassroots organizations or members of guerrilla groups who were returning to the country in what was termed "the message system" (Jonas 1991).

Upon tracing the course of human rights violations between January 1987 and May 1988, the first thing carried out by uniformed groups that stands out is the long list of abductions and torture-murders of peasants in San Marcos, Retalhuleu, Suchitepéquez, Sololá, and Chimaltenango. Given that these were areas of ORPA expansion, it is easy to assume that these crimes targeted alleged guerrilla collaborators. The total absence of detentions followed by transfer of the prisoners to the court system suggests that the army authorities in conflict zones followed a policy of abducting and disappearing suspected guerrilla collaborators. This was apparent in communities such as Santiago Atitlán.

The government-sponsored policy of repression continued to use National Police forces in the capital in actions to intimidate grassroots organizations; to seek ways to blame such actions on common criminals or on other types of violence; and to target mid-level and anonymous activists for repression in order to avoid international attention. When, in March 1987, the president was queried about the rise in human rights violations, he attributed it to common crime.

At the same time that the National Police was being equipped by the German, Venezuelan, United States, and Spanish governments, its members—controlled by military intelligence officers (D-2)—were employed for counterintelligence "dirty work" (WOLA 1989). There is sufficient evidence to indicate that this created conflicts over security policy. The institutional development and modernization of the police corps advertised by Interior Minister Juan José Rodil Peralta was used by destabilizing elements within the army. In December 1987, columnist Danilo Roca affirmed that the government was forming a presidential security super corps, led by Rodil Peralta, that might some day challenge the army. Even though this accusation may have had no basis beyond the goal of disquieting the army ranks, the White Van (*la Pánel Blanca*) case in March 1987 was symptomatic of an internal struggle for control over state security forces.

The government succeeded in portraying itself as a victim besieged by extremists from both sides who insisted on resorting to violence. Thus, in March 1987, it was able to convince the United Nations Human Rights Commission to withdraw the Special Representative for Guatemala and replace him with an advisor. The U.S. Department of State's report on human rights in Guatemala during 1987 acknowledged progress in reining in official violence. To this end, in addition to complying formally with the commitments made during Esquipulas II,[5] the Guatemalan government named a human rights ombudsman. In an attempt to neutralize the Mutual Support Group (GAM), the government recognized a dissident organization, and it passed the Law for Assistance to Widows and Orphans in order to weaken the GAM's constituency.

The government's defensive stance was most vividly evoked by the refugee issue. In a January 1987 meeting with delegates of the United Nations High Commissioner for Refugees, the government agreed to the free return of refugees. Nonetheless, the commander of Huehuetenango arbitrarily required returnees to sign an amnesty form, leading the Catholic church to conclude that it was still not safe for refugees to return.

The army's hard-line stance was reiterated in a document written by Colonel Molina Bedoya, which advised against return and recommended that returning refugees be interred in special camps. Gramajo himself, in the "27 Years of Struggle for Freedom" forum, acknowledged that this subject had been examined by the National Defense Staff, which recommended against authorizing refugee returns until "a certain amount of psychological conditioning" had taken place. In any case, on the subject of both refugees and internally displaced persons, the official view was that they were guerrilla support bases that the army was in the process of winning over. At the same time, the executive was able to get international assistance flowing for this population. It founded the Special Commission for

---

[5] In the Esquipulas II peace plan, based on the initiative of Costa Rican president Oscar Arias, in 1987 the five Central American presidents committed themselves to taking a series of steps to promote peace in their countries. Each government committed itself to democratic pluralism, free elections, and a cease fire and dialogue with its opponents. Each country also pledged not to support or provide refuge to insurgents.

Attention to Refugees (CEAR) but could not convince the army to stop treating the displaced like prisoners of war (Mack 1989).

THE CONSPIRACY, 1988-1989

The government began 1988 hoping to make up for lost time. The president called it "[the year] of accomplishments" and revisited its reforms agenda under the National Reorganization Plan. The government embarked on a period of feverish activity, with cabinet meetings every ten days. The Law of Development Councils was approved in February, on the eve of municipal elections.

As part of its populist campaign, the government signed a pact with the UASP in February and broke off conversations with CACIF. The pact included a 40 percent tax increase on commercial and industrial energy usage, a fifty quetzal wage increase in the private sector, and adjusted minimum wages. Moreover, confident in its victory on the tax-reform issue the previous year, the government approached isolated but influential business sectors with the indirect support of James Michel, the new U.S. ambassador to Guatemala.

The Bishops' Conference supported this new government approach and, on February 29, 1988, published a pastoral letter entitled "The Cry for Land." At the same time, the army defined its National Stability policy, which regarded the civilian government as a vehicle for the perpetuation of its overall counter-insurgency policy.

COUP ATTEMPTS

This series of measures set the hard-line business sectors on edge. When the Christian Democrats won a sweeping victory against the right-wing coalition in the municipal elections, the displeasure of some members of the business sector was channeled toward a group of army officers who were already plotting against the government. Thus, on May 11, a coup attempt occurred, which set the Christian Democratic government on a path toward destabilization. Prominent businessmen Edgar Heinemann (Chamber of Commerce), Edgar Alvarado Pinetta (UNAGRO), Gustavo Anzueto Vielman, and Juan Luis Bosch supported the coup attempt. Other entrepreneurs hired vehicles to transport coup-plotters between Jutiapa and Retalhuleu.

The 1988 coup attempt had immediate repercussions. The government prioritized spending on counterinsurgency policy and tried to move ahead with war-related modernization projects. The president ordered the transfer of U.S.$30 million to the Defense Ministry in "discretionary" funds for the expedited purchase of Bell helicopters and M-16 rifles, creating a liquidity squeeze in the Bank of Guatemala. The government also established its priorities through budget transfers to the Ministry of Communications and Public Works, which indirectly administered military projects, especially in areas affected by the Year-end Offensive. As a result, during 1988 the army absorbed 22.3 million quetzales of discretionary funds from the executive branch; additional transfers from other ministries expanded its operating expenses to 31 million quetzales and its investment spending to 11 million quetzales.

The United States government delivered emergency funds totaling U.S.$75 million to stabilize the financial situation in response to reports of renewed capital flight—even though the business community attributed this phenomenon to interest rate hikes in international markets.

In 1989, the governing party launched its campaign for the 1990 presidential elections, transforming itself into a vehicle for leveraging government resources. A bloc was created around presidential candidate Alfonso Cabrera. However, a second coup attempt occurred on May 9. The coup plotters issued a communiqué attacking the corrupt Christian Democratic administration, which had designs to remain in power without regard for the legal authorities; they further called for the removal of the ministers of defense and the interior.

This new blow created a situation of ungovernability that left the government in the army's hands. In August, the Presidential General Staff enhanced its control over the president by denouncing an alleged plot to assassinate him—the Manila Plan. By then repression and criminality had permeated society and the government was plagued by a lack of credibility stemming from accusations of corruption. It could be said that by then, the government had lost even its staunchest allies in the army.

The government had also lost control of the economic situation. In March, an agreement was signed with the World Bank for U.S.$120 million to be invested in the Social Investment Fund. The fund was immobilized within months, after the World Bank froze payments due to Guatemala's inability to repay its creditors. On August 20, the government reacted to its cash flow problem with a new devaluation and freed interest rates. And, although the U.S. Agency for International Development (AID) donated 75 million quetzales, the administration froze the constitutionally mandated 8 percent allocations to western municipalities, because the Finance Ministry was blocking the disbursements. The fiscal deficit reached 945 million quetzales, and the government attempted to gain control over foreign exchange allocations. The government slipped from a cash flow problem into bankruptcy, due both to falling coffee prices and the business community's tax boycott. Export tax revenues fell from U.S.$102.8 million in 1988 to U.S.$58.4 million in 1989.

THE "DIRTY WAR"

Gramajo's National Stability project was shaped by internal and external pressures until it gradually was transformed into a more sophisticated version of the National Security Doctrine. Meanwhile, Gramajo's retirement left the army in a state of confusion and with a leadership vacuum that placed it on the defensive against external pressures. This defensive posture was manifested by increased institutional violence and social controls.

An analysis of the war's progress from 1987 to 1990 shows that the guerrilla forces' offensive capability rebounded, allowing them to expand into new parts of the country. In 1990 they were closing in on the capital and had a strong influence on agroexport production.

As the guerrilla operations advanced, the "political warfare" thesis quickly became a euphemism for a policy of open repression against sectors of society suspected of providing direct or indirect support to the guerrilla forces. In fact, as the guerrillas progressed politically and militarily, the army seemed to place more emphasis on preventive intelligence operations than on offensive military campaigns.

Since 1988 the army had maintained constant pressure on displaced groups using elite troops backed by air support and, in particular, mobilizing the civil patrol network, according to a 1990 bulletin of the Guatemalan Church in Exile. The Multi-sectorial Commission, an Interinstitutional Coordination in the Ixil area, was the only counterinsurgency development project that the Christian Democratic government had been able to implement, and by 1990, most of the communities surrounding the areas where the displaced had settled (CPRs) had been revived. However, the flow of people turning themselves in decreased sharply, from 4,000 people in 1988 to 683 in 1989 (Mack 1989). In 1990 Gramajo publicly acknowledged the existence of "errant villages" of peasants in the Ixil area but, by then, representatives of the CPRs were traveling to Europe seeking international recognition.

Political warfare became psychological warfare only to deteriorate immediately into a "dirty war" that, by 1989, appeared to have spiraled out of control and become a destabilizing force for the government. In areas such as San Marcos-Quetzaltenango-Retalhuleu and Suchitepéquez-Sololá, the campaign of abductions and murders of peasants continued to accompany counterinsurgency campaigns under the responsibility and "decentralized implementation" of the military zone commander. What is more, these operations expanded into the Escuintla, Sacatepéquez, Chimaltenango, and Santa Rosa departments, paralleling the guerrilla expansion. Other human rights violations were committed in the southern part of El Quiché, northern Chimaltenango, and eastern Sololá, where a strong anti-PAC movement had emerged, led by the Mutual Support Group, the Council of Ethnic Communities—"Runujel Junam"—CERJ, and CONAVIGUA. The army's role in indoctrinating civil patrollers and military commissioners as well as its direct participation in abductions were clearly visible in these cases.

In the city, repression took the form of abductions and murders of less-well-known leaders who, nonetheless, figured prominently in civic protests, especially in June 1989 and 1990. The University Students Association, teachers' representatives, and some labor leaders from companies engaged in labor disputes, fell victim to this repression. The National Police was implicated in many of these abductions.

President Cerezo used these attacks, as well as the murder of Christian Democrat Danilo Barillas and businessman Ramiro Castillo Love, to further his image as a victim of destabilizing violence by extremist forces on both sides. He also resorted to this image when Social Democrats Héctor Oquelí Colindres (Salvadoran) and Hilda Flores (Guatemalan) were murdered in January 1990. However, such assertions ultimately came across as attempts to elude government accountability for a policy of violence that was clearly outlined by the army high command.

DIPLOMACY AND TERROR

Guatemalan foreign policy provides an example of how the army placed the civilian government at the service of its counterinsurgency policy. In March 1989 the government presented its report to the United Nations Human Rights Commission and was able to secure an extension of the expert advisor's mandate, thereby escaping stronger censure. On April 11, the Guatemalan daily *Diario Centroamérica* announced that Colonel Francisco Ortega Menaldo, Major Edgar Ricardo Bustamante Figueroa, and Captain Mauricio López Bonilla had been decorated for having written the government human rights report. At the time, Colonel Ortega was the intelligence director of the National Defense Staff (EMDN). Moreover, one aspect of Campaign Plan Advance 90 was to counteract internal and external disinformation campaigns.

The army was most adamant about its control and use of the National Police and the resources of the EMP's intelligence division *Archivo* to guarantee its ability to operate with impunity on state security matters. The army's prior control over the National Police, through then-director Colonel Julio Caballeros (an intelligence officer who had also worked in *Archivo*), was notably reinforced by these changes. This control was consolidated by the creation, in August, of the Civilian Protection System (SIPROCI), which united all of the internal security forces under the control of the EMP.

The "militarization" of the National Police (which was formally attached to the Interior Ministry), and the EMP's control over it through SIPROCI, provoked serious internal tensions that exploded when former police chief Angel Aníbal Guevara Reyes and several DIC agents participated in the 1989 coup attempt. Among their demands was the removal of the interior minister. The death squad known as Jaguar Justiciero (Avenging Jaguar) surfaced during this period, and an intimidation campaign was launched against grassroots organizations and democratic figures.

In December the abduction and torture of a U.S. citizen, Sister Dianna Ortiz, demonstrated the collusion between the National Police and military forces. This cooperation was also exposed by the Salvadoran Truth Commission's investigation into the January 1990 murder of Héctor Oquelí in Guatemala.[6] Shortly there-

---

[6] In its report the commission established that Guatemalan police agents were involved in the abduction, leaving behind abundant evidence of their participation, although the army ultimately took charge of the interrogation and ordered the murder.

after, Harvard University suspended its technical assistance program to the National Police, convinced that there was "no political will" in the institution to combat violence.

The evidence pointing to the EMP's *Archivo* has not succeeded in clarifying how these agencies, directed by former D-2 chief General Edgar Godoy, coordinated with the Intelligence Directorate, which was headed by Colonel Francisco Ortega Menaldo, and with the work team of the defense minister's personal staff (headed by Colonel Cabrera, who would later replace Ortega as intelligence chief).

THE COLLAPSE OF STABILITY

The most significant failure of the army's National Stability project was in the area of internal alliances. Gramajo himself rapidly determined that his discourse on "all-out war" involving all sectors of society in the application of counterinsurgency policy had not been heeded by the business sector (Jonas 1991).

Throughout 1989 the army took pains to court the business sector by showing that its forces were defending the agroexport economy against guerrilla attacks. But by the end of that year, Gramajo realized that this policy was not producing immediate results and he announced that both the army and the guerrillas had made advances that jeopardized all of the export crops of the *bocacosta* region. In 1990 the Pyramid Group emerged at the forefront of the business community. It concentrated on securing a presidential candidacy that would give it direct control over the executive and lost all interest in listening to the army's proposals as a powerful sector.

During the first half of the year, Gramajo increasingly showed signs of distancing himself from the government and focused on consolidating his National Stability project through political alliances chosen with a medium-term perspective.

Gramajo asserts that in 1989 he revised his National Stability thesis, distanced himself from the government, sought support among different social forces, and concentrated on institution-building; he further tried to depoliticize his ministerial responsibilities, remaining detached from current events (Gramajo 1995). This new approach coincided with the most active period of the Center for Studies on National Stability (ESTNA), which Gramajo had founded in September 1988. While ESTNA never came to be considered a "think tank," in 1989-90 it did succeed in broadening the army's sphere of influence in certain professional circles; it also served to reconvene groups that formerly collaborated with the army's developmentalist policy—including groups concerned with cooperatives and even indigenous issues.

In terms of the development component of the military plan, while it still had certain prospects in 1988, the government's development policy had been totally displaced by the implementation of economic structural readjustment by the following year. Cerezo's 500 Days Plan, which emphasized social spending (and was the basis for requests for economic aid) became merely an electoral device that could not have been applied anyway in light of the government's financial crisis.

THE ARMY LOSES LEADERSHIP

It was on August 10, following the intimidating meeting of the Council of Commanders—during which the government cabinet was in session, helicopters were flying overhead, and troops were in a state of alert at Army General Headquarters—that the correlation of forces changed definitively. The Council of Commanders reclaimed its status as the army's institutional liaison to the minister and the government. The framework of democracy was retained, in exchange for increased army control. From that moment on, human rights policy and international relations became considerably more rigid.

The country entered the pre-electoral period, which was characterized by three factors: the officially backed candidacy of Alfonso Cabrera, who tried to involve certain high-level army officers such as General Roberto Mata and Colonel Carlos Santizo Franco; the candidacy of General Ríos Montt, which had a tremendous impact on army sectors who were convinced that the political system was too corrupt and untrustworthy; and the position of the business sector, which was prepared to finance its own candidate through the Pyramid Group.

Simultaneously, the outlook for the counterinsurgency struggle became visibly bleak—due both to changes in the regional and international political scene and to the military and political progress of the URNG; economic developments in the country caused development projects to be sidelined, and potential social eruptions were predicted. Meanwhile, the president remained relatively in control of the situation thanks to the loyalty of the chief of the Presidential General Staff and the defense minister. Gramajo continued to consolidate positions inside the Council of Commanders, promoting chiefs he trusted. But his leadership, as a representative of the officers who rebuilt the army's institutional framework in 1983 and as an ideologue of National Stability, had been weakened by his role in a government that had lost the army's trust and had failed in its overtures to business sectors. This provided the backdrop for the second coup attempt of May 9, 1989, which involved high-level army commanders and even more officers than the first.

The aim of this strike was not, by all appearances, to break with the rule of law, but rather to shake up the military hierarchy. Nonetheless, as could be expected, by then the Council of Commanders felt that it was on sufficiently solid ground to refuse to make drastic high-level changes.

From that time on, the army's internal situation revolved around Gramajo's successor, since the defense minister was due to retire in June 1990. Because the army chief of staff would have retired several months earlier, in December 1989, whoever succeeded him would probably become the next defense minister. The officer chosen was General Juan Leonel Bolaños Chávez, a desk officer with no track record in the field, who had computerized the army's administrative and intelligence activities. He had also studied and proposed reforms to the Army Organic Law, the Military Code, and the Military Service Law. He was respected but lacked leadership ability among high-level officers.

For their part, army chief of staff General Juan José Marroquín and vice–chief of staff General Mata Gálvez, backed by fifteen generals who had been promoted under Gramajo (nearly all of whom had signed the proclamation of the Council of Commanders that overthrew Ríos Montt), pressured for future control over the army without exhibiting any leadership capable of uniting them. It was a delicate situation, given that destructive phenomena such as drug trafficking were beginning to weaken the army as an institution, provoking serious ideological divisions internally, and distancing its strategic ally, the U.S. government.

THE CASUALTIES

The grassroots sector was, in fact, the hardest hit by the political destabilization caused by the two coup attempts. In 1989 escalating political violence against the grassroots movement reached levels comparable to 1980. In October and November the president spoke of a destabilizing campaign. By then, however, the accusations pointed to the EMP as the origin of the repression, which was confirmed by former interior minister Juan José Rodil (*Prensa Libre*, September 17, 1989). The violence was symptomatic of a stability policy that had become mired. But it also aimed to abort any guerrilla attempt to consolidate an urban front, a possibility that had grown in the uproar of the educators' strike in mid-1989.

Furthermore, analysis of human rights violations indicates that, beginning at the time of the first coup attempt in May 1988, but particularly after the "institutional pressure" of August 10 of that year, the civilian government's stance was one of open complicity with army repression. This was the case with the September 11, 1990, murder of anthropologist Myrna Mack and a series of extrajudicial executions that occurred during this period.

Chapter Sixteen

THE SERRANO ELIAS GOVERNMENT

The arrival of the new decade was marked by the failure of the Christian Democratic government, as evidenced by the fact that one of the least likely candidates won the presidential elections. Jorge Serrano Elías took the presidency with 24.8 percent of the vote, only ten seats in Congress, and 3 percent of the municipalities. The weakness of the incoming government presented the business sector with the opportunity to establish the "rules of the game."

However, at that time a silent struggle was in progress within the business sector: some entrepreneurs attempted to monopolize new means of capital formation (especially financial); others adhered to the traditional bureaucratic systems that had enabled fortunes to be made in the seventies; still others saw privatization of the public sector as a way to harness incoming postwar aid or looked to drug trafficking for new get-rich-quick schemes. In the midst of this chaos, the inability to negotiate and share political space led the business sector to endeavor to grasp power exclusively, destabilizing the democratic system yet again through plots and fiscal boycotts.

THE BUSINESS CANDIDATE

Beginning in February, Alvaro Arzú, mayor of Guatemala City, had announced his candidacy, with prominent sugar producer Fraterno Vila as his running mate. Jorge Carpio, head of the UCN party, also sought the support of the business sector. However, CACIF's "hard-line" faction, which had governed the organization since 1987, had already designed its own corporate election strategy. Thus, the Pyramid Group, which had been operating from the shadows, emerged to support the creation of a sole candidate to whom all of the economic support of the business sector would be channeled (instead of the traditional negotiations to buy affinities in one party or the other). The Pyramid Group chose Jorge Carpio, whose nomination was quickly backed by politicians such as former interior minister Juan José Rodil Peralta and CUSG labor leader Alfaro Mijangos. In September, "the dreams of two generations of entrepreneurs came true," as one press headline put it, when Jorge Carpio and Manuel Ayau announced their run for the presidency and vice-presidency. Jorge Serrano's election victory ruined the Pyramid Group's strategy.

BATTLES OVER PEACE

During the Serrano administration the army formally consented to negotiating a political solution to the internal armed conflict, which it interpreted as the surrender of the guerrilla forces. The guerrillas accepted the negotiation proposal on the basis that an armed victory was impossible and as a vehicle for transforming its military achievements into political ones.

In this context both parties increased their military pressure, but their progress on the battlefield did not bring peace any closer. International pressure for an end to the conflict and calls for demilitarization put the army on the defensive. It responded by tightening its grip on society and allowing a hard-line faction to take over the army leadership, which ultimately provoked the attempted coup d'état of May 1993.

The first meeting established by the Oslo Accords[1] was held in May 1990, in El Escorial, Spain, between representatives of the political parties and the URNG; it created tremendous unrest within the army. At that meeting the guerrilla forces accepted the Esquipulas Accords and the Constitution as a framework for negotiations, and the political parties promised to introduce constitutional reforms. Vinicio Cerezo responded immediately by saying that the conversations that had begun were nothing less than the first step to disarming and demobilizing the URNG. Concurrently, the EMDN launched a repressive campaign against social movements considered supportive of the subversives or a challenge to its social control.

Throughout the second half of 1990 the guerrillas held meetings with diverse social sectors, which served to demonstrate to the international community their willingness to engage in dialogue. Although the URNG did take advantage of these meetings to strengthen its relationships and political alliances, it was clear that any commitment would have to be made with the government that would take over in January 1991.

The army took the initiative with its Comprehensive Peace Plan, presented by the new president, Jorge Serrano Elías, on April 3, 1991. This plan proposed a cease-fire and the immediate surrender of the guerrillas, to be followed by negotiations over the nature of their political reinsertion. Like the guerrillas' earlier proposal to demilitarize the country, this proposal essentially served to throw down the gauntlet.

Nonetheless, Serrano's Comprehensive Peace Plan was the first proposal to recognize the guerrillas as a counterpart to a negotiation process, and the army high command was well represented on the negotiating commission. Most analysts saw in this proposal a high degree of initiative on the part of President Serrano Elías. In diplomatic circles the proposal was criticized as less than solid in its content and lacking a negotiating strategy. Serrano's intention, according to

---

[1] In the Oslo Accords the parties essentially agreed to seek a political solution to the conflict and to resolve national problems by peaceful means.

analysts, was to "soften" the army so that a serious negotiation process could be undertaken two years down the line.

The guerrillas approached these proposals by evaluating the political weakness of the new president; the confusion within the army generated by international pressures; and the outcomes of its 1990 military campaigns, which had turned vital areas of the country back into war zones. A key factor for the guerrilla forces was to gain time to wear down their adversary and to assimilate the changing international panorama. The immediate outcomes of this negotiating process were in their favor: the accord on the procedure for seeking peace through political means opened doors for them to expand their political work in Guatemala and internationally. The established process created a climate for the growth of the grassroots movement, which was influenced by the URNG.

But the panorama shifted rapidly beginning in July when, after an initial rotation of the army command, the army launched operations against several guerrilla fronts, and the human rights situation again deteriorated. In December 1991, after the president instigated further changes in the military hierarchy, the army stepped up its militaristic discourse and renewed its offensives against guerrilla fronts, particularly the Central Unitary Front and ORPA's rear guard in San Marcos and Retalhuleu. This immediately translated into increased political violence and indiscriminate attacks. The new military hierarchy wanted to steer the negotiations by turning them against the guerrillas. During the first quarter of 1992, EMP chief General Francisco Ortega Menaldo had broadened his influence over the president, and the defense minister and army chief of staff were in the process of consolidating their positions.

The dialogue process had reached a dead end. The URNG reiterated the position it had adopted in the second half of 1990: it could not enter into commitments with a government that was incapable of fulfilling them. At the same time, the army continued its offensive to weaken the guerrilla fronts. The army offensive, Victoria 93, was particularly directed against the EGP's rear guard. Its purpose was to destabilize the guerrillas' permanent combat units in an attempt to inflict damage on the insurgent command structure and obtain strategic information, much as it had done in 1992 against ORPA's rear guard. But the military campaign was hampered by the return of refugees and the public emergence of the CPRs, two events that had captured international attention.

This offensive was accompanied by a new proposal, which Serrano announced on January 14 at the United Nations headquarters. It included a ninety-day deadline, accepted United Nations' verification of the accords, and even recognized the full belligerence of the URNG by proposing that it withdraw into previously determined zones. Serrano raised this plan in a complex international context. Although the government had improved its international support, especially with the formation of the Group of Friends of the Peace Process, human rights pressures and other factors—such as the award of the Nobel Peace Prize to Rigoberta Menchú and the Alternative Nobel Prize to Helen Mack—not to mention the incipient refugee returns—were severely testing his government.

WAGING WAR

Changes in the army leadership did not represent any significant change in military policy. It seemed that, while the official posts were filled by loyal disciples of the National Stability theory (for example, the international and psychological warfare team of the defense minister's personal staff remained largely unchanged), the army's methods were defined by the decisions of the Council of Commanders.

During the first half of 1991, with a new government in office, the impact of the December 1990 Santiago Atitlán massacre still fresh, and an international community alarmed by the conservatism of the new president, the formula remained unchanged. Despite the new president's pledge to wage an open war on impunity, key National Police posts remained under army control. Prominent crimes designed to intimidate were committed, such as the killings of political leader Dinorah Pérez and cleric Moisés Cisneros. The guerrilla armies launched a joint offensive in their traditional fronts, featuring repeated attacks in northern Alta Verapaz and southern El Petén departments; an attack on the oil pipeline between Chisec and Fray Bartolomé de las Casas; an aggressive armed propaganda campaign in Huehuetenango; and an attack in Villacanales, just twenty-two miles from the capital.

In June, the army regained the initiative and launched a military campaign in the Ixil and Ixcán regions of El Quiché department; it began Operation Lacandona 91 in the Petén to combat "narcoterrorism"; this operation was led by General Roberto Perussina with the support of Colonel Homero García Carillo of the army's public relations department (DIDE).

The army assaults on traditional URNG fronts did not produce spectacular results. Moreover, the intensive use of heavy weaponry and attempts to gain control over civilians in conflictive areas led to rising human rights violations that rapidly attracted the attention of international observers. Lastly, the guerrillas assembled select troops in a united central front that operated in the strategic *bocacosta* region. In the city, the campaign of threats and intimidation intensified. One striking example was the August attacks against international press offices (NOTIMEX and Inter-Press Service). In October, military control over the National Police was sealed with the appointment of Lieutenant Colonel Luis Fernández Ligorría as assistant director with operational oversight.

The army's military offensive approach was reinforced by the January 1992 appointments of General José Domingo García Samayoa as defense minister, and General Roberto Perussina as army chief of staff.

Probably the most intense combat of the preceding ten years of war took place in the *bocacosta* region and on the southern coast in 1992. The army launched a major offensive against ORPA's rear guard in these areas at precisely the moment when ORPA's forces were occupied in Escuintla and Palín. This tactic was widely used under President Serrano Elías, and it damaged, although it did not destroy, ORPA's combat units.

Campaign Victoria 93 was commanded by Colonels Víctor Manuel Argueta and Francisco Marín Golib in northern El Quiché and southern El Petén. Its purpose was not to consolidate territorial control or to establish an army presence in areas frequented by the guerrillas, but rather to prevent the EGP from concentrating its forces and launching any significant attack.

During the second half of 1992 the guerrilla forces had been relatively quiet. The negotiation process and the expanding role of different sectors of civil society—in the form of refugee returns, and campaigns for peace and against impunity—had created fissures in the guerrilla organizations. The URNG unified its stance by asserting that military pressure was the only way to produce results in the negotiations, and that the guerrillas would only disarm when compliance with all of the accords was subject to verification. However, during 1992, it lost much of the offensive capability it had built up over the preceding two years and began to exhibit serious recruitment difficulties.

Another noteworthy aspect of this period was the army's attempt to stifle and control the judiciary, which sparked public debate and a civic movement to challenge impunity that ultimately left the army on the defensive.

A CLIMATE OF INSECURITY

Beginning in 1990 the international panorama was, at best, uncertain. The collapse of socialist Europe, the electoral defeat of the Sandinista Front in Nicaragua, the failed Salvadoran guerrilla offensive, and measures to tighten the blockade of Cuba strengthened the extreme right-wing's triumphalist posture. However, a realignment of international relations was on the horizon, as signaled by the outcomes of the Malta Summit in September, which ushered in a new phase of U.S. relations with the former Soviet Union.

By all indications, aside from international pressure to end the armed conflict in Guatemala, the government, army, and much of the business sector misread the guerrillas' situation by regarding their dialogue proposal as an indication of international isolation and political weakness.

In addition, the human rights issue began to take an unexpected turn. In July, when human rights organizations asked former president Carter to lobby for the suspension of all U.S. aid to Guatemala in response to ongoing political violence, the business sector finally began to fathom the cost of the army's recalcitrant efforts to eradicate the guerrillas' political potential by pulverizing the grassroots movement. This did not, however, lead the business community to make any great effort to intervene during one of the darkest years for human rights since the installation of a civilian government.

One of the hypotheses most starkly proved by the history of violence in Guatemala was that, when international pressure became excessive, the army tightened the reins internally rather than cede to the pressure. Another hypothesis confirmed by events was that, as the moment for negotiation approached, both sides became increasingly rigid. A combination of these two hypotheses could explain the context for the extraordinary violence registered during 1990, in which repressive forces lashed out in every direction in an apparent attempt to induce generalized panic.

THE ADVENT OF GLOBALIZATION

Serrano Elías's victory immediately brought the power elite (the army and business community) face to face with its own political weakness, which was not conducive to the task of establishing medium-term objectives in such a challenging climate.

In this perilous state, the army portrayed itself as the only guarantor of political stability. Some modernist sectors of the business community began to build bridges with like-minded sectors of the army (who were commonly referred to as "constitutionalist officers"). But these business sectors argued that the army was also subject to the logic of reducing the public sector; this entailed, for example, the elimination of discretionary funds and the budget transfers through which the army leveraged additional public funds and the removal of the army from public administration posts.

OTHER AREAS OF CIVIL SOCIETY

Guatemalan civil society flourished during the Serrano administration. The struggle against human rights violations, which until that time had maintained a growing but manageable profile, grew remarkably. Denunciations and protests by local groups evolved into coordinated actions at the international level; these groups were increasingly astute at perceiving and assimilating worldwide developments at the regional level.

Serrano's formal proposals for eliminating impunity created more space for civil society's struggle against it; this was particularly true in the case of the murder of Myrna Mack. The army's defiance in the cases of U.S. citizens Michael Devine and Dianna Ortiz, its belligerent reaction to U.S. proposals for demilitarization, and evidence that high-level officers were involved in drug trafficking, led the U.S. Department of State and its Embassy to push harder on human rights issues. The United States focused directly on the army, with two concrete objectives: the dismantling of the Presidential General Staff (EMP) and the civil patrols, and the demilitarization of the National Police, both of which were recommendations found in the report by the United Nations special advisor.

At the same time, civil society began to play an increasingly important role in the life of the country, posing a challenge to army control. Events such as the public emergence of displaced populations, refugee returns, and the demands of social sectors that had been created by the repression galvanized other important sectors—such as the Catholic church and nongovernmental organizations (NGOs). This turned into a groundswell that was able to generate significant pressure, despite its lack of coordination and cohesion. The government and the army reacted by stepping up the repression and accused the civic movement of belonging to the guerrillas. Finally, the indigenous movement made an abrupt appearance on the political scene through the campaign commemorating the five-hundred-year anniversary of the invasion of the Americas. This campaign quickly evolved into a social current that carved out its own space in civil society. Against this backdrop, a new movement to occupy plantations with demands for better wages and land titles forcefully emerged.

The traditional labor movement continued to experience a pronounced down slide, however. The URNG pressured grassroots organizations to adopt a more aggressive stance in order to wear down the government, which frequently responded by striking out at these organizations in order to weaken the guerrillas politically. The repression was harshest against the civilian population in conflictive areas, and against organizations that the army deemed most directly connected to the URNG.[2]

ARMY REASSIGNMENTS

When Serrano took office, there was a certain degree of international pressure to either retain Defense Minister Bolaños, who had two years of army service remaining, or promote General Raúl Molina Bedoya. Despite this, the Council of Commanders obliged the new president to remove Bolaños and Mata Gálvez and appoint General Luis Enrique Mendoza, then vice–chief of the National Defense Staff, as the next defense minister. Mendoza chose General Humberto Angeles as his vice-minister. The Council of Commanders hoped that these changes would stabilize the promotion process by balancing the different army currents, giving it time to devise a new strategy to confront the difficult situation in which it was immersed.

Internal tensions persisted, however. The Officers from the Mountain[3] resurfaced to accuse the military hierarchy of the unexplained murders of retired Gen-

---

[2] Human rights violations increased unexpectedly during the Serrano administration. According to the Archdiocesan Human Rights Office (ODHAG), 551 extrajudicial executions were committed in 1991, 205 murders, 143 enforced disappearances, and 123 cases of torture. The human rights ombudsman reported 148 extrajudicial executions and 118 forced disappearances. These figures increased markedly in 1992. According to the Guatemalan Human Rights Commission (CDHG), between January 1 and August 18, there were 1,128 murders, of which 350 were extrajudicial executions (65 showing signs of torture), 21 detainees disappeared, and 31 executions; there were 32 arbitrary detentions, 104 death threats, 289 attacks, and 321 cases of bombardments or machine-gun strafings.

[3] This was a clandestine group of hard-line army officers and civilians who surfaced during that period. They used written communiqués to denounce army corruption and human rights violations.

eral Anacleto Maza Castellanos and Captain Jorge Méndez Barragán, former DIC chief in the National Police.

The new lineup of army commanders focused primarily on counteracting the international demilitarization campaign. Although Serrano announced cosmetic measures, what he actually did was to increase the militarization of the Interior Ministry and the National Police. Soon the Presidential General Staff began to encroach on presidential functions and threatened to do the same in other ministries such as the Finance Ministry.

The army hardened its stance toward the U.S. Embassy. Significantly, in January, it refused to allow the aircraft carrying the U.S. assistant secretary of state, Bernard Aronson, arriving for Serrano's inauguration, to land on a military airstrip. In April, the president publicly rejected the delivery of $100,000 in U.S. military aid. Meanwhile, the Embassy was sending discreet messages about military involvement in drug trafficking.

The antimilitarism debate, framed in defensive terms, harmed rather than helped the army. The army's consent to dialogue with the guerrillas as an excuse to divert international tensions disconcerted army officers. It reached the point that General Mario Enríquez began to speak of a "clean slate," affirming that no war ended with unconditional surrender, although virtually no other member of the Council of Commanders shared this opinion.

The nationalistic campaign clashed with the modernizing trend in the business sector, which was moving toward globalization. Developmentalist positions had been explicitly left off the new government's agenda, a battle that the army lost quietly. In the midst of these tensions, new army rotations took place in July 1991. These placed the most militaristic officers from the military academy's graduating classes of 1967 and 1968 in line for the Army High Command, displacing several officers from the National Stability trend (class of 1970), who previously had been promoted over the heads of senior officers.

These new readjustments and promotions could not stay the growing internal crisis, which erupted in December when the president abruptly removed the defense minister, Luis Enrique Mendoza, and National Defense Chief of Staff Edgar Godoy Gaitán. Attention soon focused on General Francisco Ortega Menaldo, chief of the Presidential General Staff, who was widely recognized as a powerful force in the army leadership. The changes brought in José Domingo García Samayoa as defense minister and Roberto Perussina as National Defense chief of staff. Mario Enríquez was the vice–chief of staff, and José Luis Quilo the vice-minister of defense. Generals Edgar Godoy and Jaime Rabanales were retired, as was Colonel Byron Disrael Lima.

This new shake-up of the command structure placed the "gentlemen from the front" squarely in power. They believed that the time was ripe for the army to win a decisive military victory over the guerrillas, and that the High Command should be made up of commanders with a track record of success on the battlefield.

The public debate over demilitarization was replaced by the issue of army reform. The campaign soon spotlighted the power wielded by the chief of the

Presidential General Staff, Francisco Ortega Menaldo, whom public opinion identified as the "strong man" of the new military hierarchy. *Crónica* magazine published an article on the power of the EMP chief, and the Public Ministry accused the EMP of being responsible for the murder of Myrna Mack.

In 1993 the international context remained bleak for the army, due to civil society's efforts. By that time, two explicit army strategies had emerged: one supported by the "gentlemen from the front," and the other by the army sector readying itself to oversee the peace process. While the first group continued to back the presidency and the EMP, the second group—whose main proponents were General Mario Enríquez, Colonel Otto Pérez, and Major Mauricio López Bonilla—began to approach groups of businessmen, politicians, and professionals who were willing to limit Serrano's autocracy.

The dubious success of "Victoria 93," and the defense minister's notorious attempted participation in privatized enterprises (as in the case of television's Channel Nine) put even more distance between the military hierarchy and the rest of society. This was the backdrop for the attempted government coup d'état of May, when García Samayoa, Roberto Perussina, and Francisco Ortega's group realized that it had lost the support of the other commanders, despite the fact that their graduating class controlled the key posts.

Chapter Seventeen

PREPARING FOR THE POSTWAR PERIOD

INTO THE VOID

On May 25, 1993, President Jorge Serrano decided, without warning, to dissolve the Congress, the Supreme Court of Justice, and the Constitutional Court, and to repudiate the human rights ombudsman. He also decreed a system of censorship and suspended several articles of the Constitution concerning individual rights. Serrano justified the coup based on the need to "put an end to the mafia and the corruption in the legislature and judiciary," and he promised to hold legislative elections immediately in order to restore the rule of law. Some observers pointed out that these measures received a modicum of public support at first, largely because the political party system was totally discredited. However, the immediate reaction of the business sector and a portion of the military hierarchy, the role of the media, international pressure, and the response of organized sectors and leaders in civil society quickly created a dismal panorama for the president.

Although EMP chief General Francisco Ortega, Defense Minister José Domingo García, and National Defense Chief of Staff Roberto Perussina backed Serrano, the Council of Commanders decided to leave the president to his own devices and watch him sink or swim. From the first moment of the coup, however, a conspiracy took shape among the "constitutionalists" in the army, headed by Intelligence Director (D-2) Colonel Otto Pérez Molina, together with certain modernist businessmen, who helped free the human rights ombudsman, Ramiro de León Carpio, and coordinated closely with civic protests.

The business community's main objective was to "clear the playing field," so that its economic modernization program (essentially, privatization of public sector corporations) could proceed without interference from political parties or government agencies. It was also interested in a more committed approach to the peace negotiations, out of conviction that this could open the doors to international finances and trade. The "constitutionalists" in the army were in agreement on this point, perceiving that the defensiveness of the militaristic officers did not solve the problem of the army's postwar role.

Epaminondas González, president of the Constitutional Court, played a critical role by refusing to recognize Serrano's measures. Five days after the coup, Defense Minister José Domingo García announced Serrano's resignation. Serrano himself maneuvered to have Vice-president Gustavo Espina replace him, but by then the opposition forces had devised their own plan. The political parties had promised that the Congress would purge itself, and the Coordinator of Civil Sectors played a key opposition role alongside the Catholic leadership, San Carlos University (USAC), Rigoberta Menchú, Helen Mack, and young businessmen like Lionel Toriello, Peter Lamport, and José Rubén Zamora. The Consensus Group was formed (comprised of CACIF, political parties, and the CGTG-CUSG), and joined the Multisector Social Forum (UASP, NGOs, San Carlos University, and indigenous groups).

The Consensus Group called for the purging of the legislative and judicial branches, and proposed drawing up a three-person slate from which a president would be selected. On June 6, former human rights ombudsman Ramiro de León Carpio was elected president by Congress. Arturo Herbruger was selected to be vice-president, under pressure from then-minister of defense, General Roberto Perussina. Although the new president hastened to dismiss García Samayoa and Francisco Ortega, the army remained off balance, as Perussina rose to the post of defense minister and Quilo Ayuso went from vice-minister to vice–chief of the National Defense staff.

It was the first time since 1990 that the military hierarchy comprised a group of officers sharing a single purpose: to design a suitable strategy for the peace negotiations and the postwar role of the army. The group included a wide range of officers—from the 62nd graduating class through the 73rd—making it possible to outline a medium-term strategy; prominent members of this group were Generals Mario Enríquez, Marco Antonio González Taracena, and Julio Balconi Turcios; Colonels Otto Pérez, Robert Letona Hora, Mario Mérida, José Luis Fernández Ligorría, and Benjamín Godoy Búrbano. They were joined by Lieutenant Colonels Otto Noack and Rolando Díez; Majors Mauricio López Bonilla, José Cabrera, Luis Alburez, and Francisco García Cuyún; and Captain Otto Spiegler.

But this command rotation did not alter the army's operational principles. According to a functional analysis of the National Stability theory (of which Otto Pérez was a staunch advocate), certain vulnerabilities could be detected within the army institution (unjustifiable human rights violations, corruption, drug trafficking); these vulnerabilities were inevitable for a number of reasons, and attempts to combat them could destabilize the institution as a whole as well as the government. The proposed solution was to manage the vulnerabilities so as to keep them from becoming threats. Thus, members of *La Cofradía* once again retained their control over key positions in the security agencies and the chain of command, independently of their class loyalty to other officers in *El Sindicato*.

The new military hierarchy was able to consolidate its position with relative ease in an institution that had experienced a vacuum of leadership since 1990, but it could not escape internal tensions. The new group leading the army sought to defend its power against pressures brought to bear by other forces such as the business sector, the demands of civil society, and the URNG. This led it to develop a postwar discourse that included partial reforms, even as the security and intelligence services kept up constant pressure on their adversaries. Once again, the international factor slipped from its grasp. In 1995, when the peace negotiations took an unexpected turn for the army, the new command structure under Enríquez quickly began to disintegrate as it attempted to deal with issues such as purging and the army role in privatization.

RAMIRO DE LEON AND THE BUSINESS COMMUNITY

Those who believed that Ramiro de León Carpio's election to the presidency meant that political stability had at last been achieved were soon disappointed. Pressure from big business, which had caused the two previous administrations to flounder, also infused de León's government with uncertainty, above and beyond his own weakness and wavering.

In Serrano's final days, a rapprochement had occurred between a "renovating" faction of high-level officials and certain segments of the business community and politicians. They were determined to establish a more advantageous strategic position vis-à-vis a peace negotiation that they regarded as inevitable in the medium term. The national political order no longer worked for the two principal power centers: military and economic. When the coup-induced crisis was settled, these two groups were the big winners.

During 1995 the president's public image plummeted. In October, *Crónica* magazine stated that "Ramiro de León is the leader who has inflicted the greatest harm on Guatemala, by strengthening the army's control over the Executive." Since May 22, the country had been governed by a so-called Crisis Committee: the ministers of defense, foreign affairs, and interior, as well as the attorney general, the president of the Peace Commission (COPAZ), the president of the Presidential Human Rights Commission (COPREDEH), and the president of the Republic. This committee was actually directed by the chief of the Presidential General Staff, General Otto Pérez Molina.

POWER STRUGGLES

The new president's crusade to purge the judicial and legislative branches, which he undertook under strong pressure from the business community, turned into a battle that left the political system in a state of perpetual crisis instead of restoring its credibility. This crisis would last until the presidential campaign was launched in August 1995, when Ríos Montt would resurface to challenge the legality of the electoral process. The business sector applied considerable pressure in 1993 to achieve an arbitrary purge that would enhance its influence over legislators, while the latter entrenched themselves in institutional legality. In November 1993 the business sector even went so far as to propose that the presidential elections be pushed forward. In the midst of this crisis, civil society—which had played a pivotal role in the May 1993 crisis—was shunted aside and ultimately became involved in the peace negotiations through the Assembly of Civil Sectors.

President Ramiro de León's initial affinity with private sector objectives dwindled and he turned to the EMP to bolster his authority. In the midst of this power struggle, which was particularly acute in 1994, pressure from the "developmentalist" army faction once again played a crucial role, this time in the form of "reconstruction plans for the postwar period." But pressures from this faction eased in 1995, when it came under attack by international public opinion and the local press and withdrew to defend the corporate interests of the institutional army.

Simultaneously, a silent tug-of-war was taking place between businessmen and army officers. Since January 1991 the business community had realized that any attempt to adjust or reduce the public sector would run up against the army's economic interests, which were apparent at every level of government. Moreover, the peace process, buttressed by recent pro-demilitarization trends in the United States, offered an opportunity to try to dislodge the army's economic power while avoiding direct confrontation.

The army initially reacted to this challenge by lashing out at the most influential business leaders (particularly under Serrano), encouraging labor and political opposition to privatization attempts, and pressuring to participate. While the army leadership apparently tried to reach an understanding with the business sector on this matter, a wave of abductions and accusations targeting army officers involved in dirty dealings occurred between 1993 to 1995. This standoff did not stop certain business circles from "knocking on the doors of army headquarters," as they had done since the seventies.

PEACE NEGOTIATIONS

One point of consensus between business circles and the army officers who had prevented Serrano's coup was the design of a postwar plan based on the immediate signing of Peace Accords in exchange for certain political concessions to the URNG. This would bring investment into the country and allow these sectors to address their priorities (internal army reorganization and economic realignment) free of national and international pressures. For this, they counted on the excellent international image of the new president and the appearance that the anti-coup movement had in fact been a powerful mobilization of all of civil society, which would now be represented in the new government.

In 1994, the economic power elite hoped to fast-track the negotiation process with the sole aim of halting the armed conflict, disarming and demobilizing the URNG, and receiving international funds for peace. But a historically more powerful business segment considered it unlikely that accords would be signed in 1994. In any event, this group did not believe that international pressure or the curse of the peace negotiations should be allowed to impose economic reforms that could diminish their privileges.

Pressures to purge the army caused new currents to surface within the institution, reviving power struggles that had been developing unseen since 1991, although the rapprochement between "constitutionalists" and "modernist entrepreneurs" had, since 1992, produced an interest group centered on finding new economic pursuits for army officers that would not impede the economic growth of the business sector. However, the government's financial setbacks—caused, in fact, by the fiscal blackmail of hard-line entrepreneurs—cast a pall over these efforts.

In January 1994, with abductions of businessmen at their height and numerous cases of army officers implicated in crimes, a new distinction in the army ranks began to be discussed in business circles: the "corrupt and the honorable." By then, most officers who had reached the rank of lieutenant colonel and colonel, led by Colonel Otto Pérez Molina, were interested in reaching an agreement with the modernist sector of the business community in order to participate in privatization or whatever economic opportunities emerged from the peace process. In response, lower-ranking classes of officers, led by certain former officials who had profited from the public holdings, announced that the companies to be privatized were strategic and should remain under government control.

THE WAR CONTINUES

The popular movement was unable to recover from the political changes of the previous year. It was not until May 17, 1994, when the Assembly of Civil Sectors began to function without CACIF, that it began to reestablish itself politically. The URNG was reluctant to allow the Assembly of Civil Sectors to play a protagonist role in the negotiation process, after its experience in May 1993 when the business sector had successfully manipulated the civic reaction to Serrano's coup. The URNG was very interested, however, in holding talks with the Christian Democratic Party, which offered a populist platform that the insurgents could use to acquire political experience.

In November 1994, the Assembly of Civil Sectors' mandate to develop proposals for the discussion of substantive issues expired, but it drafted a proposal to continue its mandate. However, rumors were spreading to the effect that the URNG might channel its political participation in the 1995 elections through the Assembly after the guerrilla organization entered into consultations concerning the possibility of proposing Bishop Quezada as a presidential candidate. Alfonso Cabrera, who was also lobbying for URNG support in the 1995 elections, revealed that Quezada was a potential presidential candidate. The bishop's subsequent resignation as president of the Assembly thwarted the Assembly of Civil Sectors' efforts. From that moment, the grassroots organizations began to revolve around the electoral candidates: on September 22, members of the Assembly and the entire URNG command met at the United Nations headquarters in El Salvador to discuss the elections and the negotiation process, and to ensure that the accords already signed would be included in the next president's agenda.

The proposal to convene an Assembly of Civil Sectors that would open the door of political participation to grassroots organizations seemed mostly attributable to the URNG's interest in legitimizing the accords and bringing a certain degree of external pressure to the negotiating table. From the outset, in fact, the subjects that seemed to be open for negotiation were a certain modernization-purging of some government agencies and a certain economic modernization. The government-army left room for concessions only in the political arena. The army leadership regarded the negotiation process as an opportunity to boost its historical legitimacy and lay the groundwork for its future hegemony. It had drafted a series of proposals, particularly concerning a partial cease-fire in advance of the final accords, and it was preparing to take control of the population affected by the conflict through aid and development programs.

The grassroots movement failed to come up with a proposal that approached reconciliation and an end to the violence as a means of resolving social conflicts; it made no community- and sector-specific proposals for reintegrating war victims and addressing the root causes of the conflict. Rather, it appeared to be dragged along by the URNG's approach to the negotiation process, and it forfeited any possible influence it might have had in the broader picture.

In this social context, grassroots activism during the de León administration followed the formula that had dominated since 1990. The struggle for land, the presence of indigenous movements, human rights monitoring, and the return or resettlement of displaced persons and refugees dominated the grassroots agenda between 1993 and 1995.

The fact that very little labor union activity was taking place did not curb the repression. The army continued to use the security forces to confront the grassroots movement, intimidate civil society, and contend with other existing powers, such as entrepreneurs and political or justice officials. By this time the army was facing a considerably more active civil society, one that had mushroomed since 1992; initiatives often addressed crucial concerns such as impunity and demilitarization.[1]

Despite the discourse about the "battle for peace," rural grassroots groups calling for demilitarization or the dismantling of the civil patrols continued to be persecuted. The army incited recent settlers in the Ixcán and the Ixil to harass former residents who had returned from refugee camps or displacement; it orchestrated a panic campaign against foreigners in the country; and, to a lesser

---

[1] In this context human rights violations in the capital city continued to rise in terms of attacks on citizens belonging to the opposition, journalists, and members of church and nongovernmental organizations. The labor and grassroots movements were attacked, as were human rights activists and the Judiciary itself. Groups such as Avenging Jaguar or the National Anticommunist Committee resurfaced, and new forms of intimidation with a lower political cost were employed: raids on offices, interrogations followed by release of the victim, and civil patrollers who stalked their victims all the way to the capital. Other forms of indiscriminate violence also occurred, such as a renewed wave of terrorist attacks in the capital in September 1994, and the murder of gang members, which were attributed to the vice–minister of the interior, Colonel Mario Mérida.

degree, corpses of civilians continued to appear in areas where the guerrilla forces were expanding their military operations. Finally, in some cases police agents investigating crimes in which army personnel or civil patrollers were apparently implicated were murdered.

THE URNG AND THE SIGNING OF THE PEACE ACCORD

In order to conserve its resources, the guerrilla forces calibrated their military operations, beginning in 1994, so that they could indefinitely sustain pressure that was not easily diffused. It concentrated its efforts on a united front, located close to the capital, to which it channeled funds and select combatants. Its traditional fronts remained engaged in harassment and propaganda activities conducted by armed combatants. Thus, the guerrillas postponed the development of a political strategy, anticipating that democratic institutions would weaken. At the same time they tested other forms of social pressure such as farm invasions.

Although the URNG had been considerably weakened politically since the beginning of the refugee return process, it stood by its "armed peace" proposal (sign the Peace Accords, but not demobilize), which would last until there was sufficient evidence that the government was in a position to fulfill the Peace Accords. For this reason, the URNG showed absolutely no interest in accepting the "honorable way out" offered by the de León Carpio administration.

In 1994, following the signing of the Free Trade Agreement with Mexico and the threat of a Zapatista uprising, bringing peace to Guatemala acquired a new importance for the United States and the international community, which increased their pressure. The accords of January 10, 1994, totally changed the formal dynamics of the negotiation: the United Nations accepted the role of mediator and the parties committed to a predetermined calendar.

The government embarked on a race to demonstrate that it was willing to do anything to prevent a single extra day of conflict. The army began to apply its "war for peace" measures and succeeded in signing a human rights accord that did not include a truth commission. This enabled it to allay strong internal pressures such as those reflected in the conspiracy led by General Quilo Ayuso.

The URNG also felt pressured to arrive as soon as possible at accords that would benefit its social base. In the end, however, the strong sense of imposition associated with the early accords, particularly the one concerning historical clarification, left neither party satisfied. On the other hand, while the human rights accord did not directly change the situation in that area, it created an unexpected predicament for the army by establishing the United Nations verification mission (MINUGUA). The URNG and grassroots organizations would be able to make good use of MINUGUA's attributes.

From the standpoint of the army, these early accords had to be offset by, at a minimum, a cease-fire which would allow it to present concrete accomplishments to its people and focus its efforts on increasing its influence in civil society through its "war for peace." The government and business sectors also needed a cease-fire so they could begin to capitalize on the business of peace. The URNG, however, had already plotted its own course and was not interested in repeating the experience of May 1993, when its combatants were demoralized by a unilateral cease-fire that lacked any long-term import. Moreover, many sectors criticized the secrecy of the negotiation process and the outcome of the truth commission accord, which put the URNG on the defensive. The negotiation bogged down once again, and both armies opted for a military push. This lasted until December 22, when the United Nations secretary general gave both parties two weeks to submit a plan to galvanize the negotiations; otherwise, it might withdraw the verification mission.

In 1995 renewed pressure from the international community served to synchronize the peace negotiation calendar with the political election calendar; this was formally accepted by the URNG in exchange for assurances that the discussion of fundamental points would not be diluted. The URNG maintained its pledge to participate in the elections, even though it lacked a well-defined strategy, while the subject of purging the army and demilitarizing society remained in the foreground. By June 1995 the United States was pressuring the army more forcefully than it ever had in the past, and General Mario Enríquez's leadership began to deteriorate alarmingly.

THE BUSINESS CANDIDATE'S VICTORY

The general elections of 1995 had special significance: they created the opportunity to invigorate the process of political institution-building begun by the army in 1984. This was particularly true since, in the interim, the 1989 crisis of the Christian Democratic government had caused the political party system and institutions critical to political stability (presidency, congress, judiciary) to become increasingly discredited in the eyes of the public. The viability of government reform, which was essential for a final peace accord and economic modernization, rested on the outcome of the 1995 elections. The victorious political party would have to meet these two challenges. As an analysis by the Myrna Mack Foundation observed:

> The electoral process emerges as the space for the realignment of political forces with the purpose of reshaping the transition that was severely derailed by the May 1993 self-coup. It is a contest among elites who are arguing over their territory in the post-conflict period....They are hegemonic groups following an international agenda that promotes a negotiated solution to the conflict, retrofitting the army, and economic modernization....Elections are the forum, *par excellence,* for changing the correlation of power at a given moment. But the November 12 elections have an additional charge: they will determine the space and the political actors who will define the physiognomy of the peace process. In other words, the scope of economic and military reforms.

Given the institutional crisis left behind by the government of Ramiro de León Carpio, the elections were seen by countries interested in the peace negotiations as an opportunity for the political system to regain credibility. Therefore, they pressed the URNG to support publicly the elections, and even to participate indirectly. Diplomatic pressure also served to influence the election authorities so that Ríos Montt's candidacy would not be accepted.

In contrast to the elections in Nicaragua and El Salvador in times of peace negotiations or postwar agreements, the organization of elections in Guatemala suffered from structural deficiencies. The voter registration campaign was a mere formality and fraught with irregularities: one-third of the population of voting age, most of whom had been affected by the war, were unable to register—they were not even given the opportunity to do so. The government refused funds from the European Union to provide free transportation on election day. Guatemala also lacked laws governing criminal funding of political parties or regulating the candidates' access to the media. And the Electoral Tribunal was totally ineffective in protecting the freedom to cast a vote and preventing politicians from using threats and blackmail against rural populations. MINUGUA refrained from taking on the democratic exercise of voting as part of its supervisory mission.

The PAN and the FRG emerged triumphant in the first round of elections; although the PAN did not win a simple majority in the presidential tally, it gained a majority in the Congress (forty-seven out of eighty seats), and one-third of the municipalities nationwide. The most unexpected outcomes were those of the New Guatemala Democratic Front (FDNG), to which polls had given 0.5 percent of the voter sample; it put six deputies in the Congress and became the third-most-powerful electoral force.

However, the PAN needed a wide margin of legitimacy to advance a government program that could, in its first year in office, confer negotiating power with influential groups in the business sector and the army. Party members were therefore discouraged by their failure to achieve the anticipated simple majority in the first round. They were even more discouraged by the extremely narrow margin with which they won the second round.

To a certain extent, the PAN victory represented an answer to the crisis experienced by the Guatemalan right wing and to the political ambitions of the business community since the advent of civilian governments in 1985. The PAN emerged as a political force after Alvaro Arzú became mayor of Guatemala City in 1985 and attracted middle-class sectors and professionals disillusioned by the Christian Democratic government. Later, the PAN took advantage of disputes between politicians and large-scale entrepreneurs under Serrano and broadened its sphere of influence by bringing in key members of parties in upheaval. During the de León administration, the PAN had become an electoral alternative for the government and a vehicle for certain economic and military groups.

Through a complicated and rough six-year process (Arzú first announced his presidential candidacy in 1989), the new president had earned the trust of some of the most powerful factions of the business sector. His primary calling card was a network of roadways and a strategy to attract funds to support the Peace Accords; but both points required another tax reform. In terms of the army, the PAN did not have a history with military officers, and it had not worked out a strategy to approach them, as the Christian Democrats had.

Once his cabinet was formed, the president defined his priorities. The first was to advance the administrative reform of the executive branch, and he sent six bills to Congress: reform of the Municipal Code, Law of the Executive Branch, Probity Law, reforms of the Comptrollership of Accounts law, and the Organic Law of the Security Forces. Subsequently, he defined his guidelines for the main ministries and unified public administration procedures. Within this framework the new government immediately established its political priorities which focused on three objectives: ending the internal armed conflict, purging the army, and negotiating with the business sector over financial support to cover the fiscal deficit.

PEACE AGAINST ALL ODDS

The negotiation process concluded in November 1995 and the *concertación* process between the URNG and President-elect Alvaro Arzú's transition team began. The insurgent leadership made no secret of its preference for Arzú and stated that his party had a long-term program that offered the security the insurgents needed to conclude the negotiations and enter into the postwar period. Informal meetings took place in El Salvador, Italy, and Mexico.

Arzú named a new Peace Commission (COPAZ), led by his chief advisor, Gustavo Porras (former EGP member) and composed of Raquel Zelaya, an influential intellectual in the previous three administrations and executive director of ASIES; Richard Aikenhead, former minister of Public Finances, who was close to the sugar producers; and General Otto Pérez Molina, army inspector general and a key figure in the transition between the de León and Arzú administrations. The new commission began to work immediately on drafts of the Accord on the Socio-Economic Aspects and Agrarian Situation, which was finally approved on May 6, 1996. The URNG had announced a cease-fire in early March, and Arzú had immediately followed suit.

In the interim, however, the optimistic tenor the process had acquired caused unease in the ranks of the URNG. The insurgent's political-diplomatic commission had higher expectations than the general command itself, which was interpreted as a hindrance to the negotiations. As a result, the four-member insurgent command decided to dissolve the commission and work directly on the negotiations.

Criticisms of the accord were not slow in coming. It was called "neo-liberal." It was said that it essentially summarized PAN's government agenda without addressing structural issues such as unequal distribution of wealth. Despite this, significant aspects were the inclusion of a national land registry, increased social spending, and the goal of raising the tax burden to 12 percent of the Gross Domestic Product by the year 2000.

The negotiations continued without obvious snags until the signing of the last substantive accord, Strengthening Civilian Power and the Role of the Armed Forces in a Democratic Society, signed in Mexico on September 19. This accord outlines a process by which society becomes involved in public institutions and contributes to their reactivation; it presents a general plan to reform the security forces, which includes the creation of a national civilian police force, the reorganization of intelligence agencies (with the aim of reducing their considerable discretionary powers), and army reform based on the country's peacetime needs (troop and budget reductions, and redefining its functions exclusively in terms of defense from an external threat).

Once this accord was signed, the question was how to preserve the peace process and follow it to its conclusion before December 1996, so that it would not exceed the budgeting schedule established by international supporters. The Arzú government, the URNG high command, and the international community, particularly the "group of friends" (Spain, United States, Mexico, and Norway), were all involved in this process.

The negotiation had also reached its most sensitive point: determining the vehicle by which members of the URNG could legalize their presence. Since early 1996, the human rights community had raised concerns that the so-called *concertación* between the parties could lead them to endorse a general amnesty: a sort of forgive-and-forget law for all combatants. This alarmed all of those who had laboriously pushed for prosecutions of state agents in the courts, and those who defended the victims' right to seek justice.

Given this risk, it was decided in June 1996 to organize an Alliance against Impunity (*Alianza contra la Impunidad*) to prevent a new general amnesty law from being enacted. The Alliance's strategy was to propose a limited amnesty, in keeping with the intent of the negotiation process, which was the reinsertion of the insurgent forces, excluding the military.

The Alliance framed the debate with a bill exclusively dealing with the reinsertion of the insurgents; it established that political crimes, and not related common crimes, were covered by the amnesty, a definition that the courts would most likely be unable to enforce. This was the first time since the beginning of the negotiation process in April 1991 that an issue at the negotiating table acquired a life of its own in civil society, becoming a subject of public debate. It could only be compared to the discussion of the rights of indigenous peoples, although the political parameters were different, as well as what, concretely, was at stake. In the present case, it was an ad hoc tool to break with the traditional political exclusion.

In October, an unexpected incident occurred that would change the course of events and, in fact, the postwar panorama. The government was obliged to make public the fact that ORPA had abducted Olga de Novella, 86 years old, a member of one of the most influential business families in Guatemala. According to the official account, the president had been forced to exchange a guerrilla commander to save the life of the octogenarian. However, few people believed this version and many criticized the government's breach of established legal procedures (see the box below). The URNG was also strongly criticized, which obliged it to remove ORPA commander-in-chief "Gaspar Ilom" from the negotiating table and introduce changes in the order of the pending operative accords. Thus, the cease-fire was moved up and, under these circumstances, the accord on reinsertion was approved.

In the end, the accord reflected the interest in amnesty that the army had never attempted to hide. The amnesty was broader for them than it was for the guerrillas. In the midst of these storms, the Accord for a Firm and Lasting Peace was finally signed during the afternoon of December 29, 1996. A new chapter in Guatemalan history would begin.

THE CONFLICT'S LAST DISAPPEARED PERSON
The "Mincho" Case

On Sunday, August 25, 1996, an ORPA urban commando abducted Olga de Novella in Zone 6 of the capital. The guerrilla group, simulating a National Police checkpoint, abducted her after disarming the Novellas' security detail.

Seven weeks went by before the EMP's anti-kidnapping squad intercepted Rafael Valdizón Nuñez ("Isaías"), the head of a guerrilla commando, chief of staff and member of the National Directorate of ORPA, and follower of ORPA commander Rodrigo Asturias ("Gaspar Ilom"). During this time, the Accord on Strengthening Civilian Power and the Role of the Armed Forces in a Democratic Society had been signed and the negotiating process was to conclude with the signing of the operative accords, including an agreement on guerrilla reinsertion.

Certain government officials privately acknowledged that on October 19 the anti-kidnapping squad detected Valdizón Nuñez and his bodyguard, Juan José Cabrera Rodas ("Mincho"), a longtime grassroots militant. On October 20, according to the official version, Isaías was exchanged for Mrs. Novella in a secluded area adjacent to Petapa Avenue in Zone 12. The incident would have ended there, a strictly guarded secret.

According to the Guatemalan Republican Front (FRG) version, however, the EMP squad stormed the house where the guerrillas were holding Olga de Novella, apprehended Isaías and Mincho, and freed the victim. Under this version, there could not have been any kind of "exchange."

Less than a week after Mrs. Novella's release, the FRG threatened to publicize the incident, stressing that, according to its version (which coincided with that of military intelligence) the government had actually freed Isaías to safeguard the peace negotiations. The government decided to seize the initiative and, on October 28, hold a press conference to inform the public of ORPA's responsibility for the Novella kidnapping. The government maintained that, for humanitarian reasons, it had freed Isaías in exchange for the safe release of Mrs. Novella. The government did not acknowledge the apprehension of Mincho; his name was never mentioned.

ORPA members left messages with Mincho's relatives suggesting that they present a complaint to human rights groups. In late October the family did so. Once the family had taken action, the Mincho case became public, even though neither the government nor the URNG had acknowledged his existence.

MINUGUA, in turn, launched an official investigation. Its verification team discovered a number of clues. However, the head of verification for the mission suspended the inquiry in November and centralized the files.

During the second quarter of 1997 a bitter controversy broke out between the Alliance against Impunity and Jean Arnault, head of MINUGUA, and between the Alliance and the government. The pressing issue was the coverup of the forced disappearance and presumed extrajudicial execution of Mincho. The former guerrillas finally acknowledged the existence of Mincho. MINUGUA issued a preliminary report about its investigation on May 20 and sent the ball back into the government's court. MINUGUA acknowledged that Mincho had been forcibly disappeared and claimed to have convincing information implicating the EMP. The government refused to back down and issued an irate response to the MINUGUA report.

From that point on, the case disappeared from the headlines. The United Nations Secretary General sent a couple of discreet missions to investigate whether the MINUGUA mission, which had generally been considered successful, had been involved in a coverup.

The Mincho case remains open. All of the mechanisms that guarantee impunity started to function once again, this time, ironically, in the name of safeguarding the peace process.

Part Four

THE VICTIMS OF THE CONFLICT

Chapter Eighteen

THE DATA COMPILED BY THE REMHI PROJECT

VIOLATIONS OF HUMAN RIGHTS
AND INTERNATIONAL HUMANITARIAN LAW

The testimonies compiled by the REMHI project represent a significant, albeit partial, sample of the massive human rights violations that took place in Guatemala during the past thirty-six years. Most of the violent acts, and victims, occurred in the early eighties, particularly in rural areas inhabited by indigenous groups. The information presented here demonstrates an overriding pattern of violence against the civilian population.

Few of the testimonies concern violence in eastern Guatemala in the sixties or urban violence in the seventies. Therefore, the firsthand data compiled do not portray the true scope of the violence during those periods. This has been taken into account in the sociopolitical analysis of violence (Part Three) and the qualitative study of people's experiences and different categories of violence (Parts One and Two).[1]

This chapter presents an analysis of the data compiled, together with some perspectives on international human rights and humanitarian law.

THE MAGNITUDE OF THE VIOLENCE

THE VIOLATIONS

The 5,465 testimonies compiled by REMHI include 52,427 documented victims of human rights and humanitarian law violations, in a total of 14,291 incidents. These figures indicate that human rights violations were often collective, targeting communities and other groups. The most frequently reported violations were individual or collective murders: 6,150 incidents resulting in 25,123 victims (47.92 percent of all victims). Other victims of violence were, in order of frequency: 5,537 victims of attacks (10.56 percent); 5,079 irregular detentions (9.69 percent); 4,620 people threatened (8.81 percent); 4,219 victims of torture and other cruel, inhumane, or degrading treatment (8.05 percent); 3,893 victims of

---

[1] The reasons for these limitations are explained in the Introduction to this report.

forced disappearances (7.43 percent); 715 people abducted who later reappeared (1.36 percent); and 152 recorded rape victims (although this figure understates the actual frequency of such cases).[2]

Victims include members of the civilian population who were targeted whether or not they were politically active, or engaged in public, legitimate religious, community-based, labor, or any other type of activities. The victims also include civil patrollers, military commissioners, and insurgent organizations who were attacked outside of combat situations in violation of international humanitarian law standards.

ACCOUNTABILITY

The cumulative government responsibility (including the army, police forces, civil patrollers, military commissioners, and death squads) is a staggering 47,004 victims, or 89.65 percent of the total violations. The army was found to be directly responsible for 32,978 victims of all types of violations (62.9 percent), and for an additional 10,602 victims (20.22 percent) in conjunction with paramilitary groups (civil patrollers and military commissioners). A total of 3,424 victims (6.53 percent) were attributed to paramilitaries acting alone.

A total of 2,523 victims of all types of violations are attributed to guerrilla organizations (4.81 percent). These guerrilla violations are divided into three groups of essentially equal proportions: killings, cruel treatment, and threats against groups or institutions (members of paramilitary groups or communities considered hostile).

PERIODS OF VIOLENCE

Despite the limitations mentioned earlier, the majority of victims of sociopolitical violence documented in REMHI's testimonies referred to events that occurred between 1980 and 1983. During that period, a total of 41,187 victims were tallied, representing nearly 80 percent of the total (see table 6 in chapter 19). These figures show that the first half of the eighties was the bloodiest period; during this time Romeo Lucas García, Efraín Ríos Montt, and Oscar Mejía Víctores respectively were the commanders-in-chief of the army, according to the army chain of command. Therefore, none of these three can escape responsibility for

---

[2] As explained in chapter 6, the stigma and shame associated with rape commonly results in the under-reporting of such cases. Western studies of rape show that only one out of every five rapes is reported. There are social and cultural reasons to believe that, in this case, the discrepancy may be much greater. Therefore, the data probably do not reflect more than a small portion of the reality.

so many victims (at least 71 percent of victims of all types of violations registered during this period were attributed to the state[3]; another 3.78 percent to the guerrillas; and the rest to unknown assailants). The highest number of victims relative to the incidents that occurred were recorded during the short de facto regime of General Ríos Montt.[4]

There was a significant increase in victims of attacks on individuals and institutions in 1987 and 1988, during the Cerezo administration, although there was a significant decrease in the number of people affected by other categories of violence. This trend illustrates the impact on the civilian population of several military campaigns, including the Year-end Offensive (see chapter 15).

THE CHARACTERISTICS OF GENOCIDE

Article two of the 1948 Convention on the Prevention and Punishment of the Crime of Genocide states:

Genocide is understood as any of the following acts, committed with the intent to destroy, in whole or in part, a national, ethnic, racial, or religious group, as such:

　a) Killing members of the group;

　b) Causing serious bodily or mental harm to members of the group;

　c) Deliberately inflicting on the group conditions of life calculated to bring about its physical destruction in whole or in part;

　d) Imposing measures intended to prevent births within the group;

　e) Forcibly transferring children of the group to another group.

---

[3] The army created, commanded, and supervised the civil patrols and military commissioners. Death squads operated as clandestine structures with direct links to military intelligence.

[4] Referring to this period, Amnesty International stated in its 1984 annual report that it was "concerned that the regular security and military forces, as well as paramilitary groups acting under government orders or with official complicity, continue to be responsible for massive human rights violations" (Amnesty International Report 1984, 157). AI also referred to special forum military tribunals created by Ríos Montt, the state of siege he decreed, and the state security forces that, despite having been officially reformed during his regime, continued to engage in the same repressive methods associated with past regimes. According to AI: "Giving his own interpretation of the strategy the army was pursuing, [Ríos Montt] replied, 'we have no scorched earth policy, we have a policy of scorched communists.' Privately he was said to have acknowledged the massacres and, on one occasion to have admitted, during a meeting held with representatives of legal political parties that, 'we are killing people, we are slaughtering women and children. The problem is, everyone is a guerrilla there'"(Amnesty International, *Guatemala: The Human Rights Record* [London, 1987], 100).

Despite this narrow definition—which excludes ideological differences as a motive for genocidal acts—it is useful to include it in the analysis of what happened in Guatemala during the first half of the eighties. Over the objections of some of the authoritative international bodies for the promotion and protection of human rights, the United Nations Special Rapporteur for Guatemala (appointed in 1983) proposed the possibility of expanding the definition and defining certain post–World War II events as genocide, including the massacre of Ache Indians in Paraguayan territory.

As shown in several earlier chapters, gross human rights violations in Guatemala were not incidental. They were the direct result of plans designed according to the needs and interests of those responsible for them. Counterinsurgency violence targeted entire communities, including noncombatant civilians and even children. It was characterized by recurrent patterns of action and acquired specific common traits in different regions. Violence against the civilian population targeted entire groups (sometimes for their religious beliefs—such as the persecution of catechists in El Quiché in the early eighties—and, in other areas, for reasons of ethnicity). All of these forms of violence, which are examined throughout the REMHI report, include certain aspects of genocide. An analysis of intentionality and of the decisions underlying these actions merit further study beyond the scope of research based solely on victims' testimonies.

PATTERNS OF VIOLATIONS

What were the patterns of violent actions from the perspective of international human rights and humanitarian law? In order to clarify the terms, we use the definition of *pattern* developed by the Salvadoran Truth Commission,[5] which identified two essential components for establishing a pattern of violence: its systematic nature and a minimum frequency. The systematic nature of violence had to do with a "regularity in its development that constitutes the repetitive functioning of certain mechanisms producing the same result, cyclically, at different moments in time." The minimum frequency means that the practice is repeated "a sufficient number of times" and affects "a calculable number of people." According to this definition, an isolated act, "the product of a particular set of circumstances lacking continuity over time," would not constitute a "pattern," nor would "any type of action that, despite being regular and cyclical, involved very few people" or was repeated only sporadically.

Based on the information compiled by REMHI, and following these general guidelines, it is possible to discern four broad categories of human rights and international humanitarian law violations associated with political violence in Guatemala. Specific patterns and typologies can be identified within each category: violations of the right to life; violations of the right to physical and psychological integrity; violations of the right to personal security; and violations of personal liberty.

---

[5] Volume II, appendices of the report *From Madness to Hope*.

VIOLATIONS OF THE RIGHT TO LIFE

LAWS AND CONVENTIONS

The Guatemalan Constitution (Article 3, Chapter 1, Section II) states that the "State guarantees and protects human life from the moment of conception." There are fundamental international norms that must be considered in conjunction with this basic provision of domestic legislation. Article 4(1) of the American Convention on Human Rights states: "Every person has the right to have his life respected. This right shall be protected by law, and, in general, from the moment of conception. No one shall be arbitrarily deprived of his life." Moreover, the International Covenant on Civil and Political Rights asserts: "Every human being has the inherent right to life. This right shall be protected by law. No one shall be arbitrarily deprived of his life" (Part III, Article 6(1)). Similar provisions can be found in the Universal Declaration of Human Rights (Article 3) and the American Declaration on the Rights and Duties of Man (Article 1).

In the framework of international humanitarian law—and its application to the Guatemalan reality examined here—human life is particularly protected by part (a) of Article 3 common to the four Geneva Conventions. This provision states, among other things, that in a situation of a "non-international armed conflict"—such as occurred in Guatemala—it is prohibited "at any time and in any place whatsoever" to attack in any manner the life of people not directly involved in armed combat, including those who belong to the armed forces of either party to the conflict who have laid down their arms or are *hors de combat* for any reason.

International human rights law considers "arbitrary deprivation of life" to be death caused by a range of circumstances, from the death penalty to deaths caused by military tactics. Forced disappearances also fall into this category, as do deaths falsely attributed to combat, deaths from torture, premeditated murders committed or tolerated by the State, and deaths caused by security forces during demonstrations.

EXTRAJUDICIAL EXECUTIONS[6]

The total number of victims of extrajudicial executions recorded by the REMHI project was 4,532. Of these, 3,307 (90.95 percent) were attributed to government

---

[6] Deaths caused by state security forces, paramilitary forces, para-state forces, and groups tolerated by these, or sufficiently organized so as to be able to carry out such an act, without a sentence given by an authorized institution or without having previously exhausted all available remedies.

forces (army or paramilitary forces). In the majority of cases, these people were killed for their prominent role as religious, social, or political leaders in Guatemalan communities and society in general.

A total of 514 extrajudicial executions (14.13 percent of the total) were attributed to the guerrillas. Most of these victims were members of paramilitary groups or alleged army collaborators who were not, at the time, engaged in combat or armed attack.

Although many deaths by torture are included in the pattern of massacres and extrajudicial executions, the testimonies include 98 victims who died as a direct result of torture. Responsibility for two out of three of these victims was attributed to government forces, 10 percent to the guerrillas, and the rest to unknown perpetrators.

FORCED DISAPPEARANCES

Forced disappearance is commonly understood[7] as the detention of a person whose fate is unknown because the detainee either becomes entrapped in a clandestine detention network or is executed and the body concealed.[8] Forced disappearance is an ongoing violation that only ends when the victim reappears alive—either free or in detention—or when his or her body is positively identified by relatives or acquaintances. The testimonies compiled by the REMHI project confirmed 3,893 victims of forced disappearance. Government forces (army and paramilitary groups) were responsible for 3,243 victims (83.5 percent of disappearances). Although the guerrillas' strategy did not include forced disappearance per se, and it cannot therefore be considered a systematic practice on their part, the testimonies report the disappearance of 294 people (7.5 percent) as a consequence of guerrilla actions.

DEATH AS A RESULT OF PERSECUTION

LAWS AND CONVENTIONS

Fundamental international humanitarian law norms prohibit the starvation of the civilian population by destroying objects indispensable to their survival. According to article 54 (2) of Protocol I additional to the Geneva Conventions of 1949:

---

[7] Truth Commission for El Salvador. Volume II of the appendices to the report *From Madness to Hope.*

[8] See Volume III of *From Madness to Hope,* which analyzes the emergence and use of enforced disappearances as a form of terror.

[It is prohibited to] attack, destroy, remove, or render useless objects indispensable to the survival of the civilian population, such as foodstuffs, agricultural areas for the production of foodstuffs, crops, livestock, drinking water installations and supplies and irrigation works, for the specific purpose of denying them for their sustenance value to the civilian population or the adverse Party, whatever the motive, whether in order to starve out civilians, to cause them to move away, or for any other motive.

Deaths resulting from persecution also constituted a very common pattern. The total of 2,659 victims in this category constituted 8.94 percent of the total deaths tabulated (see table 5 in chapter 19). This category includes people who died of hunger or illness, or from feelings of pain and anguish, while being pursued and persecuted by the army or civil patrollers. Many of these deaths occurred as whole communities and groups were suffering extreme hardship and persecution as they fled for months in the hills and forests.

CASUALTIES OF INDISCRIMINATE ATTACKS

These include civilian noncombatants who died in the course of any kind of military action attributed to one or both parties to the armed conflict. This category includes deaths caused by indiscriminate attacks by infantry troops, aerial bombardments, artillery fire, the use of other types of explosive devices, cross fire, and the use of land mines. Attacks on the civilian population that caused either severe injuries or the death of the victims constitute a "pattern" even though they occurred with less frequency.[9] Of the total of 124 victims of indiscriminate attacks, 98 percent were attributed to government forces.

MASSACRES

Massacres, defined as multiple killings of three or more people (1,090 massacres), occurred very frequently and produced a huge number of victims (18,424 victims, 94 percent of which were the responsibility of army or paramilitary forces). More than 60 percent of all fatalities tabulated by the REMHI project occurred during massacres. The analysis of massacres defined as generalized attacks on communities, or those accompanied by terror tactics or atrocities (422 massacres) as

---

[9] Most fatalities from indiscriminate attacks are associated with other victims who survived. These are described in the section of the original text on attacks that occurred much more frequently as a pattern or systematic practice.

described earlier (see chapter 7)[10] demonstrates a similar trend in terms of government, civil patrol, and military commissioner responsibility.

The guerrillas were considered responsible for 95 multiple murders for a total of 665 victims (3.6 percent of all massacre victims). These figures, which include massacres considered under the narrower definition (16 attributed to the guerrillas out of 422 analyzed), show a comparable overall trend in terms of the more selective use of collective murders—which targeted paramilitary groups or communities more actively involved in fighting the guerrillas—although there were cases in which these attacks were indiscriminate.

Sociopolitical violence in the form of mass destruction of groups and communities was a central feature of the counterinsurgency war in Guatemala, particularly from 1980 to 1983. Most of the victims of massacres occurred under the Ríos Montt regime.

VIOLATIONS OF THE RIGHT TO PHYSICAL
AND PSYCHOLOGICAL INTEGRITY

INTERNATIONAL LAWS AND CONVENTIONS

Article 3 of the Guatemalan Constitution establishes the state's responsibility to guarantee the integrity, as well as the life, of its people. In this regard, it is important to take into consideration that the four basic international instruments—two from the international system and two from the Inter-American system—do not address this matter identically, at least formally.

Article 5 of the Universal Declaration of Human Rights expressly prohibits the use of torture and "other forms of cruel, inhuman, or degrading, treatment or punishment." At the same time, the American Declaration on the Rights

---

[10] In chapter 7, however, we used a narrower definition of massacres as collective murders associated with community destruction. A systematic analysis of the last of REMHI's data produced a total of 422 massacres, instead of the 410 described. The most recently analyzed data update that chart without causing any significant modifications. Most of the massacres analyzed occurred during the 1981-82 period (70 percent). The majority of recorded massacres occurred in Quiché Department (263), followed by Alta Verapaz (63), Huehuetenango (42), Baja Verapaz (16), Petén (10), and Chimaltenango (9). Information on the perpetrators reveals the important role massacres played in the counterinsurgency strategy. The perpetrators of the massacres were the army, which was implicated in 90.52 percent of massacres (acting alone in 55 percent of the cases and jointly with civil patrollers and military commissioners in the rest); civil patrollers and military commissioners in 35.54 percent (acting on their own in 4.5 percent of cases, and otherwise in tandem with the army); guerrilla forces (3.79 percent); and unknown perpetrators (1.18 percent).

and Duties of Man discusses the humane treatment of detainees (Article 25(3)) and prohibits the use of cruel, degrading, or unusual punishments against alleged criminals, without explicitly referring to torture.

Article 7 of the International Covenant on Civil and Political Rights asserts that "no one shall be subjected to torture or to cruel, inhuman, or degrading treatment or punishment." It further discusses the protection of detainees and addresses the basic standards related to separation and treatment according to the legal status and age of the individual, as well as the fundamental aim of the penitentiary system: the reform and social rehabilitation of detainees (Article 10).

Finally, Article 5 of the American Convention on Human Rights is even more specific when it establishes that "every person has a right to have his physical, mental, and moral integrity respected" and that no one should be tortured or subjected to cruel, inhuman, or degrading treatment or punishment.

More specifically, Article One of the United Nations Convention against Torture and Other Cruel, Inhuman, or Degrading Treatment or Punishment defines torture as "any act by which severe pain or suffering, whether physical or mental, is intentionally inflicted on a person for such purposes as obtaining from him or a third person information or a confession, punishing him for an act he or a third person has committed or is suspected of having committed, or intimidating or coercing him or a third person, or for any reason based on discrimination of any kind, when such pain or suffering is inflicted by or at the instigation of or with the consent or acquiescence of a public official or other person acting in an official capacity."

Based on this definition, one can affirm that—from the international human rights standpoint—two factors are necessary to assert this type of violation. One has to do with intensity—"severe pain or suffering, whether physical or mental"—and the other with the purpose—extracting a confession from the victim or a third person; punishing the person for an act committed or allegedly committed; intimidating, or coercing him or her; and finally, any other motive based on discrimination of any kind.

There are obvious difficulties in distinguishing between torture and other types of cruel, inhuman, and degrading treatment. The former, however, must be understood as any act by state agents or private individuals exercising official functions, at the instigation of the former or with their tolerance, with the purpose of provoking—besides physical pain—feelings of fear, distress, inferiority, and humiliation, or attempting to break the person down physically or morally. According to international human rights law precepts, the expression "cruel, inhuman and degrading treatment or punishment" must be interpreted "in such a way as to provide the broadest protection possible against all types of abuses, whether physical or mental, including keeping the prisoner or detainee in conditions that deprive him, temporarily or permanently, of the use of one of his senses, such as sight or hearing, or his notion of place or the passing of time."

From the standpoint of international humanitarian law, Article Three common to the four Geneva Conventions provides that the people falling under its protection must at all times be "treated humanely, without any adverse distinction." What's more, it expressly prohibits "at any time and in any place whatsoever…outrages upon personal dignity, in particular humiliating and degrading treatment."

TORTURE AND CRUEL TREATMENT

Numerous acts that fit the definitions provided above occurred throughout the period examined. A total of 2,752 incidents were recorded in this category, for a total of 9,908 victims. A significant number of testimonies collected by the REMHI Project reveal torture to be an official, systematic practice based on the strict definitions found in the Torture Convention cited above. There are many more victims of this category of violation, since the majority of people who were tortured by government forces were subsequently killed or remain disappeared. Torture was also applied collectively: the 1,806 incidents of torture and other cruel, inhuman, or degrading treatments and punishments tabulated produced 4,219 victims, or an average of 2.34 victims per incident. These figures do not include torture during massacres, which was often the cause of death, given the numerous atrocities committed during such actions (see chapter 8).

Cases of torture or cruel, inhuman, or degrading treatment or punishment by the insurgent forces were also reported. These incidents took place particularly in some communities in the Ixcán, in Chajul, and in certain areas of Huehuetenango during the years when governmental repression intensified. Of the total victims of all types of guerrilla violations (2,523), 7.02 percent (177) reflect cruel treatment generally associated with extrajudicial executions.

RAPES

Although most torture victims (90 percent) in the data compiled were men, these figures do not include rapes. The figures show that rapes were most common during acts of collective violence. The victims' testimonies in 16 percent of massacres associated with community destruction describe rapes of women by the army, military commissioners, and civil patrollers (see chapter 5). In the individual cases, 149 rape victims were reported. According to the testimonies, for every ten women, one girl was raped, and one out of every three women raped was a young woman. As explained earlier, these figures for rape victims are under-reported.

ATTACKS

Victims of attacks[11] constitute 10.56 percent of the total victims reported in the testimonies. A total of 4,179 people were victims of attacks (44 percent of these were physically injured), representing 7.97 percent of all human rights violations. In addition, 1,358 people experienced attacks on their property (2.5 percent). Nearly all of these attacks are attributed to the army (91.16 percent) in the context of indiscriminate attacks, bombings of communities, and so forth. Another 2.92 percent of attacks are attributed to the guerrillas, including attacks on installations and harassment of some communities.

VIOLATIONS OF THE RIGHT TO PERSONAL SECURITY

This section describes deliberate acts whose purpose—overt or covert—was to instill in the victims a well-founded fear that they will experience an attempt against their life or physical integrity. These threatening acts have occurred in Guatemala for many years, essentially with the intention of preventing people from becoming actively and consciously involved in what are considered to be "opposition" activities against specific interests, whether political or economic. The goal was to break up or neutralize organizations and institutions that were labeled "enemy."

The testimonies gathered by the REMHI project contain a total of 1,577 cases of threats, representing a total of 7,378 victims. Representing 14.07 percent of the total, this constitutes the third most frequently reported violation, after the right to life (55.35 percent) and physical integrity (including torture and attacks, 18.9 percent). As discussed in the respective chapters, threats not only targeted opposition sectors[12] but were also associated with the obligatory organization of PACs.

If all of the incidents and victims associated with threats against individuals or institutions are taken into account—4,620 and 2,758 respectively—the findings

---

[11] *Atentados* are generally defined as attacks against individuals with the purpose of causing them harm or intimidating them in order to change their behavior.

[12] These findings support statements made by the Inter-American Commission on Human Rights, which, in its second report on the human rights situation in Guatemala, stated: "Despite the public statements of the authorities that these exiles [referring to the religious, writers, journalists, teachers, professionals, and politicians] can return to Guatemala when they wish, the reality is that fear prevents them from doing so. Right or wrong, they feel threatened, and the prevailing state of terror, which has been mentioned so frequently in this report, heightens the insecurity that prevents their returning to their country" (Organization of American States, Inter-American Commission on Human Rights, Report on the Situation of Human Rights in the Republic of Guatemala, OAS/SER.L/V/II.61/Doc. 47 [Washington, D.C., October 5, 1983], 120-21).

do not differ in any way from the patterns of violations discussed earlier: most incidents and victims are concentrated in the period from 1980 to 1984. Specifically, 76.60 percent of the incidents and 79.28 percent of the victims occurred during that five-year period. What is more, approximately 40 percent of the cases and victims were produced during 1982 alone, during the de facto regime of General Ríos Montt. Military and paramilitary forces were responsible for 75 percent of the threats tabulated.

According to data compiled by the REMHI project, insurgent forces were also responsible for threats; they were reported to be involved in 300 incidents in this category, representing 19.02 percent of total threats against individuals and institutions by different parties to the armed conflict (7,378). Violations of personal security accounted for 19.94 percent of the total 2,523 victims of guerrilla violations (42 threats against groups or institutions affecting 79 people; 424 victims of individual threats). This pattern of threats by guerrilla forces was part of the persecution of communities perceived as hostile or that had particularly aggressive paramilitary groups.

VIOLATIONS OF THE RIGHT TO PERSONAL LIBERTY

LAWS AND CONVENTIONS

The Guatemalan Constitution affirms that all human beings are free and equal in dignity and rights. Men and women, regardless of their marital status, have equal opportunities and responsibilities. No person can be subjected to servitude or any other status that diminishes his dignity.

Articles 6 through 19 of the Constitution contain provisions concerning legal detentions and the bringing of charges; the rights of detainees, jurisdiction over, and methods of, interrogation; the non-admissibility of extrajudicial interrogations; separate detention centers for pre-trial defendants and convicted criminals; the right to a defense and not to be prosecuted by special courts; the presumption of innocence; the public nature of proceedings; nonretroactive application of criminal law; protection from incriminating oneself or one's relatives; and the aims of the penitentiary system.

The Universal Declaration of Human Rights (Article 3) and the American Declaration on the Rights and Duties of Man (Article 1) state that all human beings "have a right to life, liberty, and security of person." The International Covenant on Civil and Political Rights (Art. 9) and the American Convention on Human Rights (Art. 7) both state that every person "has the right to personal liberty and security."

In terms of international humanitarian law, violations in this category are contemplated by Article 3 common to the four Geneva Conventions. As those protected under this provision are described earlier, we will only refer to the clauses germane to the case at hand. The following are prohibited "at any time and in any place whatsoever...": (b) "taking of hostages" and (d) "the passing of sentences and the carrying out of executions without previous judgement pronounced by a regularly constituted court, affording all the judicial guarantees which are recognized as indispensable by civilized peoples."

Similarly, Title II (Humane Treatment), Article 4 (2) of Protocol II additional to the Geneva Conventions of 1949 includes among its provisions the prohibition on taking hostages. The next article, moreover, contains specific stipulations that regulate the status of people who have been deprived of their liberty in the context of a noninternational armed conflict.

IRREGULAR DETENTIONS

The testimonies compiled by the REMHI project contain 1,405 incidents (9.83 percent of the total) and 5,079 victims (9.69 percent of total victims) of this category of systematic human rights violations. For the most part, these figures correspond to situations that the REMHI project termed "irregular detentions." This category comprises detentions carried out without regard to domestic and international law, including arbitrary and illegal detentions. These incidents occurred with great frequency, given that most prisoners of war captured during military operations were never recognized as such.[13] In other cases, forced settlement in strategic or model villages was also a form of "irregular detention," accompanied by numerous other human rights violations.

The data compiled by the REMHI Project show that such violations were frequently committed by government military and paramilitary forces, which were identified as responsible for 94 percent of cases of arbitrary or illegal detention (another 5.2 percent are attributed to unknown perpetrators, and 0.6 percent to the guerrillas).

---

[13] Regarding the failure to respect the right to personal liberty, the Inter-American Commission on Human Rights reported: "a) That under the state of siege, both *habeas corpus* (the writ ordering that a party be brought before a court) and the writ of *amparo* were suspended. This allowed Government security agencies to act with total impunity in illegally detaining persons; b) That kidnapping by security agents continues to occur, and in some cases, these have resulted in prolonged illegal detentions, which were initially denied by the authorities" (Organization of American States, Inter-American Commission on Human Rights, Report on the Situation of Human Rights in the Republic of Guatemala, OAS/SER.L/V/II.61/Doc. 47 [Washington, D.C., October 5, 1983], 131).

Chapter Nineteen

GENERAL STATISTICS

The statistics presented below contain basic, general information that has been compiled exclusively from the testimonies received by REMHI. Since a single event may produce more than one victim, and a single victim may suffer more than one human rights violation, some findings are quantified based on both incidents and victims.

TABLE 1: VIOLATIONS BY HISTORICAL PERIOD (VICTIMS)

				Period				
Violation	Unk.	60-68	69-74	75-79	80-83	84-87	88-96	TOTAL
Direct death	1,653	33	43	605	18,554	836	739	22,463
Indirect death	168	3	4	16	2,127	207	135	2,660
Forced disappearance	193	1	19	144	3,082	388	66	3,893
Disappeared, reappeared alive	35	1	1	19	598	46	15	715
Kidnapping for ransom					7	1		8
Torture and cruel treatment	172	10	23	126	3,352	340	196	4,219
Rape	13			6	127	4	2	152
Attack with injuries	18	3	3	14	1,422	227	138	1,825
Attack without injuries	44	2		11	1,117	838	342	2,354
Attack with damages	16			3	754	115	78	966
Attack without damages	46			1	299	12	34	392
Threats to individuals	129	90	33	120	3,517	318	413	4,620
Threats to inst./groups	30	1	182	24	2,423	69	29	2,758
Irregular detention	509	105	18	220	3,520	466	241	5,079
Others	25			4	288	4	2	323
TOTAL	3,051	249	326	1,313	41,187	3,871	2,430	52,427

MASSACRES

The massacres presented below do not include all cases of multiple killings with three or more victims, as reported in the last section. Rather, these are cases of collective murders distinguished by myriad factors and diverse patterns of human rights violations (extreme cruelty, rape, torture, forced disappearances, and so forth).

TABLE 2: DISTRIBUTED BY DEPARTMENT AND YEAR*

Year

Department	Unk.	78	79	80	81	82	83	84	85	88	91	95	Total
Guatemala				1									1
Baja Verapaz					4	12							16
Alta Verapaz	3	2	1	15	10	27	4					1	68
Izabal						1							1
Chiquimula					1								1
Chimaltenango	1			1	2	3	1			1			9
Quetzaltenango					1			1					2
San Marcos	3				4	3	1	1					12
Huehuetenango	2		2	2	16	20							42
Quiché	16		4	27	62	120	17	9	5	2	1		263
Petén	1				3	6							10
Mexico								1	1				2
Total	26	2	7	46	103	192	23	12	6	3	1	1	422

*Does not include years for which REMHI lacks information concerning massacres.

TABLE 3: DISTRIBUTED BY MONTH AND YEAR

Year

Month	Unk.	78	79	80	81	82	83	84	85	88	91	95	Total
Unk.	19	1	3	21	25	48	7	7	2	1	1		135
January				2	10	21	1	1					35
February	7			7	9	30	2		1				56
March			1	4	4	16							25
April				5	2	11	3		1				22
May		1	1	2	6	11	2		1	1			25
June			1		7	13	5			1			27
July				5	3	13	2	1					24
August					8	13		2	1				24
September			1		8	5	1						15
October					6	5						1	12
November					6	1							7
December					9	5		1					15
Total	26	2	7	46	103	192	23	12	6	3	1	1	422

RESPONSIBLE FORCE

Some of the testimonies compiled by REMHI describe incidents in which more than one group took part. Given the numerous combinations that occurred, the information is presented by type of violation, year, place, and massacres, with only five broad categories of responsible forces.

Table 4: Responsible Force

Violation	Data	Guerrilla	Para-military	Army	Army & Paras	Other*	Unk.	Total
Direct death**	Victims	1,252	1,546	11,628	7,062	26	949	22,463
	Incidents	613	545	2,304	580	18	612	4,672
Indirect death***	Victims	37	50	1,765	243	19	546	2,660
	Incidents	34	44	668	175	16	537	1,474
Forced disappearance	Victims	294	356	2,421	466	1	355	3,893
	Incidents	79	225	1,025	222	1	273	1,825
Disappeared, reappeared alive	Victims	35	29	556	67		28	715
	Incidents	18	23	162	43		18	264
Kidnapping for ransom	Victims	1		6	0		1	8
	Incidents	2		6	1		1	10
Torture and cruel treatment	Victims	177	391	2,871	555	8	217	4,219
	Incidents	125	255	1,063	260	4	99	1,806
Rape	Victims	4	13	119	9		7	152
	Incidents	2	12	66	8		7	95
Attack with injuries	Victims	107	44	1,600	33	5	36	1,825
	Incidents	41	35	159	31	5	35	306
Attack without injuries	Victims	31	62	2,194	55		12	2,354
	Incidents	20	37	120	22		11	210
Attack with damages	Victims	21	50	863	25		7	966
	Incidents	15	10	200	26		6	257
Attack without damages	Victims	4	0	375	10		3	392
	Incidents	2	2	61	12		1	78
Threats to individuals	Victims	424	395	3,478	150	22	161	4,620
	Incidents	258	252	488	117	5	124	1,244

* Witnesses report government and insurgent forces were both involved in the incident (victims of cross fire, for example).

** Includes deaths by massacre, extrajudicial execution, forced disappearance (when the victim was found dead), indiscriminate attacks, bombardments, artillery fire, explosives, mines, cross fire.

*** Includes deaths resulting from persecution: suicide, starvation, disease, accidents, and others.

Violation	Data	Guerrilla	Para-military	Army	Army & Paras	Other*	Unk.	Total
Threats to insts./groups	Victims	1,379	98	1,124	1,238	7	212	4,058
	Incidents	42	53	175	36	3	24	333
Irregular detention	Victims	32	394	3,743	641	2	267	5,079
	Incidents	28	232	884	225	1	35	1,405
Others	Victims	25	6	235	48	2	7	323
	Incidents	23	6	236	41	2	4	312
Total Victims		3,823	3,424	32,978	10,602	92	2,808	53,727
Total Incidents		1,302	1,731	7,617	1,799	55	1,787	14,291

TABLE 5: VIOLATIONS AGAINST LIFE BY INCIDENTS AND VICTIMS

Force(s) Responsible

	Data	Unk.	Army	Af-PM	FM	G	Others	Total
Death caused by…								
Massacre*	Incidents	38	615	249	93	95		1,090
	Victims	322	9,704	6,695	1,038	665		18,424
Extrajudicial	Incidents	562	1,736	362	458	514	4	3,636
executions	Victims	621	2,357	430	520	599	5	4,532
Indiscriminate	Incidents	4	35	7	4	5		55
attack	Victims	3	36	7	3	4		53
Bombing	Incidents	1	19	1				21
	Victims	2	18	1				21
Artillery	Incidents	1	2					3
	Victims	1	4					5
Explosives	Incidents	4	14			2		20
	Victims	6	14			2		22
Mines	Incidents		8			3		11
	Victims		10			4		14
Cross fire	Incidents	1	2	3		2	1	9
	Victims	1	2	3		2	1	9
Undetermined	Incidents	19	35	14	13	10		91
	Victims	21	39	13	14	11		98
Death by persecution								
Suicide	Incidents	2	5	2	1	1		11
	Victims	2	4	2	1	1		10
Starvation	Incidents	12	241	86	10	3	2	354
	Victims	21	438	121	14	3	2	599
Illness	Incidents	504	243	55	15	9	3	829
	Victims	504	960	92	15	11	3	1,585
Accident	Incidents	7	21	3	2	4		37
	Victims	7	20	3	2	4		36
Grief, sorrow,	Incidents	7	105	28	11	13		164
etc.	Victims	7	112	29	12	13		173
Others	Incidents	5	53	12	5	4		79
	Victims	5	231	10	6	5		257
Disappearance								
	Incidents	273	1,025	223	225	79		1,825
	Victims	355	2,421	467	366	294		3,893
Total Incidents		1,440	4,159	1,045	837	744	10	8,235
Total Victims		1,878	16,370	7,873	1,981	1,618	11	29,731

* In these cases massacres were considered incidents in which three or more people died.

TABLE 6: DISTRIBUTION BY HISTORICAL PERIOD BY INCIDENTS AND VICTIMS

Period

Forces	Data	Unk.	60-68	69-74	75-79	80-83	84-87	88-96	Total
Army	Victims	2,320	154	70	811	25,042	2,734	1,847	32,978
	Incidents	593	15	38	247	5,585	810	329	7,617
Army and	Victims	223	43	13	163	9,601	426	133	10,602
Paramilitaries	Incidents	107	16	6	25	1,389	182	74	1,799
Paramilitaries	Victims	121	41	28	105	2,636	231	262	3,424
	Incidents	104	24	21	74	1,231	137	140	1,731
Guerrillas	Victims	202	2	1	113	1,982	130	93	2,523
	Incidents	143	2	1	80	1,001	45	30	1,302
Unknown	Victims	182	9	214	109	1,860	347	87	2,808
	Incidents	110	9	33	77	1,329	152	77	1,787
Others*	Victims	3			12	66	3	8	92
	Incidents	3			2	39	3	8	55
Total Victims		3,051	249	326	1,313	41,187	3,871	2,430	52,427
Total Incidents		1,060	66	99	505	10,574	1,329	668	14,291

*This group includes cases in which witnesses report the participation of both government and insurgent forces, such as cases of cross fire, among others.

TABLE 7: MASSACRES DISTRIBUTED BY DEPARTMENT AND YEAR*

Forces: A = Army; P = Paramilitaries; G = Guerrillas; U = Unknown

Department	Force	Unk	78	79	80	81	82	83	84	85	88	91	95	Total
Guatemala	A+P				1									1
Total Guatemala					*1*									*1*
Baja Verapaz	A						1							1
	A+P					4	11							15
Total Baja Verapaz						*4*	*12*							*16*
Alta Verapaz	A	1	1	1	6	5	11	2					1	28
	A+P		1		6	4	13	2						26
	P	2			2		2							6
	G						1							1
	U				1	1								2
Total Alta Verapaz		*3*	*2*	*1*	*15*	*10*	*27*	*4*					*1*	*63*
Izabal	A						1							1
Total Izabal							*1*							*1*
Chiquimula	A+P					1								1
Total Chiquimula						*1*								*1*
Chimaltenango	A	1				2	1	1						5
	A+P			1			2				1			4
Total Chimaltenango		*1*		*1*		*2*	*3*	*1*			*1*			*9*
Quetzaltenango	A					1			1					2
Total Quetzaltenango						*1*			*1*					*2*
San Marcos	A	2				3	3	1	1					10
	A+P	1				1								2
Total San Marcos		*3*				*4*	*3*	*1*	*1*					*12*
Huehuetenango	A	1		2	1	16	16							36
	A+P				1		3							4
	P						1							1
	G	1												1
Total Huehuetenango		*2*		*2*	*2*	*16*	*20*							*42*
Quiché	A	11		3	21	29	59	9	8	2	1	1		144
	A+P	4			6	23	48	4	1	3	1			90
	P	1				6	2	3						12
	G			1		4	8	1						14
	U						3							3
Total Quiché		*16*		*4*	*27*	*62*	*120*	*17*	*9*	*5*	*2*	*1*		*263*
Petén	A	1				1	3							5
	A+P					2	3							5
Total Petén		*1*				*3*	*6*							*10*
México	A+P								1	1				2
Total México									*1*	*1*				*2*
General Total		26	2	7	46	103	192	23	12	6	3	1	1	422

*Years for which REMHI lacks information concerning massacres are not included.

TABLE 8: VIOLATIONS BY DEPARTMENT (1)

Violation	Data	Unk.	Guatemala	Baja Verapaz	Alta Verapaz	Progreso	Izabal	Zacapa
Direct death	Victims	29	132	1,490	3,294	8	325	17
	Incidents	26	39	219	866	3	127	16
Indirect death	Victims	14	7	16	849		25	
	Incidents	14	6	15	779		21	
Forced disappearance	Victims	44	122	145	635	6	190	7
	Incidents	42	73	98	299	3	83	5
Disappeared, reappeared alive	Victims		14	10	25	3	40	1
	Incidents		11	7	21	1	14	1
Kidnapping for ransom	Victims		0		2			
	Incidents		1		3			
Torture and cruel treatment	Victims	22	26	335	608	8	153	4
	Incidents	13	21	124	272	3	69	3
Rape	Victims	2	3	10	9		0	
	Incidents	2	2	8	6		1	
Attack with injuries	Victims	1	11	11	43		10	4
	Incidents	1	9	11	38		8	3
Attack w/o injuries	Victims		6	8	28	2	9	1
	Incidents		7	9	20	2	7	1
Attack with damages	Victims		4	53	106		1	
	Incidents		3	10	17		2	
Attack w/o damages	Victims		1	3	4		1	
	Incidents		1	2	6		2	
Threats to individuals	Victims		62	212	177	1	56	73
	Incidents		36	102	146	1	41	4
Threats to institutions/groups	Victims		6	100	228	0	22	
	Incidents		7	15	23	1	12	
Irregular detention	Victims	5	25	404	463	10	109	70
	Incidents	3	17	102	189	4	46	1
Others	Victims		2	2	14		2	
	Incidents		1	2	16		1	
Total Victims		117	421	2,799	6,485	38	943	177
Total Incidents		101	234	724	2,691	18	434	34

TABLE 9: VIOLATIONS BY DEPARTMENT (2)

Violation	Data	Chiqui-mula	Santa Rosa	Juti-apa	Sacate-péquez	Chimal-tenango	Escuintla	Sololá	Totoni-capán
Direct death	Victims	17		7	3	156	25	10	40
	Incidents	12		6	3	50	15	8	24
Indirect death	Victims	1				1		1	4
	Incidents	1				1		1	4
Forced disappearance	Victims	3	3	1		66	20	12	25
	Incidents	2	2	1		30	18	3	19
Disappeared, reappeared alive	Victims					6	5	1	11
	Incidents					3	2	1	6
Kidnapping for ransom	Victims								
	Incidents								
Torture and cruel treatment	Victims	4	1	5		37	18	4	18
	Incidents	3	1	5		20	13	4	14
Rape	Victims					2			1
	Incidents					1			1
Attack with injuries	Victims			1		4	3	2	2
	Incidents			1		5	3	2	2
Attack w/o injuries	Victims	2				0	2		6
	Incidents	1				1	2		4
Attack with damages	Victims	0		0		0			4
	Incidents	1		1		1			1
Attack w/o damages	Victims								0
	Incidents								1
Threats to individuals	Victims	2	1	2		16	12	10	12
	Incidents	2	1	2		6	11	5	14
Threats to institutions/groups	Victims			0		7	6	1	0
	Incidents			1		3	3	2	1
Irregular detention	Victims	14	1	1		37	16	5	13
	Incidents	6	1	1		22	10	5	12
Others	Victims						1		
	Incidents						1		
Total Victims		43	6	17	3	332	108	46	136
Total Incidents		28	5	18	3	143	78	31	103

TABLE 10: VIOLATIONS BY DEPARTMENT (3)

Violation	Data	Quetzal-tenango	Suchite-péquez	Retal-huleu	San Marcos	Huehue-tenango	Quiché	Petén	Méx-ico	C.A.	Total
Direct death	Victims	188	8	14	606	2,681	12,743	624	41	5	22,463
	Incidents	129	3	13	133	460	2,272	222	22	4	4,672
Indirect death	Victims	9			8	54	985	39	647		2,660
	Incidents	9			8	32	524	24	35		1,474
Forced disappearance	Victims	123	4	2	171	177	1,718	408	10	1	3,893
	Incidents	95	4	2	96	56	703	193	7	1	1,825
Disappeared, reappeared alive	Victims	15		1	19	63	434	67			715
	Incidents	14		1	14	16	122	30			264
Kidnapping for ransom	Victims	1					5				8
	Incidents	1					5				10
Torture and cruel treatment	Victims	102	7	5	249	538	1,818	250	6	1	4,219
	Incidents	71	3	5	82	214	754	103	6	3	1,806
Rape	Victims	2			2	9	92	20			152
	Incidents	3			3	8	47	13			95
Attack with injuries	Victims	22		2	7	413	1,262	23	4		1,825
	Incidents	14		2	8	14	158	23	4		306
Attack w/o injuries	Victims	8			18	46	1,748	15	454	1	2,354
	Incidents	7			5	10	114	16	3	1	210
Attack with damages	Victims				57	7	664	5	65	0	966
	Incidents				13	9	189	6	3	1	257
Attack w/o damages	Victims				1	7	365	6	4		392
	Incidents				2	6	49	4	5		78
Threats to individuals	Victims	68	1	3	1,333	275	1,587	264	453		4,620
	Incidents	56	1	4	61	160	510	77	4		1,244
Threats to institutions/groups	Victims	7	4		76	46	2,024	223	8	0	2,758
	Incidents	6	1		14	53	169	15	6	1	333
Irregular detention	Victims	50	3	1	167	450	3,079	150	5	1	5,079
	Incidents	34	2	1	58	149	668	78	3	3	1,405
Others	Victims			1	4	10	282	5			323
	Incidents			1	4	10	271	5			312
Total Victims		595	27	29	2,718	4,776	28,806	2,099	1,697	9	52,427
Total Incidents		439	14	29	501	1,197	6,545	809	98	14	14,291

C.A. = Central América

THE PATH TO SOCIAL RECONSTRUCTION

Recommendations of the REMHI Project

REPAIRING THE DAMAGE

Given its responsibility for systematic human rights violations, the Guatemalan state should take measures to provide a minimal form of restitution and offset the damages. These measures should include compensation, victim assistance programs, moral reparations, and the restitution of truth and the collective memory of the victims.

REPARATIONS

In recent years, victims of human rights violations have increasingly demanded reparations; this is reflected in the testimonies compiled by the REMHI project. The State has the responsibility to institute economic, social, and cultural measures that partially compensate for the victims' losses and the harm they suffered. The government should enact laws and procedures for compensation, based on criteria of equity, social participation, and cultural respect. Similarly, the government is obliged to prevent the diversion of funds earmarked for compensation.

Restitution measures must support community development; therefore, they must include opportunities for the active involvement of the affected communities and surrounding communities. Forms of economic compensation should be guided by a community development rationale, including support for access to agricultural production (land, credit, inputs, training, technology transfer, markets) and avoiding onerous debts. These measures must foster local participation to avoid creating dependency, which has occurred with some of the assistance programs currently in progress (including the government's Fund for Peace—FONAPAZ—programs).

Material Restitution

These measures are used to restore as nearly as possible the victims' circumstances prior to the violence (employment, properties, repatriation, and so forth).

Restitution of material losses caused by the violence is fundamental, particularly since often one of the objectives of the violence was to cause such losses. In cases of mass destruction, the government should compensate the survivors for lost crops, livestock, seeds, farm equipment, destroyed symbols and belongings, and the loss of land, among other things.

The plight of the internally displaced is especially likely to be overlooked, given that these cases usually involve individuals or family groups. It is therefore essential to formulate public policies that address their situation.

Compensation Measures

These are measures to provide financial compensation for damages suffered, for example, physical or moral harm, loss of opportunities and education, loss of supplementary income due to the violence, and attacks on people's reputations and honor.

An important component of reparation measures relates to the needs of children and young people, especially war orphans or those who were unable to go to school when their families were left in a state of severe economic hardship. Although the government has the responsibility to guarantee a basic education to the entire population, educational programs can also be specifically targeted in explicit recognition of the harm inflicted. In addition to these measures, the government should reform its current economic policy, which threatens to discontinue, or increase the cost of, basic services including education.

HUMANITARIAN ASSISTANCE FOR VICTIMS AND SURVIVORS (MEDICAL, PSYCHOLOGICAL, SOCIAL, AND LEGAL REPARATIONS)

The purpose of "readaption measures" is to cover the costs of medical, psychological or psychiatric care, as well as social and legal services, and so forth.

Medical and psychological and social services for survivors must not become another form of victimization, stigma, or discrimination. These services must incorporate individual, family, and community-centered therapeutic approaches, imbued with social awareness of the experience and sensitive to the fact that, above all, the dignity of the survivors must be respected. Programs should avoid rigid clinical models focusing on decontextualized individual care and should respect cultural differences.

Without excluding health programs offered through the public health system, psychological and social services should be provided in an atmosphere of trust and community participation often lacking in public services. The government should support psychological and social services offered by social groups, churches, nongovernmental organizations, and others who have a sufficient understanding of the situation, experience in providing services to victims, and professional expertise. In any case, these services should be free of charge as a basic right of the population affected by the violence.

Training programs should be designed for health and education professionals specializing in serving victims of violence. University and vocational training centers should revise their curricula to increase their involvement in activities to serve and support victims (in the fields of medicine, psychology, social work, law, etc.).

Social and legal services should make available the legal procedures and assistance survivors need to normalize various legal matters that were affected by the conflict: identity documents, property titles, hereditary rights, and so forth.

COLLECTIVE MEMORY

STATEMENT OF GOVERNMENT RESPONSIBILITY

The government should publicly acknowledge the facts and its responsibility in the massive, systematic violation of the human rights of the Guatemalan people. The URNG and other armed actors should do likewise. They should acknowledge that this happened, that it was unjust, and that they are committed to taking the necessary measures to avoid any recurrence. This official acknowledgment must be included in informational and educational programs to ensure that it reaches all sectors of Guatemalan society, particularly those most affected by the war.

The government must avoid measures that contradict this overall position. Such measures would include decorating or honoring human rights violators, including former presidents responsible for state terrorism.

OFFICIAL HISTORY

For many years Guatemalan society has been subjected to censorship, manipulation of information, and social isolation, keeping it from acquiring a real understanding of its history. The government, and particularly education officials, have the obligation to carry out curricular reforms and incorporate into textbooks relevant historical and official documents that provide an accurate account of what happened during the armed conflict in the country, beginning with the findings of REMHI and the Historical Clarification Commission. The work of expert commissions should be supplemented by establishing working groups to design plans and activities that turn this history into a genuine pedagogical tool. The media also have a historic responsibility to acknowledge the role they have played in this information process, adhering to their ethical and professional obligation to truth in reporting.

The production of materials, including this history, must be sensitive to the multilingual, pluricultural reality and the oral, nonliterate traditions of many rural communities. It must avoid contributing once again to a memory that is segregated from the vast majorities who have been the protagonists of this history.

INVESTIGATION OF CASES: STATEMENTS CONCERNING THE DISAPPEARED

Numerous testimonies and evidence indicate that military bases maintained clandestine jails and cemeteries. Providing public information about such cemeteries or, in some cases, conducting investigations and providing official information should be the first step in enabling survivors to locate the remains of their family members. This would require the creation of an official agency, with sufficient resources and an unlimited time period, to coordinate with public authorities to support the investigations necessary to clarify the fate of these people. The works of REMHI and the Historical Clarification Commission should form the basis for these investigations. This agency should be authorized to collect testimonies and conduct on-site investigations of military files, units, and bases, subject to the applicable due process guarantees.

The responsible individuals in the army and police, paramilitary groups (former military commissioners or civil patrol chiefs), and the URNG have the obligation to provide reliable information about cases to establish the fate of people detained, disappeared, abducted, or murdered during the armed conflict. Relatives of the victims have the right to know what happened to them and to have access to all information that governmental authorities may possess or obtain concerning the case. To undertake these cases the Public Ministry should reinforce its investigatory capacity, including its ability to conduct exhumations.

HONORING THE VICTIMS

Public, symbolic reparation measures, such as commemorations, monuments, and tributes to the victims, are a necessary contribution to honoring the victims of human rights violations.

Ceremonies and Monuments

The government should promote forms of remembering and honoring victims that can become a permanent fixture in the collective memory of present and future generations; for example, changing the names of plazas, streets, or places in memory of people or events that have a collective significance and epitomize the struggle for human rights. Commemorations should redeem the values and struggles for human dignity that many victims were engaged in and that remain convictions that inspire much of society.

The memory of atrocities cannot coexist with monuments to evil figures in history who are deeply implicated in violence against the civilian population. Two cases in point are the monument to Germán Chupina Barahona in front of the National Police General Headquarters, and the plaque honoring Efraín Ríos Montt on the corner of 6 Av. and 8 Calle in Guatemala City Central Park.

The Joint Commission on Sacred Sites created by the Peace Accords should contribute to researching and creating monuments or symbols of indigenous collective memory in traditional Mayan sacred sites that were desecrated during the armed conflict.

Commemorations and ceremonies infuse memory with public meaning and acknowledgment. More than just a remembrance of pain, these ceremonies are also a memory of solidarity. Since many families have been unable even to bury their dead or observe their cultural or religious rites, the authorities have the obligation to facilitate public ceremonies, exhumations, funerals, and burials in accordance with meaningful religious and cultural traditions.

Legal procedures

Although they may be convinced that their loved one is dead, many relatives have faced bureaucratic red tape forcing them to take further action, suffer new humiliations, or incur prohibitive expenses, given their impoverished circumstances. The authorities have the moral obligation, and should also have the legal obligation, to research and process name changes, accommodate traditional inheritance systems, or clarify land use rights, all without charge. Some necessary measures include providing the services of municipal notary publics and government-appointed attorneys who can process these matters, as well as making these rights known to the general public.

EXHUMATIONS

Exhumations can help clarify many incidents and should contribute to a family and community mourning process. Adapting exhumations and handling remains in culturally appropriate ways, and providing specific information about the process, should be part of the compensatory nature of exhumations.

Exhumations are inherently a demand for justice, since many families regard the search for their relatives as a path toward obtaining justice. People involved in exhumations should provide the most reliable information possible to help families evaluate the effort, possible outcomes, and limitations they may encounter during this process.

In any event, it is essential that the rhythm and demands of the community govern the actions of those technically, legally, or socially involved in exhumations. There should be a law regulating exhumations that provides for simplified procedures, given the magnitude of these demands and the political, legal, or procedural obstacles encountered.

Families have the right to exhume their dead, and this right should be officially guaranteed, given that the army was directly responsible for the vast majority of clandestine burials. The authorities with jurisdiction over these cases should have the resources they need to apply the personal documentation law.

RESTORING MEMORY TO THE PEOPLE

The government should facilitate the process of returning memory to the affected communities and groups, following up on the investigations carried out by the Historical Clarification Commission in coordination with other social institutions or movements.

As mentioned earlier, in addition to their long-term significance as part of the country's official history, the findings of recent investigations into the past must be restored to society as a whole through documentary and educational materials that symbolically acknowledge the experience described in the testimonies, provide a systematic accounting of violent episodes and their impact, and honor the victims.

To the extent possible, these efforts to restore memory must help explain, clarify, and elucidate what happened, as well as extract lessons and conclusions for the present. They must confer meaning on the experience and reconstruct what happened with an emphasis on the positive aspects for collective identity. Moreover, memory must avoid fixation on the past, obsessive repetition, and stigmatization of the survivors as victims. Memory's usefulness as a form of reparation goes beyond reconstructing the facts; it is a moral judgment that ethically repudiates the perpetrators.

THE ROLE OF OTHER SOCIAL SECTORS

THE RELIGIOUS COMMUNITY: DEMANDS AND EXPECTATIONS

Churches, and particularly the Catholic church, must play a key role in educating and guiding communities to combat stigma, foster community life, and prevent all forms of violence.

Some religious denominations must reframe the concepts of reconciliation, forgiveness, and peace from the standpoint of the values of truth and justice, which are widely exploited.

These concepts must be revisited in the context of the collective memory as it has been reconstructed by the REMHI project and the deliberations of the Historical Clarification Commission. Part of this process includes publicly recognizing the responsibilities incurred.

Together with other social and religious institutions, the Catholic church must play an active role in monitoring the Peace Accords and the State's compliance with social demands. As part of its social and religious activities, the Catholic church must further its commitment to the task of social reconstruction, incorporating the systematic accounting of past experiences by the REMHI project. It must likewise become actively involved in community-based initiatives, particularly those related to collective memory.

INTERNATIONAL PRESENCE

The international presence in Guatemala continues to play an important role in the initiatives, institutions, and efforts undertaken by the affected populations to meet the challenges of postwar reconstruction. However, this international presence must not be confined to information campaigns on peace and so forth. Appropriate accompaniment and monitoring of local social reconstruction efforts are required; without them, peace may never go beyond abstract discourse and have a local impact.

International assistance for social reconstruction in Guatemala should oversee the government's compliance with its obligations but should avoid creating new forms of economic dependence in political agreements for development projects. Governments and nongovernmental organizations providing international assistance must ensure that it is managed transparently and efficiently, with an emphasis on local initiatives and the participation of the beneficiaries in decisions that affect their lives.

The URNG

The URNG should account for the deaths and disappearances that it was responsible for during the armed conflict. It should inform relatives about what happened and help locate missing victims in order to bring closure to the survivors' grief. To this end, it should also acknowledge the murders of noncombatant civilians.

The demand that the guerrilla forces publicly admit their errors also entails modifying their conduct to make their discourse and actions more consistent. This demand for political consistency refers not only to the past, but to the former guerrillas' role in the postwar social reconstruction process.

The former guerrilla forces have a direct responsibility for monitoring the Peace Accords signed with the Guatemalan government. Therefore, the URNG should unfailingly promote, supervise and, if need be, denounce noncompliance with these agreements.

PREVENTING HUMAN RIGHTS VIOLATIONS

The right to reparation includes *guarantees* that people's rights will not continue to be violated. These include dismantling paramilitary armed groups and clandestine bodies that operate from within the state apparatus and rescinding exceptional measures, legislative or otherwise, that are conducive to violations, as well as administrative or other measures concerning government agents implicated in violations and atrocities.

RESPECT FOR HUMAN RIGHTS

Public awareness of individual and collective rights is an important tool for preventing future violence. Public oversight institutions should have greater authority and capacity to investigate human rights violations.

These actions must be reinforced by local and regional structures that guarantee freedom of association and contribute to reweaving the social fabric in consonance with traditional forms of grassroots or indigenous organization; government agencies should recognize the interlocutory role of these local organizations.

In the context of severe social discrimination against indigenous groups, the demand for respect for human rights encompasses measures that promote their collective identity.

JUSTICE AND SOCIAL SANCTIONS

For victims and survivors, the impact of the violence on their lives, their families, and the life of the communities has left a deep sense of injustice, not only because of the painful loss, but because those responsible have never been punished.

Without social sanctions, the potential for a recurrence of violence is much greater, given the rupture of basic standards of coexistence. Unless they acknowledge the facts and submit to social condemnation, the perpetrators will never have the opportunity to confront the past, rebuild their identity, and reshape their everyday relationships with victims and society.

Besides facilitating legal investigations of cases brought by victims' families, the government should pledge to take administrative measures to control and sanction people implicated in the violence. Appropriate legislative and administrative measures include limiting the rights and privileges of those implicated in serious human rights violations and barring them from public service; eliminating the army's preferential treatment of former military commissioners and civil patrollers; and proposing legislative reforms that strengthen civilian control over the military.

The Public Ministry should fulfill its obligation to investigate cases of violations, particularly crimes against humanity, so that the courts can punish the perpetrators. Forgiveness is a voluntary act that is born inside an individual who has learned the truth and experienced justice; it cannot, therefore, be imposed.

PREVENTING SOCIAL AND COMMUNITY VIOLENCE

Without a clear sense of moral condemnation of the atrocities that have been committed, and absent a system of investigation, control, and legal sanction, violence could become a behavioral pattern with implications for the future of society, and especially for young people. Reforms of the security forces and current law-enforcement models are essential to prevent new forms of violence emanating from the concentration of authority.

The types of social and community violence currently being observed are the result of impunity, socioeconomic decline (including a deficient reinsertion model for demobilized members of the security forces), corruption, and a culture of violence (such as exemplary terror), which were fostered during the conflict.

Therefore, violence prevention must include reforms of diverse government institutions and a concerted effort to combat organized crime. Simultaneously, a long-term crime-fighting policy should be designed and implemented that enables different government institutions to adopt a comprehensive approach to preventing, investigating, prosecuting, and punishing crime, as well as effectively rehabilitating offenders.

The intention of involving the army in public security, besides violating the accord on "Strengthening Civilian Authority and the Role of the Army in a Democratic Society," precludes a security policy in keeping with a democratic system and respect for human rights. The National Civilian Police must be the agency to develop preventive measures to create a climate of security and respect for the people. Prolonging the army's involvement in internal security matters leads to increased fear in communities.

LEGISLATIVE AND JUDICIAL REFORMS

METHODS FOR MONITORING LAW ENFORCEMENT

Many methods of civilian oversight of the government are found in existing laws; thus, government agencies and the justice system must effectively enforce recognized individual and collective guarantees.

At the same time, it is necessary to adopt effective methods to inform and involve citizens in government oversight activities. Laws that are ambiguous or contain discretionary provisions must be replaced by clear, explicit laws. This is particularly important in the case of laws that can be interpreted in ways that reinforce the ability to commit crimes with impunity.

TRADITIONAL AUTHORITY AND LAW

Restoring the social fabric in Mayan communities throughout the country entails fostering, strengthening, and respecting their own authorities and their specific methods of administration of justice.

THE JUDICIARY

Judicial reform must be accomplished by thoroughly implementing the recommendations made by the Commission to Strengthen the Justice System, particularly those having to do with judicial governance, the independence of judges, and the judicial profession. Ongoing training of justice officials is imperative to ensure professional excellence, and evaluation methods that ensure transparency in the application of laws.

SOCIAL CHANGES FOR PEACE

DEMILITARIZATION

Demobilization and Army Reforms

The demilitarization of society is essential to real peace. This refers to demobilization and military reform as well as reducing the army's influence in society. It includes demobilizing the military units, officers, and soldiers most implicated in atrocities; dismantling clandestine security apparatus; and extensive reform of the intelligence system.

In addition to the measures contemplated in the Peace Accords, the Presidential General Staff (EMP) must be abolished and its activities thoroughly investigated. The intelligence system must be reorganized to remove all operational functions from the Secretariat for Strategic Analysis. The legislature and judiciary must oversee its operations, jurisdiction, and budget so that correctional measures can be applied in a timely manner. Laws regulating intelligence activities must be explicit rather than vague.

Since military intelligence has spent the last several decades spying on the everyday lives of many Guatemalans, the government must effectively protect individual privacy. It should also set up a freedom-of-information (*habeas data*) system so citizens can exercise their right to know what the intelligence services have investigated and what information these services hold about them. Files containing information about people's political or personal lives should be turned over to them or be destroyed.

The military instruction systems for officers, soldiers, and specialists must undergo a comprehensive reform process, because the existing systems pose an ongoing threat to social peace. The precepts underlying military instruction must be reformulated, and the functions, organization, and equipping of army bases and special units reoriented. At the same time, centers that epitomize the aggression waged against the population, such as the Ranger School, must be closed.

At the Local Level

Demilitarization at the local level refers to concrete measures, such as decreasing military presence in the communities, overall changes in how the army relates to the population, especially in local religious ceremonies, which army soldiers attend in uniform. Procedures must be established to confiscate, destroy, or abolish weapons-trafficking in communities. Demilitarization of daily life also means refraining from extolling the army in "civic" educational or social events.

Demilitarization means reforming local power structures. This includes restoring the role of civic and traditional authorities. In some areas, civil patrols were recently converted into Development Committees, which could serve as a new form of social control by leveraging assistance and development projects. These committees represent attempts to perpetuate the same structures under a new name. They should therefore be dissolved and replaced by truly democratic structures respectful of community organizational methods. Legal reforms are needed so that local committees can serve as new forms of representation that respect the people's will.

Recruitment and the Right to Conscientious Objection

Obligatory military service for young people should be abolished based on the recent, tragic history of violence against people, the impact that forced recruitment has had on young people and their families, and the cultural repercussions of the militaristic socialization of youth. The children and relatives of victims must be exempt from any type of service. The government must also desist from exploiting young people by offering military service as the only route to meeting their basic needs (literacy, an income, etc.). A conscientious objection law is needed, along the lines currently being proposed by various social sectors.

EXERCISING PERSONAL FREEDOMS

In the testimonies compiled, demands for freedom are related to the possibility of expressing identity and culture. This includes freedom to celebrate rites and ceremonies, unimpeded access to sacred sites, and the ability to express personal beliefs. The government should also facilitate participatory structures to replace the current system of political exclusion of the Mayan people.

The exercise of freedoms must reach into areas of economic and labor relations, which continue to be off limits. The semi-feudal relationships that persist on many plantations must be abolished. In these areas, civic freedoms have not been respected or have been limited by private property. Dignified living conditions, and freedom of association, religion, and so forth are urgently needed and must include changes in the attitudes and policies of employers. In any case, existing systems to protect human rights in general must have the capacity to supervise and monitor this category of rights as well.

ADDRESSING THE LAND ISSUE

In recent years, war-induced displacement has exacerbated a historically unjust system characterized by skewed property distribution and access to land; a recent history of fraudulent purchases; legal obstacles; economic exploitation in rural areas; and the concentration of property in a few hands. Improved land distribution is not only a form of reparation but, more important, it is a way to avert new problems and social conflicts.

Conflict resolution mechanisms are urgently needed to handle land disputes in rural areas. The government, as part of its historic responsibility, must shoulder the task of resolving land disputes caused by the violence. It should not delegate these problems to be addressed in dealings between social agents, such as landowners and potential buyers. Land purchases cannot become a new form of enrichment for landowners and brokers at the expense of people's needs. Moreover, the government must implement a national agrarian development policy that includes effective, broadly targeted measures for access to land. It must institute measures for the provision of soft credits for social groups most affected by the violence, such as widows. Agriculture-based community-development projects must be accompanied by appropriate government-sponsored technical assistance for peasants.

A national land registry is urgently needed to correct the illegalities and injustices that have accompanied boundary determinations and property sales. The populations affected by the violence must have access to free and trustworthy legal assistance as part of the necessary guarantees of restitution for which the government is responsible. The legalization of communal lands is another important measure, so that they are no longer susceptible to fraudulent purchases or looting.

BIBLIOGRAPHY

Adams, Richard. *Crucifixion by Power*. Austin, Tex.: University of Texas Press, 1970.

————. "Conclusions: What Can We Know about the Harvest of Violence?" In *Harvest of Violence*. Edited by R. C. Carmack. Norman, Okla.: University of Oklahoma Press, 1988.

Aguilera Peralta, Gabriel, and Jorge Romero Imery. *Dialéctica del terror en Guatemala*. San Jose, Costa Rica: EDUCA, 1981.

————. *La contrainsurgencia rural en Guatemala*. Instituto Centroamericano de Documentación e Investigación Social. 1985. Mimeo.

Aitkenhead, Richard. *Los ochenta, crónica de una década difícil*. Thesis. Universidad Rafael Landívar [Guatemala], 1989.

Albizures, Miguel Ángel. "Luchas y experiencias del movimiento sindical, período 1976-junio 1978." *Estudios Centroamericanos, Guatemala: Drama y conflicto social* (número extraordinario) 356/357. Universidad Centroamericana José Simeón Cañas. El Salvador. 1978.

————. *Tiempo de sudor y de lucha*. México: Editorial Praxis, 1987.

Alvarado Pinetta, Edgar. *La agricultura en Guatemala*. Guatemala: Cámara del Agro de Guatemala, 1981.

Americas Watch. *Clandestine Detention in Guatemala* 5, no. 2 (March 1993).

Amnesty International. *Human Rights in Guatemala*. Guatemala, 1980.

————. *Guatemala: Programa gubernamental de asesinatos políticos*. London, 1981.

Arias, Arturo. "El movimiento indígena en Guatemala, 1970-83." In *Movimientos populares en Centroamérica*. Compiled by Daniel Camacho and Rafael Menjívar. San José, Costa Rica: EDUCA, 1985.

Arriola, Aura Marina. *Guatemala: contrainsurgencia y guerra de exterminio*. México D.F.: ENIAL, 1982.

ASIES. *IV Seminario sobre realidad nacional* [Guatemala] (May 1988).

AVANCSO. *Política exterior y estabilidad estatal*. Cuadernos de Investigación no. 5. Guatemala, 1990.

————. *¿Dónde está el futuro? Procesos de reintegración en comunidades de retornados*. Cuadernos de Investigación no. 8. Guatemala, July 1992.

Barillas, Danilo. *La Democracia Cristiana y su posición ante el Ejército de Guatemala hoy*. Guatemala, 1974. Mimeo.

Bauer Paiz, Alfonso, and Iván Carpio Alfaro. *Memorias de Alfonso Bauer Paiz. Historia no oficial de Guatemala*. Guatemala: Rusticatio Ediciones, 1996.

Beltranena Falla, Francisco Fernando. *Guatemala: pretorianismo y democracia estratégica*. Thesis. Universidad Francisco Marroquín, Instituto de Estudios Políticos [Guatemala], September 1992.

Bendaña Perdomo, Ricardo. *La Iglesia en Guatemala. Síntesis histórica del catolicismo*. Guatemala: Artemis-Edinter, 1996.

Beristain, Carlos Martín. *Viaje a la memoria. Por los caminos de la milpa.* Lallevir. Barcelona, Spain, March 1997.

Bettelheim, B. *El corazón bien informado.* México: Fondo de Cultura Económica, 1976.

Breton, André. *El complejo ajaw y el complejo mam.* Memorias del II Coloquio internacional de mayistas. Volume I. México: UNAM, 1989.

Cabrera Ovalle, Julio. *Consuela a mi pueblo (Selección de homilías).* Guatemala: Voces del Tiempo, 1997.

Cáceres, Carlos. *Aproximación a Guatemala.* Universidad Autónoma de Sinaloa, Culiacán, Sin. Mexico, 1980.

Cambranes, J. C., ed. *500 años de lucha por la tierra. Estudios sobre propiedad rural y reforma agraria en Guatemala.* Volumes 1 and 2. Guatemala: FLACSO, 1992.

Camús, Manuel. "Mujeres mayas en el mercado de la terminal." Presentation made at the Second Congress of Maya Studies, Universidad Rafael Lanívar, August 5-7, 1997.

Carmack, Robert M., comp. *Guatemala: cosecha de violencia,* San José, Costa Rica: FLACSO, 1991.

Casaus Arzú, Marta. *Guatemala: linaje y racismo.* San José, Costa Rica: FLACSO, 1992.

Centro de Investigación y Documentación Centroamericana. *Violencia y contraviolencia: desarrollo histórico de la violencia institucional en Guatemala.* Guatemala: Editorial Universitaria, 1980.

Centro ESTNA. *Situación de defensa y seguridad en Guatemala* (Curso 1989-90. Sesión 89019). Guatemala, September 1989.

Cerezo, Vinicio. *El Ejército: ¿una alternativa?* Unpublished, no date.

COLAT. *Psicopatología de la tortura y el exilio.* Madrid: Fundamentos, 1982.

———. *Así buscamos rehacernos.* Brussels: CELADEC, 1987.

Colom, Yolanda. *Mujeres en la alborada.* Guatemala: Editorial Artemis and Edinter, 1996.

Commission on Human Rights, United Nations Economic and Social Council. *The Right to Repatriation.* E/CN.4/Sub.2/1996/18.

Comité Nacional de Unidad Sindical. *Revista Unidad* (various issues). México, 1986.

Comité Pro Justicia y Paz en Guatemala. *Los derechos humanos en Guatemala.* Guatemala, 1986.

Conferencia Episcopal de Guatemala. *Al servicio de la vida, la justicia y la paz. Documentos de la CEG 1956-1997.* Guatemala, 1997.

Corby, M. *La necesaria relatividad cultural de los sistemas de valores humanos: mitologías, ideologías, ontologías y formaciones religiosas. Análisis epistemológico de las configuraciones axiológicas humanas.* Universidad de Salamanca, Instituto Interdisciplinario de Barcelona, 1983.

Cox, Glenn. *Guatemala insurrecta: violencia y orden pretoriano.* 1995. Mimeo.

Crosby, Benjamín. *Crisis y fragmentación: relaciones entre los sectores público y privado en América Central.* Latin American and Caribbean Center, Florida International University, Occasional Papers Series, May 1985.

Cullather, Nicholas. *Operation PBSUCCESS. The United States and Guatemala 1952-1954.* History Staff, Center for the Study of Intelligence, Central Intelligence Agency, Washington, D.C. 1994.

Dary, Claudia. *El derecho internacional humanitario y el orden jurídico maya. Una perspectiva histórica.* Guatemala: FLACSO, 1997.

Davis, S. H. "Introduction: Sowing Seeds of Violence." In *Harvest of Violence.* Edited by R. C. Carmack. Norman, Okla.: University of Oklahoma Press, 1988.

Debray, Regis. *Les epreuves du feu (La critique des Armes, 2).* Paris: Editions du Seuil, 1974.

Diócesis del Quiché. *Y dieron la vida por El Quiché.* Guatemala, 1992.

———. *El Quiché: el pueblo y su Iglesia (1960-80).* Santa Cruz del Quiché, Guatemala, July 1994.

Dowdeswell, Jane. *La violación: hablan las mujeres.* Madrid: Editorial Revolucíon, 1987.

EAFG (Equipo de Antropología Forense de Guatemala, Guatemalan Forensic Anthropology Team). *Las masacres en Rabinal.* Guatemala, 1995.

EGP. See Ejército Guerrillero de los Pobres below.

Ejército de Guatemala, Escuela de Inteligencia. *Manual de interrogatorio.* January 1980.

———, Estado Mayor General del Ejército-Centro de Estudios Militares (Comisión de trabajo). *Plan Nacional de Seguridad y Desarrollo.* Guatemala, April 1, 1982. Mimeo.

———. *Manual de contrainsurgencia.* 1983.

———, Estado Mayor de la Defensa Nacional. *Doctrina de Asuntos Civiles.* Guatemala, August 8, 1986. Mimeo.

———. *Foro 27 años de lucha por la libertad.* Guatemala, August 1987. Typewritten version.

———, Estado Mayor de la Defensa Nacional. *La tesis de la Estabilidad Nacional,* Guatemala, 1988. Mimeo.

———. Inforpress Centroaméricana Cetnroamérica 1990, Anexo capitulo 3.

———, Ministerio de la Defensa Nacional. "Reglamento para el servicio militar en tiempo de paz." *Diario de Centro América,* July 1, 1991.

———, Estado Mayor del Ejército, Division de Inteligencia, *Manual de área.* Guatemala, March 1996.

Ejército Guerrillero de los Pobres (EGP). *La lucha democrática, revolucionaria y popular contra el poder de los ricos. Manifiesto al pueblo de Guatemala.* October 1978. Mimeo.

———. COTRAM, *El desarrollo del trabajo amplio de masas en la coyuntura actual.* 1981. Mimeo.

———. *Informador guerrillero* (several issues), 1982.

———. *Orientaciones provisionales para que los cuadros de dirección intermedia expliquen a los miembros de la Organización las interrogantes previsibles que surgirán con motivo de la muerte de Camilo a manos del enemigo.* August 15, 1983. Mimeo.

———. Internal document dated 1984.

———. Internal document "Number 20."

———. *Línea de masas.* Mimeo, no date.

———. *Los cinco principios.* Mimeo, no date.

Equipo Ak'kutan. *Evangelio y culturas en Verapaz.* Guatemala, 1993.

Escoto, Jorge, and Manfredo Marroquín. *La AID en Guatemala. Poder y sector empresarial.* Guatemala: CRIES/AVANCSO, 1992.

Escuela de Ciencia Política. *Revista Política y Sociedad* (Número extraordinario). Instituto de Investigaciones Políticas y Sociales, Facultad de Ciencias Jurídicas y Sociales, Universidad de San Carlos de Guatemala. Guatemala, April, 1978.

Falla, Ricardo. *Quiché rebelde*. Guatemala: Editorial Universitaria, 1978.

———. *Preparatory work to Massacres in the Jungle* (Unofficial title). 1987. Unpublished.

———. "Introducción al resumen (Agosto 1990)." In Joaquín Noval, *Resumen Etnográfico de Guatemala*. Guatemala: Editorial Piedrasanta, 1992.

———. *Masacres de la selva. Ixcán, Guatemala (1975-1982)*. Editorial Guatemala: Universitaria, 1992.

———. *Historia de un gran amor. Recuperación autobiográfica de las experiencias con las Comunidades de Población en Resistencia. Ixcán, Guatemala*. May 1993.

Farías, P. "Central and South American Refugees." In *Amidst Peril and Pain: The Mental Health and Well-being of the World's Refugees*. Edited by A. J. Marsella, T. Bornemann, S. Ekblad. and J. Orley. Washington, D.C.: American Psychological Association, 1994.

Fernández Fernández, José Manuel. *Comunidades indígenas y conflicto social en Guatemala*. Universidad Complutense de Madrid, Facultad de Ciencias Políticas y Sociología, Madrid, 1988.

Fernández Poncela, Ana. "Relaciones de género y cambio socio cultural." 1997.

Figueroa Ibarra, Carlos. *El proletariado rural en el agro guatemalteco*. Editorial Universitaria de Guatemala, 1981.

———. *El recurso del miedo. Ensayo sobre el Estado y el terror en Guatemala*. San José, Costa Rica: EDUCA, 1991.

———. "Violencia política e insurgencia en Guatemala (1954-95)." In *América Latina, violencia y miseria en el crepúsculo del siglo*. México: Universidad Autónoma de Puebla-Asociación Latinoamericana de Sociología. 1996.

Flores, Marco Antonio. *Fortuny: un comunista guatemalteco (Memorias)*. Óscar de León Palacios, Palo de Hormigo y Universitaria. Guatemala, 1994.

Fundación Friedrich Ebert, comp. *Acuerdos de Paz*. Guatemala, February 1997.

Fundación Myrna Mack. *Hacia un sistema de inteligencia para la democracia en Guatemala (preliminary working document)*. Guatemala, October 1997. Mimeo.

Galeano, Eduardo. *Guatemala país ocupado*. México: Editorial Nuestro Tiempo, 1971.

Garnier, Leonardo. "La economía centroamericana en los ochenta." In *Historia General de Centroamérica*. Tomo VI. San José, Costa Rica: FLACSO, 1993.

Gramajo, Héctor Alejandro. *Lección inaugural, X Promoción. Curso comando y Estado Mayor*. Centro de Estudios Militares. Guatemala, April 30, 1987. Mimeo.

———. *Liderazgo militar y el futuro del Ejército de Guatemala*. Guatemala: Editorial del Ejército, May 1990.

———. *De la guerra. a la guerra. La difícil transición política en Guatemala*. Fondo de Cultura Editorial, Guatemala, 1995.

Guerra Borges, Alfredo. "El desarrollo económico de Centroamérica." In *Historia General de Centroamérica*. Tomo V. San José, Costa Rica: FLACSO, 1993.

Gutiérrez, Edgar. "La difícil transición en Guatemala." In *Revista Verdad y Vida*, Año II, Núm. 5. Guatemala: ODHAG, January-March 1995.

Handy, Jim. *Gift of the Devil*. Boston: South End Press. 1984.

Harnecker, Martha. *Pueblos en armas (Entrevistas)*. ERA, Serie popular. México, 1984.

Hofstede, G., *Cultures and Organizations*. London: McGraw-Hill, 1991.

Hoyos de Asig, María del Pilar. *Fernando Hoyos ¿dónde estás?* Guatemala: Fondo de Cultura Editorial, 1997.

IIDH (Instituto Inter-Americano de Derechos Humanos). *Estudios básicos de derechos humanos*, Tomo IV. San José, Costa Rica, 1996.

Iglesia Guatemalteca en el Exilio. *Cronología de una experiencia pastoral (Veinte años de vida y de muerte de fe y esperanza cristianas)*. Mimeo, no date.

ILAS. *Trauma psicosocial y adolescentes latinoamericanos*. Eds. ChileAmérica. CESOC, Santiago de Chile, 1994.

Immerman, Richard H. *The CIA in Guatemala: The Foreign Policy of Intervention*. Austin, Tex.: University of Texas Press, 1995.

Inforpress Centroamericana. *Elecciones 1985*. Guatemala, 1985.

———. *Guatemala 1986: el año de las promesas*. Guatemala, 1986.

———. *Centroamérica 1987*. Guatemala, 1988.

———. *Compendio del proceso de paz*. Guatemala, 1995.

———. *Inforpress* (various issues). Guatemala, 1972-96.

Jimenez, Dina. "El movimiento campesino en Guatemala." In *Movimientos populares en Centroamérica*. Compiled by Daniel Camacho and Rafael Menjívar. San José, Costa Rica: EDUCA, 1985.

Jodelet, D. "Memoire de masse: le cote moral et affectif de l'histoire." *Bulletin de Psychologie* 45 (1992): 239-56.

Jonas, Susanne. *Guatemala: plan piloto para el continente*. San José, Costa Rica: EDUCA, 1981.

———. *The Battle for Guatemala*. Boulder, Colo.: Westview Press, 1991.

Las Dignas. *Las relaciones de género y la subjetividad en los proyectos revolucionarios*. El Salvador, 1995.

Le Bot, Ivon. *La guerra en tierras mayas. Comunidad, violencia y modernidad en Guatemala (1970-1992)*. México: Fondo de Cultura Económica, 1995.

Lira E., and M. Castillo. *Psicología de la amenaza política y del miedo*. Santiago de Chile: ILAS, 1991.

Macías, Julio César. *La guerrilla fue mi camino, Epitafio para César Montes*. Piedrasanta, Guatemala, 1998.

Mack, Myrna. *La política de desarrollo del Estado guatemalteco 1986-87*. Avancso, Cuadernos de Investigación no. 2. 1989.

———. *Política institucional hacia el desplazado interno en Guatemala*. Avancso, Cuadernos de Investigación no. 4. Guatemala, January 1990.

Martín-Baró, Ignacio. "Guerra y salud mental." In *Psicología social de la guerra*. El Salvador: UCA Eds., 1990.

———. "Political Violence and War as Causes of Psychological Trauma in El Salvador." *International Journal of Mental Health* (1989).

McClintock, Michael. *The American Connection*. Vol. 2, *State Terror and Popular Resistance in Guatemala*. London: Zed Books, 1987.

Melville, Thomas and Marjorie. *Tierra y poder en Guatemala*. San José, Costa Rica, EDUCA, 1982.

Nairn, Allan. "Guatemala Can't Take Two Roads." *The New York Times* (July 20, 1982).

Nairn, Allan, and Jean-Marie Simon. "The Bureaucracy of Death: Guatemala's Civilian Government Confronts the Internal Enemy." *New Republic* (1986).

Noval, Joaquín. *El estado y la violencia*. Guatemala, November 1970. Mimeo.

Oficina de Derechos Humanos del Arzobispado de Guatemala. *Informe Anual* (Informes correspondientes: 1991, 1992, 1993, 1994, and 1995).

Opinión Política (several issues). México, 1985.

ORPA. *La guerra necesaria e inevitable*. Guatemala, February 1979.

———. *El racismo*. Guatemala, 1980.

———. *La verdadera magnitud del racismo (Racismo II)*. Guatemala, 1978.

———. *Historia nuestra*. Guatemala, 1980.

Páez D., and N. Basabe. "Trauma político y memoria colectiva: Freud, Halbwachs y la psicología contemporánea." *Psicología política* 6 (1993).

Payeras, Mario. *Los días de la selva*. Havana: Casa de Las Américas, 1980.

———. "The Guatemalan Army and U.S. Policy in Central America." *Monthly Review* (1986).

———. *El trueno en la ciudad. Episodios de la lucha armada urbana de 1981 en Guatemala*. Juan Pablos Editor. México, 1991.

———. *Los fusiles de octubre (Ensayos y artículos militares sobre la revolución guatemalteca, 1985-1988)*. Juan Pablos Editor. México, 1991.

Pérez Sales et al. *Muerte y desaparición forzada en la Araucaria: una aproximación étnica*. Santiago de Chile: De. LOM, 1998.

PGT (Partido Guatemalteco de Trabajo). Internal document dated 1962.

Poitevin, René. *El proceso de industrialización en Guatemala*. San José, Costa Rica: EDUCA, 1977.

Popkin, Margaret L. *The Civil Patrols and Their Legacy*. Washington, D.C.: Robert F. Kennedy Memorial Center for Human Rights, June 1996.

Presidencia de la República, Comité de Reconstrucción Nacional. *Política de los frijoles*. Guatemala, undated. Mimeo.

Procurador de los Derechos Humanos/Human Rights Ombudsman et al. *Los comités de defensa civil en Guatemala*. PDH, Guatemala, July, 1994.

Ramírez, Ricardo. *Documento de marzo de 1967*. Mimeo.

———. *Lettres du front guatemalteque*. Masperó. París, 1970.

REMHI. *Evolución de los modelos políticos y económicos en Guatemala, 1960-1995*. August 1995. Mimeo.

———. *Insurgencia y contrainsurgencia. Conceptos y elementos de análisis*. October 1995. Mimeo.

———. *El movimiento sindical y popular guatemalteco. Recomposición, auge y desarrollo, resurgimiento y situación actual (1960-1995)*, February 1996. Mimeo.

———. *Historia reciente de la Iglesia católica de Guatemala* (discussion paper. part 1). May 1996. Mimeo.

———. *Evolución de las políticas sociales, indígenas y de integración territorial del Estado guatemalteco, 1960-1995*, October 1996. Mimeo.

———. *El Ejército de Guatemala, 1985-95*. 1996. Mimeo.

———. *Empresarios y violencia, 1954-96*. 1996. Mimeo.

———. *Casos de sacerdotes y religiosas víctimas de la violencia política*. 1996. Mimeo.

———. *La vida religiosa en el fuego del conflicto armado en Guatemala*. 1997. Mimeo.

———. *Memoria de las masacres contra la aldea Salquil Grande de Nebaj y contra el resto del pueblo ixil*. Volumes 1 and 2. 1996. Mimeo.

————. *Principales expresiones del movimiento revolucionario entre 1975-96 (Estrategias, descisiones y desarrollo organizativo).* 1996-97. Mimeo.

————. *Esbozo histórico del movimiento guerrillero guatemalteco, 1962-1968.* February 1997. Mimeo.

————. *Informe final de Sololá.* March 1997. Mimeo.

————. *Organización del campesinado y huelga en la costa sur en 1980.* March 1997. Mimeo.

————. *La guerra en Ixcán (Desde los primeros colonizadores hasta 1993).* April 1997. Mimeo.

————. *Chimaltenango y el Frente Guerrillero Tecún Umán de FAR.* May 1997. Mimeo.

————. *Una mirada retrospectiva al proceso político-organizativo revolucionario en la región noroccidental de Huehuetenango.* May 1997. Mimeo.

————. *El movimiento estudiantil de educación media en Guatemala. Demandas, luchas, represión.* July 1997. Mimeo.

————. *Temario para una investigación sobre Petén.* May 1997. Mimeo.

————. *Informe sobre Santiago Atitlán.* July 1997. Mimeo.

————. *El terrorismo estatal y los sindicatos* (fourth version). July 1997. Mimeo.

————. *Análisis jurídico de la violencia en Guatemala.* Volume 1, 1954-70, Volume 2, 1970-86. 1997. Mimeo.

————. *Aproximación histórica a la represión en el K'iche,* 1997. Mimeo.

————. *Contexto del conflicto armado en la Arquidiócesis de Los Altos. Los mecanismos de la guerra.* 1997. Mimeo.

————. *El conflicto armado en San Marcos.* 1997. Mimeo.

————. *Insurgencia y contrainsurgencia, su choque en la Universidad de San Carlos y el movimiento estudiantil.* 1997. Mimeo.

————. *La Iglesia guatemalteca en la segunda mitad del siglo XX. Reflexiones sobre su itinerario.* 1997. Mimeo.

————. *Las Patrullas de Autodefensa Civil.* 1997. Mimeo.

————. *Los polos de desarrollo y sus aldeas modelos. ¿Centros de desarrollo o campos de concentración?* 1997. Mimeo.

————. *Movimiento indígena y conflicto armado.* 1997. Mimeo.

————. *Presencia y acción de la Iglesia en el conflicto armado* (version 1.1). 1997. Mimeo.

————. *Resumen de la historia inmediata de Guatemala.* 1997. Mimeo.

————. *Movimiento indígena y conflicto armado.* 1997. Mimeo.

————. *La violencia en Guatemala ¿cómo se realizó? (Los patrones de las violaciones a los derechos humanos).* January 1998. Mimeo.

Rivas Cifúentes, Álvaro Gabriel (Tnte. Coronel). *Medidas para recuperar a la población en resistencia.* Editorial del Ejército, 1990.

Samper K., Mario. "Café, trabajo y sociedad en Centroamérica, 1870-1930. Una historia común y divergente." In *Historia general de Centroamérica.* Tomo IV. San José, Costa Rica: FLACSO, 1993.

Sandoval Alarcón, Mario. *Memorándum al general Ríos Montt.* Guatemala, January 18, 1983. Photocopy.

Saravia, Raquel, and Santiago Otero. *Memoria y Profesia. Historia de la Conferencia de Religiosos de Guatemala (1961-1996).* Guatemala: Ediciones San Pablo, 1997.

Sarti Castañeda, Carlos. "El proceso de estructuración de la dictadura militar contrarrevolucionaria." In *Revista Polémica*. San José, Costa Rica: FLACSO, 1983.

Schirmer, Jennifer. "The Guatemalan Military Project: An Interview with General Héctor Gramajo." *Harvard International Review* 13, no. 3 (Spring 1991).

Schlesinger, Stephen, and Stephen Kinzer. *Bitter Fruit: The Untold Story of the American Coup in Guatemala*. New York: Doubleday, 1982.

Simon, Jean-Marie. *Guatemala, Eternal Spring, Eternal Tyranny*. New York: W. W. Norton and Company, 1987.

Silva Girón, César Augusto. *Cuando gobiernan las armas. Guatemala 31 años de miseria*. Guatemala, 1987.

Solórzano Fernández, Valentín. *Evolución económica de Guatemala*. Cuarta edición. Guatemala, 1997.

Solórzano Foppa, Mario. "El nacionalismo indígena, una ideología burguesa." In *Revista Polémica*. No. 3. San José, Costa Rica: FLACSO, 1982.

Staub, E. *The Roots of Evil: The Origins of Genocide and Other Group Violence*. Cambridge: Cambridge University Press, 1989.

Stoll, David. *Between Two Armies in the Ixil Towns of Guatemala*. New York: Columbia University Press, 1993.

Tedlock, B. *Time and the Highland Maya*. Albuquerque, N.M.: University of New Mexico Press, 1992.

Thompson, E. *La voz del pasado*. Valencia: Ediciones Alfons El Magnanim IVEI, 1988.

Toriello Garrido, Guillermo. *Guatemala: más de 20 años de traición (1954-1979)*. Guatemala: Editorial Universitaria, 1979.

United Nations High Commissioner for Refugees. *Report on the Situation of Refugees around the World*. Madrid: Icaria, 1994.

Urrutia, Edmundo. *El movimiento revolucionario guatemalteco 1949-1967. Constitución y crisis de su identidad política*. Thesis. México, D.F.: FLACSO, 1986.

URNG. *La situación actual y las perspectivas en Guatemala. Visión de la URNG*. Guatemala. December 1985.

———. *Línea política de los revolucionarios guatemaltecos*. México: Editorial Nuestro Tiempo, 1988.

———. *Cuatro años de gobierno democristiano*. Guatemala, January 1990. Mimeo.

Villagrán Kramer, Francisco. *Biografía política de Guatemala. Los pactos políticos de 1944 a 1970*. Guatemala: FLACSO, 1994.

Wearne, P. *The Maya of Guatemala*. London: Minority Rights Group International, 1994.

Wilson, Richard. *Ametralladoras y espíritus de la montaña*. Los efectos culturales de la represión estatal entre los Q'eqchies. Textos Ak'kutan, Cobán, Alta Verapaz, 1994.

———. *Maya resurgence in Guatemala: Q'eqchi' experiences*. Norman, Okla.: University of Oklahoma Press, 1995.

Washington Office on Latin America (WOLA). *The Administration of Injustice: Military Accountability in Guatemala*. Washington, D.C., December 1989.

———. *Habits of Repression: Military Accountability for Human Rights Abuses under the Serrano Government in Guatemala, 1991-1992*. Washington, D.C., December 1992.

———. *Military Intelligence and Human Rights in Guatemala: The Archivo and the Case for Intelligence Reform*. Washington, D.C., March 30, 1995.

Worden, W. *Grief Counseling and Grief Therapy: A Handbook for the Mental Health Practitioner*. London: Tavistock/Routledge, 1991.